DATE DUE			

WITHDRAWN

THE PROCESS OF SOCIAL ORGANIZATION

The Process of
Social Organization:
POWER IN SOCIAL SYSTEMS

Second Edition

MARVIN E. OLSEN

Battelle Human Affairs Research Centers

HOLT, RINEHART AND WINSTON
New York, Chicago, San Francisco, Dallas
Montreal, Toronto, London, Sydney

Copyright © 1968,1978 by Holt, Rinehart and Winston

LIBRARY OF CONGRESS CATALOGING IN PUBLICATION DATA

Olsen, Marvin Elliott.
  The process of social organization.

  Includes index.
  1. Sociology. I. Title.
HM51.045 1978 301 77-85511 ISBN 0-03-040631-5

Printed in the United States of America
890   038   987654321

Preface to the Second Edition

Although there is considerable intellectual continuity between this edition of *The Process of Social Organization* and its predecessor—both books center around the twin themes of process and social organization—in large measure this is an entirely new book. The contents have been almost entirely rearranged to provide more logical continuity and organization and to place greater emphasis on certain key themes. A considerable amount of new material has been added, primarily in expanded discussions of the six major theoretical perspectives on the general nature of social organization. And virtually every paragraph has been totally rewritten to give the presentation greater clarity and precision.

Even more crucial are two other changes in this volume. First, the original version was justifiably criticized for lacking overall theoretical unity. In an attempt to rectify that deficiency, I have incorporated two additional central themes into this work. As reflected in its new subtitle, these are social power and the social system model. I have become increasingly convinced during the past years that power pervades all social interaction and organization and is in fact the principal dynamic medium of organized social life, analogous to energy in the physical world. Although I do not try to construct a general power theory of social organization, I do emphasize the power (or alternatively, influence or control) aspects of all social processes and theories discussed here. The general social system model, meanwhile, provides a useful analytical framework and set of concepts for examining social organization as a dynamic process. Stripped of its functional implications and overtones, this analytical perspective—it is not a substantive theory—is being widely adopted by contemporary sociologists as a framework for studying social organization that transcends the social-psychological and behavioral approaches that have dominated the discipline for so long.

The second major change in this edition is that it is no longer designed for introductory sociology students. To my surprise, I discovered that the first edition was being widely used by upperclass and graduate students, at least partially because there apparently was a great need for a book that treated social organization in a generic sense as the core concern of modern sociology. Consequently, I have attempted to raise somewhat the intellectual level of this revised edition, aiming it primarily at upperclass sociology majors and graduate students. Instructors may also find it appropriate for undergraduate courses in the principles of social organization (which are usually intended for beginning sociology majors), although they will undoubtedly want to supplement it with numerous additional readings. Finally, I also hope that my professional colleagues will find this presentation of social organization as a dynamic ongoing process, pervaded by power exertion and analyzable within a social systems framework, to be a stimulating and suggestive theoretical approach to the study of social life.

All of the thoughts expressed in the Preface to the First Edition are also applicable to this present work, with the exception of the statement that the book is intended for introductory students.

In addition to all of the people who contributed to the first edition, I especially want to express my great appreciation to the graduate students in my courses in social organization at Indiana University during the nine years I taught there. Many of the ideas for revision were contributed by them as we collectively struggled to bring intellectual and theoretical coherence into the discipline of sociology. Finally, deepest thanks to Cindy Perry, who cheerfully and skillfully typed this present manuscript, and to Val Fonseca, who critically but gently gave it a final polishing.

M.E.O.

Seattle, Wash.

Preface to the
First Edition

For many students, both beginning and advanced, the field of sociology is a chaotic jumble of unrelated or contradictory ideas, concepts, and propositions. They are confronted with a vast array of terms such as "social interaction," "social organization," "culture," "social system," and "institution," each perhaps meaningful by itself but none fitting together to form a logically consistent and unified analytical framework with which to examine social life. Study of specific topical areas—such as the family or race relations or stratification—often proves rewarding and challenging to students, but all too often they fail to understand or appreciate the common phenomenal and conceptual core that pervades all these topics and binds together the field of sociology.

This intellectual fragmentation and confusion among students reflects the multiplicity of perspectives and approaches abounding among sociologists today. When large numbers of professionals in a field disagree on the meanings of basic concepts, or do not fully synthesize these concepts into a unified whole, it is no wonder that students turn away from that discipline in dismay. They may be willing to forgive sociology's lack of methodological rigor or theoretical definitiveness, but not what appears to be conceptual chaos.

The underlying premise of this book is that sociology is ultimately concerned with a fundamental phenomenal reality—the process of social organization—which can be studied from a single encompassing analytical perspective incorporating the major concepts in sociology. The explicit purpose of the book is to present the basic concepts and theories of social organization as coherently and comprehensively as possible, within this overall analytical perspective.

Two major themes pervade the book: *process* and *social organization*. The continual stressing of these analytical perspectives gives the work whatever overall unity it possesses. Above all, I conceive of social reality as a continual ongoing process of activity or becoming. Dynamic processes, not static objects, are the ultimate essence of human life. Social order grows out of the constant patterning of social interactions and relationships, and all social structures must be seen as particular instances of ongoing processes.

The second pervasive theme is that of social organization. The unique concern of sociology, I argue, is with social processes and phenomena that transcend the individual personality. Social organization, in all its various forms, always has an existence and properties that are not reducible to characteristics of its individual members. The whole is more than the sum of its component parts and can only be understood and explained as an entity in itself. I use "social organization" as a generic term, referring to all processes and instances of organized social life, and not in the narrower sense of "formal associations." The study of social organization must, of course, take into account individuals' actions and interactions, for it is through these processes that organization arises. But interpersonal phenomena are not, in themselves, the primary focus of the sociologist concerned with social organization. They are, I would suggest, the proper objects of study for social psychologists. In the opposite direction, cultural phenomena, such as values, norms, and technology, are relevant for social organization only to the extent that they reflect or influence ordered social life.

This is not a textbook in the usual sense. No attempt is made to discuss extensively either empirical generalizations or the research on which they are based, and many topics usually included in introductory texts (such as the family, religion, education, race relations, or criminology) are omitted here. Nor is it a theoretical treatise, since it does not attempt to set forth, develop, or test any specific theories. Its purpose, instead, is to provide the student of sociology with a systematic introduction to the fundamental concepts and ideas necessary for examining and analyzing the process and forms of social organization, so that he may have a relatively firm foundation on which to base his further studies. Its intended use is as a supplement to whatever standard text or additional readings an instructor chooses to assign. I have not attempted here the infinitely more demanding task of constructing a systematic general theory that would incorporate all sociological concepts into a set of interrelated propositions. The creation of such theories must remain the ultimate goal of sociology, but that endeavor is still considerably beyond our abilities.

I make no claim of being either eclectic or definitive in this work. Many sociologists may not fully agree with all that I have said here, and undoubtedly other authors would have treated many of these ideas somewhat differently. To achieve logical coherence and consistency, however, one must employ a dominant unifying theme, which in turn largely dictates one's selection and use of more specific conceptualizations. Although I have judiciously attempted to keep the discussion as close as possible to the mainstream of contemporary sociological thought, to maintain uniformity and continuity it has been necessary to treat certain ideas in a manner that may seem slightly unconventional to some readers. The intended effect of these alterations is not idiosyncrasy, but rather clarification and redirection of conceptual thinking in sociology. The intellectual venture undertaken in this book is far from completion; scientific analysis, like social life itself, is a continual process of development. But perhaps the best means of enlarging one's own thinking is to put one's ideas down on paper and then invite one's colleagues to evaluate and criticize them.

The viewpoint presented here was developed in the course of my lectures to introductory sociology students at The University of Michigan and Indiana University during the past several years. Although the book is thus essentially designed for beginning students, it attempts to demand somewhat more of the reader than do many standard introductory texts. Hopefully, therefore, it will also prove challenging to upperclassmen and to graduate students.

My intellectual debt to Alfred North Whitehead and the other developers of process philosophy is fully apparent. The substantive ideas developed here are drawn from extremely diverse sources, but four names deserve particular mention: the teachings of Guy E. Swanson and Amos H. Hawley, and the writings of Émile Durkheim and Talcott Parsons. Needless to say, they are in no way responsible for this book, and some of them might even be surprised to find their names linked in this manner, but their influences on my thinking are inexorably interwoven throughout this work.

I also express my deep gratitude to all those persons who have unselfishly contributed to this book through their innumerable suggestions, criticisms, and encouragement: to James Moulton, who first prompted me to begin this project; to Professors Guy E. Swanson, Paul E. Mott, Walter Buckley, Don C. Gibbons, J. Eugene Haas, and Richard L. Simpson, who critically read earlier versions of the manuscript and offered countless ideas for improvement; to my wife, Katherine, for her unlimited confidence and encouragement; to Betty Beedie, who diligently typed the manuscript; and to all my students who have served as critical audiences for my thinking.

Finally, a special word of appreciation is due to Professors John H. Burma and Thomas E. Lasswell, who first awakened in me a vision of "the sociological imagination."

M.E.O.

Contents

Part III ENACTING SOCIAL ORGANIZATION *203*

Part IV TRANSFORMING SOCIAL ORGANIZATION *305*

PART I

Examining Social Organization

THE process of social organization—or the emergence of patterns of social ordering and shared cultural meanings in social life—pervades all human activity from simple friendships to total societies. Through this process we create stable organizational entities within the dynamic flow of ongoing social existence.

The purpose of the three chapters in this first section is to lay a groundwork for conceptualizing and analyzing the process of social organization. The fundamental perspective and analytical framework to be used throughout the book are presented here.

Chapter 1 begins with the thesis that all social life is a dynamic process of emerging development. It explores the essential nature of social organization as an ongoing process that incorporates interacting personalities, patterns of social ordering, and shared cultural ideas. The organizational forms that emerge through this process are viewed as real entities that are not reducible to their component parts. In addition, this chapter briefly sketches the parameters or boundaries of

1

organized social life. Finally, it discusses the social system model as an analytical tool with which to conceptualize the dynamic processes occurring within all social organization.

To provide an overall theoretical perspective for explaining the process of social organization, Chapter 2 argues that the exercise of social power constitutes the crucial dynamic core of social organization. It then discusses numerous characteristics of social power, four main types of power, and two general theories of the creation of social power. The chapter also explores the process through which power is exercised and some ways of analyzing this process, and suggests several uses of power by social organizations.

Chapter 3 examines the organizational units that are created through the process of social organization. Several ways in which organizations are delineated from their social environments are discussed, and a typology of the various kinds of organizational units is sketched. Also presented here are the concepts of functional specialization versus functional autonomy and the processes of segmentation versus absorption that occur between organizations and their component subunits.

1

Process and Social Organization

"THE actual world is a process. . . . The flux of things is one ultimate generalization around which we must weave our philosophical system."[1] Thus Alfred North Whitehead expressed the fundamental principle of process philosophy that underlies our contemporary understanding of the nature of the physical universe, human social life, and ultimate reality. Every phenomenon of which we are aware—from electrons to galaxies, from amoebae to human beings, from friendships to societies, from nursery rhymes to cosmologies—exists in a state of continual "becoming," which Whitehead describes as "a creative advance into novelty." As expressed by Wilmon Henry Sheldon, there are "no fixed entities, no ultimate terms; a thing, a being, even being *qua* being, is not what it is but what it is going to be. Transition, a pure relation, is the ultimate fact. . . ."[2]

The dynamic nature of our existence frequently escapes our attention,

[1] Alfred North Whitehead, *Process and Reality* (New York: Macmillan Co., 1929), pp. 33, 317, 42.
[2] Wilmon Henry Sheldon, *God and Polarity* (New Haven, Conn.: Yale University Press, 1954), p. 542.

3

primarily because of our perceptual and conceptual limitations. These limitations are not insurmountable, however. Not long ago most people believed that the earth stood still (presumably at the center of the universe), while the sun revolved around it. Today, as the result of scientific research in astronomy, we know that we inhabit a spinning globe which continually circles the sun as the entire solar system revolves around the core of a galaxy which is hurtling through space at unimaginable speeds—even though we still appear to be motionless. Biological science, meanwhile, demonstrates the marvelous complexity of the continual life cycle of all living organisms, from creation through growth and adaptations to death. More recently, psychology has begun to understand some of the processes involved in the development of the human mind and the emergence of mature personalities.

The Nature of Social Organization

IF this conception of reality as a continual ongoing process applies to the physical, biological, and psychological realms of existence, must it not also be relevant to human social life? Are not all of our relationships with one another, as well as the patterns of social ordering and cultural ideas that emerge from these interactions, constantly fluctuating and developing? In this book, *we view all social life as a dynamic process of becoming* rather than a static state of being.

DYNAMIC SOCIAL REALITY

To become fully aware of the dynamic nature of social organization, we must learn to transcend the time limitations inherent in our everyday perceptions of the social world that often lead us to view it in static terms. We must come to view social life as a process that is continually being created and recreated as individuals seek to bring order and meaning into their collective social life. If we perceive any instance of social life as static rather than dynamic, therefore, it is only because we are focusing solely on forms and ignoring processes, or else are limiting our time perspective too severely. Charles Warriner lucidly expressed this idea in the following passage:

> The only realities which we as humans can directly observe are events within a relatively limited time and space location. Any unity . . . whose structural processes are too slow or too fast for our perception must be inferred from partial observations made via instruments or through time series. The fact that we cannot directly perceive their unity does not detract from their essential empirical reality; it merely reflects the human limitation. . . . Whenever we are dealing with a unity that exceeds our

perceptual facility, we postulate that unity from the observation of sequences of events that appear to have a continuity and a degree of causal connection. We create a conceptual unit. . . . We cannot "see" persons any more than we can see groups: both are realities which extend beyond the range of human perception. Both are abstractions from and summaries of our observations of more limited aspects of the reality. . . . The action orientation says that persons and societies are to be known through what they do, are to be postulated from continuities in action and conduct and that both are equivalent inferences from these observations.[3]

This conception of social reality as a dynamic process whose nature and unity are inferred from empirical observations can also be illustrated by an analogy. Imagine the human mind to be a motion picture camera. Suppose that it is presently focused on a specific instance of social interaction—a man and a woman in conversation, with the man reaching out his hand to the woman. The camera records a continuous stream of static pictures of the ongoing interactions, no one of which tells us much about the nature of the dynamic relationship being enacted by these individuals. Whatever pattern of social organization they are creating, whether it be a marriage or a sales transaction or a play production, existed as an ongoing process before any single picture was recorded, and will continue into the future. Each picture "freezes" this dynamic process into a static form that is isolated in time and not representative of social reality. From a succession of pictures taken through time, however, we can construct an image of the dynamic social process that is actually occurring. We then perceive, perhaps, the enactment of an employer-employee relationship in which an executive is giving a secretary instructions for the day's work. Note, however, that the existence of this ongoing relationship must be inferred by the observer from a series of separate static observations. To accurately draw such inferences about dynamic social processes and determine how these processes interrelate to form patterns of social ordering, one's perceptions of social life must constantly be attuned to the ongoing nature of all social organization.

PERVASIVE SOCIAL ORGANIZATION

The process of social organization necessarily involves at least two interacting persons, as in the above example, but it can also become extremely extensive and complex. There are four billion people in the world today, each of whom interacts with many other individuals every day. Out of these billions of social interactions arise millions of continuing social relationships, from which emerge countless numbers of families, groups,

[3]Charles K. Warriner, *The Emergence of Society* (Homewood, Ill.: Dorsey Press, 1970), pp. 7–8.

associations, and communities, which in turn comprise the more than one hundred societies that today constitute human civilization. This process of social organization can assume or produce unlimited specific forms, such as friendships, informal groups, nuclear families, schools, churches, mobs, businesses, special-interest associations, social classes, cities, governments, economic markets, societies, and international confederations, so that all aspects of human social life involve social organization. Thomas Hobbes's classic description of "presocial" human life—as "solitary, poor, nasty, brutish, and short"—may be poetic fiction, but it provides a dramatic suggestion of what human life might be like if humans were not capable of creating social organization.

Regardless of its size, location, or particular form, however, social organization develops whenever individuals create stable social relationships that display patterns of social ordering and become infused with shared cultural ideas. Expressed more formally, *social organization is the process of bringing patterns of social ordering and shared cultural meanings into human social interaction through time.* Although we sometimes view process and order as antithetical, both are in fact integral aspects of dynamic social organization. Processes are ongoing streams of interrelated actions and events occurring through time. Patterns of ordering develop within these processes as their component parts become interrelated in various ways and persistent through a period of time, or as several processes become interwoven into stable arrangements. Order is therefore not a static condition, but a dynamic pattern or set of patterns persisting through time with relative stability and predictability. Social processes and social ordering simultaneously constitute the essence of social organization.

The term "social organization" can be confusing, since it is commonly used to refer both to ongoing processes and to established social entities. It designates both the process by which social relationships become ordered into recurrent patterns, and also the identifiable outcomes or products of this process. Thus, we might first speak of social organization as the process through which individuals create a friendship group or a political party or a business firm, and then go on to describe each of these as a particular type of social organization that exists as a recognized entity with an established boundary and structure. There is a crucial semantic reason for this double meaning of the term. *The entities that we call organizations are always the products or outcomes of the ongoing process of social organization.* They are relatively stable patterns of activity resulting from dynamic social processes.

Moreover, the organizational entities that emerge through the general process of social organization are themselves composed of numerous specific processes. These include social conflict, control, cohesion, and coordination, each of which gives rise to recurrent and meaningful patterns of social ordering. In addition, all forms of organization, from the smallest and simplest group to the largest and most complex society, are constantly developing and changing through time. Using the term "social organization" to refer to both processes and entities should therefore continually remind us that social reality, no matter what form it displays at any given moment, is forever in a process of becoming, and that dynamic social organization pervades all human existence.

LEVELS OF ORDERING

All aspects of human social existence are to some extent interrelated. But within this totality of existence occur many distinguishable types of ordering, or patterning of dynamic processes. In broadest terms, we can distinguish among atomic, physical, biological, personal, social, and cultural ordering. Each type of ordering is interrelated with other types but also displays its own unique characteristics and properties. Moreover, these six types of ordering can be viewed as a hierarchy of levels, with atomic ordering being the lowest level and cultural ordering the highest. Social and cultural ordering are therefore more removed from (and less constrained by) physical existence than are the organic and personal levels. For understanding human social life, consequently, the levels of atomic and physical ordering are largely irrelevant; organic ordering is only indirectly relevant; personal and cultural ordering are directly relevant insofar as they affect social processes; and social ordering becomes the central focus. Let us examine the latter three levels of ordering in more detail.[4]

Personal ordering gives coherence and stability to the various cognitive and affective psychological processes occurring within an individual. Diverse motives, needs, beliefs, feelings, traits, and attitudes are constantly being ordered by the mind into a relatively unified entity that is perceived by oneself and others as a distinct personality. Focusing on this level of ordering gives one a psychological perspective on human life and leads to a concern with such psychological processes as motivation, learning, thinking, personality development, and mental illness.

Social ordering grows out of the interactions and relationships of individuals as these activities become patterned and recurrent through time. Although personalities create social ordering, they do not constitute it. Conversely, organized social life also creates personalities through the process of socialization, although personalities are never totally determined by their social environments. The principal focus at this level of social

[4]This concept of levels of ordering is derived largely from the writings of Talcott Parsons. See Talcott Parsons and Edward Shils, eds., *Toward a General Theory of Action* (New York: Harper & Row, 1962), chap. 1.

ordering is on such social processes as conflict, cooperation, and change, and on social collectivities such as families, communities, and societies. Sociology, political science, economics, and the other social sciences are all concerned primarily with this social level of ordering.

Cultural ordering refers to sets of knowledge, meanings, values, and symbols that are shared by a set of people. Cultural ideas can exist in random isolation (such as entries in an encyclopedia), but as they pervade people's lives and constitute a living culture they normally display considerable patterning and regularity. Such disciplines as law, philosophy, religion, linguistics, and literature all attempt to understand various aspects of cultural ordering.

To the extent that these levels of ordering are separately identifiable in human life, each is characterized by the three basic qualities of emergence, autonomy, and interpenetration. Each level of ordering develops out of those below it and exists as a reality in its own right, but is also interwoven with other levels below and above it. Thus, social ordering develops as personalities interact and in turn gives rise to sets of shared cultural ideas. When we speak of the total process of social organization, therefore, we are including personal ordering insofar as it enables individuals to create and sustain social relationships, all patterns of social ordering that develop out of these relationships, and cultural ordering insofar as it reflects and affects this social ordering. Thus social organization centers on patterns of social ordering but also incorporates portions of both individual personalities and shared cultures. Figure 1-1 depicts the process of social organization in terms of these three interpenetrating levels of ordering. The diagram is necessarily static, since it is only a single representation of an ongoing process, but it does indicate the flow of time and hence by implication the dynamic nature of this process.

THE EMERGENCE OF SOCIAL ORGANIZATION

Social organization develops as individuals interact to create ongoing relationships that form patterns of social ordering that become infused with shared meanings. That is, organization emerges from the actions of individual personalities and can never be completely separated from them. If the members of a group all cease to interact with one another, the group will no longer exist. Similarly, cultures are outgrowths of collective social activities, and become mere museum relics when the social ordering that created them or the individuals who carry them disappear. The concept of emergence thus refers to the fact that each succeedingly higher level of ordering develops out of the levels below it and is always dependent to some extent on those lower levels, yet displays distinctive properties of its own not found in those lower levels of ordering. The decision-making

FIGURE 1-1. Interpenetration of Personality, Social Order, and Culture in the Process of Social Organization

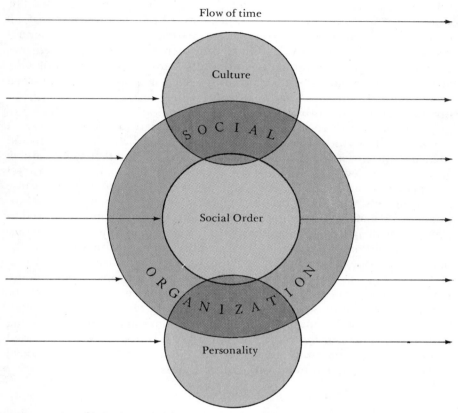

process of an organization, for instance, is not a personality characteristic of any of its individual members.

The crucial notion here is that the interactions of the units comprising any level of ordering produce patterns or configurations that are unique to that ordering. Each level of ordering, in other words, possesses some degree of emergent unity and autonomy, and is not merely the sum of its constituent parts. The characteristics displayed by each level are not fully determined by any lower levels, so that it is impossible to explain any given instance of ordering solely in terms of lower levels. A personality is something more than just an acting organism, and cannot be explained entirely by biological concepts and processes. A group is something more than just several interacting personalities, and cannot be adequately explained with psychological concepts and processes. And a culture is something more than just a symbolic reflection of society, and cannot be understood solely in terms of its social setting. Thus every instance of social or cultural ordering displays a unique patterning of characteristics that gives it emergent reality. The community of "Jonesville," for example, may contain a power structure, an economic pattern, and an ethnic heritage that persist through several generations and distinguish it from all other communities. This emergence is itself a dynamic process that is continually being created. If we look only at the static structure of an organization—such as portrayed by a formal organizational chart—we shall miss entirely the process through which the organization is constantly emerging from the actions of its members.

Finally, because each level of ordering is partially autonomous as well as emergent from those below it, processes at that level often act back on and influence the lower levels from which they emerge. In other words, influences between levels of ordering are always reciprocal, so that each level interpenetrates those both above and below it. Personal tensions cause stomach ulcers, while poor health often affects one's personality. Communities exercise many constraints upon the actions of their members, as well as provide for their biological welfare, while at the same time the sustenance needs and personality characteristics of individuals continually affect the nature and scope of community activities. And at the cultural level, beliefs and ideas can shape societies, change personalities, and even produce martyrs, while concurrently such cultural phenomena always reflect the social life, personality structures, and organic characteristics of their components. Because of this interpenetration of personal and cultural ordering with social ordering, the concept of emergence is applicable to the total process of social organization whereby individuals create patterns of social ordering that become infused with cultural ideas.

THE REALITY OF SOCIAL ORGANIZATION

If social organization is an emergent process, the organizational entities that result from it must exist as real phenomena. They are not just conceptual abstractions derived from generalizations about the behaviors of individuals, but can and must be explained in terms of unique and distinctive principles applicable only to this level of reality. This idea that the process of social organization creates new entities that are qualitatively different from their constituent parts is expressed by Walter Buckley:

> Thus, if social groups are not "real entities," then neither are individual organisms, organs, cells, molecules or atoms, since they are all "nothing but" the constituents of which they are made. But this "nothing but" hides the central key to modern thinking—the fact of *organization* into systemic relationships. When we say that "the whole is more than the sum of its parts," the meaning becomes unambiguous and loses its

> mystery: the "more than" points to the fact of *organization*, which imparts to the aggregate characteristics that are not only *different* from, but often *not found in* the components alone; and the "sum of the parts" must be taken to mean, not their numerical addition, but their unorganized aggregation.[5]

To substantiate this thesis, we begin by observing that social organizations exhibit numerous properties that are not inherent in their individual members. Typical organizational properties include size, complexity, formality, power arrangements, rate of change, operational requirements, and integration or cohesion. All of these properties are qualitatively distinct from the personal characteristics of the individuals who create or perpetuate that organization. Knowing the personality profiles of Tom, Dick, Harry, Bill, and Bob tells us nothing about the basketball team they comprise— nothing about the duties of the various positions on the team, the coordination of their ball handling, their stability as a team under pressure, their rate of improvement during the season, or their overall ability to win basketball games. If features such as these are not inherent in individual members, then they must be properties of the organization itself.

Carrying this line of reasoning one step further, if a phenomenon exhibits properties that are distinctly its own, then it must have existence of its own. It must be something more than just interacting components. In other words, *social organization possesses a unity that is always greater than the sum of its component parts.* Émile Durkheim, one of the intellectual founders of sociology, expressed this idea nearly a half-century ago:

> A whole is not identical with the sum of its parts. It is something different, and its properties differ from those of its component parts. . . . By reason of this principle, society is not a mere sum of individuals. Rather, the system formed by their association represents a specific reality which has its own characteristics. . . . We must seek the explanation of social life in the nature of society itself.[6]

Durkheim's illustration of the fallacy of reductionist thinking, or trying to explain a social phenomenon solely in terms of its component parts, is also worth noting:

> It will be said that, since the only elements making up society are individuals, the first origins of sociological phenomena cannot but be psychological. In reasoning thus, it can be established just as easily that

---

[5] Walter Buckley, *Sociology and Modern Systems Theory* (Englewood Cliffs, N.J.: Prentice-Hall, 1966), p. 42.

[6] Émile Durkheim, *The Rules of Sociological Method*, trans. by Sarah A. Solovay and John H. Mueller (New York: Free Press, 1933), pp. 102–103.

organic phenomena may be explained by inorganic phenomena. It is
very certain that there are in the living cell only molecules of crude
matter. But these molecules are in contact with one another, and this
association is the cause of the new phenomena which characterize life,
the very germ of which cannot possibly be found in any of the separate
elements.[7]

To assert the reality of social organizations from their constituent
members is easier than to demonstrate objectively this reality. Since social
organization, like gravity, cannot be directly observed by human senses, we
must ascertain its existence through its effects on other phenomena, just as
the effects of gravity are demonstrated by a falling apple. The consequences
of the existence of social organization can be witnessed both in individuals'
actions and in cultural ideas.

On the individual level, Durkheim's concepts of *exteriority* and *constraint* provide two classic illustrations of the effects of social ordering and
organization. The exteriority of social organization to individuals is seen in
the fact that its patterns may continue to exist over time despite changes, or
even a complete turnover, in its membership. Anything short of total
simultaneous withdrawal by all members will not necessarily destroy a
group, a community, or a society. In fact, many organizations—of which a
university is an excellent example—establish ordered procedures for the
departure of old members and the acquisition and training of new members.
As a result of the relatively stable persistence of social organization through
time, individuals must treat these patterns of relationships as external to
themselves. Social ordering is already there when the individual comes onto
the scene, and he or she has no choice but to recognize its existence and to
take account of its demands. One may conform to these demands, deviate
from them, or attempt to change them, but one cannot ignore them.

The constraints of established social organization on individuals are
seen in the ways in which it influences their actions. Patterned social
arrangements limit or obstruct some kinds of behavior and simultaneously
provide opportunities for other kinds. Most members of an underdeveloped
agricultural society cannot obtain a college education no matter how
intelligent they may be, because their society does not have adequate
economic surpluses to build schools, train teachers, or free students from
productive labor for four years. They are not, however, forced to adhere to
rigid work schedules or file income tax returns. In the United States, on the
other hand, it is quite difficult for children from an affluent family to avoid
college, no matter how unintelligent (within normality) they may be,
because of the strong social pressures from all directions that push them to

7 Ibid., p. 102.

enroll. And most people in this society do enjoy annual paid vacations and the economic security provided by old age insurance. In a more direct manner, individuals are punished for doing some things (e.g., stealing) and for not doing other things (e.g., not paying income taxes), and rewarded for doing some things (e.g., performing a job) and for not doing some things they might wish to do (e.g., awarded a military decoration for defending a position rather than retreating under fire). Finally, individuals are often provided with entire ready-made sets of actions, or roles, which they simply act out with little or no individual modifications (as illustrated by American dating rituals or workers following detailed job descriptions).

On the cultural level, ordered social life will often influence common values, beliefs, traditions, norms, and other ideas over time. Widespread practices of racial discrimination and segregation will result in cultural beliefs and traditions that justify and support these actions, while extensive equal-status interaction across racial lines will produce strong values and norms favoring racial equality. Our contemporary ideas of nationalism and patriotism are outgrowths of the development of the nation-state as the dominant political unit in Europe doing the seventeenth and eighteenth centuries. And one researcher has argued that religious monotheism among primitive peoples is more likely to occur in societies containing three or more levels of sovereign organization (such as families, communities, and tribes) than in societies that lack this degree of complexity.[8]

These arguments for the reality of social organization and its partial autonomy in relation to its constituent members are not totally conclusive from a philosophical perspective. Nevertheless, they are strong enough to convince most social scientists that exclusive reliance on the psychological level of analysis is not adequate to explain organized social life. At the same time, we must remember that the autonomy of social organization is never total. Individual personalities, patterns of social ordering, and cultures always interpenetrate each other's existence and functioning. On the one hand, social organization must ultimately be created by, and expressed through, the behaviors and thoughts of individuals, and shared cultural ideas can shape and alter existing organizations. On the other hand, apart from ordered social life the individual remains only a biological organism that never becomes human, and cultural ideas are utterly meaningless.

In sum, emergent social organizations exhibit their own unique properties that are distinct from those of their members, they are real phenomena that produce discernible consequences for human life, and they possess a unity that is greater than the sum of their component parts. Social organization exists not solely in individuals or cultural ideas, but in ordered

[8]Guy E. Swanson, *The Birth of the Gods* (Ann Arbor, Mich.: University of Michigan Press, 1960), chap. 3.

patterns of social relationships that persist through time and are infused with shared cultures. Social organization is an emergent, partially autonomous reality in which personalities, social ordering, and culture continually interpenetrate in an ongoing dynamic process.

Parameters of Social Organization

SOCIAL organization never occurs in a vacuum. This process is only part of the totality of ongoing existence and can be understood only in relation to its setting. The sociologist must therefore always be aware of, and take into account, the various factors that constitute the parameters of all organized social life. These parameters are not themselves part of the process of social organization, nor do they ever fully determine its nature, but they do always impose limits on social organization and continually influence it.

Four crucial parameters of all social organization consist of psychological, demographic, environmental, and technological factors. (Portions of both the personality and culture are component parts of the process of social organization, but the psychological characteristics and technological knowledge discussed below lie outside that process.) Figuratively speaking, these four sets of factors comprise the frame that bounds the ongoing process of social organization. They can also be viewed as prerequisites for social organization, since without them there could be no social ordering or culture. In addition, when examining any particular instance of social organization, its social environment constitutes another inescapable parameter that continually influences, limits, and shapes its activities.

PSYCHOLOGICAL PARAMETERS

Sociology is essentially concerned with social interactions among individuals and the patterns of social ordering and shared cultural ideas that result from these interactions. Sociologists do not normally study individuals' psychological processes or personalities, but they do make several assumptions about human beings as psychological entities that are taken for granted as constants or parameters for the study of social organization. If individuals did not possess these qualities, they could not interact to create social ordering or culture.

The most important of these assumptions about humans is that they are inexorably dependent upon other persons (and hence collectively interdependent) for the satisfaction of a wide variety of imperative biological, emotional, and cognitive needs. All societies must first of all provide some organized means whereby their members can obtain food, shelter, clothing, and other necessities for physical survival. The manner in which the economy of a society functions to perform this task may affect many other aspects of social life. Beyond these primary physical requirements, the human being possesses a host of emotional needs (such as for response, acceptance, and affection) and cognitive desires (such as for information, new experiences, and creativity). In all these cases, the individual normally turns to other people as sources of need fulfillment or as companions in an effort to achieve gratification. In fact, psychologists and social psychologists have amassed considerable evidence to support the contention that the entire process of personality formation and growth is totally dependent on social interaction with others. Left entirely to itself, a human baby will never become anything more than a helpless animal—if it even manages to survive—and total isolation can produce psychosis in an adult.

Sociologists also assume that the human beings who participate in social organization possess at least a minimum amount of intelligence (the ability to learn and solve problems) and that they are capable of symbolization and symbolic communication (the ability to think and communicate in abstract symbols). It is possible to have organized collective life based solely on common instincts, as in ant and bee colonies, but virtually all human interaction clearly involves symbol manipulation and communication. As a result of their ability to symbolize, human beings can relate to and take into consideration one another's thoughts as well as overt behaviors, and thus modify their own thoughts and actions on the basis of what they believe and discover other persons to be thinking or feeling. Persons who lack these cognitive capabilities—such as the mentally retarded, brain-damaged, or mentally ill—often cannot engage in normal social interaction or participate fully as members of organizations.

A third assumption sociologists make about human beings is that they are normally motivated to achieve a wide variety of goals, ranging from mere survival to full maximization of their lives. Beyond the basic demands of survival, no attempt is made to prescribe the exact nature of these goals or to define "maximization of life." Those decisions are made by the participant individuals. But the sociologist must assume that all people normally seek desired goals and expend effort to achieve them. Notice the word *normally* in this statement. It is certainly true that at times some individuals do not seek goals, or do not even wish to interact with others. This withdrawal may be temporary (as in the case of a person under the influence of alcohol or other drugs) or it may be permanent (as in the case of severe psychosis or suicide). But to the extent that individuals withdraw from social life in these ways they no longer contribute to the process of social organization. Sociologists do not reify social organization by assuming the existence of a "group mind," since only individuals can think and formulate future intentions. However, the members of any organization can share common goals that they seek to attain through their joint actions and that become identified with that organization. We therefore often use the term "organizational goals" as a shorthand way of saying "goals shared and jointly sought by the members of an organization." With this understanding, we can assume that social organizations normally seek to survive and attain goals, just as individuals do.

When studying the process of social organization, sociologists assume that the participating individuals all possess these characteristics of dependence, intelligence, and goal seeking, and hence can engage in meaningful social interaction. Consequently, all participants are assumed to be interchangeable, and the particular nature of any one individual's personality is not theoretically relevant for understanding social organization. In reality, of course, individuals' personality characteristics do sometimes affect social organizations, especially if these people occupy key organizational positions. But such individual characteristics must be treated as random variations by sociologists when constructing theories to explain broad social processes.

DEMOGRAPHIC PARAMETERS

A second fundamental type of parameter for social organization consists of the demographic characteristics of populations. By itself, a population is nothing but a number of individuals; it has no organization of any kind. But it does provide the raw material for the creation of social organization, since organizations are always composed of relationships among the members of a population. Social organization develops as a population of people acts collectively to attain shared goals.

In a fundamental sense, social organization is always a property of populations, not of single individuals. As population phenomena, social organizations are highly influenced by the characteristics of the populations that comprise them. A number of sociologists, beginning with Émile Durkheim,[9] have argued that population size or density is a major factor determining the organizational complexity of a society. Other social scientists consider additional variables equally important, but no one would deny that the size of an organization's population is a crucial determinant of its social structure and functioning. A community with a million inhabitants will never achieve the personal intimacy of a village with a dozen families, but it is able to support a vast array of specialized activities far beyond the capabilities of the village. Apart from absolute size, the rate at which a population is growing or declining may also have multiple ramifications for social organization. Endless problems in education, housing, transporta-

---

[9]Émile Durkheim, *The Division of Labor in Society*, trans. by George Simpson (New York: Free Press, 1933), pp. 102–103.

tion, and recreation have been encountered in the United States as the result of rapid population growth. And on a broader scale, many experts agree that most nonindustrial societies will be unable to raise their standards of living unless they first curb their present population "explosions."

In addition to size, other demographic characteristics of a population are also important for social organization. For instance, societies differ markedly in their age distributions, and a predominantly "young" society faces problems quite different from those encountered by "aging" societies. The racial composition of a society may likewise influence many aspects of its social life if the members of the society believe race to be socially important. Serious imbalances in the sex ratio of a population will certainly alter marriage and family patterns and create numerous social problems. In short, the demographic characteristics of a population—unlike the personality characteristics of its individual members—will always affect the process of social organization within that population.

ENVIRONMENTAL PARAMETERS

That human life is totally dependent on the natural environment in which we live is obvious. As biological organisms, we cannot exist without oxygen, water, food, and a limited temperature range. The flow of human activities, and even our conception of time, are shaped and regulated by the rotation, tilt, and movement of the earth. And all societies draw on the natural environment for a vast array of natural resources—from wood for fires to oil for engines—for survival and the achievement of collective goals.

It is easy to see the ways in which the social organization of primitive societies is shaped by the natural environment, but what about contemporary "advanced" societies? To some extent, modern technology is enabling us to utilize and control the natural environment and its resources more effectively than ever before. The influence and limitations of the natural environment are still pervasive and profound in the modern world, however. Patterns of living in a warm climate, such as in Mexico, are very different from those in a cold climate such as in Norway. A heavy snowfall can virtually immobilize a large city, and a severe earthquake or hurricane quickly reminds us of our inescapable dependence on nature. All industrialized nations, finally, are heavily dependent at the present time on fossil fuels, as the current energy crisis is demonstrating so dramatically.

Human societies not only draw on the natural environment for necessary resources, but also alter the environment in the process. Until recently, these alterations were generally not extensive or serious, but gradually we have begun to realize that modern industrialized societies are producing massive and often irrevocable changes in the environment. Air, water, and land pollution in many forms have finally come to be seen as one of humanity's most fundamental problems. Modern technological man is slowly relearning the basic maxim that guides all "primitive" societies: humanity is always dependent on "spaceship earth," and must live in harmony with the natural environment to survive.

Spatial arrangements and distributions also significantly affect the ways in which people interact and the kinds of organizations they create. People living on opposite sides of a busy highway are unlikely to become close friends despite their physical proximity, for the flow of traffic typically acts as a barrier to social interaction. Most communities contain numerous "natural areas"—neighborhoods bounded by highways, rivers, or other spatial landmarks—that display distinctive social characteristics. And all political systems are organized as geographical units such as countries, states, or provinces, on the assumption that people living near one another will share common interests and problems. Thus, all attempts to create social organization are shaped and influenced by the natural environment.

TECHNOLOGICAL PARAMETERS

The fourth type of parameter affecting social organization is material technology. This includes all human knowledge concerning the use of physical objects and forces for the attainment of desired goals. Such knowledge might include techniques for obtaining natural resources, preparing food, constructing shelters, making tools, manufacturing goods from safety pins to automobiles, curing diseases, utilizing forces such as magnetism or electricity, synthesizing chemical compounds to produce new products such as plastics, smashing atoms, and so on. The range of material technology is unlimited, from the most primitive tools to yet undreamed-of means of exploring space. All of these techniques, nevertheless, share the common feature of enabling people to deal with and more effectively utilize the natural environment.

The creation of social organization does not depend on the possession of material technology beyond that required for physical survival. Primitive societies have existed without even a knowledge of fire making, and the internal combustion engine is certainly not a prerequisite for organized social life. The technological knowledge used by a population does, however, have tremendous consequences for the social organization it creates. Revolutionary turning points in human societies have been marked, for instance, by the development of knowledge about grain cultivation, which made possible settled communities, about steam engines, which introduced widespread industrialization, and about public sanitation and rapid transportation, which are necessary for large-scale urbanization. Today we are witnessing the manifold ramifications of electronic communications and air travel, as our social world steadily "shrinks" and becomes increasingly interdependent. As for tomorrow, we can only speculate about the possible dynamic social effects of atomic energy and space travel.

Perhaps even more important for human civilization than any specific technological inventions, however, is humanity's ability to harness energy. Each new source of energy exploited by us—from water power to the steam engine to fossil fuels to atomic fission—has opened vast new opportunities for economic and social development. Without abundant energy, modern industrial societies could not long continue to survive, and existing patterns of social organization would be radically altered. Material technology is thus always inseparably linked with social organization, as both cause and consequence of ongoing social processes. Technology does not unequivocally determine social organization, but technological innovation is a prime instigator of social change, and the effects of applied technology pervade all realms of contemporary social life.

SOCIAL ENVIRONMENT

Any particular social process or organization occurs not only within a setting consisting of the four parameters discussed above, but also within a social environment composed of innumerable other social processes and organizations. Although the social environment is by definition part of the total process of social organization, for any given instance of social life it acts as an additional parameter for that situation. A political party, for example, must constantly compete with other associations for the commitment of its members, must depend on the economy to produce enough surplus wealth to support nonproductive political activities, must formulate programs to deal with an unending stream of community and national problems, must compete with one or more other parties for control of the government, and must even take the interests of other societies into account in the formulation of its major policies. Complex bonds of interdependence thus link this organization with its social environment in countless ways.

If either individuals or organizations are to survive over time or achieve whatever goals they seek, they are almost inevitably forced to interact with others in their social environments. The resulting social interdependence can be either cooperative—as when federal, state, and local governments work together to alleviate poverty—or conflicting—as when the construction of a new highway is blocked by the protests of a homeowners' association. As further illustrations of this interdependency throughout all spheres of organized social life, consider families entrusting the education of their children to schools, businesses and labor unions negotiating work contracts, suburbs relying on the central metropolis for their economic livelihoods and many municipal services, and wealthy nations establishing foreign-aid programs based on the realization that their own welfare ultimately depends on the ability of underdeveloped societies to raise their standards of living. In short, individuals and organizations always exist within complex social environments with which they are interdependent and with which they must constantly interact.

PARAMETERS AND SOCIAL ORGANIZATION

The four sets of nonsocial parameters discussed above—psychological, demographic, environmental, and technological—as well as the social environment surrounding every occurrence of social organization, continuously influence, limit, and shape all social relationships, processes, and organizations. Although none of these factors totally determines the exact ways in which people organize their collective activities, their effects can never be escaped.

At the same time, established social organizations repeatedly affect all of these parameters through dynamic reciprocal processes. For instance, an extensive program of mass public education may markedly raise the intellectual capabilities of a population and alter the goals sought by individuals. An organized movement for more effective birth control may have profound effects on the birth rate of a society and eventually on its total population size. Governmental efforts to control industrial pollution may eventually be effective in reversing our destruction of the natural environment. And the establishment of large-scale research programs often leads to major technological discoveries. From this reverse perspective, therefore, we are also led to conclude that social organization is intertwined with the larger setting in which it occurs and cannot escape the bounds of its parameters.

The Social System Model

ALL of the sciences—physical, biological, psychological, social, and cultural—find it useful to construct models as heuristic analytical tools. A model is neither a true description of reality nor a substantive theory. Rather, it is a conceptual device designed to facilitate the entire scientific process, from the formation of propositions to the design of research. Put differently, *a model is an abstract but simplified representation of some real phenomenon* which is used to increase our understanding of that phenomenon. It rarely portrays all the features and details of the phenomenon being studied, since it selects only those aspects or characteristics that are crucial for the question under investigation, and omits many others. These selected features are combined into a unified conceptualization according to predetermined logical principles. A model therefore differs from reality precisely to the degree that we arbitrarily abstract it from real existence.

Some models are believed to correspond quite closely to reality—such as the contemporary astronomical model of the solar system—while others are recognized as convenient fictions—such as the economic model of a perfectly rational business firm.

Although models cannot describe or directly explain empirical phenomena, they do have considerable scientific usefulness. First, a model can help us gain insight into the essential nature of a real phenomenon, by emphasizing significant features and ignoring nonessential ones. Second, use of a model facilitates scientific analysis because the abstract concepts and symbols that comprise it are easier to manipulate than is the phenomenon they represent, and also because a model is usually more internally consistent than our observations of reality. Finally, a model can alert us to similarities existing among several seemingly different phenomena.[10]

Nonetheless, when we use a scientific model we must remember that it is only a conceptual and analytical tool, and cannot be substituted for either theory or research. Models can be evaluated only in terms of utility, never of validity. As summarized by Theodore Caplow:[11]

> The study of a model should not be confused with the study of the real world. Predictions derived from the study of the real world are more or less *probable*, but predictions derived from analysis of the model are either *correct* or *incorrect*. The model contains only what we put into it. The real world contains more than we can ever get out of it. No model is an exact replica of its subject, but a useful model identifies and simplifies strategic variables so as to produce a fairly good—never a perfect—fit between effects in the arena of observation and effects obtained by manipulating symbols. The tests of an analytic model are its internal consistency, the amount of simplification achieved, and whether it can be used to predict real events.

SOCIAL SYSTEMS AND CYBERNETICS

By far the most widely used analytical model in contemporary sociology is that of a social system. System models of various kinds are used in many fields besides sociology, so a social system can be thought of as the application of a system model to social phenomena. Very generally, a system consists of a set of interrelated activities that is distinguished from its environment by some kind of boundary, that interacts with its environment in a variety of ways, that exhibits numerous dynamic internal processes, that displays patterns of ordering which are relatively stable through time, and

[10] May Brodbeck, "Models, Meaning, and Theories," in Llewellyn Gross, ed., *Symposium on Sociological Theory* (New York: Harper & Row, 1959), pp. 373–403.
[11] Theodore Caplow, *Principles of Organization* (New York: Harcourt, Brace & World, 1964), pp. 90–91.

that constitutes a single entity with its own distinctive characteristics. Expressed more briefly, *a system is a bounded and unified set of interrelated, dynamic, stable processes.*

As applied to social phenomena, the social system model is not a substantive theory of social organization. Rather, it is a highly general, content-free conceptual framework within which any number of different substantive theories of social organization can be constructed. Nor does the social system model refer to any particular kind of social organization. It is an analytical model that can be applied to any instance of the process of social organization, from families to nations. Real organizations or networks of interrelated organizations may approximate the social system model—which often leads us to speak loosely of an organization such as a university as a system, or of the economic and political systems of a society— but this approximation is never perfect and should not tempt us to confuse real organizations with the analytical model.[12]

The analysis of social systems is frequently termed *cybernetics,* which is usually defined as the scientific study of methods of control and communication. Cybernetics, in other words, is concerned with understanding the dynamics of social system functioning, on the levels of both social ordering—via control processes—and cultural ordering—via communication. Most recent attempts to apply cybernetics to social phenomena have tended to stress communication processes,[13] but the primary focus throughout this book will be on control processes, on the grounds that they are central to all social organization. Communication processes are also important for social life and cannot be ignored, but their primary relevance is to cultural systems. From the perspective of social organization, communication can be viewed as one means of effecting social control. This focus on control processes leads us to see social power as the basic dynamic medium pervading all social organization—as will be elaborated in the next chapter. Power is basic to social systems in the same sense that energy constitutes the medium of physical systems, "life" (or more properly, biochemical processes) the core of biological systems, and information the basis of cultural systems.

SOCIAL SYSTEM PROPERTIES

The most distinctive feature of the social system model is its emphasis on *the totality of the whole system.*[14] A system is seen as possessing

---

[12] Two introductory discussions of the social system model are Walter Buckley, *Sociology and Modern Systems Theory* (Englewood Cliffs, N.J.: Prentice-Hall, 1966), and Joseph H. Monane, *A Sociology of Human Systems* (New York: Appleton-Century-Crofts, 1967).
[13] An excellent example of this approach is Karl W. Deutsch, *The Nerves of Government* (New York: Free Press, 1966).
[14] A. D. Hall and R. E. Fagen, "Definition of a System," *General Systems,* 1 (1956): 18–28.

distinctive properties and a unity of its own, so that it is more than just the sum of its component parts. Emphasis on the totality of a system does not imply that its parts have no functional autonomy, but it does suggest that the parts can be thoroughly understood only in relation to the encompassing system to which they belong. Viewing these parts as completely separate entities negates the social system model. Use of the social system model is therefore appropriate whenever a sociologist wishes to focus on any type of social organization as an entity in and of itself. In fact, many social scientists, when discussing real social organizations, call them social systems to emphasize their overall totality or unity. This practice entails no serious difficulties as long as we remember that in using systematic terminology we are viewing social organization from an abstract analytical perspective and are not directly describing social reality.[15]

The following paragraphs briefly describe several other crucial properties of all social systems.

Open Boundaries. To designate a particular social system, it must be bounded in some manner so as to separate it from its social environment. Since a social system is analytically constructed rather than empirically observed, its boundaries are always arbitrarily defined by the social scientist. System boundaries are often drawn so as to approximate real organizational boundaries, but for some analytical purposes it is useful to establish entirely artificial boundaries to set off some particular set of activities. Because the boundaries of all real social organizations are at least partially open to the natural and social environments, enabling them to interact with other organizations and individuals, social system boundaries are normally conceptualized as open to varying degrees. Social systems are therefore usually described as open systems, although the extent to which a particular system model is open or closed to its environment is determined by the social scientist constructing it. The greater the degree of openness, the more the system is dependent on and influenced by its environment, and the less vulnerable it is to entropy, or eventual decay due to loss of vital resources.

Inputs and Outputs. Because an open system is interdependent with its surrounding natural and social environments, it must engage in exchange transactions with these environments. Inputs are flows of items— such as energy, raw materials, entering personnel, influences, or

---

[15] The social system model is sometimes contrasted with a coercive model, as in Ralf Dahrendorf's *Class and Class Conflict in Industrial Society* (Stanford, Calif.: Stanford University Press, 1959), chap. 5. The coercive model can be incorporated within the social system model, however, as long as one allows for some functional autonomy among the component parts. See Alvin Gouldner, "Reciprocity and Autonomy in Functional Analysis," in Llewellyn Gross, ed., *Symposium on Sociological Theory.*

information—that are taken into the system either because they are needed by the system or because they are forced onto the system by its environment. Conversely, outputs are flows of items—such as completed products, wastes, exiting personnel, influences, or information—that are given out by the system, either because it is finished with them or because they are demanded by its environment. Flows of inputs and outputs travel through openings in the system's boundaries, called gateways, that are specifically designated and equipped to handle external exchange processes. In general, the effectiveness of the system in conducting these transactions will greatly affect, if not determine, its ability to survive through time, maintain internal stability, and achieve whatever goals it seeks.

Feedback and Feedforward. Social systems, in contrast to mechanistic systems, are flexible and can adapt to changes in their natural and social environments, thus facilitating the processes of system survival, maintenance, and goal attainment. The primary means through which a system adapts to its environment is feedback, or flow of information and influence from the environment back into the system as additional inputs. These feedback flows tell the system how its natural and social environments are responding to its outputs and how adequately it is achieving its external goals. It compares these feedback messages against its intended effects or desired goals, and then modifies its subsequent activities in light of this criteria testing. Thus, social systems are guided or controlled by dynamic external feedback rather than by predetermined internal mechanisms as occurs in closed physical systems. Moreover, because a system can often respond to feedback in a variety of ways, it can transcend fixed cycles of reciprocal causes and effects to achieve flexible adaptability. Feedback messages received by a system operate in two directions, with opposing consequences for that system. Positive feedback encourages the system to continue or increase its present activities because they are producing intended consequences or leading to desired goals. Negative feedback, on the other hand, tells the system to cease or alter its activities because they are producing unintended consequences or not leading to desired goals. Both types of feedback are vital for adequate system functioning, but an excess of either type can eventually destroy a system through unchecked rapid growth or stagnation.

Feedforward is not as common as feedback, for it requires the presence within a social system of individuals capable of exercising rational foresight and planning. In this process, individuals within the system attempt to anticipate the probable consequences of proposed activities for the system and its environment before the enactment of these activities. They then modify the intended actions in light of these anticipated consequences in hopes of more effectively achieving system goals. To the extent that a system utilizes feedforward, therefore, it gains even greater control over its activities.

Internal Ordering. In addition to delineating the boundaries of the social system model being created, a social scientist must also specify its component parts and the existing relationships among them, which are often termed its "state variables." System parts may be of any number, size, and nature, depending on the purposes for which the model is being constructed. Moreover, the major parts may themselves be composed of numerous subparts, sub-subparts, and so on, thus giving the system considerable structural complexity. Since by definition these component units are parts of a total system, they will always be interrelated to some extent. Again, however, the exact nature of these patterns of relationships, or internal ordering, are specified by the model builder. One could, for instance, choose to have every part interrelated with every other part, or to have all the parts connected only through their common ties to a single central unit. Total interrelatedness among all the parts of a social system is not mandatory, however, so that the analyst can give the parts considerable amounts of functional autonomy if desired, so long as they retain some minimal ties to the whole system. To the extent that the parts are interrelated, actions of any one part will either directly or indirectly affect many or all of the other parts, as well as the total system. Once the model has been constructed and set in motion, consequently, a principal concern of the analyst is to observe changes occurring in the parts and their relationships as they respond to external inputs (including feedback) and to each other's actions.

To the extent that any given system overlaps and interlocks with other systems, it can also be viewed as part of a larger and more inclusive system. At the same time, as long as its own parts possess some amount of functional autonomy, they can be analyzed either as systems in their own right or as subsystems of the original system. Furthermore, any given subsystem may simultaneously be a part of two or more overlapping systems, so that a "total social system" can become an extremely complex model. This interrelatedness of social systems at varying levels of complexity and inclusiveness does not, however, negate the essential unity of any given system.

Key Functionaries. By virtue of their particular locations within a system and relationships with other parts, certain parts are capable of performing crucial activities or functions for the total system. These key functionaries are of several types: (1) Gatekeepers mediate or control the flow of inputs and outputs with the natural and social environments through system gateways. (2) Channelers provide pathways or channels for the flow of influence and messages among system parts as they interact. (3) Switchers are located at vital decision points within the web of relationships among system parts and thus direct the flow of activities occurring within the system. (4) Storers provide storage places for whatever resources and information are not currently being used by the system but that may be needed in the future. Although each type of key functionary performs a unique function for the system, they all share one feature in common. Because the system continually depends on adequate performance of their functions for its overall survival and operations, they are capable of wielding considerable power over other parts and the entire system. As a result of their locations and activities, key functionaries are thus centers of power within social systems.

SOCIAL SYSTEM PROCESSES

As described thus far, the social system model is relatively static in nature. If it is to be applicable to ongoing social processes and organizations, however, the model must also incorporate dynamic processes. Unlike closed mechanistic systems that respond only to predetermined internal programs, open social systems are continually being impinged upon by external forces that create tensions within the system. Similarly, inside the system the actions of any one part will create tensions for all the other parts with which it is interrelated. Thus, social systems are constantly tension-ridden. In the words of Walter Buckley: "Far from seeing any principle of 'inertia' operating in complex adaptive systems, with 'tension' occurring only occasionally or residually as a 'disturbing' factor, we must see some level of tension as characteristic of and vital to such systems though it may manifest itself as now destructive, now constructive."[16]

As a result of these pervasive external and internal tensions, social systems display two basic types of processes: morphostasis and morphogenesis. The first type refers to all those processes that tend to preserve or maintain a system's present conditions or overall state, giving it stability through time. The second type refers to those processes that tend to alter or elaborate a system's conditions or state, producing change or growth through time. The following paragraphs explore both types of system processes in greater detail.[17]

[16]Buckley, *Sociology and Modern Systems Theory*, p. 52.
[17]The following discussions of both morphostatic and morphogenic processes are drawn largely from Ludwig von Bertalanffy, "General Systems Theory," *General Systems* 1 (1956); 1–10; and from Buckley, *Sociology and Modern Systems Theory*, chaps. 2 and 3. For applied conceptualizations of these processes see Robert Chin, "The Utility of System Models for Practitioners," in Warren G. Bennis et al., eds., *The Planning of Change* (New York: Holt, Rinehart and Winston, 1951), pp. 201–214.

Morphostasis. Social systems are morphostatic, or self-maintaining, to the extent that they are able to cope in some manner with external and internal tensions and thus maintain their overall stability and unity. If a system is not capable of adapting to impinging tensions, pressures will continue to build up to the point where the system is either radically altered or totally destroyed.

The simplest and most common morphostatic process is balancing, in which an increase in some external force or internal activity is balanced by a corresponding decrease in some other system activity or part, or vice versa. For example, social systems frequently tend to maintain at least a rough balance between member input and output, with resulting population stability. Depending on the effectiveness of the system's control mechanisms, balancing can occur virtually automatically and continuously or only randomly and sporadically. In all cases, however, balancing processes involve only those particular aspects of the system that are linked in a balanced relationship, and not the entire system.

Homeostasis is a somewhat more complex morphostatic process in which the system's tension-coping efforts are focused on certain critical system features. These critical features are typically activities or parts that are crucial for system survival or that wield dominant power in the system, such as boundary maintenance, vital resource inputs, basic patterns of ordering, decision-making procedures, or various key functionaries. Whenever disruptive tensions threaten those critical features that the system as a whole is protecting, adjustive actions are taken by the system to counter the tensions and maintain system stability.

The process of homeostasis thus necessitates considerable activity and alterations by many or all system parts not being protected. These compensatory system activities are guided and controlled by feedback messages, both from the natural and social environments and among system parts. For example, if an environmental threat to the system's boundaries is countered with a defensive action of some kind, the system must then receive feedback concerning the effectiveness of its strategy so that it "knows" whether to continue this action or try some other tactic. The language used to describe homeostatic processes often appears to impute teleology, or minded purpose, to social systems, but this inference is not warranted. A common illustration of a homeostatic process, for instance, is a furnace controlled by a thermostat that registers a drop in room temperature, which in turn activates the furnace to provide more heat so as to keep the room at a constant temperature.

A third kind of morphostatic process is equilibrium maintenance, which perpetuates the system in a steady state. Equilibrium exists in a social system when all the parts maintain a constant relationship to each other, so that no part changes its position or relation with respect to any of the other parts.[18] Disruptive tensions may temporarily upset this equilibrium, creating periods of disequilibrium, but sooner or later the system neutralizes or eliminates whatever disruptive forces are impinging upon it and thus restores its equilibrium. Whereas in homeostasis only one or a few selected features of the system are protected through the actions of other parts, in equilibrium maintenance every part is preserved in a constant relation to every other part, preserving equilibrium throughout the total system.

A change in any one part of an equilibrium system will necessarily produce a corresponding change in every other part. Equilibrium can therefore occur only when all the system's parts are interrelated in some manner, which is a rather artificial condition that social system analysts rarely assume because of its inapplicability to most real social organizations. In addition, equilibrium also assumes that the system's boundaries are closed to the environment and that its parts exercise no functional autonomy. Given these necessary conditions, the analyst then opens the boundaries of the system in a carefully controlled manner and interjects a precisely defined and measured disruptive force, which creates disequilibrium. After reclosing the boundaries, one observes and records whatever activity occurs in the system as it acts to reassert equilibrium. To enable one to measure this activity and determine when equilibrium is restored, all variables in the system must be mathematically quantified. Because at present we cannot quantify many important sociological variables, sophisticated analysis of equilibrium processes is extremely difficult, although the use of simulation techniques with computers offers considerable promise for the future.[19]

Equilibrium social systems are commonly divided into two basic types: stationary and dynamic. A system in stationary equilibrium will always return to its initial state after disruptive forces have been dispelled. A system in dynamic equilibrium, in contrast, may assume new forms as the result of its reequilibrating activities. In both cases, though, the overall pattern of relationships among all parts of the system remains constant. The point on which equilibrium centers can either remain at rest or move, but the basic form of the system never changes. Finally, stationary and dynamic equilibrium should not be confused with stable, neutral, and unstable equilibrium, which are simply three ways of describing the strength of the disruptive force that must be introduced before system equilibrium is upset. If the equilibrium of a system is unstable, the slightest disruption will upset whatever equilibrium exists; if the equilibrium is stable, a considerable amount of

[18] This definition, as well as the following discussion of equilibrium, is drawn primarily from two sources: David Easton, "Limits of the Equilibrium Model in Social Research," *Behavioral Science* 1 (1956): 96–104; and Everett Hagen, "Analytic Models in the Study of Social Systems," *American Journal of Sociology* 67 (September 1961); pp. 144–151.

[19] Jay W. Forrester, *Urban Dynamics* (Cambridge, Mass.: The M.I.T. Press, 1969).

force is required to initiate reequilibrating activities; and if the equilibrium is neutral, nothing will disturb it.

Morphogenesis. All morphostatic processes cope with disruptive tensions by attempting in one way or another to maintain the system in its present condition. In contrast, a unique feature of open systems—both organic and social—is the ability to adapt to tensions through system change or growth. That is, they display morphogenic as well as morphostatic processes. In morphogenesis, a system develops toward increasing order, complexity, unity, or operational effectiveness. It need not develop in all these directions at once, and development along any one line does not automatically produce growth in all other areas. In general, though, morphogenesis enables a system to deal more effectively with its environment and its own subsystems. As a consequence, it grows both structurally, in terms of increased internal complexity and ordering, and functionally, in terms of effective ability to control its activities and attain its goals. In contrast to closed mechanistic systems, which tend toward entropy—that is, to "run down" and eventually disintegrate—open adaptive systems can develop and grow through time as they deal with tensions.

For morphogenesis to occur, however, two conditions must prevail in a system. First, the system must preserve a favorable ratio of inputs over outputs, which gives it a surplus of resources to devote to its own growth. These slack resources are converted by key functionaries of the system into power that can be used in various ways to expand or improve existing activities and parts, or to add new activities and parts to the system. Second, the system must incorporate and utilize feedback processes that constantly provide it with information from the natural and social environments and from its own subsystems. On the basis of this information, key functionaries can learn to direct and control the system more effectively in the future, and the system gains greater self-awareness of its own dynamics.

The use of such terms as "learning" and "self-awareness" does not imply that morphogenesis necessarily involves purposeful or rational thought, any more than does morphostasis. Much system growth is undoubtedly similar to the biological process of natural selection, in which random occurrences that prove beneficial to the system are incorporated and retained, while nonbeneficial occurrences are discarded. Growth can also take place through manipulation of the system, even though the actors involved in these processes are not aware of the consequences of their activities for system development. For example, participants in a social system might for some reason increase the flow of resources into the system, improve intrasystem communication, create new subsystems, or strengthen existing relationships among system parts—all without any conscious awareness that these activities were increasing the complexity or functional effectiveness of the total system.

The actual process of system growth can occur in countless different ways, ranging from sporadic but extensive jumps that shift the system from one state to another, to continuous but minute alterations whose cumulative effects are observable only over a long span of time. More generally, systems are often portrayed as growing either linearly or exponentially, depending on their rate of growth. A linearly growing system increases by a more-or-less constant amount (say 10 units) during a given time period (say one year), so that when charted, its growth approximates a straight line. An exponentially growing system, in contrast, increases by a constant percentage (say 10 percent) during a given time period, with the result that its growth line rises at a steadily increasing rate. Within a short period of time, such a system can become very large: with a 10 percent growth rate per year, it will double in size in just seven years and in fourteen years it will be four times its original size. This kind of almost unrestrained growth, which often results from an excess of positive over negative feedback, can quickly have disastrous consequences for a system. A current illustration of this process is the "world model" that predicts total collapse of the world's economic and ecological systems during the twenty-first century if present exponential population and industrial development rates are not limited.[20]

The public concern aroused by this prediction raises a question often confronted by users of system models that incorporate morphostasis and morphogenesis. To what extent do either or both of these system processes exist in real social organizations? Morphostatic and morphogenic processes occur in social systems because the analyst builds them into the model. But is it valid to assume inherent tendencies toward morphostasis or morphogenesis in real organizations? Although this is a topic of considerable debate, most sociologists would probably answer in the negative. It is certainly true that actions by members and subunits of social organizations often produce morphostatic or morphogenic processes within that organization. In fact, since individuals are capable of purposeful social activities, they may intentionally seek to promote organizational maintenance or growth, and such collectively oriented perspectives and actions are commonly viewed as effective leadership. But the fact that morphostatic and morphogenic processes frequently occur in real social organizations, either intentionally or unintentionally, does not warrant the assumption that these processes are inherent in all organizations. The degree to which morphostasis and morphogenesis actually occur in any real organization must always remain a problematic question for sociological research.

[20] Donella H. Meadows et. al., *The Limits to Growth* (Washington, D.C.: Potomac Associates, 1972).

The Concept of Social Organization

IN summary of this first chapter, let us recapitulate its major ideas:

The creation of social organization occurs within a setting imposed by the parameters of the human personality, population characteristics, the natural environment, material technology, and the surrounding social environment. As a result of a variety of causal factors, individuals interact with one another and influence one another's actions and thoughts. Through time many of these interactions develop into enduring social relationships that form interrelated and recurrent patterns of social ordering. The resulting collective activities in turn give rise to shared cultural ideas that give meaning to organized social life.

Out of this emergent process of social organization arise many relatively stable organizational forms. To describe and analyze social organizations, we are forced by the limitations of our perceptual abilities to freeze these ongoing processes into static pictures, but by combining many such observations through time, we can learn to see social organization as a dynamic process. Emergent social organizations are exterior to individual personalities and continually constrain or influence the actions of their members. The partial autonomy of social organization is also evident in the fact that organizations display properties of their own that are not inherent in their constituent members. At the same time, individual personalities, patterns of social ordering, and cultural ideas always interpenetrate each other so that none of them can exist entirely apart from the others.

To represent the interrelated wholeness of social organization, we frequently employ the social system model. This model is not a representation of reality, but an analytical tool that enables us to conceptualize social organizations as dynamic entities that continuously display both morphostatic and morphogenetic processes which simultaneously function to maintain and alter social organizations.

In short, the process of social organization occurs as individuals interact in patterned and recurrent relationships to create social ordering that becomes infused with common cultural meanings. The crucial idea here is that through the emergent process of organization the whole becomes more than the mere sum of its parts, gains unity, and exists as a real phenomenon. Whitehead saw this principle of emergent organization as the basis of all existence: "The ultimate metaphysical principle is the advance from disjunction to conjunction, creating a novel entity other than the entities given in disjunction. . . . The many become one, and are increased by one." [21]

---

[21] Whitehead, *Process and Reality*, p. 32.

RECOMMENDED READING

Bertalanffy, Ludwig von. "General Systems Theory." *General Systems* 1 (1956): 1–10.
>A broad description of the system model, outlining its major characteristics and distinctive features..

Bertrand, Alvin L. *Social Organization.* Philadelphia: F. A. Davis, 1972.
>An examination of the total process of social organization, as viewed from the perspective of social role theory and social systems analysis.

Braude, Lee. *A Sense of Sociology.* New York: Praeger, 1974.
>An overview, for nonsociologists, of the problems, prospects, and pleasures of the field at the present time, viewing it as both an intellectual perspective and a science.

Buckley, Walter. *Sociology and Modern Systems Theory.* Englewood Cliffs, N.J.: Prentice-Hall, 1967.
>A comprehensive exploration and analysis of the social system model as applied to social processes and organizations.

Durkheim, Émile. *The Rules of Sociological Method,* trans. by Sarah A. Solovay and John H. Mueller. New York: Free Press, 1938; chap. 12.
>The classic statement of the reality of social phenomena apart from their constituent individuals.

Meadows, Paul. "Models, Systems, and Science." *American Sociological Review* 22 (February 1957): 3–9.
>An argument that various kinds of system models pervade all sociological theory, and an outline of mechanistic and organistic system models.

Monane, Joseph H. *A Sociology of Human Systems.* New York: Appleton-Century-Crofts, 1967.
>A general, nontechnical discussion of social system properties and processes.

Warriner, Charles K. "Groups are Real." *American Sociological Review* 21 (October 1956): 549–554.
>An argument for the reality of groups and organizations, as opposed to nominalistic, neonominalistic, and interactionalist perspectives on social organization.

2

Power and Social Organization

TO explain the fundamental dynamics of organized social life, philosophers and sociologists have relied on principles as diverse as biological instincts and "the spirit of an age" (*Zeitgeist*). Somewhere in between these biological and spiritual extremes lies the mundane but pervasive arena of social power exertion. The idea that social power constitutes the core of all social ordering and organization has been suggested by social philosophers since antiquity, from Plato to Machiavelli to Thomas Hobbes. Yet most twentieth-century sociologists have given relatively little attention to power processes, and have not viewed the process of social organization as a manifestation of the exercise of social power.

A few recent writers have attempted to draw attention to the crucial importance of power in social life, as in Robert Bierstedt's argument that: "Power supports the fundamental order of society and the social organization within it. . . . Power stands behind every association and sustains its structure. Without power there is no organization and without power there is no order."[1] But not until the 1960s did social power become a major

[1] Robert Bierstedt, "An Analysis of Social Power," *American Sociological Review* 15 (December 1950): 730–738.

concern of sociological theorizing, and it still remains one of the least understood aspects of social life. Nevertheless, if we conceive of social interaction as a process in which one actor affects another, then every instance of interaction and every social relationship involves the exercise of power. And as these processes give rise to broader patterns of social ordering and delineated organizations—from families to societies—all organized social life becomes infused with power exertion. As expressed by Amos Hawley: "Every social act is an exercise of power, every social relationship is a power equation, and every social group or system is an organization of power. Accordingly, it is possible to transpose any system of social relationships into terms of potential or active power. Perhaps such a transposition is nothing more than the substitution of one terminology for another."[2]

The Nature of Social Power

SOCIAL power can be viewed analytically as both a cause and a consequence of social organization, although in reality these are but two sides of the same coin. On the one side, power exertion is a fundamental process contributing to the creation and perpetuation of all social organization. As power is created through social activities, it can be used to impose social ordering and cultural ideas upon any realm of collective social life. Conversely, inability to exercise power effectively may seriously impede or prevent the creation of social organization. On the other side, power is continually being generated through the process of social organization and is an inevitable outcome of this process whenever and wherever it occurs. Organized power exertion enables actors to perform collective activities and attain common goals that none of them could achieve individually.

The fundamental theoretical postulate underlying this entire volume is that *the exercise of social power pervades all social organization and all its component processes.* Although social power is neither the sole cause nor the only outcome of the process of social organization, it must always be taken into consideration if we wish fully to understand organized social life. Because its existence and exertion can only be indirectly inferred from its effects on social activities, we are often led to disregard or minimize its critical significance, but to ignore social power is to overlook the very core of the process of social organization.

THE CONCEPT OF SOCIAL POWER

Power in social life is analogous to energy in the physical world: wherever we look we observe its effects, and all activities are an expression of

[2]Amos H. Hawley, "Community Power and Urban Renewal Success," *American Journal of Sociology* 68 (January 1963): 422-431.

it. We talk freely about the uses of power and energy, even though neither can be directly observed or measured. The most general way of conceptualizing social power, therefore, is to think of it as the essence of all social activities. Just as all physical phenomena are ultimately reducible or convertible to energy, so all social phenomena are in an ultimate sense manifestations of power. This is the meaning of Hawley's statement that social power and social relationships are merely alternative terminologies for the same reality.

There are at least two practical problems with this conceptualization of social power, however. One is that it leaves the idea of power both vague and redundant, since it has no meaning apart from the ideas of social interaction and organization. If we could precisely measure social power, it would provide an extremely useful common denominator for analyzing all social phenomena, but since we cannot do this at the present time, it remains just another item in the sociological lexicon. The second problem is linguistic, in that "power" is a noun rather than a verb, and hence is not readily applicable to a process conception of social life. To convert it into an active process, we must either use a phrase such as "exercise power," or else employ a partial synonym such as "influence" which can be used as a verb.

For these reasons, the idea of social power is used in this book only as a generic sensitizing concept. As a generic concept it provides a single inclusive term encompassing such phenomena as influence, control, force, dominance, authority, and attraction. As a sensitizing concept it alerts us to view all social activities as power processes and to attempt to explain these activities in power terms insofar as possible. From this perspective, *social power is the ability to shape the process of social organization through time, despite resistance.*

CHARACTERISTICS OF SOCIAL POWER

Social power always exists within social relationships. Hence it is meaningful only within interactional or organizational settings. Individuals may possess a certain amount of physical strength, special knowledge or competence, strong personality qualities, or particular interaction abilities such as leadership skills, but none of these personal capabilities constitutes social power. One's personal characteristics can contribute to his or her power in a particular situation, but social power always resides within social relationships. The chairperson of a committee, for instance, might exercise power over the actions of the other members and the activities of the committee as a whole, but this power lies in the person's relationships within the committee. If this individual should be removed from office or leave the group, he or she will no longer wield the power created by the group, even though he or she retains extensive personal skill at conducting meetings. Similarly, organizations do not possess power in isolation, but only as they potentially or actively relate to other organizations. Consequently, in any power relationship the actions of the recipient are as important as those of the exerter, for the manner in which the recipient responds to the exerter largely determines the outcomes of that power transaction.

Social power can be exercised by individuals or organizations. Although power always occurs within social relationships, the actors who exert it and the recipients of their actions can be individuals, subunits of larger organizations, or whole organizations. Although interpersonal influence or control is relatively easy to conceptualize, interorganizational power exertion often is not. While interactions among subunits or organizations are carried out by individuals representing those entities, it is the collectivity that is exercising power in this case. The representatives of a labor union and a business firm who meet to bargain on a new contract are able to exert power on each other only because they both represent organized collectivities, regardless of their personal bargaining skills. Moreover, real social life exhibits endless diverse combinations of interpersonal and interorganizational power. A husband who determines how much money his wife spends on household expenses is wielding interpersonal power, while the family as a social unit exerts organizational power in relation to other organizations with which it interacts, including local businesses, perhaps a church or school, and to some extent the entire community. Similarly, one member of a national legislature may wield interpersonal power over another member, while the legislature as a whole exercises organizational power over its component parts (such as committees) and over many other organizations within the society, as well as the entire nation. This situation is further complicated by the fact that individuals acting as representatives of organizations often use their roles and positions to further their own interpersonal power. It is true that we frequently label our power acts as either personal ("Do this for me") or organizational ("This office opposes . . ."), but our actions do not always substantiate our words.

Different definitions of power reflect this distinction between interpersonal and interorganizational power processes. For instance, an interpersonal perspective is reflected in the statement that "a person may be said to have power to the extent that he influences the behavior of others in accordance with his own intentions."[3] An organizational perspective, in contrast, is seen in the definition of power as "the generalized capacity of a social system to get things done in the interest of collective goals."[4] Edward

[3] Herbert Goldhamer and Edward Shils, "Types of Power and Status," *American Journal of Sociology* 45 (September 1939): 171–182.
[4] Talott Parsons, *Structure and Process in Modern Societies* (New York: Free Press, 1960), pp. 180–181.

Lehman's conceptions of "intermember" and "systemic" power catch this distinction quite clearly.[5] He notes that "The study of [intermember] power relations focuses primarily on the competition over scarce resources in a system. Unequal control of resources is a major basis of success in such intermember struggles, and hence it also provides the basis for greater and greater slanting in the distributive process and consequently of greater and greater inequality in power." Conversely, "In its systemic form, power refers to the capacity of some unit acting as an agent of the system to overcome the resistance of members in setting, pursuing, and implementing collective goals."

Social power varies in determinateness from influence to control. The terms "influence" and "control" are frequently used as synonyms for social power, although they might more properly be thought of as the two end points of a continuum of power determinateness or outcomes. Social influence is power exertion in which the outcomes are problematic. Influence can only be attempted, not predetermined, and the recipient retains some leeway in accepting or rejecting the influence. In contrast, social control is power exertion in which the outcomes are largely or totally predictable. Control can be exercised regardless of the wishes of the recipient, with little or no doubt concerning its results. To mention one example, a railroad company might be able to exert only moderate influence over a large metropolis, but be able to control the economic fate of a small business that relied on rail shipment of its products. In short, the exercise of social power varies from mild influence to total control, depending on the amount and types of power being exerted and the relative power of the other actors involved.[6]

Social power is generated through the use of resources. Before either an individual or an organization can exert influence or control, this actor must have access to resources that are relevant to the situation. A resource is anything that is desired or valued by others, and hence can be used by an actor to generate power in relation to them. Resources can be either tangible items such as money, land, material goods, and organizational members, or relatively intangible assets such as knowledge, skills, legitimacy, and organizational unity. Whatever their nature, these available resources provide the basis on which an actor's power rests. By drawing on them—or threatening to do so—an actor gains the ability to exert power. Unlike power, which

---

[5] Edward H. Lehman, *A Macrosociology of Politics* (New York: Columbia University Press, 1977).

[6] Some writers (cf. William Gamson, *Power and Discontent* [Homewood, Ill.: The Dorsey Press, 1968]) apply the term "influence" to attempts by individuals to affect organizations and "control" to organizational actions directed toward individuals. This restriction appears unnecessarily limiting, however, and does not accord with everyday usage of these terms. Those two specific situations might well be termed "participation" and "regulation," respectively.

occurs only in social relationships, however, resources can be possessed by an individual or organization alone. In general, the greater the resources of the power wielder in relation to the recipient, the more likely the wielder is to attempt to control the recipient. Conversely, the weaker the resources of the wielder in relation to the recipient, the more likely it is that only influence will be attempted.

Social power may be either potential or active in nature. An actor is often said to have potential power when he or she or it possesses relevant resources and is capable of employing them if desired. Power then becomes active when these resources are converted into actions toward others. This distinction reminds us that (1) resources must be readily available for use before they can be drawn upon for power exertion, and (2) an actor can be viewed by others as capable of wielding power even though no overt action occurs. The first point can just as well be made by always speaking of "available resources." The second point is more important, however, since an actor's potential for exerting power is often assessed and taken into account by possible recipients. These assessments are essentially probabilistic expectations of the actor's willingness to use available resources and his or her skill at converting them into actions, based on knowledge of his or her past activities and the immediate situation. In this latter sense, "potential power" is a useful concept for sociological analysis, although use of the alternative term "perceived power" would remind us that the accuracy of these assessments is often affected by values, statuses, and other characteristics of the assessors.

Social power can be exercised either intentionally or unintentionally. If a social actor purposefully attempts to affect others to achieve some desired outcome, this power exertion is clearly intentional in nature. In other cases, however, the same outcome might come about even though the actor had no purposeful intention of wielding power. Often a given action has both intended and unintended power consequences, as when a newspaper union calls a strike to gain higher wages for its members, but the strike also has extensive side effects on stores, theaters, voluntary associations, and other community organizations. For analytical and empirical convenience, the process of power exertion is often limited to intentional goal-seeking activities and their immediate consequences. But in reality, much power wielding is relatively or wholly unintended, so that more encompassing investigations of power must also take these effects into consideration. Closely related to this distinction is the difference between direct and indirect power exertion. Power is exercised directly when it flows from the power wielder straight to the recipient. It becomes indirect when it passes through one or more intermediate actors before reaching its ultimate destination. Indirect social power frequently takes the form of ordering social situations in particular ways, which in turn affects the actions that individuals or organizations can take. In general, intentional power exertion is usually fairly direct, while unintentional power wielding is often rather indirect, but it is possible to intentionally try to exert power indirectly or to unintentionally have direct social effects on others.

Social power exertion necessitates overcoming resistance. Many definitions of social power include the idea of overcoming resistance from recipients. Resistance can occur in the form of active opposition through the exertion of countervailing power, which usually results in conflict between the wielder and the recipient. It can also take passive nonconflicting forms such as reluctant compliance, avoidance of the situation through alternative courses of action, or indifference to the effects of the attempted power exertion. Regardless of the nature of the resistance, nevertheless, the exercise of power is almost always a reciprocal process among the involved actors, and is rarely completely determined by a single actor no matter how unequal the situation may appear. If the resistance by others to an actor's attempted power exertion is sufficient to prevent that actor from having any effect on them, the actor remains powerless in that situation. More common, however, are situations in which the resistance of the recipients is sufficient to alter or limit but not completely block the attempted power exertion. Even though power relationships are thus usually asymmetrical in strength, the recipients may in turn mobilize their own resources to exert some other kind of power back on the original actor. Thus all power transactions can be described as exchanges among the involved participants.

Social power exertion can be either balanced or unbalanced. The exchanges that occur in power transactions can vary in nature from evenly balanced to grossly unbalanced. In a relatively balanced situation, each actor exerts approximately the same amount of influence or control on the other actor(s). The forms of power exercised by the various actors may differ, but the outcome is a more or less even exchange in which all the participants receive approximately equal benefits. Consequently, they usually feel that the transaction has been fair and nonexploitive. In a highly unbalanced situation, conversely, one or a few actors exert much greater influence or control than the rest. Regardless of the manner in which this power is exerted or the extent to which it is willingly accepted by the recipients, the power wielders—often termed *elites*—typically receive much greater benefits than the other participants. The recipients of this power exertion therefore frequently feel manipulated or exploited.

Social power can either promote or prevent actions. The exercise of power can enable actors to accomplish activities that otherwise would not occur, or to prevent actions that otherwise would occur. Those sociologists who emphasize the restrictive side of power often speak of it as "control *over* others" and tend to deplore its occurrence because of an underlying ideological belief that power is antithetical to freedom of action. In contrast, those who emphasize the activating side of power describe it as "influence *with* others" for the attainment of collective goals, and view it as necessary and desirable for organized social life. It would seem clear that if sociologists are to study power objectively, they must as far as possible put aside all such ideological beliefs and explore the ways in which power exertion both promotes and prevents social actions.

Types of Power

THE exercise of social power occurs whenever a social actor shapes the process of social organization in some manner. To facilitate the analysis of power, however, it can be categorized into four different types, depending on the nature of the resources employed and the intentionality of the action. Power exertion can also be described as taking one of three forms, depending on the degree of balance or unbalance in the power transaction.

FOUR TYPES OF SOCIAL POWER

Four fairly distinct types of social power often identified by sociologists are force, dominance, authority, and attraction.[7] As mentioned above, the major differences among these types lie in the nature of the resources on which they are based and whether they are exerted intentionally or unintentionally. Force involves the intended utilization of previously uncommitted and valued resources, dominance occurs unintentionally from the performance of existing social roles, authority rests on the intentional exercise of normative legitimacy, and attraction results primarily from the unintended growth of affective feelings. The following paragraphs discuss these four types of power in greater detail.

Force.   To exert force over others, an actor must intentionally convert resources into overt pressures or coercion or at least convincingly threaten to

[7]This typology is drawn from several different schools of thought that have not before been combined. The major, though not the only, sources of the ideas presented here are Robert Bierstedt, "An Analysis of Social Power," *American Sociological Review* 15 (December 1950): 730-738; Robert Dubin, "Power, Function, and Organization," *Pacific Sociological Review* 6 (Spring, 1963): 16-22; Amitai Etzioni, *The Active Society* (New York: Free Press, 1968), pp. 314-323; John R. P. French, Jr., and Bertram Raven, *Social Power* (Ann Arbor, Mich.: The University of Michigan Institute for Social Research, 1959), chap. 9; Seymour Martin Lipset, *Political Man* (New York: Doubleday, 1960), chap. 3; Robert E. Park, *Human Communities* (New York: Free Press, 1952), chap. 13; and Max Weber, *The Theory of Social and Economic Organization*, trans. by A. M. Henderson and Talcott Parsons (New York: Free Press, 1947), pp. 324-363.

do so. The actor must purposefully invest previously uncommitted resources in the relationship and be prepared to use them to back up his or her demands and overcome resistance. Even if one successfully bluffs the recipients into following one's wishes, these goods or assets are committed to that power relationship for the duration of its existence and cannot simultaneously be used elsewhere. More commonly, however, a person will have to expend part or all of these committed resources to gain his or her goal. To the extent that many resources are limited in quantity or availability, any one actor's ability to exercise force is correspondingly restricted, although great disparities occur among actors in the amount of force they can exert toward one another.

Three frequently identified subtypes of force are inducement (also called compensation), constraint (also called deprivation), and persuasion (also called convincement). Inducement involves providing desired objectives or conditions in return for obedience. Constraint involves applying punishments or withholding desired benefits as a consequence of nonobedience. Persuasion involves the manipulation of information, emotions, attitudes, or values. Each kind of force has a different consequence for the actor employing it. Constraint can be accomplished through threats without actually expending resources or it may require elaborate negative sanctioning procedures, but in either case the obedience obtained from others is given grudgingly and remains highly unreliable. As soon as the constraint is lifted, obedience will normally cease. Inducement requires the continual bestowing of benefits, rewards, or other positive sanctions, but because the recipients usually feel that they are also gaining from the relationship this kind of force can become considerably more stable and reliable. Finally, since persuasion often produces relatively permanent motivational or attitudinal changes in the recipients, its effects can be extremely stable and reliable through time, and may continue long after the initial persuasion has occurred.

Dominance. To exercise functional dominance, an actor must effectively perform activities or roles within a social organization, but one need not intentionally seek to affect others or draw on additional resources. Functional specialization and interdependence among the members and subunits of an organization tend to make each of them highly vulnerable to the actions of the other participants. As actors perform their routine activities and roles within the organization, therefore, they often unintentionally influence or control the actions of many other interdependent actors, as well as the functioning of the entire organization. To the extent that this occurs, functional dominance is being exerted. The resource base for the exertion of dominance is thus an actor's ability to effectively perform organizational activities and roles, and does not depend on access to any additional goods or assets. In practice, an actor may seek to use a position of dominance to also exert force by drawing on organizational resources for one's own use or by threatening to withhold services until one's demands are met, but this overlapping does not erase the analytical distinction between force and dominance. Whereas force always requires the intentional utilization of additional resources, dominance flows unintentionally from the routine performance of functional activities within an organization.

Dominance is often observed in such activities as information flows, economic transactions, transportation services, and allocative decision making, although it can occur within any kind of organized activity in which the participants are functionally specialized and interdependent. Actors occupying positions at the top or the center of an organization, as well as key functionaries such as boundary gatekeepers and communication channelers, are often in a particularly advantageous location to exert dominance over a wide range of organizational activities. Nevertheless, any person or unit within an organization can exercise some amount of dominance over others to the extent that they are functionally dependent on this actor. As all realms of social life in modern societies become increasingly interdependent and highly organized, functional dominance emerges as a crucial and extremely stable and reliable type of power exertion.

Authority. To exercise authority, an actor must first be granted legitimacy by those subject to his or her directions or commands. They must in some way voluntarily accord this actor the legitimate right to make binding decisions for them, direct their activities, or otherwise influence or control them. This grant of legitimacy then becomes the actor's resource base for exercising authoritative power, so that authority can be described as the intentional utilization of legitimacy. The power exerter in this case purposefully draws on these grants of legitimacy to request or demand compliance with his or her dictates, and the recipients voluntarily comply because they view these dictates as legitimate and proper. Legitimacy is sometimes given to an actor through direct procedures such as formal votes or informal agreements, but more commonly it is indirectly expressed as one joins an organization, remains a member, and supports the actions of those who claim legitimacy. To the extent that legitimacy is granted in any of these ways, a government can exercise authority over all other parts of a society, the personnel office of a company has the authority to hire and fire employees, and a committee chairperson has authority to conduct meetings.

Four grounds on which legitimate authority often rests, as identified by Max Weber, are traditional values and beliefs, legal prerogatives established through more or less rational agreements, special expertise or knowledge relevant to the situation, and charismatic appeal by revered leaders.[8] To the extent that an actor draws legitimacy from all four sources, as when he or she is particularly well qualified for a position, obtains it through legal procedures, adheres to established values, and is seen as possessing unusual charisma, his or her grounds for exercising authority are particularly strong. In addition, legitimacy can also be acquired through the effective performance of organizational functions or even the successful employment of force, especially over long periods of time. Organizational leaders and others with established legitimacy frequently supplement their authority at times by exercising dominance through their activities and by exerting force derived from organizational resources, although if carried too far such activities can erode their legitimacy rather than enhance it. Because authority is a highly stable and reliable type of social power, organizational leaders almost invariably seek to protect and extend their legitimacy, no matter how they acquire their positions or how extensively they also utilize force and dominance in particular situations. Even if a government comes to power through violent revolution and controls its society through coercion, it will still seek to create an image of legitimacy through such devices as plebiscites and mass communications. It can hardly afford to do otherwise, since without legitimacy its ability to govern is constantly in jeopardy and its ability to provide leadership is severely restricted.

Attraction. To employ attraction, an actor must first be appealing to others in some way. They must like some characteristic or ability of that actor, and for this reason voluntarily follow his or her lead. This appeal then becomes the actor's resource for exerting attractive power. Appeal to others is sometimes purposefully cultivated, but more commonly it is simply unintentionally present, so that attraction can be described as the predominantly unintentional utilization of social appeal. Others will then shape their actions in accord with the ideas or activities of the actor to whom they are attracted, regardless of whether or not that actor is aware of the example he or she is setting.

Three common sources of attraction are cognitive identification with another person or an organization, affective feelings or "liking" toward an individual or organization, and charisma, or the attribution of "superhuman" or "divine" qualities to a person or organization (although charismatic appeal is in no way limited to religion). Thus individuals might comply with the demands of a political party because they identified with its policies, because it had always been their family's party, or because they believed that the party or its leaders were carrying out some "ultimate

[8]Weber, *The Theory of Social and Economic Organization.*

mission." Because attraction is determined largely by the unintended appeal that others feel toward an actor, rather than by his or her purposeful actions, this type of power tends to be quite unstable and unreliable, though at times it can become extremely strong. In practice, moreover, attraction often shades into force, as the appealing actor seeks to manipulate others' feelings as a means of exerting pressure on them, or into authority, as charismatic or affective appeals are employed as a claim to legitimacy.

All four of these types of power—force, dominance, authority, and attraction—occur throughout all realms of social life, on both the interpersonal and interorganizational levels, in both potential and active states, with both positive and negative effects, and in all degrees of determinateness from weak influence to total control. In use, they commonly become highly interwoven, as actors convert one type to another or use one form to supplement another. Nevertheless, the four types are quite distinct in their basic nature and consequences for social organization.

THREE FORMS OF POWER EXERTION

All four types of power can occur in situations ranging from evenly balanced to totally unbalanced. Although degree of balance in a power relationship is a continuous gradient, it is often useful to describe the poles of this continuum as distinctive forms of power exertion. The tripartite classification of power suggested by Amitai Etzioni—utilitarian, coercive, and persuasive—provides terms that are applicable here.[9] With *utilitarian* power exertion, all the participants exercise more or less equal amounts of power upon each other and all benefit from the exchange. With *coercive* power exertion, one or a few actors wield grossly disproportionate amounts of power, so that the situation is highly unbalanced and the benefits are quite unequal. With *persuasive* power exertion the situation is also relatively unbalanced, but in this case the power wielder is able to persuade the recipient(s) that the inequality is justified or at least acceptable because of overriding ethical or normative considerations, or because of unique personal factors of some kind. Etzioni claims that these three forms of power exertion are mutually exclusive and theoretically exhaustive, and many sociologists use this conceptual scheme.[10] Regardless of the validity of that claim, his terms aid us in describing the exertion of social power in balanced and unbalanced situations. And as we shall note in Chapter 7, each form of power exertion if most evident at a different level of ordering within the process of social organization.

[9] Etzioni, *The Active Society*, chap. 14.
[10] Gamson, *Power and Discontent*.

The Creation of Social Power

TWO metatheoretical or philosophical perspectives on the nature of social life pervade all contemporary sociological thinking. Ralf Dahrendorf's terms of "coercion" and "consensus" are widely used labels for these two perspectives.[11] although the older concepts of "conflict" and "cooperation" refer to essentially the same notions. Whichever terminology one prefers, the philosophical distinction between the two perspectives remains remarkably consistent across all theoretical schemes in sociology. The first of these perspectives stresses *differences* among individuals and groups in interests, resources, and values. These differences cause actors to become dependent on one another, so that social ordering is a functional necessity based on mutual interdependence and compulsion. The second perspective stresses *similarities* among individuals and groups in activities, interests, and values. These similarities give rise to consensus among actors, so that social ordering results from shared commitments and compliance. These metatheoretical perspectives on social organization are reflected in the two major sociological theories of power creation sketched below.

DEPENDENCY THEORY

The dependency theory of power creation, which stresses differences among actors, has been formulated most concisely by Richard Emerson.[12] The central thesis of this argument is that *"power resides in the mutual dependency which occurs in all social relationships."* That is, one actor (A) can exercise power over another actor (B) to the extent that B depends on A for some goal he or she seeks, and vice versa. This power becomes manifest as A uses B's dependency to make demands upon B that result in changes in B's actions, despite resistance. More formally, the theory states that the dependency of B on A is directly proportional to B's motivational investment in goals mediated by A, and inversely proportional to the availability of those goals to B outside of this relationship. In turn, the power of A over B is determined by the degree of B's dependency on A and by the amount of resistance by B that A can overcome. In short, "the power of A over B is equal to, and based on, the dependence of B upon A." This idea is expressed symbolically by the equation $P_{ab} = D_{ba}$.

---

[11] Ralf Dahrendorf, *Class and Class Conflict in Industrial Society* (Stanford, Calif.: Stanford University Press, 1959), chap. 5.

[12] Richard M. Emerson, "Power-Dependence Relations," *American Sociological Review* 27 (February 1962): 31–41. See also Peter M. Blau, *Exchange and Power in Social Life* (New York: John Wiley & Sons, 1964), pp. 19–25. For a more recent elaboration of this theory, see Richard M. Emerson, "Exchange Theory," in Joseph Berger et al. eds., *Sociological Theories in Progress*, Vol. II (Boston: Houghton Mifflin, 1972), pp. 38–87.

In some situations power is balanced, in that A's power over B is confronted by an equal opposing power of B over A. Emerson argues that in such a balanced condition power is not necessarily neutralized or removed from the relationship, for each actor may exert considerable influence or control over the other. Quite commonly, however, power relationships are initially unbalanced, so that one actor has a power advantage over the other. A power disadvantage may simply be accepted or endured by the weaker party, although this actor will likely attempt to reduce the psychic, social, economic, or political costs of acquiescence in some manner. Cost reduction, no matter how effective, nevertheless leaves the relationship unbalanced and hence unstable. Consequently, actors involved in a power relationship will usually seek to bring their relationships as closely into balance as possible. Balance can be attained either by decreasing B's dependence on A or by increasing A's dependence on B. More specifically, Emerson discusses four ways in which balance can be restored to power relationships: (1) B reduces his or her interest in goals mediated by A—a process of motivational withdrawal or goal alteration; (2) B cultivates alternative sources for achieving his or her goals—a process of creating new relationships that extend the power interactions to other actors; (3) A increases his or her interest in goals mediated by B—a process of granting higher status to the weaker participant; or (4) A is denied opportunities for exerting power in pursuit of his or her goals—a process of coalition formation between B and other disadvantaged participants in the relationship.

In general, this dependency theory is most applicable to the creation of force and dominance, which are commonly exercised through pressures or coercion of various kinds. From this theoretical perspective, therefore, social power can be described as imposed *compulsion*. We shall use this term as a convenient way of referring to both force and dominance.

TRUST THEORY

The trust theory of power creation, which stresses similarities among actors, comes principally from the writings of Talcott Parsons.[13] According to this thesis, *the basis of all social influence and power is people's investment of trust in others and in the relationships that bind them together in organizations.* This investment of trust in collective activities occurs when individual participants believe that the other people involved or the organization as a whole will normally act in ways that are beneficial to them. In relatively small, informal organizations, the existence of shared

[13]Talcott Parsons, "On the Concept of Influence," *Public Opinion Quarterly*, Spring 1963, pp. 37–62. See also James Coleman, "Comment on 'On the Concept of Influence,'" ibid., pp. 63–82. Parsons discusses his concept of the "power bank" in more detail in "Some Reflections on the Place of Force in Social Processes," in Harry Eckstein, ed., *Internal War* (New York: Free Press, 1964), pp. 57–65.

common values is enough to assure the individual that an investment of trust will benefit him or her, at least in the long run. Shared values and common interests are also vital in larger and more formal and complex organizations, but in these situations individuals often demand some kind of guaranteed protection—such as legal contracts or established control procedures—before they will render themselves vulnerable to others by investing trust in the organization. In either case, though, this investment of trust in a relationship or an organization by its participants gives the collectivity resources that it can draw upon in order to exercise power in the attainment of its goals. Thus, as individuals commit themselves to a relationship or organization and act as trusting and responsible participants in it, both the collectivity as a whole and they, as parts of it, can exercise increasing amounts of social power.

Parsons goes on to draw an analogy between organizational trust investment and banking. A bank creates financial resources by recirculating the money deposited in it through the extension of credit loans, thereby increasing the total amount of money in circulation. Bank deposits thus do double financial duty, serving as economic resources both for the depositors and the borrowers. A similar process occurs when a person invests trust in an organization by joining it and giving it his or her support. The organization can in turn utilize this trust as a resource for exerting influence or control, either directly in goal attainment or indirectly in support of other organizations or social activities. The creation of social power, as with money, is thus ultimately limited not by the amount of the initial investment, but only by public confidence in the mediating organization. As expressed by William Gamson in respect to political systems: "The effectiveness of political leadership . . . depends on the ability of authorities to claim the loyal cooperation of members of the system without having to specify in advance what such cooperation will entail. . . . The importance of trust becomes apparent: the loss of trust is the loss of system power, the loss of a generalized capacity for authorities to commit resources to attain collective goals." [14]

In general, this trust theory is most applicable to the creation of attraction and authority, which are commonly exercised through suggestions and commands. From this theoretical perspective, therefore, social power can be described as consenting *compliance*. We shall use this term to refer to both authority and attraction.

These two theories of power creation are not logically incompatible, and in practice both processes can—and often do—occur together in varying degrees and reinforce each other. Nevertheless, they offer quite contrasting explanations of how social power is ultimately created. In the former case, stress is laid on mutual dependency, so that the exercise of influence and

[14] Gamson, *Power and Discontent*, p. 43.

control is seen as "power over others." In the latter case, stress is laid on shared trust, so that the exercise of influence and control is seen as "power with others." A theoretical synthesis of these two theories of power creation would clearly further our ability to explain the process of power exertion.

The Exercise of Social Power

THUS far we have been discussing power in descriptive and relatively static terms, but power exertion is actually a dynamic process that occurs in ongoing social relationships and organizations. If we wish to use power as a fundamental explanatory principle of all social organization, we must be able to conceptualize this process, measure it, and evaluate it. The following paragraphs sketch the key ideas to be considered in any analysis of the exercise of social power.

POWER EXERTION

The process of exerting power involves the three factors of capacity, commitment, and conversion. *Capacity* refers to available and relevant resources. Although resources are often categorized as either tangible or intangible, a more analytically important distinction is between limited and unlimited resources. Limited resources are restricted in supply, so that every use of them diminishes the total amount available to an actor, at least temporarily. All tangible resources—including wealth and all material goods—are inherently limited, but so are many intangible resources such as organizational positions, functional dependency, social privileges (which come to be seen as rights if extended too broadly or frequently), and symbolic punishments (which lose meaning if applied too often). Unlimited resources, in contrast, are not diminished by use as long as they are not abused or overextended, and may in fact (as in the case of learned skills) develop and expand with use. Other common examples of unlimited resources include knowledge, trust, legitimacy, reputation, affection, established operational procedures, and organizational cohesion.

In general, it is more desirable to draw on unlimited rather than limited resources for power exertion if at all possible, since once one has them they are not lost through use. This is not always possible, however, for unlimited resources such as knowledge, trust, or legitimacy are often transformable into power only within specific contexts or specified ranges of activities. Outside these appropriate conditions the resource may be worthless. Although this is also true of limited resources—currency is technically valueless in a foreign country—their boundaries of applicability are often much broader and more flexible (banks will usually exchange foreign for domestic currency, and gold is valued almost universally).

The amount and kind of an actor's available resources provide a basis for power exertion, but do not determine it. The second factor in this process is *commitment*, or willingness to apply one's available resources to a given situation in order to exert power. An actor who is willing to commit all of his or her limited resources to a particular relationship may be able to exert considerably more power than an actor with more extensive resources that he or she does not wish to employ.

The third factor in the power exertion process is resource *conversion* effectiveness, or the ability of an actor to transform available and committed resources into action. This conversion can be done either positively, by employing or distributing valued resources, or negatively, by restricting or withholding resources desired by others. To take a simple example of conversion effectiveness, an outright offer of a million dollars to a public official for a political favor might be indignantly rejected as attempted bribery, whereas much less money invested in a political action organization might easily produce the desired goal. Knowing when, where, and how to use one's resources—especially when combined with a certain amount of finesse and subtlety—can often be more crucial than the sheer amount of these resources.

An actor's potential power, or perceived ability to exert power, is thus a resultant of his or her (1) available relevant resources, (2) willingness to commit them to a particular situation, and (3) ability to convert those resources into overt influence or control. In the absence of overt action, all of these factors must be calculated by others on the basis of their perceptions of the actor, their knowledge of his or her past actions, and their probability assessments of his or her commitment and motivation. On the other hand, if one actually initiates this process one is enacting an overt "power attempt" which affects others. In sum, *power attempt = committed resources × conversion effectiveness.*

At this point, the other actor(s) in the power relationship must respond to the power attempt in some manner. They can merely acquiesce to the pressures or commands of the would-be power exerter, but more commonly they will offer resistance of some kind. Active resistance by the recipients can take either (or both) of two forms: (1) power neutralization, in which they attempt to remove the basis (either functional dependency or normative trust) on which the exerter's power rests, or (2) power opposition, in which they exert countervailing power of their own back on the exerter (which can lead to conflict or power balancing or both). Passive resistance by the recipients, in contrast, can occur through (1) appeals to shared values or beliefs that stress antipower or egalitarian themes, (2) indifference to the effects of the power being exerted on them, or (3) total withdrawal from the situation. Regardless of the nature of the resistance encountered, however, the would-be power exerter must overcome it in some way if he or she is to actually wield power. To the extent that this occurs, power is actively exercised. *Power exertion = committed resources × conversion effective-nes – resistance.*[15]

POWER ANALYSIS

The above equation might provide a useful tool for analyzing power exertion if we could quantitatively measure all the variables comprising it. This we cannot do at the present time, however, with the result that our power analyses normally rest on crude subjective estimates (such as "little influence," "some influence," or "much influence") or relative rankings (such as "most influential," "next most influential," "least influential").

To be able to analyze power processes objectively, we will need to measure quantitatively a number of relevant variables, including resources, resource conversion effectiveness, and resistance. We will also need to develop standardized measures of quantities of power exertion, or the outcomes of these processes. Conceptually, the total quantity of an actor's power exertion in a particular situation can be described as a product of the strength and field of his power. Strength of power is in turn composed of its intensity (amount at any given time) multiplied by its duration (the length of time it is exerted), while field of power is the sum of its scope (the number of activities affected) plus its domain (the number of actors affected). Thus total quantity of power = (intensity × duration) × (scope + domain).

Beyond these problems of measurement lie broader questions of analytical strategies. Two main analytical approaches are commonly used in power studies. *Distributive analysis* examines the way in which the total amount of power being exerted at any one time within a given situation is divided among the participating actors. It usually addresses such questions as these: "Is power being wielded equally by all participants, almost exclusively by a single actor, or does some other condition prevail?" "Who are the power elites in this organization?" "What is the prevailing balance of power here?" The usual result of distributive analysis is either a static picture of the distribution of potential power or power attempts among the various actors at a particular time, or a description of shifts in the relative distribution of power that have occurred through time. *Developmental analysis* investigates increases and decreases occurring through time in the total amount of power being exercised within a given relationship or organization. Typical questions in this case include: "To what extent has the accumulation of resources or the creation of social organization through time increased the total amount of power of the total system?" "Has the depletion of available

---

[15] For a basically similar but much more elaborate description of the power exertion process, see H. M. Blalock, "Toward a General Theory of Social Power," read at the 1973 meeting of the American Sociological Association.

resources or growing social disorganization through time reduced the ability of an organization to exert power?" The usual outcome of developmental analysis is an explanation of temporal changes in overall patterns of power processes or usage. As an example of the differences between these two types of analysis, a study showing that business people presently exert more influence on community decisions than do politicians would be distributive in nature, while a study of growth in the effectiveness of community decision-making procedures during the past twenty years would be developmental in nature.

Both of these approaches to power analysis are equally valid, and in fact distributive and developmental changes in power relationships often accompany and reinforce each other. Growth or decline in the total amount of power being exercised often stimulates shifts in power distributions, while a "struggle for power" among actors can significantly strengthen or weaken the power potential of the total organization. It is nevertheless important that social scientists differentiate between these two analytical approaches, for they require contrasting initial assumptions. For distributive analysis we must assume "zero-sum" conditions in which the total amount of power being exerted remains constant, so that one actor's gain is another's loss. For developmental analysis, on the other hand, we must assume "variable-sum" conditions in which the total amount of power being exerted can be constantly increasing or decreasing through time. These simplifying assumptions, which the analyst temporarily accepts as a basis for performing either distributive or developmental analysis, are in no way contradictory as long as the time factor is kept clearly in mind. Unfortunately, not all writers have done so. For instance, if we demonstrate that large businesses, the executive branch of the federal government, and the military have all increased their power exertion in the United States during the past thirty years, this is clearly developmental analysis. On the basis of this information alone, however, we cannot simply assume that other parts of the society—such as Congress, state and community governments, schools, churches, labor unions, political parties, and voluntary associations—have necessarily all declined in power exertion. If such a conclusion were reached without additional information concerning these other realms of society, we would be assuming a zero-sum conception of social power when our developmental analysis requires a variable-sum conception. The total amount of social power being exerted in the United States might have increased considerably during this period, so that these other unexamined parts of the society could have grown in power at equal or even faster rates than businesses, government, and the military.[16]

---

[16] This illustration is drawn from C. Wright Mills, *The Power Elite* (New York: Oxford University Press, 1956).

POWER OUTCOMES

Once social power has been created in a relationship, what consequences does its exercise have for social organizations? How do organizations use social power? The major consequences of power exertion can be divided into four general categories: internal ordering, internal coordination, external procurement, and external attainment.[17] The first two processes occur among the subunits comprising a power-wielding organization; the last two involve its relationships with the natural and social environments.

The primary necessity of any social organization is survival. No organization will survive long if the stresses and strains that continually disrupt it are not dealt with. If an organization has achieved a relatively high degree of internal cohesion and has also developed effective conflict-management techniques, it may be able to tolerate and even benefit from a considerable amount of social conflict. Lacking these characteristics, however, an organization must rely upon the use of power—especially force—as a means of maintaining social order. And even strongly cohesive organizations frequently employ power to cope with disruptions that cannot be handled by other means. Thus, the most basic use of social power by organizations is for the *protection and perpetuation of patterns of internal ordering*.

Beyond mere survival, most organizations normally strive to increase the effectiveness and efficiency of their internal functioning. As the size and internal complexity of an organization increases, so does the functional specialization, or division of labor, among its subunits. This in turn requires a certain amount of centralized coordination, communication, regulation, and planning. It also requires overall direction of the internal distributive process, by which the benefits of collective action are allocated to the members of the organization. To establish and operate such centralized coordination and administration, an organization must utilize power. Any (or all) of the four major types of power can be used, although authority is particularly advantageous because of its predictability and stability. In general, a second way in which all organizations use power is for the *promotion of internal coordination*.

Turning outward, all social organizations depend upon their natural and social environments for the procurement of resources necessary for their operation. Whether they be goods, people, services, or information, these vital resources are frequently acquired by using some type of power. Although organizations often gain necessary resources through balanced

[17]This suggested classification is in some ways analogous to Talcott Parsons' AGIL scheme, but it is not intended to be a direct application of that scheme and it was not derived from Parsons' writings.

exchange relationships, most of the time they must also seek to influence or control portions of the external world. This generalization holds whether the organization relies on forceful pressures, functional dominance, legitimate authority, or voluntary attraction to obtain its resources. Therefore, a third way in which all organizations use social power is for *procurement of necessary resources* from the environment.

Finally, to obtain whatever goals they seek, social organizations must further influence or control other organizations, individuals, or natural phenomena. Depending on the nature of the organization, goal attainment may involve selling goods and services (as in the case of business concerns), disseminating information (in the case of communication media), providing personal services (in the case of hospitals), educating and training individuals (in the case of schools), providing public services (in the case of communities), or dealing with other societies (in the case of national governments). As in the process of resource procurement, organizations may employ force, exploit dominance, exercise authority, or rely on attraction to gain the goals they seek, but all such activities involve the exertion of power. Thus, a fourth use of social power by all organizations is for the *attainment of goals* through activities in the environment.

All of these uses of social power have been described from the point of view of the organization exercising power—and hence appear to be beneficial to it. From the viewpoint of other organizations, however, this power exertion can be quite detrimental. These other organizations may be forced to provide resources or benefits to the power-wielding organizations against their "wishes" or best interests, their own actions may be severely controlled or curtailed by it, or they may even be totally destroyed by it. It is also possible, however, for these other organizations to benefit in numerous ways from their interaction with the more powerful organization. The process of power exertion is itself functionally and morally neutral, but the ways in which power is exercised and the purposes for which it is executed can vary in their consequences from mutual reinforcement to sheer exploitation.

Our concern in this chapter has been to gain a basic understanding of social power because of its central importance for all organized social life. Arising out of interdependence and shared trust among actors and occurring in all social relationships and organizations, social power in the form of force, dominance, authority, and attraction, is utilized by social organizations for a wide variety of vital purposes. The principal conclusion we might draw from this discussion is that social power pervades all social life and is the principal dynamic medium through which most social activities occur. Hence we cannot adequately understand and explain the process of social organization without taking into account the ubiquitous exercise of social power.

RECOMMENDED READING

Bierstedt, Robert. "An Analysis of Social Power." *American Sociological Review* 15 (December 1950): 730–738. (Also Bobbs-Merrill reprint S-343.)
> A conceptual analysis of the phenomenon of social power.

Emerson, Richard M. "Power-Dependence Relations." *American Sociological Review* 27 (February 1962): 31–41.
> A theoretical explanation of the creation of social power through differential dependence among interacting actors.

Etzioni, Amitai. *The Active Society*. New York: Free Press, 1968, chaps. 13 and 14.
> Examines the nature and dynamics of power exertion in organized social life.

Lasswell, Harold D., and Abraham Kaplan. *Power and Society*. New Haven, Conn.: Yale University Press, 1950.
> Sets forth a sociopolitical conception of society focusing on the use of social power in all social processes.

Lehman, Edward W. "Toward a Macrosociology of Power." *American Sociological Review* 34 (August 1969): 453–465.
> Distinguishes between organizational and interpersonal conceptions of social power and discusses various features of organizational power.

Lipset, Seymour Martin. *Political Man*. New York: Doubleday, 1959, chap. 3. (Also Bobbs-Merrill reprint S-175, pp. 86–103 only.)
> Analyzes the concept of legitimacy, and points out several social factors that promote and destroy it.

Parsons, Talcott. "On the Concept of Influence." *Public Opinion Quarterly* (Spring 1963): 37–62.
> A theoretical explanation of the creation of social power through investment of trust in collectivities.

Weber, Max. *The Theory of Social and Economic Organization*, trans. by A. M. Henderson and Talcott Parsons. New York: Free Press, 1961, pp. 324–363.
> The classic discussion of traditional, rational-legal, and charismatic bases of authority.

3

Units of Social Organization

AS the process of social organization occurs through time, it is shaped by its participants into various kinds of delineated and identifiable units. The resulting organizations—also termed collectivities—are specific instances of the general process of social organization. A social organization is thus both a manifestation of an ongoing process and a distinct social entity. In this chapter we explore several aspects of the organizational units that develop through the process of social organization.

One way of conceptualizing social organizations is to think of them as collections of individuals who have joined together to carry out common activities. For example, isn't a university actually a collection of students, faculty, and administrators who are jointly engaged in the tasks of acquiring and disseminating knowledge? This conception of social organization as a number of interacting individuals is extremely common, but sociologically it is inadequate. An organization must have members in order to exist, but these individual members do not, in and of themselves, constitute the organization. Any social organization can over time experience a complete turnover of membership and yet remain the same entity. In fact, if the organization is to last longer than the human life span, it must change members. Whether it is the Thursday Afternoon Bridge Club or the United States, its membership is constantly changing, without any necessary changes in the organization itself. Social organization is created as people interact, but the organizational units that develop through this process cannot be equated with any particular individuals.

Delineation of Organizations

AS an ongoing process, we have described social organization as the merging of social interactions into recurrent patterns of social ordering that become infused with cultural ideas. But how do selected portions of this process become delineated into specific organizations that exist as identifiable entities? This question is crucial, since a social organization exists as a separate unit only if it is delineated from its social environment in some manner that is recognized by the participating actors.

What are the boundaries that set organizations apart from their surrounding social environments? Some organizational boundaries are totally arbitrary, as in the case of the imaginary line running down the middle of a street that separates a city from its adjoining suburb. Usually, though, some basis for identifying organizational boundaries does exist in the underlying patterns of social organization—such as who attends meetings and who doesn't, or who shares our values and who doesn't. Such existing "breaks" in ongoing interactional and cultural processes are in turn often clarified and strengthened through shared conceptualizations of membership and boundary lines.

Because of our human perception of time, boundaries of physical and biological objects usually appear to be fairly definite. The rate of exchange between the object and its surrounding environment is slower than our ability to perceive change, so that its boundaries seem to be well defined and permanent over time. We all agree without argument where a table stops and a chair begins. Boundaries of social organizations (and also personalities), however, tend to be considerably less sharp and stable to our senses. Consequently, organizational boundaries are frequently either vague and blurred or else based largely on arbitrary definitions.

For example, what are the boundaries of the nuclear family? We commonly think of a family as consisting of a married couple and their minor unmarried children. But what about a grandparent who lives with them, or an unmarried adult son or daughter still living at home, or a foster child cared for by the parents? As another example, some churches count as members all persons living in their area who were ever baptized in that faith, regardless of the present convictions or actions of these people. Other churches count as members only individuals who have formally requested membership and who are currently active in the church. Communities are also often perplexed by this question of boundaries. Do the social boundaries of a community correspond to the legal city limits, do they include neighboring suburbs, or do they extend outward to include the entire surrounding area that is functionally and culturally dependent on the central urban area? And on the societal level, nations often establish rather arbitrary definitions of citizenship. The United States is quite inclusive in this respect, granting citizenship to all persons born within the geographical limits of the country or its territories, regardless of the citizenship of their parents, as well as to persons born abroad whose parents are American citizens.

A few common types of organizational boundaries are described below, although this list is far from complete:

1. Formal membership rosters, on which the names of all members of the organization are listed. Formal membership status is frequently contingent upon some action by the individual, such as paying dues, professing a certain belief, or undergoing an initiation ritual.
2. Interpersonal identification of members with each other, as in the case of most small friendship groups. One becomes a member of such a group when he or she is tacitly accepted by the other members.
3. Geographical location, or physical presence in a specified area such as a neighborhood or a community.
4. Self-identification by a person with an organization, as employed by some political parties and religious bodies.
5. Limitations on social relationships, based on observations or prescriptions concerning who interacts with whom in what ways on a regular basis.
6. Willingness to defend the organization against disruptive forces—"If you're with us, stand and fight for us."
7. Shared cultural values and norms, as in the case of ethnic classes and professional associations.

These various types of organizational boundaries are not mutually exclusive, and many organizations use several of them simultaneously or under differing conditions. But all of them do serve to delineate an organization from its social environment.

Types of Organizations

AT the present time, sociology does not have a rigorous taxonomy for classifying the various organizational forms that are created through the process of social organization. To describe the wide variety of organizational units existing in the contemporary world, some sort of typology is nevertheless required. This section therefore sketches a preliminary typology of nine kinds of organizational units: aggregates, classes, groups, families, communities, associations, networks, societies, and federations.[1] In addition, populations are discussed as social categories that underlie all social organizations. This typology is useful as a heuristic tool for descriptive purposes, but it is in no sense a refined taxonomy.

The typology is arranged in rough order of increasing social complexity, as determined by such characteristics as the number of subunits within the organization, the degree to which these subunits are functionally specialized and interdependent, and the extent of overall organizational coordination and control. The ranking of associations as more complex than communities is perhaps the most arbitrary feature of this typology, since New York City is clearly a much more complex organization than a corner grocery store. When communities and associations of equal size are compared, however, associations usually tend to have more complex social structures. Finally, organizational size usually increases with complexity, but not always so. A social class is larger than a family, but typically contains a less complex set of relationships.

POPULATIONS

Individuals are often classified by social scientists into various populations based on common characteristics, actions, ideas, or other criteria. There are endless possibilities, such as: (1) male or female; (2) single, married, separated, divorced, or widowed; (3) urban, suburban, or rural residents; (4) "liberals" or "conservatives"; (5) Protestants, Catholics, or Jews; (6) manual versus nonmanual workers; (7) Republicans, Democrats, or Independents; (8) grammar school graduates, high school graduates, or college graduates. The important point is that the "members" of a population do not necessarily interact, form patterns of social ordering, or share a common culture. (If they do carry out these processes, they cease to be merely a population.) They are assigned a common designation by an outside observer on the basis of arbitrary criteria, not through their own social interactions. A population is thus not, in and of itself, an organization.

Nevertheless, identifiable populations are very important social phenomena, both for the creation of social organization and for sociological

---

[1] This typology includes most kinds of organizations commonly identified and studied by contemporary sociologists. It is, in effect, a composite of numerous other, less extensive typologies. A few broad categories, such as "secondary groups" and "multi-bonded groups," have been omitted on the grounds that they are so inclusive as to be analytically useless. Also omitted are social entities that are purely political in nature, such as townships, counties, states, and nations.

analysis. A population provides the setting in which social organization occurs, and organization is in one sense a population phenomenon. By identifying populations that evidence several common characteristics, social scientists can often discover potential or developing social organizations. This category of populations is therefore included within our typology as a means of distinguishing populations of individuals from types of established social organizations and at the same time stressing the relevance of population phenomena for social life and social science. Formally defined, *a population is a set of unorganized individuals that is identified by an observer on the basis of one or more common characteristics.*

AGGREGATES

Collective phenomena such as crowds, mobs, publics, and audiences are examples of aggregates. These phenomena are, in effect, populations of people who interact transiently and temporarily, so that the resulting patterns of social ordering and shared culture are highly ephemeral. Nonetheless, they do evidence some minimal amount of social organization. Because of their ephemeral nature, and also because most of them have relatively few effects upon established patterns of social life, these phenomena have not been extensively studied by social scientists as a form of social organization. They cannot be totally dismissed from the study of social organization, however, since they provide unusual insights into the processes through which organization is created, and also because they occasionally produce extensive social change.

Students of these phenomena, both sociologists and psychologists, have commonly referred to them as "collective behavior." To the extent that these scientists have been concerned largely with the behaviors of individuals within such collectivities, this term has been appropriate. When we consider the collectivity as a social entity, however, we need a new generic organizational term such as "aggregate," which means "a collected but relatively unorganized whole."[2] More precisely, *an aggregate is a social organization that is relatively spontaneous in origin, temporary in duration, and minimally ordered.*

CLASSES

When loosely unified social organizations become somewhat stable through time, when they exercise some amount of social power, and when they can act collectively to achieve shared goals, we call them social

---

[2]The term "collectivity" might at first seem a more logical choice, but this term is frequently used as a synonym for all social organizations. Such phenomena as fads, panics, and crazes are also commonly included under the heading of "collective behavior," but these are forms of social activity, not delineated social organizations.

classes. "Class" is one of the most ambiguous concepts in sociology, and almost everyone gives it a slightly different meaning. It is usually associated with the phenomenon of social stratification, but in practice it refers sometimes to purely economic conditions, sometimes to social prestige and deference, sometimes to social power, sometimes to people who share common interests and values, sometimes to populations of individuals who frequently interact, sometimes to abstract statistical categories, and frequently to several of these phenomenon in combination.

We shall apply the concept of class directly to social stratification in a later chapter; here we limit the term to its most general meaning. Expanding upon an idea developed by Ralf Dahrendorf,[3] we suggest that *a class is a loosely ordered and unified social organization based on the similar power, privileges, and prestige of its members.* A class exists when persons who occupy approximately similar positions within the distributive (or stratification) process of a society, community, or other encompassing organization begin to interact in ordered and perpetuated patterns and to develop a unique culture. The common interests and social conditions of these people lead them to organize themselves in some manner for the collective attainment of shared goals. These attempts will often lead them into conflict with competing classes and other organizations, so that the use of power becomes a pervasive aspect of class activities. Little internal differentiation of subunits occurs within a class, however.

This conceptualization of social class is broad enough to include the various classes within a feudal type of society (such as serfs, peasants, artisans, nobility), the castes of India, the three "estates" of prerevolutionary France, Marxian conceptions of class (such as bourgeoisie and proletariat), and whatever social classes exist in the contemporary United States (such as a "power elite" or an "upper-middle class" or the "socially dispossessed"). Whether or not these phenomena actually constitute organized social classes is always a problematic question. To qualify as organizations, they must evidence some patterns of social ordering and a distinctive culture; otherwise they remain simply unorganized populations. Under these criteria, a stratum of individuals with similar socioeconomic status (based on such criteria as occupation, education, and income) who did not interact with one another in any ordered manner would not constitute a class.

Following the ideas of Max Weber,[4] most sociologists have either explicitly or implicitly conceived of classes as based ultimately on economic factors. Only recently have we begun to think of classes in the broader

---

[3] Ralf Dahrendorf, *Class and Class Conflict in Industrial Society* (Stanford, Calif.: Stanford University Press, 1959), chap. 5.
[4] Max Weber, "Class, Status, and Party," in H. H. Gerth and C. W. Mills, eds., *From Max Weber: Essays in Sociology* (New York: Oxford University Press, 1946), chap. 7.

context of power suggested here.[5] To the extent that economic power dominates a society, it will form the primary basis of all classes. But as other forms of social power—such as legal authority or technical knowledge—grow in functional importance within the society, they provide new foundations for different social classes.

GROUPS

For many social scientists the word "group" is synonymous with social organization—or at least with all organizations smaller in size than a total society. In this typology, however, the term is given a more restricted and precise meaning. Groups are almost always smaller in number of members than are classes. Nevertheless, most groups tend to be more tightly unified than classes, and sometimes they also display at least rudimentary structural differentiation into partially autonomous subunits. Such unification and internal ordering are outgrowths of the strong interpersonal bonds that normally join the members of a group, based largely on personal identification of the members with each other. That is, *a group is a social organization whose members identify and interact with each other personally as individuals.*

This diverse category includes such phenomena as friendship cliques, work crews, neighborhood *kaffee klatsch* gatherings, teenage gangs, sports teams, juries, discussion groups, and committees of all kinds. The interpersonal identification that characterizes all groups is immensely aided by small size and frequent interaction among members, although neither of these factors is absolutely necessary for the creation of a group. Finally, groups can exist either as relatively autonomous social entities, as in the case of a neighborhood gathering, or as parts of larger organizations, as in the case of committees.

Some groups, such as friendship cliques or youth gangs, are frequently described by sociologists as "primary groups."[6] The interactions among the members of these groups are especially personal and intimate, and the interpersonal bonds are extremely strong. Technically, we should speak of "primary relations" rather than "primary groups," since "primariness" is a variable that exists to some extent in all groups and also in more complex organizations. Groups vary, that is, in the degree to which the relationships among their members are "primary" in nature. Nonetheless, the concept of "primary group" provides a convenient means of designating those groups in which the interpersonal relationships are especially close, so that the members tend to respond to one another's total personalities.

[5] Gerhard E. Lenski, *Power and Privilege* (New York: McGraw-Hill, 1966).
[6] Charles H. Cooley, *Social Organization* (New York: Free Press, 1956), chap. 3.

FAMILIES

What is a family? Does this type of social organization include just two spouses and their children, or must we also take into account grandparents, in-laws, uncles and aunts, cousins, and nieces and nephews? The meaning of "family," and hence its boundaries, is culturally determined and differs widely from one society to another, and often even within a single society. In one society the biological father of a child acts as its male parent, while in another society the mother's brother assumes this duty. In a third society a marriage consists of one male and several females, while in another several males may marry one female.

Despite these many variations, the idea of kinship (however culturally defined) is present in all known societies. Some version of the family as a type of social organization exists everywhere. In its most universal conception, *a family is a social organization that is characterized by ties of kinship among all its members.* In other words, a family is united by either biological or marital kinship bonds among its members, as well as by interpersonal identification. These kinship ties normally give the family more stability and unity than exists in nonkinship groups.

Sociologists also usually include families under the heading of "primary groups," but once again the degree of intimacy or "primariness" in family social relationships varies considerably from society to society, and even from one family to another. The fact that several people are related and live together is no guarantee that they will relate intimately to each other.

COMMUNITIES

Although the family as a social entity can sometimes be relatively self-sufficient, most families do not live by themselves, isolated from all others. For many reasons, ranging from economic interdependence to shared cultural values, families normally band together to form communities. The community, rather than the family, then becomes the social setting for most everyday economic, political, religious, educational, recreational, and similar activities. As communities become larger and more complex, other types of organizations are often established within the community to perform these various activities. Nevertheless, the community as a whole remains the social unit within which all such social functions usually take place. In brief, *a community is a social organization that is territorially localized and within which people satisfy most of their daily needs and deal with most of their common problems.*[7]

[7] This definition is adapted from Amos H. Hawley, *Human Ecology* (New York: Ronald Press, 1960), pp. 257–258. The concept of community is sometimes used in sociology in quite a different sense, as when we speak of "the intellectual community" or "the business community." Often this is just a convenient means of referring to an identifiable but completely unorganized population of individuals. Sometimes, though, this population will develop

In modern societies, communities are never totally self-sufficient, as they may be in very primitive societies. But normally they are more self-contained, in terms of the range of needs satisfied and services rendered, than any other type of social organization except societies. Communities vary widely in size and complexity, from "Crossroads Junction" to New York City, but this diversity should not obscure their many similarities. The fact that communities always occupy a definite geographical area has given rise to a proliferation of sociological studies of community spatial patterns, although the requirement of spatial location does not exclude nomadic communities as long as they retain their organization as they move about.

As a final point, the sociological concept of community must be distinguished from the legal term "city." Many of the activities of almost all communities extended beyond the legal city limits to include suburbs and other immediately surrounding areas. In some cases, though, a community may be smaller than its legal city, as in the case of a relatively self-contained immigrant settlement or ghetto. There is no definite point at which the community as a social organization ends and its surrounding hinterland begins, so that when studying large communities many sociologists prefer to use such units as the "Standard Metropolitan Statistical Area" as defined by the U.S. Census Bureau, or the even broader concept of "metropolitan region."

ASSOCIATIONS

As social life becomes increasingly complex, with social actors pursuing a wide variety of goals through collective action, they create various kinds of relatively specialized organizations. Each of these organizations is limited in its range of activities, focusing on only one or a few aspects of social life. Its goals are restricted to its area(s) of particular concern and competence, and most or all of its actions are aimed in these directions. Such functional specialization tends to deprive these organizations of operational self-sufficiency, so that they become highly interdependent. The generic name for all such specialized organizations is associations. *An association is a social organization that is more or less purposefully created for the attainment of relatively specific and limited goals.* In contemporary societies this is by far the broadest and most inclusive type of social organization.

The goals sought by associations, and hence their organizational

---

enduring patterns of social ordering and a shared culture—as might be true of a "business community." The emerging organization should then be referred to as a social class, as we have defined this term. Finally, some writers also speak of "supernational communities" or "international communities"—primarily to emphasize that societies are today becoming increasingly interdependent, so that the organizational setting in which one lives is slowly becoming the entire world.

characteristics, vary almost infinitely. As examples of the more common forms of associations we might cite the following: governmental departments, agencies, and legislatures; factories and industries of all kinds; retail, wholesale, and service businesses; schools, colleges, and other educational organizations; churches, sects, and similar religious bodies; labor unions and occupational and professional associations; fraternal and service organizations; legal and financial firms; special-interest associations, from antique collectors to zoology enthusiasts; civic, charitable, and welfare agencies; political parties and lobbies; social and recreational associations; military services and units; hospitals, clinics, and related health organizations; libraries, museums, orchestras, theaters, and other literary and artistic bodies; scientific laboratories and institutes; civil rights and ethnic associations; protective organizations such as police and fire departments.

Because of the wide variety of different kinds of associations, several writers have devised schemes for categorizing them into subtypes. For illustrative purposes, let us briefly examine one of these. Peter Blau and Richard Scott divide associations into four categories on the basis of who benefits from the attainment of their dominant goals and the kinds of organizational problems they encounter.[8]

Business associations include all associations whose dominant goal is to benefit their owners by making money, such as industries, stores, construction and repair concerns, communication and transportation companies, and all other private businesses. Their distinctive organizational problem is promoting operating efficiency, since the association must operate efficiently if it is to show a profit.

Mutual benefit associations include all associations whose dominant goal is to benefit their members in some way, such as occupational and professional associations, labor unions, political parties, literary and artistic bodies, civil rights associations, social and recreational organizations, special-interest associations, and churches. Their distinctive organizational problem is maintaining internal control by the members over activities of the association, so that it will directly benefit them.

Service associations include all associations whose dominant goal is to provide services of some kind to clients, such as schools and colleges, hospitals, charitable and welfare agencies, law firms, police departments, and prisons. Their distinctive organizational problem is preventing exploitation of the relatively dependent clients—or in other words, maintaining professional operating standards in the association.

[8] Peter Blau and Richard C. Scott, *Formal Organizations* (San Francisco, Calif.: Chandler, 1963), pp. 46–67. For a formal taxonomy of associations based on many different dimensions, see J. Eugene Hass, Richard H. Hall, and Norman J. Johnson, "Towards an Empirically Derived Taxonomy of Organizations," in Raymond W. Bowers, ed., *Studies on Behavior in Organizations* (Athens, Ga.: University of Georgia Press, 1966), chap. 8.

Commonwealth associations include all associations whose dominant goal is to serve an entire community or society, such as governmental organizations of all kinds, military units, public health services, scientific institutes, and libraries and museums. Their distinctive organizational problem is maintaining external (or public) control over the association's activities, to ensure that it always benefits the common welfare.

Associations range in size from a two-person partnership to General Motors Corporation or the United States Government. Increasingly, however, they are tending to become not only large, but also highly complex and formally organized. There are numerous exceptions, but this dominant trend is clear in modern society. As a result, the claim is sometimes made that large, complex, formal associations are relatively new phenomena in human affairs. In an absolute sense this is not true, since some types of complex associations, such as armies, have existed since the beginning of recorded history. But in a relative sense, the predominance of such associations in all facets of social life is one of the most significant features of contemporary societies.

NETWORKS

Functionally interdependent groups, families, communities, and associations must interact with each other within extensive networks of patterned relationships if they are to satisfy their survival and operational requirements, coordinate joint activities, and achieve common goals. In the past, the setting for most such interorganizational exchange relationships has been the local community, within whose confines more specialized groups and associations normally functioned. These arrangements are altered, however, as associations grow in size and span several communities or an entire society, and as means of transportation and communication increasingly link together all communities within a society. This process of expansion beyond the local community leads to the growth of organized functional networks.

Formally defined, *a network is a functionally specialized social organization that links together numerous associations, groups, and other types of interrelated organizations, all of which deal with a common set of activities.* Included within this category are such phenomena as political networks (including national and local governments, as well as related associations such as political parties and pressure groups—all of which are sometimes referred to as the "polity" of a society); educational networks (public and private schools, colleges and universities, some aspects of the mass media, and technical training programs); economic networks (either the total economy of a society, including factories, distributors, stores, and services establishments, or specialized sectors of the economy such as agriculture or heavy industry); legal networks (composed of courts, law firms, police departments, prisons, and similar associations); religious networks (churches, synagogues, seminaries, religious orders, and so on); military networks (the various armed services and the local militia); communication networks (television and radio stations, newspapers, magazine and book publishers, and movie producers); socialization networks (families, nursery schools, youth groups, parts of the mass media, and many other related activities); and medical networks (clinics, hospitals, laboratories, public health services, and other medical facilities).

The term "network," as used in this typology, was first suggested by S. F. Nadel, who stressed that all of the social relationships comprising a social network are to some degree interrelated.[9] Activities or changes in one part of such a network will therefore have effects throughout many other parts of the network. Notice that any given network will often include several different kinds of associations and groups, and sometimes also families, classes, and communities. Concurrently, one specific kind of group or association may fit into two or more different networks, according to its various activities. Thus schools are part of the socialization as well as the educational network of our society; families perform educational and religious as well as socialization actions; governmental agencies may become involved in economic, educational, and legal as well as political events; and the mass media frequently become engaged in all these networks. The unifying feature of any given network, regardless of which or how many other organizations it incorporates, is its focus on a particular kind of activity or set of related activities. All the various parts of a network are involved in some manner with a broad social concern—be it economic, political, legal, educational, religious, communicative, or socializing. Finally, since most functional networks are societywide in the scope of their activities, networks are usually described as the major subsectors of a society.

SOCIETIES

Societies are the most inclusive and complex type of social organization in today's world. Most other organizations exist within the confines of a society, all aspects of human social life are encompassed by a society, and to a large extent the way in which a society functions will influence all the patterns of social ordering and subcultures that comprise it. In recent years the term "society" has come into wide popular usage, but for social-scientific purposes it can be defined in this manner: *a society is a*

---

[9]S. F. Nadel, *The Theory of Social Structure* (New York: Free Press, 1957), pp. 16–17. Sociologists often refer to networks as social institutions, since they are highly institutionalized subparts of society, but this usage is confusing, since the process of institutionalization can occur in any organization, and is not limited to networks.

broadly inclusive social organization that possesses both functional and cultural autonomy and that dominates all other types of organization.[10]

The ideas of societal functional and cultural autonomy require some elaboration. Functional autonomy can be demonstrated in several different ways. First, most social relationships occur within the boundaries of a society, with only a small minority of all relationships involving actors from different societies—and in these latter cases the society retains control over their continuation. Second, a society is relatively self-sufficient, or independent of other societies. Self-sufficiency does not mean that a society provides all of its necessary resources or satisfies all the needs of its members, but rather that it establishes the social procedures and mechanisms by which all resources are procured and all needs are satisfied. Third, a society possesses functional autonomy in decision making. It is the ultimate decision-making unit for all its members, and hence has sovereignty over all decisions concerning them. Fourth, a society is the supreme organization to which its members give loyalty and which they defend against disruptive external and internal forces.

A society possesses cultural autonomy to the extent that its members share a common, distinctive, and unique culture. Any number of specific traits of this culture may be shared with other societies, including technical and scientific knowledge, customs and traditions, language, norms, and values. At the same time, many subparts of a society may hold numerous cultural ideas of their own that are not shared throughout the whole society. Nevertheless, the common culture of the total society—and especially its dominant social values and norms—forms a distinctive and unified set of ideas that is unique to that society.

Like communities, societies have historically been located within a defined territorial area, and some theorists include the requirement of spatial unity in their definition of a society. As long as communication and transportation facilities were severely limited, spatial unity was a requisite for functional and cultural autonomy. Given the technological developments of the twentieth century, however, this necessity no longer exists. We have already discarded the idea that a society must be territorially contiguous, and in the not too distant future, space travel and space stations may permanently obliterate the spatial unity of many societies.

The terms "state" and "nation" are frequently used interchangeably with "society," but technically each has a different meaning. A state is a specifically defined political entity, centering around a government. It is, in effect, a political network, or polity. In many instances the boundaries of a state are conterminous with those of its total society; the state is then the

[10]This definition is adapted from Ronald Freedman et al., *Principals of Sociology*, rev. ed. (New York: Holt, Rinehart, and Winston, 1956), p. 78.

whole society as viewed from a purely political perspective. In Africa, though, many political states still contain several relatively anonymous native societies, while the separate states of the United States are clearly not societies (although the United States as a whole is simultaneously a state and a society). In short a state is a political unit, while a society is a considerably more inclusive social organization, of which its government is only one aspect. A nation, in the contemporary sense of the word, exists when a political state coincides with a total society and when the polity is the dominant social network within the society. In other words, a nation is the particular kind of society that happens to be prevalent in today's world. Indeed, because all major contemporary societies are also nations, it is difficult for us to realize that this is not a theoretical imperative. Historically, however, societies have not always been nations—as demonstrated by military and early colonial empires, in which a single political unit spanned many separate societies. Conceivably, too, a society might exist in which the religious, educational, or some other major network was the dominant sphere of power.

FEDERATIONS

Some day the entire world may constitute a single society, organized as an international federation. Such an organization would be infinitely more inclusive and complex than any single nation, and would constitute a logical final category in our typology of social organizations. Formally defined, *a federation is an organization of societies that retain their basic political sovereignty, but cooperate in collective activities and grant limited portions of their autonomy to a central coordinating body.* As yet, this category of international federations is only a potentiality rather than a reality. No existing international organization begins to compete with national societies in inclusiveness, complexity, or power. In fact, only a few of them—most notably the European Economic Community—possess any political authority above that of their member nations.

Because true international federations do not yet exist, our present discussion is limited to international confederations or loosely organized combination of autonomous societies who cooperate in some joint activities without relinquishing their separate sovereignties. Confederations are considerably less complex than societies (and even many communities and associations), so that by discussing them as the final category in our typology, we are violating our underlying principle of increasing organizational complexity. We do this, however, on the grounds that presently existing confederations may eventually evolve into true international federations.

Examples of contemporary international confederations are the United

Nations, the Organization of American States, the European Free Trade Association, the North Atlantic Treaty Organization, the Nordic Council, the Council of Europe, and the Latin American Free Trade Association.[11] The significant feature of all such organizations is that their members are nations, not individuals or other types of organizations.[12] They are, in effect, essentially stable relationships among national governments.

In conclusion, it must be reiterated that the definitions of these various types of social organizations, and indeed the whole typology itself, are entirely arbitrary. This classificatory scheme is presented not as a finished taxonomy of all social organizations, but merely as a heuristic device for describing and illustrating the vast range of different kinds of organizational units that develop through the process of social organization.

Organizational Subunits

WE now shift attention from organizations as whole entities to their component parts. Most social organizations contain a number of subunits, each of which normally exercises some degree of autonomy and can therefore be examined as an organization in its own right. Moreover, most "whole organizations" are simultaneously parts of larger social units. Consequently, whether a given organization is studied as a separate entity or as a part of a more encompassing whole is largely an arbitrary decision of the researcher, depending on the problem under investigation.

FUNCTIONAL SPECIALIZATION AND AUTONOMY

The two conditions of functional specialization and functional autonomy normally exist among the subunits of any organization, though in varying degrees in different organizations and at different times within the same organization.

On the one hand, *in any organization more complex than a simple friendship group there will be some degree of functional specialization, or division of labor, among the subunits.* The various subunits (and sub-subunits and so on) will tend to become specialized in their actions, performing different kinds of activities. To the extent that these specialized functions mesh with each other and contribute to the overall functioning of

---

[11] The European Economic Community is at present primarily an international confederation, but the limited amount of political sovereignty it possesses gives it some characteristics of a true international federation.

[12] Many associations today cross national boundaries to become international in scope. However, the limited ranges of activities of all international associations, plus the fact that they are composed of individuals or private associations, disqualifies them as confederations.

the larger organization, it will become strongly unified. In any case, however, each subunit will tend to lose self-sufficiency as it increasingly performs one or a few specialized activities, so that if left to itself it could not long survive. It relinquishes to other subunits the responsibility for satisfying most of its survival requirements and hence becomes highly interdependent upon them. In return, by concentrating all of its actions on the activities it performs most effectively, it gains functional efficiency.

On the other hand, *the subunits of most organizations also normally possess some degree of functional autonomy, or limited ability to act independently of the larger organization.*[13] Each subunit will evidence its own unique patterns of social ordering and sets of activities. The encompassing organization may attempt to limit and control the functional autonomy of its component parts to a considerable degree, so as to acquire overall stability and unity. In anything less than a completely monolithic organization, however, this control can only be partial, leaving the subunits with some latitude to act on their own. Moreover, it is usually to the long-run benefit of the encompassing organization to grant its component parts considerable leeway within broadly specified limits, for this greatly increases the flexibility of the organization and its ability to deal with changing circumstances—even though this procedure does multiply the short-run administrative and coordination problems of the larger organization.

The degree of subunit functional autonomy varies widely among different organizations and even among various subunits of the same organization. As a general proposition, however, it has been suggested that the process through which the larger organization is created may influence the relative autonomy of its component parts. If the larger organization is established through the merging of what were once relatively independent units, these units often retain more functional autonomy than do subunits that are initiated by a more inconclusive organization.[14]

From a theoretical viewpoint, these two conditions of functional specialization and autonomy are mutually contradictory, since as a subunit becomes increasingly specialized it must relinquish self-sufficiency. In actual practice, though, the two conditions usually coexist to some degree. Each subunit will simultaneously evidence some specialization and some autonomy. This is not an accidental outcome of poor organization, but rather an attempt to gain the functional advantages of both conditions. However, since both conditions raise numerous problems of communication, coordination, and control for the organization as a whole, they both contribute to a

---

[13]The concept of functional autonomy has been extensively discussed by Alvin Gouldner, "Reciprocity and Autonomy in Functional Theory," in Llewellyn Gross, ed., *Symposium on Sociological Theory* (New York: Harper & Row, 1959), pp. 241–270.
[14]Seymour M. Lipset, *Political Man* (New York: Doubleday, 1963), chap. 12.

pervasive tendency toward administrative centralization in complex organizations.

SEGMENTATION AND ABSORPTION

As the extent and scope of functional autonomy increases or decreases among the subunits comprising an organization, one of two opposing processes may become predominant. To the degree that subunits gain functional autonomy, segmentation frequently occurs, though this is not inevitable. In contrast, as subunits lose functional autonomy—through either narrow functional specialization or pervasive control by the encompassing organization—absorption often occurs.[15] *Relatively segmented units of an organization act primarily as autonomous actors,* seeking their own goals in as expedient a manner as possible. In contrast, *relatively absorbed units act primarily as involved parts,* seeking to meet the functional requirements of the encompassing organization and to contribute to the attainment of collective goals.

These two processes of segmentation and absorption are mutually incompatible, since an increase in one leads to a corresponding decrease in the other. Both, however, can occur simultaneously among various subunits of the same organization or even within one subunit at different times. We must also guard against subjective bias toward one or the other of these processes. Neither one is exclusively beneficial or detrimental for any social organization. Both are vital for organizational survival and functional operation, although an excessively strong movement in either direction can harm any organization.[16] Let us examine both of them in greater detail.

The concept of segmentation was first used by Émile Durkheim to describe societies composed of communities and other organizations (such as clans) that are all relatively similar to each other.[17] Because of this similarity, segmented units of an organization are not highly specialized or interdependent; each can exist and act with relative autonomy. They will continue to be subunits of a more encompassing organization as long as they at least periodically interact with each other in patterned ways and share a common culture. But they also retain the capacity to function autonomously when-

[15] Some sociologists use the term "institutionalization" in this context, but its many diverse meanings can cause considerable conceptual confusion.
[16] Segmentation should not be equated with disintegration, and absorption with integration, as is sometimes done. Excessive segmentation will cause disintegration, while a certain amount of absorption is necessary for integration. But within limits the degree of segmentation or absorption of subunits can vary without disturbing the overall integration of the organization. This dimension of segmentation-absorption refers to relationships of subunits to the larger organization, whereas integration or disintegration is a property of the organization as a whole.
[17] Émile Durkheim, *The Division of Labor in Society,* trans. by George Simpson (New York: Free Press, 1933), p. 175.

ever such actions are expedient or necessary. In addition, they often possess relatively distinct cultures of their own, or cultural autonomy. As these subunits become increasingly segmented, their relationships with the larger organization may move in several possible directions: (1) The subunit seeks to influence the larger organization, and perhaps eventually dominate it. (2) The larger organization seeks to regain tighter control over the subunit, leading to increased conflict. (3) The subunit and the larger organization maintain an uneasy "truce" while continually trying to influence or change each other. (4) The unit completely severs its ties with the parent organization and becomes wholly autonomous in relation to it.

In a relatively segmented organization, in which many or most of the constituent subunits possess much functional autonomy, internal conflict and balancing of power are critical social processes. As each subunit acts to protect its own interest and attain its own goals, it will almost inevitably come into conflict with other subunits. The larger organization will therefore constantly be threatened with disintegration if it cannot cope with these pervasive conflicts. If such conflicts cannot be permanently resolved—as often they cannot—stability must then be obtained through the balancing of power among contending subunits. The threat or overt exercise of power is met with one or more countervailing pressures from other units, with the results that each unit respects the interests of the other unit and at least minimal overall stability is maintained. The twentieth-century international scene, with its alternating periods of open warfare followed by peace based on a delicate balance of power, is a clear example of this kind of situation. The overriding concern of a relatively segmented organization is therefore the management of tensions and conflicts and the maintenance of approximate power equality among all its subunits. Out of the process of segmentation, however, can come social changes that may be of great benefit to the larger organization, enabling it to adapt to shifting environmental pressures.

In the process of absorption, the subunits of an organization become oriented toward the total organization and away from their own particular interests. They accept responsibilities of membership in the larger entity, share its values, norms, and other cultural ideas, act to fulfill its functional requirements, and contribute to the attainment of whatever goals this organization seeks. Because the various subunits often concentrate their efforts on different organizational activities, extensive division of labor occurs among them. The result of such functional specialization is interdependence; the subunits lose much of their functional autonomy and become highly dependent upon each other and the encompassing organization. Loss of functional autonomy can occur without functional specialization, however. Judicious use of power—in the form of either force or authority by the larger organization to control its subunits—can effectively limit or destroy their ability to act independently or to survive outside the organization. In short, any social phenomenon becomes an absorbed subpart of a larger organization to the extent that it supports and contributes to overall patterns of social ordering and cultural ideas. To the extent that highly absorbed subunits act to fulfill functional requirements and achieve goals for the larger organization, this organization will tend to become highly unified.

In organizations whose subunits are highly absorbed, the critical social processes are promotion of overall unity and collective goal attainment. To the extent that the component units are functionally specialized, there is a continuing demand for unified coordination of their interrelationships. If the larger organization is relying on power to control its subunits, it must constantly exert force or authority to maintain internal order. Given overall coordination and stability in the organization, plus the satisfaction of its functional requirements through the actions of responsible parts, the organization then can direct most of its efforts toward obtaining its collective goals. The various academic departments within a college, for example, are highly absorbed subunits that have limited functional autonomy because of their extensive specialization and interdependence. Hence their activities must be coordinated by the offices of various deans if they are to cooperate in the common endeavor of educating students. The overriding concern of an organization with a high degree of absorption among its subunits is therefore the coordination of internal relationships and the directing of organizational activities toward collective goals. Nevertheless, if the subunits of an organization become too highly absorbed, the organization can become rigid and incapable of changing to meet new problems and conditions.

In sum, the central thrust of this discussion of segmentation and absorption is that these contradictory processes are always occurring in all social organizations to some degree, and although both tendencies can have beneficial consequences for organizations, either one can become harmful if carried to an extreme.

The Web of Organizations

THE various types of social organizations and their component subunits that we have examined in this chapter rarely exist side by side as separate and wholly unrelated entities, like books randomly placed on a shelf. Almost universally, *organizations overlap and interlock with each other, forming a gigantic social web, the totality of which is organized social life.* Societies, because of their relative self-sufficiency, come closer than any other type of existing social organization to fitting the bookshelf analogy. But even here, international confederations bind societies together to some extent. All other types of social organizations exist today within the confines of enveloping societies. They cannot escape the pervasive influences of their society, and in a legal sense they owe their very existence to the larger society. Networks, in turn, normally encompass portions of numerous associations, communities, groups, and even families. Going still further down the line, associations and classes frequently cut across scores of communities and other organizations, while a community often contains hundreds or thousands of associations, groups, families, and aggregates. Groups, finally, are normally found within almost all other types of organizations.

ORGANIZATIONAL LINKAGES

This interlocking web of social organizations is bound together in two different ways. First, individuals are almost invariably members of more than one organization. The typical person in a contemporary society is probably a member of a family, several small groups, a church or other religious body, a labor union or business or professional association, a community, possibly a class, sometimes an aggregate, at least sporadically most of the major social networks, and always the total society. Through such overlapping memberships, the activities of all the organizations comprising a society become interrelated and at least partially coordinated.

Second, the organizations themselves crosscut and overlap each other in their actions. To take a simple example, a business concern influences many families through the work schedules and pay rates of its employees; many friendship cliques and committees are formed within the business; this organization must deal with labor unions, a chamber of commerce and other associations; it pays taxes to the local community as well as to the federal government; the manner in which it is organized may contribute to the formation of "working" and "management" social classes; it plays an active part in maintaining the economic network of the society; it may rely heavily on business contracts from the national government, and in times of crisis it is called upon to help defend the society by carrying its burden of the national defense effort.

ORGANIZATIONAL TENSIONS

Social organizations can act either as relatively autonomous social actors or as parts of some larger and more inclusive social organization. A hospital, for example, may be viewed both as a relatively independent association (as when it provides various medical services, assigns doctors and nurses to duty shifts, or sets fees for patients) and as an integral part of the medical network of the community and the society (as when it cooperates with other hospitals, clinics, and public health services to control communicable diseases or deal with a natural disaster). The hospital, in turn, is composed of many smaller organizations, such as medical service teams, shifts of nurses, laboratories, and kitchens. These are usually thought of as subunits of the total hospital, but normally they do possess limited amounts of functional autonomy.

Because any organization can act as either an independent actor or an involved part of a larger collectivity, *organizations often experience both centrifugal and centripetal forces in relation to both their constituent subunits and the larger organizations of which they are a part.*

On the one hand, organizations generally attempt to increase their functional autonomy in relation to more inclusive organizational entities, so as to maximize their chances of obtaining whatever goals they seek. They also attempt to keep their own subparts relatively dependent on them (or absorbed), so as to prevent tensions and disruptions and thus ensure their own continued survival. Since organizations at all levels of size and complexity are simultaneously pushing in both these directions, tension and conflict are inherent in all social organizations.

On the other hand, these pressures are limited by counterforces which also occur in almost all organizations. The push toward increasing functional autonomy is mitigated by functional interdependency. To the extent that any organization is interdependent upon other organizations, it must join with them in creating and maintaining more inclusive and unifying patterns of social ordering and cultural ideas, thus taking on responsibilities as a part of a larger social entity. The push toward increased control over subunits, meanwhile, is mitigated by the need for functional flexibility. If an organization is to remain flexible and adaptable, and thus retain its stability over time, it must allow its own parts a certain amount of autonomy so that they can deal with constantly changing situations and demands.[18] The most basic operational requirement for all social organizations, therefore, is to establish a working balance between these opposing pressures toward simultaneous segmentation and absorption in both upward and downward directions.

We might summarize this entire discussion of the web of social organizations by saying that despite the untold number of organizational units that arise from the continual ongoing process of social organization, all of these organizations are to some extent interwoven with each other to form a single dynamic whole. To paraphrase John Donne: "No social organization is an island, entire of itself."

---

[18] These ideas are developed at some length by Alvin Gouldner in "Reciprocity and Autonomy in Functional Theory."

RECOMMENDED READING

Faris, Ellsworth. "The Primary Group: Essence and Accident." *American Journal of Sociology* 38 (July 1932): 41–50. (Also Bobbs-Merrill reprint S-81.)
> A reanalysis of Cooley's "primary group" concept, pointing out that the essence of the "primary group" is the existence of social relationships that are highly personal.

Gouldner, Alvin. "Reciprocity and Autonomy in Functional Theory." In Llewellyn Gross, ed., *Symposium on Sociological Theory.* New York: Harper & Row, 1959, pp. 241–270.
> The processes of functional autonomy and functional reciprocity among the parts of a social organization are extensively examined and analyzed.

Hall, Richard H. *Organizations: Structure and Process.* Englewood Cliffs, N.J.: Prentice-Hall, 1972, chap. 2.
> Describes the major characteristics and types of associations.

Hawley, Amos H. *Human Ecology.* New York: Ronald Press, 1950, pp. 222–233.
> Examines the structural and functional differences between the polar types of "dependent" and "independent" communities.

Linton, Ralph. *The Cultural Background of Personality.* New York: Appleton-Century-Crofts, 1945, pp. 15–19.
> A brief enumeration of the common characteristics of all societies.

McIver, Robert M. *Community: A Sociological Study.* New York: Macmillan Co., 1928, pp. 22–28.
> A classic discussion of the differences between societies, states, communities, and associations as types of social organizations.

PART II

Creating Social Organization

THUS far we have been laying a foundation for examining social organization. We have described social organization as an ongoing dynamic process that is continually being created, we have seen that organized life can be anlyzed using a social system model, we have explored the nature of social power as the principal medium through which social organization occurs, and we have discussed the various kinds of organizational units.

In this second section we focus directly on the process of social organization, looking at its various components and examining six theoretical perspectives on the creation of social organization. Our goals will be to gain a broad conceptualization of this process and to develop an overall theoretical perspective focusing on the exercise of power in social life.

Since the creation of social organization begins with social interaction, chapter 4 discusses interaction processes and social relationships, placing them in a social action frame of reference. Exchange and symbolic interaction theories are described as two *complementary views of the creation of social organization from an interaction perspective.*

As social interactions and relationships become interwoven and recurrent they form patterns of social ordering that often remain relatively stable and predictable through time. Chapter 5 begins with an overview of the nature of social ordering. Coercion and ecological ordering theories are then examined as two perspectives on the creation of social organization that focus specifically on ordering processes.

Patterns of social ordering in turn acquire meaning for their participants as they become infused with shared cultural ideas. Chapter 6 introduces the concept of culture and its major components. Normative and value cultural theories are sketched as two approaches to understanding the creation of social organization from a cultural perspective.

Chapter 7 then pulls together the major ideas from the preceding three chapters to formulate an overall theoretical perspective on the creation of social organization that views social power as the central dynamic of organized social life.

4

Interaction Processes and Theories

SOCIAL interaction first of all requires two or more social actors capable of acting. Although we commonly think of actors as individuals, organizations can also interact as social actors. If a government contracts with a construction firm to build a highway, for instance, it is the government that agrees to provide the necessary funds and the construction company that agrees to lay the highway, not the individuals who negotiate and sign the contract as representatives of their respective organizations. Thus social actors may be either individual persons or social organizations acting as units.

Individuals who perform social acts, either on their own behalf or as representatives of organizations, must be sufficiently socialized to be capable of interacting with others. Although the process of socialization is a primary concern of social psychologists, for the analysis of social organization this process is normally assumed to have already transpired. The existence of socialized individuals is therefore a psychological parameter for social organizations. Social actors, whether individuals or organizations, are also assumed to be seeking goals through their actions, although the nature of these goals need not be specified. To attain their goals, actors must exercise social power in some form and to some degree, so that power exertion becomes the basic medium through which all social action occurs.

Social Interaction

CONSIDERABLE debate has raged among sociologists and philosophers over the years concerning whether or not scientific analysis requires that the actions of social actors be predetermined by causal forces. Positivists, ranging from behavioral psychologists to organistic sociologists, argue that rational scientific analysis is impossible unless we assume that all actions are caused in some manner by either external or internal forces impinging on the actor. Their principal opponents have been the utilitarians, who argue for ethical individualism, or the idea that each person is ultimately responsible for his or her own actions as one acts with more or less rationality in pursuit of desired goals. Positivism thus rests on an assumption of determinism, whereas utilitarianism is based on an assumption of voluntarism.

Although these two philosophical positions appear to be diametrically opposed, Talcott Parsons has proposed a synthesis that is widely accepted by contemporary sociologists.[1] His notion of "voluntaristic positivism" or "the action frame of reference" argues that social acts are always voluntaristic from the perspective of the actor choosing a course of action, but that from the broader perspective of the scientific observer these choices are always guided—though not fully determined—by culturally prescribed norms that are either internalized by the actor or enforced by others. Voluntarism is therefore preserved in the dual sense that actors are free to make voluntary choices within normatively acceptable limits, and that these limitations apply only to means or courses of action, not to the ends or goals being pursued. At the same time, a considerable degree of determinism is also retained in the form of normative prescriptions and proscriptions, thus allowing for positivistic social science. Many sociologists differ with Parsons in two main respects: they view most normative limitations as less binding on actors than does Parsons, while at the same time adding other kinds of limitations imposed by the parameters of population, the natural environment, and technology. Nevertheless, Parsons' basic conception of subjective voluntarism within objectively imposed limits provides a philosophical foundation for humanistic social science, while also answering the seemingly paradoxical question of how one can simultaneously be individually autonomous and socially responsible.

[1] Talcott Parsons, *The Structure of Social Action* (Glencoe, Ill.: Free Press, 1949), chap. 2.

In terms of social systems analysis, this conception of limited voluntarism avoids many of the logical pitfalls into which systems analysts can easily fall. If we adopt a closed system model, borrowed from the physical sciences, we are led to assume the existence of several inherent tendencies within the system, including entropy (eventual dissipation of all dynamic energy), equifinality (fixed outcomes regardless of the course of action followed), and homeostasis or equilibrium (either key features or all relationships in the system remaining stable). Yet there appear to be no bases in social reality for arbitrarily making any of these assumptions. In contrast, even limited voluntarism requires that we adopt an open system model that continually interacts with its environment. In an open system, entropy, equifinality, homeostasis, and equilibrium are not necessarily assumed to occur, but rather become problematic issues for empirical investigation.

THE NATURE OF SOCIAL INTERACTION

The creation of social organization begins with social interaction between two or more social actors. *Social interaction occurs whenever the actions of one actor affect the actions or thoughts of another actor in some manner.* Actions do not become interaction if the intended recipient totally ignores them or if they produce no discernible effects. But if an action modifies the recipient's actions or thoughts in any way, interaction is occurring, regardless of whether or not the recipient responds back to the initiator. Thus if a television commercial persuades a viewer to try a new brand of soap there has been interaction, but only in one direction. Most social interaction is reciprocal, however, with each actor affecting the other participant(s). Social interaction can occur between any number of actors and with all degrees of complexity. A casual two-person conversation is an obvious instance of interaction, but so is an agreement among dozens of nations to jointly lower trade tariffs.

As emphasized by Max Weber,[2] not all human interaction is social in nature. Actions and interactions are social only to the extent that actors attach meanings to their own and others' acts. These meanings need not be similar, so that different actors may interpret a given act in quite diverse ways. Nevertheless, social interaction always consists of actions that are meaningfully oriented to meaningful actions of others. Meanings attached to actions are frequently symbolized and conveyed to others through communication, so that many sociologists use the terms "social interaction," "symbolic interaction," and "communication" almost synonymously. More precisely, however, social interaction can occur—with much confusion—even if meanings are not shared among the actors, as long as

[2] Max Weber, *The Theory of Social and Economic Organization* (Glencoe, Ill.: Free Press, 1947), chap. 1.

each one is acting in terms of his or her own meanings and those that he or she attributes to others. Symbolic interaction is therefore a special case of social interaction in which the participants overtly attempt to convey the meanings of their actions to one another. Communication occurs when this process is successful to some degree, so that the recipient correctly understands the meanings of the sender, although it is not necessary for the recipient to accept or share these meanings. Actions that do not carry any meanings lead to behavioral rather than social interaction, in which each participant relates only to the overt behaviors of the others. People sometimes interact on a purely behavioral level, as when two persons round a corner from opposite directions and accidentally bump into each other, push past each other, and continue on their separate ways. The ability to attach symbolic meanings to actions and interactions is nevertheless the unique feature of human social intercourse, not shared by animals (except perhaps chimpanzees and dolphins).

THE DIMENSIONS OF SOCIAL INTERACTION

All social interaction can be described analytically in terms of six dimensions. As originally identified by Talcott Parsons, these dimensions (which he termed "pattern variables") pertained to actors' subjective orientations toward interaction, but they also provide a useful scheme for classifying and analyzing overt social interaction.[3] Although each dimension is a continuum with infinite gradations from one extreme to the other, Parsons brought voluntarism into this scheme by insisting that each one also contains a midpoint, or "choice-point," from which the actor must choose to move in one direction or the other as he or she acts. At the same time, these dimensions also describe the social framework within which all interactions are located.

The first two dimensions, as conceptualized by Parsons, pertain to actors' subjective orientations toward social organizations. More generally, however, they describe ways in which specific interactions contribute to the overall process of social organization.

Self—Collective. To the degree that an actor is self-oriented, he or she (or it, in the case of an organization) is seeking a private goal and is concerned only with how the interaction will affect him or her personally. The actor is guided by expedient calculations of costs involved and benefits to be obtained through participation in the interaction. Conversely, to the

---

[3] All but the second of these "pattern variables" are discussed in Talcott Parsons, *The Social System* (Glencoe, Ill.: Free Press, 1951), chap. 2. The final one was added later in Talcott Parsons, "Some Comments on the State of the General Theory of Action," *American Sociological Review* 18 (December 1953): 618–631.

degree that an actor is collectively oriented, he, she, or it is seeking a collective goal in collaboration with others and is concerned with how the interaction will contribute to their common welfare. In this case the actor is guided by moral (in the broadest sense of the term) considerations regarding the obligations and responsibilities of participation in the interaction. Participation in social interaction through time often produces a shift from self to collective orientations, so that the actors begin to think in terms of "we" rather than "I," but in any given situation they may display a preponderance of either type or a mixture of both.

This distinction between self and collective orientations is critically important for understanding all organized social life, for one of the basic problems inherent in any attempt to create social organization is reconciling personal and collective interests. This dilemma occurs not just on the level of simple interaction, but throughout all kinds of organizations from informal clubs to nations. As expressed by Robert MacIver: "The problem of human society everywhere is the adjustment of the ego interest and the group interest. This is the problem not merely of social order but of every social relationship. . . . Every human organization of every kind, whether it be a family, a business, a state, or a church of God, finds some way of reconciling the interest of the individual and the interest of the whole."[4]

Instrumental—Expressive. Whereas the previous dimension indicates how actors relate to their interactions with others, this one describes the nature of the goal they are seeking through interaction. Instrumental interactions are means to the attainment of some other end, as when a store clerk sells merchandise to a customer or several community agencies join forces in a fund-raising drive. Expressive interactions, in contrast, are valued for their own sake regardless of the outcome, as in a casual chat between friends or a religious ceremony. Many interactions are predominately either instrumental or expressive in nature, but others (such as competitive games and sports) are designed to produce simultaneously both instrumental goal attainment and expressive enjoyment.

Actors can act either instrumentally or expressively with either a self or a collective orientation; these two dimensions of social interaction are conceptually and empirically distinct. For example, two members of a city council, interacting for the wholly instrumental purpose of deciding where to build a new park, might relate to each other with either self orientations ("Which location would most benefit my own constituents, or perhaps my own wallet?") or collective orientations ("Which location would most benefit the entire community?"). Similarly, if they were debating each other for the sheer expressive pleasure of matching wits, they might also hold

[4]Robert M. MacIver, *The Web of Government*, rev. ed. (New York: Free Press, 1965), p. 310.

either self orientations ("How can I counter his last point, so as to have the final word?") or collective orientations ("How can I respond to his last point, so that we will better understand each other?").

The next two dimensions, as conceptualized by Parsons, pertain to actors' orientations toward social actions. More generally, however, they describe the degree to which interactions are guided by and reflect existing social norms and practices.

Ascribed—Achieved.   An ascribed course of action is largely or wholly specified in advance by norms or expectations held by others for that interaction. The actor exercises little or no discretion in what he or she does in the interaction. Participants are evaluated not by what they do (unless they deviate noticeably from the prevailing prescriptions), but rather by how adequately they carry out their assigned actions. An achieved course of action, on the other hand, is largely or wholly created by the actor, who can therefore exercise wide latitude in what he or she does in the interaction. In this case, participants are evaluated in terms of their skills in both devising courses of action and performing them.

Universal—Particular.   Whereas the previous dimension concerned the specificity of existing norms and expectations for a course of action, this one indicates the degree to which the resulting interaction reflects previously established practices. Universal interaction follows a standard pattern and is more or less similar to all others of that same type, whereas particular interaction is essentially unique to that specific situation. Most social interactions obviously fall toward the universal or customary end of this dimension, but there can be considerable variation along the continuum, and most interactions involve at least some particularistic features. Universal or prescribed actions clearly tend to result in standardized interactions, while particular or unspecified actions produce unique interactions. It is also quite possible, however, for actors to interpret or combine existing prescriptions in novel ways, or choose to interact as others have done in similar situations.

The final two dimensions, as conceptualized by Parsons, refer to actors' orientations toward other actors. More generally, however, they describe ways in which actors act toward one another.

Diffuse—Specific.   When individuals interact in a diffuse manner, each one acts as a total person and also responds to the other participants as total persons. They view one another as whole personalities rather than as functionaries performing a duty, and are concerned with who the other persons are as well as with what they do. Highly specific interaction is just the opposite. The participants deal with each other only as impersonal functionaries enacting a specific role, and they don't care who the other people are as long as they carry out their side of the interaction. When the involved actors are organizations, the individuals representing them are likely to interact in a relatively impersonal manner, and many social critics have lamented the presumed decline of personal interaction in modern highly organized societies. Nevertheless, numerous observers have pointed out that even in the most formal bureaucratic settings people frequently bring personal interests and concerns into their interactions. Many social interactions are therefore complex mixtures of both diffuse and specific actions.

Affective—Neutral. Regardless of whether one acts toward others as total persons or as functionaries, one may approach them with varying degrees of either cathectic emotions or cognitive rationality. In affective interaction, actors react primarily to their own and others' feelings, whereas in neutral interaction the actors give primary attention to one another's ideas. Quite obviously, many interactions involve both feelings and ideas, but often one or the other of these tends to predominate. Affectivity is undoubtedly more prevalent when people interact on a personal basis, while neutrality is more common when the interaction is impersonal. The opposite combinations are quite possible, however, as when spouses rationally discuss their financial situation or when a person becomes angry at a persistent door-to-door salesman.

This dimension of affective versus neutral interaction was a central focus in the writings of Max Weber, who perceived a long-term historical trend in Western societies toward greater rationality in social organization.[5] He divided each pole of this continuum into two categories: affective interaction could be either affectual (wholly emotional) or traditional (tied to the past) in nature, while neutral or rational interaction could be either *wertrational* (rational efforts to realize given or absolute values) or *zweckrational* (rational efforts to obtain expedient goals). Weber used this scheme to explain the rise of modern bureaucratic organizations in place of more traditionally or affectually based organizations, as well as other aspects of modern societies.

By classifying interactions along these six dimensions, we can analyze the process of social interaction with some preciseness and understand better the various forms it takes. But it is important to remember that (1) these dimensions are all continua with many intermediate gradiations, not simple

[5] Weber, *The Theory of Social and Economic Organization.*

dichotomies, and that (2) our ability to quantitatively measure interactions and place them at particular points on any of these dimensions is presently extremely crude. Nevertheless, these six dimensions clearly indicate the complexity of all social interaction.

THE DYNAMICS OF SOCIAL INTERACTION

Thus far we have been discussing social interaction in static terms, ignoring the fact that this is an ongoing process. To begin thinking more dynamically, let us ask what kinds of factors cause actors to interact with one another and perpetuate those interactions through time? These underlying causes are almost as diverse as the specific kinds of interaction that result, but most of them can be classified into one of the six broad categories sketched in the following paragraphs.

Personal Needs. Individuals constantly initiate social interaction to satisfy personal needs of various kinds. These may be biological needs such as food, shelter, or sex; they may be emotional needs such as security, friendship, or love; or they may be intellectual needs such as understanding, stimulation, or growth. But all such needs usually lead people to seek out others who may be sources of gratification and begin interacting with them. To the extent that one's needs are met through this interaction, one will quite likely seek to continue and perpetuate it.

Common Interests. Another basis of much social interaction is common interests and goals. Regardless of whether or not actors particularly care for each other, mutual concerns may bring them together and lead to ongoing interaction. To attain a commonly sought goal, they may more or less purposefully agree to cooperate in joint activities. The resulting social interaction will likely be more impersonal and rational than in the case of need satisfaction, but these bonds of cooperation can become quite enduring over time.

The Exercise of Force. Although in many societies physical force does not account for much interpersonal interaction outside of custodial organizations, it is plainly visible in autocratically controlled states and in international relations. Much more common than physical coercion, however, is the exercise of force through compensations and deprivations. In addition to the obvious economic forces of wages, prices, fines, and so on, these also include providing or withdrawing opportunities for communication, giving or withholding services, or administering symbolic rewards and punishments. An even more subtle kind of force is based on the possession of expert knowledge and/or persuasive ability. Whatever form it takes, the use of force underlies much social interaction in all societies.

Functional Interdependence. The more complex the social environment in which actors live, the more likely they are to depend on one another in countless ways. And if actor A depends on actor B for something, and vice versa, they will likely attempt to arrange an exchange. Functional interdependence is perhaps most evident in cooperative economic activities, in which a chain of reciprocal interactions often reaches from suppliers of raw materials to manufacturers to transporters to wholesalers to retailers to the eventual customers. In a university, the students, faculty, and administrators are all highly interdependent, even though they may not share common interests. And much public policy formation in modern societies results from compromises among political factions who find that they need each other's support despite strong ideological differences. Pervasive functional interdependence in modern societies has thus necessitated the creation of extremely complex patterns of social interaction.

Expectations and Obligations. In the course of our daily lives all of us encounter innumerable social expectations and obligations concerning our dealings with others. In response, we often interact with others out of a sense of duty or responsibility. The resulting interactions may be based on long-standing traditions (such as the fealty bond between feudal lord and peasant), on ethical or moral convictions (as in the professional obligation of physician to patient), or on formal contracts (as in the case of a manufacturer who guarantees his product against defects). There are many diverse kinds of social expectations and obligations throughout all facets of social life, and they often reinforce one another to make interaction almost imperative.

Shared Values. When actors discover that they share a set of basic values—whether social, political, economic, religious, philosophical, ethical, or aesthetic—they will likely identify with each other and feel linked by a common bond. This attraction can then lead to interaction aimed either at jointly expressing and reaffirming these values or collectively acting to achieve goals derived from the values. Although interests and goals can converge on purely pragmatic grounds, when reinforced by shared values they constitute quite compelling grounds for interaction. Shared values can also reinforce social expectations and obligations, as well as legimate force and interdependence as bases of interaction.

Some of the interactions that result from these causal factors are one-time affairs, while others are repeated so sporadically that no continuity develops. Many other interactions, however, are renewed time after time in a fairly similar manner. Occasional dates grow into a "steady" routine, the members of a hobby club gather periodically to share their common concerns, sporadic sales between a manufacturer and a retail store evolve into a standing arrangement, and wartime alliances between nations lead to permanent treaties. When social interactions are repeated or perpetuated in this manner, we often speak of this process as the development of social relationships. *A social relationship is an instance of enduring social interaction.* There is no definitive point at which repeated interaction becomes a social relationship, so that the nature of the situation being analyzed largely determines which term is used. Nevertheless, this concept of ongoing, relatively enduring social relationships provides an extremely useful way of describing much social interaction.

Through what process are continuing relationships created out of sporadic interactions? This question takes us to the heart of the process of social organization, as well as the contention that social phenomena have a reality apart from their component actors. The process of establishing an ongoing social relationship involves a profound change in the actions of the participants, as they shift from acting as *autonomous social elements* to *involved social parts* of that emerging relationship.[6] When they first initiate social interaction, actors are always acting as autonomous elements in respect to one another, for there are no established social bonds between them. Very likely, of course, they will already be participating members of many other relationships (and may even interact with one another in some of those settings), but they enter the new interaction as independent elements. Once an ongoing social relationship develops between these actors, however, their actions and interactions begin to change. To maintain their relationship as a viable social linkage they must at least some of the time act as involved parts of this encompassing social entity they have created, carrying out the duties and responsibilities of membership. If the actors choose to remain autonomous social elements and do not act as involved social parts when necessary, their relationship will soon disintegrate. If no one is willing to serve as chairperson of the newly established neighborhood clean-up committee, the neighborhood will undoubtedly stay dirty. And when even a few nations refuse to pay their dues to the United Nations, the entire organization is severely weakened.

The essential point is that social actors act differently—at least part of the time and to some degree—when participating as responsible parts of an ongoing social relationship than when acting solely as autonomous social elements. Membership in an established social relationship invariably alters the actions of the participating actors, and if something has discernible consequences it must surely exist. Hence the argument that social relationships are real phenomena, even though we cannot directly observe them.

Perhaps the clearest example of this transition of social actors from

[6] I am indebted to Guy E. Swanson for these concepts of "elements" and "parts" in reference to social relationships.

elements to parts is a marriage. Each person must independently pledge that "I will" form this bond, and either one is free to halt the process by refusing to commit himself or herself. (The reasons why people initiate this relationship are not directly relevant here. Regardless of whether the underlying causal factors are attraction, goal seeking, obligations, interdependence, or force, the result is a marriage.) Once the commitment is made, however, each person is expected to "love, honor, and cherish" his or her spouse and to fulfill the responsibilities of marriage.

Although the distinction between acting as a social element and as a social part is most clearly seen in the initial creation of a social relationship, it applies throughout all social life. In any situation, social actors may be acting either as elements or as parts in reference to a given relationship. On the individual level, a person is acting as an element when he or she says, "Let's join forces and cooperate on this job," but as a part when he or she says, "It's my duty as supervisor to distribute this work among all of us." On the organizational level, two railroads exploring the possibilities of a corporate merger are acting as elements on this occasion, but are participating as parts of a larger transportation network when they coordinate their respective time schedules. As these examples suggest, any social actor may act as either an element or a part, depending on the situation, and may frequently shift back and forth from one mode to the other.

The concepts of "elements" and "parts" are analogous to terms used in chemistry. By themselves, chemical elements—sodium and chlorine, for example—exhibit characteristics peculiarly their own, by which each can be separately identified. This condition holds true even if elements are mixed together, as long as there is no chemical reaction between them. Through a process of atomic interaction, however, the elements can combine to form an entirely new substance—in this case, salt. The elements of sodium and chlorine have now both lost their individual identities and characteristics and have instead become parts of a more inclusive chemical compound which has properties not belonging to either of its components by themselves. In an emergent process such as this, the original elements are transformed into parts of a new entity. The analogy between chemicals and social actors is not perfect, since social relationships are rarely as thoroughly unified as chemical compounds, with the result that actors are constantly alternating between acting as elements and as parts. Nevertheless, the analogy does help us to visualize the essential features of this process.

To summarize these concepts of social elements and parts: *Social actors are elements to the extent that they participate in a particular social situation as relatively independent units, autonomously determining their own actions toward others. Social actors are parts to the extent that they participate as involved members of an encompassing social relationship, with their actions determined by the demands of that relationship.*

The six basic dimensions of all social interaction also apply to ongoing relationships, although the most critical of these is the tendency for actors to develop collective orientations toward their relationship as it develops. A change from self to collective orientations is not mandatory for the creation of a social relationship, but to the extent that this occurs it greatly facilitates and reinforces the participants' willingness to act as involved parts of that relationship. These two alterations that occur as actors create enduring relationships—shifting their actions from those of elements to those of parts, and changing their orientations from themselves to the collectivity—are easily confused, especially since they often accompany and affect each other. The obvious parallel is that actors who act as relatively autonomous elements tend to be self-oriented, while those who participate as relatively involved parts of a relationship tend to be collectively oriented. In the great majority of cases this is what occurs. Social actors enter into a new relationship as elements with expedient orientations because they believe the relationship will benefit them in some way, but as the relationship develops they begin to carry out their responsibilities as involved parts because of their growing moral concern with the welfare of their common endeavor. However, the two alternatives do not always neatly coincide. Actors may maintain a self orientation while performing the responsibilities of membership in a relationship, as in the case of an employee whose chief concern is his or her weekly paycheck but who nevertheless adequately carries out all assigned tasks. Conversely, the employee might be strongly oriented to the collective welfare of his or her work unit, but nevertheless find it impossible to act with more than minimal involvement as a part of that unit because of conflicts with the supervisor.

Most sociological discussions of interaction and relationships regrettably treat social actors either as self oriented elements or as collectively oriented parts, without distinguishing between actions and orientations or combining these two facets of all social relationships into a unified theory. This theoretical dichotomy is clearly evident in the exchange and symbolic interaction theories sketched in the following two sections. Both of these theoretical perspectives attempt to explain the process of social organization by focusing primarily on interaction, but their basic conceptualizations of this fundamental social process are quite different.

Exchange Theory [7]

THIS theoretical perspective focuses on the basic social process of exchange among social actors, using it as the primary key to understanding

---

[7] The six theoretical perspectives on the creation of social organization sketched in this and the following two chapters are not rigorous theories in the sense of a set of logically interrelated and

social organization: "Exchange is . . . : a social process of central significance in social life, which is derived from simpler processes and from which more complex processes are in turn derived."[8] Although exchange theory does not attempt to explain every type of interaction, it is applicable to all situations in which actors are seeking extrinsic goals—that is, to all instrumental as opposed to expressive interactions. It envisions actors entering exchange interactions for purely self-oriented reasons, but through time developing collective orientations toward the emerging relationship.

Exchange theory rests on several initial assumptions about social actors and activities: (1) a social actor will seek to interact with others who can satisfy his or her needs or facilitate attainment of desired goals; (2) all actions entail costs to the actor, such as time, energy, or resources expended; (3) social actors generally seek to keep the costs of their action proportional to (that is, equal to or less than) the outcomes or benefits of those actions; (4) when choosing among alternative courses of action, actors tend to select actions that are most economical in terms of costs and benefits; (5) an actor will terminate a course of action whose costs consistently exceed its benefits.

The basic principles of exchange interaction theory—as developed most extensively by Peter Blau—pertain largely to the four processes of transaction, differentiation, stabilization, and organization, as described in the following paragraphs.[9]

TRANSACTION

Social interaction begins when a social actor—either an individual or an organization—gives something to another actor in hopes of receiving some desired benefit in return. If the other actor reciprocates in an appropriate manner, an exchange transaction occurs. The basis of this mutual attraction, and hence the nature of the exchange, can take many forms: each actor has objects that the other desires, each can perform services for the other, each can satisfy a need of the other, or each can assist the other in reaching a desired goal. In any case, however, the resulting transaction will follow the fundamental principle of exchange interaction: "An individ-

---

exhaustive propositions, but together they represent the full scope of current theoretical thinking concerning the process of social organization. Any classification of theoretical writings into broad perspectives, as done here, is somewhat arbitrary, but this approach enables us to see the major strands of theoretical thinking that presently cut across sociology, and also to appreciate the intellectual bonds uniting theorists working within each perspective. In all cases there are numerous differences among the various proponents of each perspective, but for our present purposes the major ideas shared within a theoretical perspective are more relevant than any internal disagreements.

[8] Peter M. Blau, *Exchange and Power in Social Life* (New York: John Wiley & Sons, 1964), p. 4.
[9] Blau also discusses attraction and integration as basic social processes, but attraction is merely a necessary precondition for interaction in his scheme, while integration is entirely an interpersonal process that is only indirectly relevant for the creation of social organization.

ual who supplies rewarding services to another obligates him. To discharge this obligation, the second must furnish benefits to the first in turn. . . . If both individuals value what they receive from the other, both are prone to supply more of their own services to provide incentives for the other to increase his supply and to avoid becoming indebted to him." [10]

Initially, an emerging exchange relationship may be quite precarious. Unless the participants already share a common "norm of reciprocity" ("If I do something for you, you are obligated to do something for me in return") or are constrained by external power of some sort, no actor has any guarantee that his or her first overtures will be reciprocated by others. If these initial trial overtures are not reciprocated, the transaction will quickly end. To protect their own self-interest, however, recipients are usually led to return some compensatory benefit, for otherwise it would be extremely difficult for them to receive any further benefits from the first actor. Thus the self-interested need to reciprocate for benefits received in order to obtain additional benefits in the future serves as a basic "starting mechanism" [11] for all social interaction. In Blau's words: "When people are thrown together, and before common norms or goals or role expectations have crystallized among them, the advantages to be gained from entering into exchange relations furnish incentives for social interaction. . . . It is a necessary condition of exchange that individuals, in the interest of continuing to receive needed services, discharge their obligations for having received them in the past." [12]

An exchange relationship that has been initiated in this manner will likely be perpetuated as long as three conditions continue to prevail: (1) it is rewarding to the participants, in the sense that each one's benefits equal or exceed his or her costs; (2) no other alternatives are available to the actors that offer greater benefits at significantly lower costs; and (3) the actors' needs and goals remain unsatisfied. Conversely, if an actor experiences any of these conditions—excessive costs, more attractive alternatives, or need satisfaction—he or she will normally withdraw from the relationship. This may not occur immediately, especially if the actor feels a sense of responsibility for the welfare of the relationship or has affective links with other participants, but sooner or later a relationship that is either unrewarding or satisfactorily completed will almost certainly be terminated. While it lasts, however, an exchange relationship is pervaded by reciprocal obligations that bind the participants into a single unit. This collectivity displays properties and processes of its own distinct from those of its members, so that it must be viewed as an emergent real phenomenon.

The social transactions that occur in these exchange relationships differ

[10] Blau, *Exchange and Power in Social Life,* pp. 89–90.
[11] Alvin W. Gouldner, "The Norm of Reciprocity," *American Sociological Review* 25 (April 1960): 161–178.
[12] Blau, *Exchange and Power in Social Life,* p. 92.

from economic transactions in at least four crucial ways. (1) There is no quantitative medium, such as money, for social exchanges— although as we shall see later, influence serves as such a medium in a very imprecise manner. (2) As a result, social exchanges usually involve only vague and unspecified reciprocal obligations rather than stipulated contractual terms, so that "payment" for benefits received need not be an exact equivalent as long as it is appropriate to the situation and acceptable to the recipient. (3) Social exchanges are generally less rational than economic exchanges, in that people rarely pursue one goal to the exclusion of others, they are often inconsistent in their preferences, and they almost never have complete knowledge of the costs and benefits involved in a course of action.[13] (4) In most social exchanges, the actors are not attempting to maximize their profits by obtaining the greatest amount of benefits for the least costs, but rather are concerned primarily to obtain benefits at acceptable (that is, proportional) costs, so that the process of social exchange operates on a "satisfying" rather than a "maximizing" principle.[14]

In addition, the social contexts within which these transactions occur profoundly affect them in several ways: (1) Each participant also has numerous relationships with other actors that provide both resources and limitations for the exchange transaction. (2) The entire set of transactions occurring among a group of actors will establish "going rates" of exchange that affect each specific transaction. (3) Exchanges may transpire indirectly through complex chains of many interrelated actors (A gives to B, who gives to C, who gives to D, and so forth) rather than directly between just two actors. For all these reasons, exchange interaction theory should not be thought of as simply an extension of basic economic theory to the social realm, or as an attempt to treat social actors as isolated "economic men."

These basic features of exchange transactions are summarized in the following three principles:

PRINCIPLE 1: **The greater the probability that a potential exchange transaction will prove rewarding (benefits equal to or greater than costs) to an actor, the more likely one is to initiate it.**

PRINCIPLE 2: **The greater an actor's obligations to reciprocate for benefits previously received from another, the more likely that actor is to complete an exchange transaction.**

PRINCIPLE 3: **An exchange relationship will be perpetuated as long as it proves rewarding to the participants, they have no other more attractive alternatives, and their needs and goals remain unsatisfied.**

[13] Jonathan H. Turner, *The Structure of Sociological Theory* (Homewood, Ill.: Dorsey Press, 1974), p. 266.
[14] Robert A. Dahl and Charles E. Lindblom, *Politics, Economics, and Welfare* (New York: Harper & Row, 1953).

DIFFERENTIATION

Interdependence among actors creates the underlying basis for all exchange transactions, but as we saw in Chapter 2, interdependence also creates social power. Hence it is not surprising that the processes of social exchange and power exertion are closely interwoven. Broadly speaking, all social interaction involves power in some form, so that an exchange transaction can be viewed as one particular form of power exertion. As expressed by Blau: "Power refers to all kinds of influence between persons or groups, including those exercised in exchange transactions. . . ."[15]

If two actors are to complete an exchange transaction, each must be able to offer the other something of value. This indicates that each actor is dependent on the other in some manner, which in turn implies that each can exert influence on the other. Thus an exchange transaction is essentially a balanced power interaction in which each participant is able to exert some amount of influence on the other. In short, social exchange is the exercise of balanced reciprocal influence. Balanced influence does not necessarily require equality of resources or power-wielding ability among the actors, but merely requires that each one is able to exert enough influence on the other to make possible a reciprocal exchange transaction. In this sense, influence functions as a common medium for all exchange transactions, for each participant exerts influence on the other(s) in an effort to acquire desired benefits, while simultaneously responding to the influence exerted by the other(s). Because influence is such a vague and imprecise medium, many social exchanges fall far short of perfect equality. Nevertheless, as long as the influence balance is sufficient to permit reciprocal and acceptable exchanges, interaction can occur. To the extent that an exchange relationship is balanced, in the sense that all participants have sufficient resources to influence the others and alternative courses of action they can pursue, if necessary, it will tend to exhibit at least four characteristics: (1) voluntarism of action by the participants, (2) stability through time, (3) relative equality among the participants, and (4) distributive justice, so that each actor's overall benefits are at least roughly proportional to his or her total investments.

As Blau points out, however, many exchange relationships tend to become unbalanced through time, as one actor acquires more resources than another or as one becomes overdependent on another. The result is a differentiation of power between the participants, so that the relationship shifts from reciprocal influence exchanges to unilateral control exertion. In his words: "By supplying services in demand to others, a person establishes

---

[15] Blau, *Exchange and Power in Social Life*, p. 116.

power over them. If he regularly renders needed services they cannot readily obtain elsewhere, others become dependent on and obligated to him for these services, and unless they can furnish other benefits to him that produce interdependence by making him equally dependent on them, their unilateral dependence obligates them to comply with his requests lest he cease to continue to meet their needs."[16] Actors who find themselves at a power disadvantage in an exchange relationship will often attempt to reestablish relative balance through any of four procedures: (1) supplying the more powerful actor with other goods or services he or she needs, (2) satisfying their needs through alternative courses of action with other actors, (3) attempting to force or persuade the more powerful actor to meet their needs without a reciprocal exchange, or (4) resigning themselves to doing without the needed goods or services or else finding substitutes for them.[17]

If the disadvantaged actor is unsuccessful in all of these efforts, he or she has no choice but to acquiesce to whatever demands are made by the more powerful actor. In this case of severely differentiated power wielding among actors, a form of exchange is still occurring—with subservience being traded for needed goods or services—but it is no longer the kind of balanced reciprocal transaction that is the focus of exchange interaction theory. The relationship becomes one of unbalanced control, or coercion, thus losing voluntarism, stability, equality, and distributive justice. As a consequence, sooner or later conflict is likely to erupt between the stronger and weaker actors. Unless they are so deprived of resources or so thoroughly socialized into their subordinate status that they are incapable of acting, the weaker actors will attempt to challenge or destroy the relationship in order to escape from the controls being imposed on them. The stronger actors, meanwhile, will attempt to maintain or increase the imbalance in the relationship so as to preserve their control and avoid the costs of mutual exchange transactions. These and similar conflicts within exchange relationships keep them continually dynamic and provide a stimulus for constant social change.

This argument concerning power differentiation in exchange relationships is summarized by the following principle:

> **PRINCIPLE 4:** **To the extent that a relationship becomes unbalanced as a result of power differentiation and cannot be rebalanced in some manner, it will be transformed from reciprocal influence exchange to coercive control exertion.**

[16]Ibid., p. 118.
[17]Richard M. Emerson, "Power-Dependence Relations," *American Sociological Review* 27 (February 1962): 31–41. The same argument is presented in Blau, *Exchange and Power in Social Life*, pp. 118–119.

STABILIZATION

Initial exchange transactions between actors can arise out of sheer self-interest, without any collective concerns or common values. If the emergent relationship is to remain adequately stable and viable through time, however, these transactions must be buttressed by shared beliefs and orientations among the participants. This stabilization process also functions to limit—though not fully prevent—the development of gross power imbalances in exchange relationships, and to facilitate the resolution of conflicts that result from such imbalances. Stabilization occurs in three main ways in exchange relationships: creation of mutual trust, emergence of shared norms, and development of legitimate leadership.

The creation of a climate of mutual trust among the participants in an exchange relationship is an absolute requirement if that relationship is to persist for any length of time. An actor who initially offers a benefit to another does so on purely speculative grounds, in hopes of receiving a desired return, but with no assurance that this will occur. Consequently, exchange interactions typically begin with small transactions that require little trust because they involve little risk to the initiator. As these transactions are reciprocated and repeated through time, however, the participants begin to develop trust in one another. And as trust builds, the actors feel increasingly secure in committing more and more of their available resources to this exchange relationship—which expands the scope and depth of the relationship while simultaneously generating increasingly interdependence and mutual commitment among the participants. As described by Blau: "By discharging their obligations for services rendered, if only to provide inducements for the supply of more assistance, individuals demonstrate their trustworthiness, and the gradual expansion of mutual service is accompanied by a parallel growth of mutual trust. Hence, processes of social exchange, which may originate in pure self-interest, generate trust in social relations through their recurrent and gradually expanding character."[18]

To initiate an exchange transaction it is not necessary that the actors share any common norms, but ongoing exchange relationships can be considerably strengthened and stabilized by the emergence of shared social norms. Three kinds of norms have been identified as especially relevant for exchange relationships: (1) "reciprocity," which says that an actor who receives something from another is morally obligated to reciprocate that action in some manner[19] (thus facilitating the growth of mutual trust among the actors); (2) "fair exchange," or norms that stipulate fair rates of exchange between costs and benefits in a transaction[20] (which will affect but not necessarily determine the actual going rates); and (3) "distributive

18 Blau, *Exchange and Power in Social Life*, p. 94.
19 Gouldner, "The Norm of Reciprocity."
20 Blau, *Exchange and Power in Social Life*, p. 155.

justice," which asserts that through time all the participants in an exchange relationship should receive benefits that are proportional to their investments[21] (thus mitigating against the development of gross resource inequality among the actors). All of these moral norms are outgrowths of ongoing exchange relationships—not preconditions for their creation—but as they develop they further stabilize and perpetuate those relationships. "Social norms are necessary to prohibit actions through which individuals can gain advantage at the expense of the common interests of the collectivity. . . ."[22]

Finally, an exchange relationship also becomes stabilized as one or more actors assume leadership roles to coordinate the ongoing transactions and serve the collective interests of all the participants. Such leadership must, however, be legitimate in the eyes of the other actors so that their compliance is voluntary rather than coerced through imposed controls. In general, leaders acquire legitimacy and the right to exercise authority by making significant contributions to the collective welfare of a relationship or an organization. As other participants come to respect and desire these contributions, the leaders' actions are collectively legitimated and the others obligate themselves to comply with the leaders' directives. Blau describes the process thus: "If the benefits followers derive from a leader's guidance exceed their expectations of a fair return for the costs they have incurred . . . , their collective approval of his leadership legitimates it. Their joint obligations for his contributions to their welfare and their common approval of his fairness . . . generate group pressures that enforce compliance with his directives. . . . Legitimate leaders command willing compliance, which obviates the need for sanctions to compel or induce others to comply with directives, because the group of subordinates exerts pressures on its members to follow the leader's orders and suggestions."[23]

Thus mutual trust, shared norms, and legitimate authority are all outgrowths of ongoing exchange interactions which in turn stabilize these relationships. In short:

> **PRINCIPLE 5:** Exchange relationships become stabilized through time to the extent that they develop mutual trust, shared norms, and legitimate leadership.

ORGANIZATION

Thus far we have been focusing on exchange interactions and relationships, but this theoretical perspective purports to be applicable to

---

[21] George C. Homans, *Social Behavior: Its Elementary Forms* (New York: Harcourt, Brace, & World, 1961), p. 75. Homans conceptualized distributive justice as an individual sentiment rather than a shared moral norm, but Blau and others have argued that it does operate as a norm.

[22] Blau, *Exchange and Power in Social Life*, p. 257.

[23] Ibid., p. 202.

the total process of social organization, and Blau speaks of organization as the outcome of exchange interaction. How might the exchange perspective be expanded into a general theory of social organization?

We begin with the observation that social organization is a dynamic process arising from continual interplay between reciprocal exchange and unilateral control, as mediated by such stabilizing factors as trust, norms, and authority. Or, in Blau's terms, organization is a dialectic process in which balancing trends are always countered by unbalancing trends, out of which grow synthesizing trends. Moreover, this dynamic dialectic process occurs within complex systemic-like social settings—which Blau calls "social structures"—composed of multiple levels of subunits, sub-subunits, and so on.

As the scope of the organizational process expands in size and complexity (as we move from what Blau calls "microstructures" to "macrostructures"), exchange processes shift from direct interpersonal interactions to indirect chains of transactions among organizational units.[24] The economic and political systems of modern industrial societies such as the United States illustrate the extremely complex patterns of exchange relationships that can develop within large organizational units. In such social settings, interpersonal exchange transactions are replaced by interorganizational exchange arrangements, contracts, and networks. These systems of activities sometimes resemble the classical economic model of a self-regulating market, but more frequently they are unified through the process of functional cohesion (discussed in Chapter 10), in which relationships among interdependent actors are coordinated (but not necessarily controlled) by a central administrative unit.

Conflict, meanwhile, tends to develop within relationships among units comprising these systems, as these units struggle to maintain functional autonomy despite their interdependence. Blau identifies two forms of subunit interdependence that lead to conflict in large organizations: "First, substructures are dependent on each other, which means that changes in one lead to changes in the others. This kind of interdependence . . . does not conflict with [a unit's] autonomy except when one of them becomes a dominant power that can and does organize the others in accordance with its interests. . . . The second kind of interdependence . . . involves the dependence of the substructures, not on each other, but on the larger social structure, because a centralized authority in the larger collectivity coordinates and directs the major courses of action of its subgroups. It is this second type of interdependence of the component parts due to centralized control in the system that directly conflicts with their autonomy. The

[24]Ibid., pp. 283–301.

conflict is inevitable, since both some centralized coordination and some autonomy of parts are necessary for organized collectivities." [25]

These large and complex organizational systems require stabilization just as do simple relationships. Each of the three stabilizing processes discussed previously—trust, norms, and leadership—has a counterpart in more inclusive social settings. (1) Interpersonal trust is replaced by broadly shared values, so that "consensus on social values serves as the basis for extending the range of social transactions beyond the limits of direct social contacts and for perpetuating social structures beyond the life span of human beings." [26] These values provide a common set of meanings and expectations for conducting the complex chains of indirect exchanges among organizational units. (2) The informal norms of interpersonal relationships become formalized into what Blau calls "institutions," or sets of formal rules that are enforced by established power centers. "Institutionalization involves formalized procedures that perpetuate organizing principles of social life from generation to generation." [27] Institutions thus function to regulate and perpetuate complex exchange patterns in large organizations. (3) Finally, leadership roles are expanded and formalized into established political units such as governments that exercise legitimate authority derived from the beneficial functions they perform for the entire organization. The most basic of these political functions is guiding the overall organizational process: "An important function of legitimate authority is to organize collective effort on a large scale in the pursuit of ends commonly accepted." [28] Equally important in complex exchange networks is the function of coordinating and regulating all the myriad sets of transactions continually transpiring within the system, as well as mediating or resolving disputes among conflicting organizational units.

In general, this process of organization, or expansion of fundamental exchange principles to large and complex organizational systems, has not been developed as thoroughly or systematically as the more basic aspects of the theory. The tendency has been merely to "blow up" or enlarge those basic principles and apply them uncritically to all levels of organization. Consequently, there are no principles of exchange theory that are unique to the macro or systemic level of organization. Moreover, in Blau's writings exchange as a process tends to become subordinate at the organizational level to other social processes such as value consensus, institutionalization, and the exercise of legitimate political authority.

[25] Ibid., pp. 302–303.
[26] Ibid., pp. 263–264.
[27] Ibid., p. 273.
[28] Ibid., p. 213.

COLLECTIVE ACTION

Although Blau's treatment of exchange theory becomes rather weak at the level of large and complex organizations, Mancur Olson has identified a vital mechanism through which individual exchange transactions can be aggregated into organized collective actions.[29] He begins with the economic concept of "collective goods," or benefits that, once provided, are available to everyone regardless of whether or not they helped secure them, such as national security or public highways. The problem of collective goods is that they cannot be obtained through voluntary contributions by individuals, since it makes no economic sense for any single individual to make such a donation. As long as someone else is willing to pay for a collective good, so that it becomes available to all, nothing is to be gained by entering into that exchange process. "Though all of the members of the group . . . have a common interest in obtaining this collective benefit, they have no common interest in paying the cost of providing that collective goal. Each would prefer that the other pay the entire cost, and ordinarily would get any benefit provided whether he had borne part of the cost or not."[30]

In small groups, where people know each other personally, individuals may be willing to contribute voluntarily to the attainment of collective goods for several reasons, including (1) a presumed common norm of reciprocity, (2) interpersonal trust, obligations, and pressures, (3) altruistic concern for the welfare of the group as a whole, and (4) the realization that one will still benefit from the collective good even if one contributes a disproportional share of its cost. As the number of actors involved becomes larger, however, the effectiveness of all these inducements to unilateral participation steadily diminishes, so that the problem of how to induce collective action to attain common goals becomes increasingly acute. As Blau suggested, norms can be formalized into rules that are enforced through coercion, trust can be expanded into consensus on basic social values, and altruistic concern for the public welfare can be replaced by governments exercising legitimate authority. But all of these solutions to the problem of collective action, Olson argues, lie outside the realm of exchange relationships. There are two ways, he suggests, in which the exchange approach can be broadened to produce organized collective action:

Oligarchy. In any particular sphere of activity—automobile manufacturing, for instance—all the participating actors can be organized (either intentionally or through competition and consolidation) into a

---

[29] Mancur Olson, Jr., *The Logic of Collective Action* (Cambridge, Mass.: Harvard University Press, 1965).
[30] Ibid., p. 21.

handful of large and powerful social units. Internally, each of these units (firms, associations, governments) will operate through some combination of consensus, coercion, and authority—but not exchange transactions. (An exception to this generalization occurs when a subunit—such as a labor union—becomes strong enough to challenge the larger unit and pressure it into engaging in bargaining and exchanges.) Relationships among this handful of large units can continue to function on an exchange basis, however, since the field of action has essentially been narrowed to a small group in which actors will voluntarily contribute to collective activities with reasonable assurance of receiving benefits in return. According to John Kenneth Galbraith[31] and other commentators on contemporary American society, oligarchy is the principal form of organization in the economy and many other realms of this society.

Selective Incentives. To encourage actors to contribute to collective actions for the attainment of public goods, each participant is provided some kind of additional reward (benefit, privilege, status) in proportion to his or her contribution. It then becomes rational for the actor to participate in collective activities, for doing so also brings additional rewards not available to those who consume public goods without helping to produce them. In Olson's words: "Only a separate and 'selective' incentive will stimulate a rational individual in a latent group to act in a group-oriented way. In such circumstances group action can be obtained only through an incentive that operates, not indiscriminately, like the collective good, upon the group as a whole, but rather selectively toward the individuals in the group. The incentive must be 'selective' so that those who do not join the organization working for the group's interest, or in other ways contribute to the attainment of the group's interest, can be treated differently from those who do."[32] This approach preserves exchange transactions throughout an organized social system, no matter how large, since every act is balanced by a reciprocal beneficial act. It does not, however, eliminate the requirement in all large and complex organizational settings for overall coordination and regulation of activities, so as to ensure that all the numerous exchange transactions actually do result in a collective public good. Nor does this approach give most actors real control over the course of their actions, beyond the initial decision to participate and receive the selective incentives being offered by the system. This last consideration—maximizing each actor's ability to exert social power, especially in matters that directly affect him or her—is not incompatible with an exchange interaction approach to

[31] John Kenneth Galbraith, *Economics and the Public Purpose* (Boston: Houghton Mifflin, 1973).
[32] Olson, *The Logic of Collective Action*, p. 51.

social organization, but it requires a more complex systemic form of organization than envisioned by Olson.

Symbolic Theory

AS with the exchange perspective, symbolic interaction begins with actors who initially engage in social interaction as autonomous elements Through this ongoing process they create social organization, which in turn affects their action to the extent that they become involved parts of these collective activities and share their cultures. Both of these theoretical perspectives thus share a number of basic ideas in common: initial focus on the interaction level, voluntarism of action by social actors, creation of organization as a dynamic process, participants in this process shifting from elements to parts, and regulation of social action by cultural norms.

Nevertheless, there are also several crucial differences between the exchange and symbolic theories. Most importantly, exchange theory focuses on overt transactions involving services, goods, or other activities that directly benefit the participant. Symbolic theory, in contrast, is concerned primarily with the subjective meanings that individuals attach to their own and others' actions, and hence is equally applicable to expressive and instrumental activities. With this focus on subjective meanings, symbolic theory contains no concept of interaction costs or concern with balancing costs and benefits. Instead, this perspective emphasizes the processes of communicating and interpreting meanings among actors. Finally, symbolic theory makes no reference to power processes, which are of considerable importance for exchange theory, nor does it make any use of the social system model for analyzing social organization.

The major contributors to symbolic interaction theory have been Charles Horton Cooley, George Herbert Mead, Herbert Blumer, and Charles Warriner, all of whose ideas are incorporated into the following discussions of mind and self, symbolic interaction, social ordering, and shared culture.

MIND AND SELF

Whereas all other theories of social organization merely assume that individuals are minded, self-aware beings capable of communicating and interacting with others, the symbolic interaction perspective explains the process through which they acquire these capabilities, and then rests its entire conception of social organization on this basic process. In the words of George Herbert Mead: "Human society as we know it could not exist without minds and selves, since all its most characteristic features presuppose the possession of minds and selves by its individual members; but its individual members would not possess minds and selves if these had not arisen within or emerged out of the human social process. . . ."[33]

The human mind is formed, according to Mead, as individuals learn to "take the role of the other." This process begins in early childhood as a person (ego) realizes that his or her actions are eliciting responses from others (alters), and that these responses have consequences for oneself. As ego not only becomes consciously aware of the consequences of his actions, so that they have meaning for him, but also attributes this same conscious awareness to others, he attempts to anticipate the meanings that others give to his actions. In other words, during interaction, ego temporarily puts himself in the place of alter, views himself through alter's eyes, and tries to determine how he would interpret and respond to his own actions if he were alter. It is as if he continually asked himself, "What would I think and do in this situation if I were he or she and were receiving this action?" As the individual thus "takes the role of the other" in social interaction, he learns to view himself as others see him, from a partially objective rather than a wholly subjective viewpoint. On the basis of countless "external" perceptions of himself through the eyes of others, he develops a mind that is aware not only of its social environment but also of itself. This self-conscious mind is capable of paying attention to itself as well as others and engaging in "imaginative rehearsals" of potential courses of action prior to their enactment.

People have personalities as well as minds, however, and this same process of taking the role of the other also enables the individual to develop a self-conscious conception of his or her self as an integrated personality and a social actor. As ego temporarily puts himself in the place of alter and views himself and his actions from this external perspective, he acquires conceptions of himself as a social object toward which others respond. These self-conceptions become fused, over time, into a fundamental self-identity around which his entire personality becomes organized. Thus the person's spontaneously acting self—which Mead called the "I"—as well as his or her total personality structure, are largely shaped through symbolic social interaction. At the same time, taking the role of the other also enables the individual to anticipate others' probable responses to his intended actions before he overtly acts. He can then shape or modify his own actions on the basis of these anticipated responses. Although one's ability to anticipate the responses of others is never perfect, over time this process largely determines the social conception one holds of oneself in relation to others—which Mead

[33] George Herbert Mead, *Mind, Self and Society* (Chicago: University of Chicago Press, 1934), p. 227.

called the "me." Thus both sides of one's self-conception—the internally formed "I" and the externally shaped "me"—are direct outgrowths of symbolic social interaction. As described by Charles Horton Cooley, each of us possesses a "looking-glass self" acquired by using other people as mirrors to view ourselves as they see us.[34]

Herbert Blumer's account of Mead's explanation of this process through which the individual develops a social self is worthy of quotation at some length:

> Mead regards this ability of the human being to act toward himself as the central mechanism with which the human being faces and deals with his world. This mechanism enables the human being to make indication to himself of things in his surroundings and thus to guide his actions by what he notes. . . . The conscious life of the human being, from the time that he awakens until he falls asleep, is a continual flow of self-indications—notations of the things with which he deals and takes into account. . . . The significance of making indications to oneself is of paramount importance. The importance lies along two lines. First, to indicate something is to extricate it from its setting, to hold it apart, to give it a meaning or, in Mead's language, to make it into an object. An object . . . is different from a stimulus; instead of having an intrinsic character which acts on the individual and which can be identified apart from the individual, its character or meaning is conferred on it by the individual. . . . The second important implication of the fact that the human being makes indications to himself is that his action is constructed or built up instead of being a mere release. Whatever the action in which he is engaged, the human individual proceeds by pointing out to himself the divergent things which have to be taken into account in the course of his action. . . . His action is built up step by step through a process of self-indication.[35]

This initial argument of symbolic interaction theory can be stated as follows:

PRINCIPLE 6:   The human mind and self, which are the foundation of all social organization, are created through symbolic interaction as the individual takes the role of the other and views itself as an object.

SYMBOLIC INTERACTION

This theoretical perspective takes its name from the dominant emphasis it places on the symbolic meanings that individuals assign to their

[34] Charles Horton Cooley, *Human Nature and the Social Order* (Glencoe, Ill.: Free Press, 1956), chap. 5.
[35] Herbert Blumer, "Society as Symbolic Interaction," in Arnold Rose, ed., *Human Behavior and Social Processes* (Boston: Houghton Mifflin, 1962), pp. 181–182.

own and others' actions, and the process through which these meanings are exchanged. All animals are capable of recognizing signs in their environments, or stimuli to which they have learned to react. More intelligent animals may even be able to associate simple ideas with these signs, so that when they hear the word "food" they mentally anticipate eating as well as physically salivate. But human beings (and perhaps chimpanzees and porpoises) impute meanings to signs—as intended by the sender and interpreted by the receiver—and thus convert them to symbols. In symbolic interaction, human beings assign meanings to, or define, each other's actions as symbols instead of merely reacting to these actions as signs. One's response to another's action is therefore based not on the action itself, but on the meaning that one assumes the other actor is attempting to convey through his or her action. As an individual engages in social interaction, therefore, he or she is continually interpreting or defining everything happening in that situation, and his or her subsequent actions are largely shaped by these "definitions of the situation." In short, social interaction is constantly being constructed as actors attach meanings to each other's symbols and define situations in terms of inferred intentions and expectations.

Meanings and definitions of situations are expressed and exchanged among actors through symbolic communication, so that from this theoretical perspective the processes of human interaction and communication are inexorably interwoven. The extent to which any interaction results in valid communication is always highly problematic, however, for people often enter interaction situations with quite divergent "catalogs" of meanings that they attach to various symbols. Only as interaction continues through time are the participants able to test the validity of their understandings of each other's meanings, thus decreasing the problematic character of the communication process. Communication can therefore be conceptualized as the process through which actors increase the probable validity of the inferences they make concerning one another's intended meanings in an interaction situation. Charles Warriner describes this as an "adjustment process":

> The generally problematic character of communication . . . , as well as the fact that in societies such as ours actors have widely different catalogs of reference, means that in any new interactional system there is at the start much disconfirmation or only partial confirmation. The problem then is, given some lack of commonality of the actors' catalogs of reference, how is the probable validity of the inferences increased? In general we can speak of this as the adjustment process. Adjustment does not necessarily occur. If the inferences are not confirmed it may be that the interactional system ceases, the actors withdraw from each other. But if they are to continue interaction it is necessary that the problematic character of the communication be reduced. Some adjustment may be

accomplished by random "search behavior," but more frequently it results from a metalanguage use of other signs. . . . Finally, interaction may . . . result in the development of totally new signs and meanings of the particular interactional system.[36]

The following two principles, both of which rest on the thesis that the human mind and self develop through symbolic interaction, are therefore central to this theoretical perspective:

PRINCIPLE 7: **To the extent that actors respond to the intended meanings they infer from the actions of others, rather than to overt behaviors, they are engaging in symbolic interaction.**

PRINCIPLE 8: **Symbolic interaction results in valid communication to the extent that the actors correctly interpret the meanings that others attach to their actions.**

SOCIAL ORDERING

As actors perpetuate the process of symbolic interaction through time they create ongoing social relationships exhibiting some degree of valid communication and sharing of meanings. Shared meanings and definitions of situations in turn make possible coordination or patterning of collective activities. Social ordering therefore consists of patterned collective actions based on shared meanings among communicating individuals. More succinctly, common definitions of situations produce similar actions. Since social situations are never fully and permanently defined, however, social interactions and relationships are constantly being reinterpreted and reconstructed by the participants, so that social ordering is always a dynamic creative process. As expressed by Warriner: "Society . . . is that coordination of action which is created and sustained by . . . the meanings that emerge from interaction."[37]

A slightly different, though not contradictory, conception of the nature of social ordering is offered by Blumer, who sees it as a "framework inside of which action takes place"—as a setting but not a determinant of social interaction. "Social organization enters into action only to the extent to which it shapes situations in which people act, and to the extent to which it supplies fixed sets of symbols which people use in interpreting their situations."[38]

In neither case, however, do these theorists present a clearly articulated conception of social ordering as an emergent process distinct from symbolic

[36] Charles K. Warriner, *The Emergence of Society* (Homewood, Ill.: Dorsey Press, 1970), p. 119.
[37] Warriner, Ibid., p. 126.
[38] Blumer, "Society as Symbolic Interaction," pp. 189–190.

interaction. Social ordering to them is essentially just recurrent interaction, without major theoretical significance in and of itself. As observed by Jonathan Turner: "Although the patterned aspects of . . . social structure can enter into the course of interaction as 'objects' of the situation which shape the interpretative, evaluational, definitional, and mapping processes of actors, symbolic interaction appears to be concerned primarily with the *process of interaction*, per se. . . . The vagueness of the links between the interaction process and its social structural products leaves symbolic interactionism with . . . little in the way of carefully documented statements about how, when, where, and with what probability interaction processes operate to create, sustain, and change varying patterns of social organization." [39]

Moreover, an uncritical reading of the symbolic interaction literature can easily lead one to the unjustified assumption that a direct relationship exists between the degree to which meanings are shared among a set of actors and the amount and complexity of social ordering they will create. Some degree of shared meanings is a necessary prerequisite for social ordering, but it is not a sufficient condition or a determinant of this process. The extent to which actors share meanings may set a maximum potential for social ordering in a particular situation, but does not guarantee that the upper limit will be approached. Other variables in the situation—such as the exercise of social power—will also affect the amount and complexity of social ordering that emerges, but unfortunately symbolic interaction theory says nothing about these additional crucial variables.

In regard to social ordering, therefore, symbolic interactionism proposes merely that:

> PRINCIPLE 9:   Social ordering becomes possible to the degree that actors share meanings and definitions of situations and act collectively on the basis of these common interpretations.

SHARED CULTURE

Common cultural ideas, centering around shared meanings held by interacting individuals, are much more important for symbolic interaction theory than are patterns of social ordering. As people communicate the meanings of their actions to each other and work out shared interpretations of activities and definitions of situations, they develop a common culture that is shared by all the participants. Shared culture in turn influences and guides—but does not fully determine—these people's collective activities by providing them with interpretations of social life, role expectations, common definitions of situations, and social norms.

---

[39] Turner, *The Structure of Sociological Theory*, pp. 189–190.

The culture shared by a set of interacting people is common to all of them, since it consists primarily of common interpretations of their collective activities, and all of these participants are normally aware of their shared culture. Their own personal attitudes and values need not necessarily correspond to these common cultural ideas, however, which allows for autonomy of action if actors choose to ignore their shared culture. "Communication involves a totally new phenomenon, that of a *collective* meaning. Although this collective meaning exists in the separate minds of the individual actors, its content is defined by their communication and by the implicit and explicit agreements that this is the meaning that things shall have for them *in their interaction*. It is in this sense that it is collective and social, not individual, for each participates in collective meanings that may differ from the individual meanings which he may use at other times."[40]

Early symbolic interaction theorists gave considerable attention to the process of socialization, in which cultural meanings and norms become internalized into individuals' personalities. They believed that if fundamental socialization processes in small primary groups were fairly uniform throughout a society or other organization, all its members would acquire a common core of basic interaction patterns, role expectations, norms, and values—which they often referred to as "human nature." To the extent that a common "human nature" is internalized into all people's personalities, social organization became possible.[41] Contemporary cultural theories of social organization are rooted in this concern with socialization and norm internalization, so that they share several points of convergence with symbolic interaction theory. Paradoxically, however, contemporary symbolic interaction theorists have moved away from that early emphasis on learned "human nature," so that they now differ from cultural theorists on at least two major counts: (1) They see the entire process of social interaction and organization as beginning with actors acting as autonomous elements in relation to each other, not as socialized role players acting as involved parts of previously established social systems. (2) They view social interaction and ordering as dynamic processes that are continually being created and recreated through individuals' actions and symbolic interactions, not as routine enactment of pre-established cultural norms and role expectations.

Symbolic interaction theorists do share one crucial idea with cultural theorists, however. With some oversimplification, both of their conceptions of social organization can be described as consisting of minded, socialized individuals who communicate symbolically to create and sustain shared cultural meanings. Both theoretical perspectives tend to jump directly from interacting individuals (who interpret situations and guide their actions by

---

[40] Warriner, *The Emergence of Society*, p. 133.
[41] Cooley, *Human Nature and the Social Order*.

these meanings) to the level of shared culture (which is created through the sharing of meanings in symbolic communications). Although symbolic interaction theory does not deny the existence of social ordering, it largely ignores processes at this level of ordering, or else incorporates them into the concept of shared culture.

A final principle of symbolic interactionism, pertaining to shared culture, is that:

> PRINCIPLE 10: Social organization is maintained and perpetuated to the extent that social actors share a common culture composed of collective meanings and norms.

Theoretical Convergence

EXCHANGE and symbolic interaction theories have developed from completely different intellectual roots; the former perspective grew out of behavioral psychology and economics, while the latter is an outgrowth of eighteenth-century philosophy and contemporary social psychology. Nevertheless, there are a surprising number of points of convergence between these two theories, as noted by Peter Singelmann.[42] In this final section we shall briefly examine the most crucial of these commonalities (common themes) and complementarities (complementary explanations).

COMMONALITIES

1. *Voluntarism.* Both theories assume voluntarism of action by individuals acting as autonomous elements, who through their interaction create normatively guided social organization in which they participate as involved parts.

2. *Symbolic transactions.* Both theories view individuals as minded, self-conscious actors engaging in transactions. Exchange theory is not merely behavioralistic, but always involves numerous symbolic elements, such as establishing the values of actions and objects and thus defining terms of exchange, or temporarily taking the role of the other in negotiating transactions. Similarly, symbolic theory is not merely cognitive, but always postulates numerous exchange transactions, such as verifying common interpretations of symbols, or communicating images of one another's selves.

3. *Interaction.* Both theories share similar conceptions of the interaction process as "continuously being constructed and reconstructed by

---

[42] Peter Singelmann, "Exchange as Symbolic Interaction: Convergences Between Two Theoretical Perspectives," *American Sociological Review* 37 (August 1972): 414–424.

actors who 'test' the adequacy of their actions in relation to the response of others."[43] In this dynamic process, the participants constantly emit and receive symbols in order to exchange ideas, goods, and services.

4. *Social ordering.* Both theories conceptualize social ordering as patterns of relationships created through the actions of individuals, which provide the context within which interaction occurs.

5. *Conflict and change.* Both theories see conflict as an expected— though not major—aspect of social life, arising from divergent interests and definitions of situations among actors. As a consequence, change is a ubiquitous feature of all social organization.

6. *Norms.* Both theories place heavy reliance on shared norms as a vital component of social organization, functioning primarily to stabilize and give continuity to social relationships.

COMPLEMENTARITIES

1. *The occurrence and meaning of interaction.* Exchange theory explains the occurrence of social interaction, as actors seek to gain benefits for themselves, while symbolic theory explains why these interactions are meaningful to the participants. "Thus it is not sufficient to postulate that a significant part of human interaction consists in mutual barter for the exchange of rewards. It is equally important to recognize that the rewards exchanged have symbolic significance for the interactants. . . ; they are 'rewards' only in so far as the interactants assign that meaning to them."[44]

2. *Instrumental and expressive interaction.* Exchange theory emphasizes instrumental interactions in which the participants are seeking goals extrinsic to the interaction process, although persistent transactions can over time become rewarding for their own sake. Symbolic theory is applicable to both kinds of interaction also, but is especially relevant to expressive interactions in which the actors are focusing on the interaction process itself.

3. *Beneficial and costly interaction.* Exchange theory easily explains the perpetuation of interaction whose benefits equal or exceed its costs, but must shift to a power perspective to account for relationships that continue despite overwhelming costs to one or more of the actors. Symbolic theory adds the proposition that such relationships are often perpetuated because of overriding symbolic meanings or the need to protect one's self concept.

4. *Complex patterns and shared meanings.* Exchange theory views

[43] Ibid.
[44] Ibid.

social ordering as complex patterns of exchange transactions among interdependent actors, but symbolic theory is needed to explain the shared meanings, climate of mutual trust, and common values that make such complex patterning possible.

5. *Compulsive and compliant power.* Exchange theory gives considerable attention to the exercise of power, but emphasizes primarily compulsive pressures (in balanced situations) and coercion (in unbalanced situations). It assumes that formal authority becomes paramount in complex organizational settings, but fails to explain the communication process through which the legitimacy of this authority develops. Symbolic theory does not deal explicitly with power at all, but can easily be extended to account for compliant suggestion (in symbolically balanced situations) or command (in symbolically unbalanced situations). Thus in relatively balanced transactions in which influence is exercised, exchange theory predicts a preponderance of functional dominance, while symbolic theory stresses attraction. In relatively unbalanced transactions in which control is exerted, meanwhile, exchange theory emphasizes the use of force while symbolic theory can account for the exercise of legitimate authority based on shared definitions of situations.

In sum, *exchange and symbolic interaction theories nicely complement each other, with each perspective filling in theoretical gaps left unexplained by the other.* Because social organization is both an objective and a subjective process, both of these perspectives are necessary to capture its dual nature. "The dynamics of social organization rests with the paradox the 'realities' have subjectively assigned as well as objectively given significance for human actors. 'Objective' realities constrain behavior, but the subjective interpretations of such realities direct actors to change these boundaries. There is a continuous dialectical process in which objective realities become 'subjectified' by human actors. 'Reality' can thus be conceived only as simultaneously objective *and* subjective."[45] Thus we might well consider discarding the adjectives "exchange" and "symbolic" and speak only of a single social interaction theory of social organization. As seen in this chapter, social interaction theory contributes significantly to our understanding of the process of social organization. Nevertheless, by itself this theoretical perspective is incomplete because it cannot explain the nature or dynamics of patterned social ordering. In the following chapter, therefore, we turn to two additional theoretical perspectives that focus explicitly on the process of social ordering. Nor does social interaction theory by itself

[45] Ibid.

provide all the conceptual tools needed to analyze organizations as unified social systems functioning through the exercise of social power, which is our basic concern throughout this work.

RECOMMENDED READING

Blau, Peter. *Exchange and Power in Social Life.* New York: John Wiley & Sons, 1964, chaps. 1, 2, 4, 5, 6, 10.
>An elaborate, sophisticated discussion of exchange theory, emphasizing its application to social organization.

Blumer, Herbert. "Society as Symbolic Interaction." In Arnold Rose, ed., *Human Behavior and Social Processes.* Boston: Houghton Mifflin, 1962, pp. 179–192.
>An attempt to expand symbolic interaction theory from the interpersonal to the organizational level.

Cooley, Charles H. *Social Organization.* Glencoe, Ill.: Free Press, 1956.
>The original conceptualization of social organization as a process of symbolic interaction.

Homans, George C. "Social Behavior as Exchange." *American Journal of Sociology* 62 (May 1958): 597–606 (Bobbs-Merrill reprint S-122). See also his *Social Behavior: Its Elementary Forms.* New York: Harcourt, Brace & World, 1961, chaps, 3, 4, 18.
>The article outlines, and the book elaborates, his conceptualization of exchange theory on the individual behavioral level.

Mead, George Herbert. *Mind, Self, and Society.* Chicago: University of Chicago Press, 1934, pt. 4.
>The classic discussion of symbolic interaction theory and its relevance for understanding social organization.

Olson, Mancur, Jr. *The Logic of Collective Action.* Cambridge, Mass.: Harvard University Press, 1965, chaps. 1, 2.
>Uses an exchange perspective to answer the question of why people contribute to collective efforts to attain public goods.

Parsons, Talcott. *The Structure of Social Action.* New York: Free Press, 1949, chaps. 2, 19.
>Formulates a conceptualization of social interaction that unites ideas from utilitarianism, positivism, and idealism.

———. *The Social System.* Glencoe, Ill.: Free Press, 1951, pp. 58–112.
>Describes the basic set of five pattern variables and uses them to analyze social interaction processes.

Singlemann, Peter. "Exchange as Symbolic Interaction." *American Sociological Review* 37 (August 1972): 414–424.
>Proposes a synthesis of exchange and symbolic interaction on theories.

Warriner, Charles K. *The Emergence of Society*. Homewood, Ill.: Dorsey Press, 1970.
Sketches a theoretical conception of social organization based on symbolic interaction theory and stressing communicative processes.

Weber, Max. *The Theory of Social and Economic Organization*, trans. by A. M. Henderson and Talcott Parsons, ed. by Talcott Parsons. New York: Free Press, 1947, pp. 112–120.
A classic statement of the concepts of social action, interaction, and relationships.

5

Ordering Processes and Theories

SOCIAL relationships provide the threads of organized social life, but separate threads do not by themselves constitute a fabric. Countless ongoing relationships of numerous hues and textures must be endlessly interwoven in complex patterns and sustained through time to create the continuously flowing material of social ordering. As social actors interweave their relationships to form stable patterns of social ordering, they are creating the essential core of all social organization.

Social Ordering

ILLUSTRATIONS of social ordering can be drawn from all areas of human life. To cite some common examples: (1) Most adults live together in pairs consisting of one member of each sex, and year after year share countless daily activities with their partner. (2) Store clerks smoothly carry out numerous exchange transactions with streams of customers, most of whom are total strangers to them. (3) Expressway traffic flows primarily into

114

a city between seven and ten o'clock in the morning, but out of the city between three and six o'clock in the evening. (4) The members of a bridge club gather at a specified location every Monday evening at eight o'clock to engage in predictable and ritualized interactions. (5) Members of audiences at lectures remain quietly seated, rather than running about or shouting to one another. (6) Children usually progress through school at the rate of one grade per year, so that if they complete college they do not enter the labor market until after age twenty-one. (7) In most communities, stores and offices tend to be located in some areas, factories in other areas, and residences in yet another area. (8) Individuals who violate legal statutes are judged and punished through established, impersonal procedures, rather than by the persons whom they have harmed. (9) Millions of people in the United States participate in a nation-wide involuntary medical care program as the result of decisions made by a few hundred legislators. (10) Scores of nations cooperate with each other in highly complicated financial and trade arrangements.

THE NATURE OF SOCIAL ORDERING

The process of social ordering occurs as interactions and relationships coalesce into multidimensional patterns or arrangements that remain relatively stable through time. Through this process, social activities become increasingly interrelated, routinized, and predictable. As a result, actors are able to act collectively to attain goals that they could not obtain if they acted separately. Social ordering thus magnifies the total functional effectiveness of a set of actors, transforming their total action capability from .e mere sum of their separate actions into a multiplicative product of their patterned interactions. The process of social ordering therefore introduces a qualitatively new level of reality that transcends social interaction, so that the emergent whole is more than the sum of its component parts.

Like all aspects of human social life, social ordering is never a static condition, but always a dynamic process of "becoming," characterized by continual fluctuation and variation through time. Concurrently, however, patterns of social ordering become relevant and meaningful to their participants only as they persist with some degree of stability through time. Paradoxical as it may appear, social ordering is simultaneously dynamic and stable. That is, the basic features of a particular arrangement of social relationships must persist through time with some stability if a pattern of social ordering is to exist, yet (1) the interactions and relationships comprising this pattern are themselves continually being created and recreated, and (2) the pattern itself will constantly be changing in at least minor ways through time. For example, the social relationships that constitute a community all vary from day to day, and the total community will likely change considerably from year to year, yet the community persists through time as a more or less stable set of ordered social patterns.

The resolution of this seeming paradox lies in the distinction between static and stable ordering. A totally static order is unvarying through time, never evidencing any alterations in either its component parts or its total configuration. A stable social order, in contrast, may continuously experience dynamic activity and change without losing its overall patterning. Although organized social life is never completely static, it can display infinite degrees of stability versus instability, depending on the external stresses and internal strains acting upon it. Nor is any degree of stability ever inevitable or permanent in social life, for disruptive forces and tensions may upset or destroy patterns of social ordering at any moment. As long as a minimal amount of stability is maintained through time, however, social ordering will endure.

Carrying this paradox one step further, social stability is often achieved through constant fluctuation and change, not in spite of it. Patterns of social ordering sometimes endure for long periods of time by strongly resisting all change and remaining as rigidly static as possible, as in the case of an isolated primitive society that is perpetuated practically unaltered for hundreds of years. Such a society is potentially quite unstable, however, for if it suddenly encounters disruptive social forces too powerful to resist—such as economic pressures from Western nations—its inability to adjust to new conditions may likely result in its rapid destruction. The more highly interrelated any social ordering is with its social environment, the more frequently it must change in many small ways if it is to remain stable and preserve its fundamental structure.

Patterns of social ordering exist as real phenomena regardless of whether or not their participants or others are aware of them. Recognition of these patterns by the actors involved can further enhance their stability, however, to the extent that the participants identify with and purposefully seek to perpetuate their social ordering. For instance, consider a number of families who have been living in an area and interacting with one another for years, creating a pattern of ordering we would call a community. If they do not recognize this pattern and do not think of themselves as members of a common social order, they are not likely to act collectively to protect, perpetuate, or develop it. If they should become aware of the community as a relatively stable and enduring pattern of social ordering, however, it will become increasingly salient and meaningful to them. Not only will they begin to think of it as "our community," but they will also be more likely to cooperate in establishing collective activities, such as schools or a government, that will further stabilize its social ordering.

Although there is no standard scale for measuring stability of social ordering, the term "institution" is frequently applied to patterns of ordering that are strongly established, widely recognized and accepted, and highly stable over time. In this usage, institutionalization is the process of strengthening, stabilizing, and perpetuating a pattern of social ordering. Sociologists sometimes assign additional meanings to this concept of institution, but at the very minimum it connotes stable ordering.

In sum, *social ordering emerges from social interaction as ongoing relationships become interwoven into relatively stable and predictable patterns.* More succinctly, social ordering develops as social interactions become patterned and recurrent.

THE DIMENSIONS OF SOCIAL ORDERING

Stabilization through time is an integral part of the process of social ordering, but the amount of stability exhibited by a particular social pattern is also a fundamental dimension of that ordering. Three additional basic dimensions of all social ordering are size, complexity, and formality, as described in the following paragraphs.

Size. How large is this instance of social ordering? That seemingly simple question is not easily answered in most cases, for there are no universally accepted conceptual or operational definitions of size in relation to social units. At least three different criteria are often used to measure size in sociological research: number of actors, number of relationships, and volume of activity.

1. The most obvious means of determining the number of actors involved in a particular instance of social ordering is to take a simple count of the participants or members—provided there is agreement on what constitutes membership or participation, and the total configuration is not too large. In reality, however, there are often countless shades of involvement, from nominal but completely inactive membership to sporadic participation to total commitment. And shall we include actors who are not socially defined as members but who nevertheless interact on a continual basis with actors within the collectivity? Moreover, with large units such as total societies, head counts become quite demanding and often unreliable. In spite of these difficulties, the number of participating actors is usually much easier to ascertain than any other criterion.

2. If we are seeking a more sophisticated conception of size, we might argue that since patterns of ordering are composed of social relationships we should count them rather than separate actors. Theoretically this is an admirable approach, but in practice it is virtually impossible to implement. What criteria define the existence of a relationship, given the numerous dimensions along which all relationships can occur? Short of simply relying

on the actors involved to tell us what relationships exist—which would require a commonly accepted definition of participation—there is no easy way of identifying social relationships. In addition, the number of potential relationships that could exist in a given social configuration increases much more rapidly than the number of actors. Whereas three actors can have only three pair relationships, seven actors can have 21 such relationships and fifteen actors can have 105. And if we also count all compound relationships (one actor relating to another pair, a triad relating to a coalition of four, etc.), seven actors have 966 potential relationships.[1] This approach is obviously totally impractical in all but very small groups.

3. If we are concerned more with the functioning of a social unit than with its structure, we might decide to use some measure of activity flow as an indicator of size. Business corporations are frequently compared in terms of their total economic assets, the size of their gross profits, or similar monetary criteria. Hospitals and other service organizations that deal with large numbers of nonmember clients are perhaps most meaningfully measured in terms of the extent and nature of services provided. And a newspaper may measure the size of its communication network in terms of the number of copies sold daily. The point is that there is no single all-purpose indicator of size for social ordering. Rather, the best measure in any particular situation is determined by the reason for which size is being determined. The number of individuals listed on a membership roster may be the most relevant indicator of size in one situation, in another case we may include only kinship relationships involving first-cousin or closer ties, and in a third instance we might compare the relative sizes of different governmental budgets. "Size follows function," to paraphrase a classic architectural dictum.

Regardless of how the size of a particular social unit is measured, *the size of any pattern of social ordering has extensive consequences for most of its other characteristics.* Size is directly related to both complexity and formality, as we shall discuss in a moment. From a functional perspective, expanding size offers the possibility—though does not guarantee—that the scope and effectiveness of a collectivity's actions may increase, owing to greater availability of resources, functional specialization among subunits, overall efficiency of operation, and similar factors. At the same time, the larger the size the greater the potential for internal strains and conflicts, the more attention members must give to communication processes, and the

---

[1] The formulas for determining the number of relationships possible among a given number of actors are as follows: (a) pair relationships = $N(N-1)/2$; (b) total relationships = $3^{n-2}(n+1) + \frac{1}{2}$.

These formulas are taken from William M. Kephart, "A Quantitative Analysis of Intragroup Relationships," *American Journal of Sociology* 55 (May 1950): 544–549.

more difficult it may be for the collectivity to maintain its stability and unity.[2] Finally—and perhaps most crucial—size significantly affects the distribution and exercise of power within all patterns of social ordering. The available empirical evidence indicates that as the size of a unit increases, the proportion of its members performing central control functions tends to decline, and in general its internal power distribution tends to become more diffused. Large size apparently minimizes the amount of power that any single actor or small set of actors can exert within a collectivity, thus reducing the amount of control exercised by elites and providing more opportunities for other actors to wield at least some influence.[3]

Complexity. In addition to sheer size, patterns of social ordering differ immensely in terms of internal complexity. *Complexity results from differentiation among the component parts of a social unit.* As activities and relationships become specialized, distinct subunits with some degree of autonomy are created, these parts become increasingly interdependent and interrelated, and the overall patterning evidences extensive diversity. In short, complex social ordering is differentiated, diverse, and complicated. Families, friendship cliques, and other small groups are rarely very complex, whereas corporations, universities, governments, cities, and total societies often display extremely complex patterns of ordering. Especially important in producing social complexity is the existence of numerous subunits within the total configuration, each of which has its own distinct pattern of ordering, all of which are interdependent in their activities, and all of which relate to some kind of central coordinating unit.

Differentiation can occur both horizontally and vertically. Horizontal differentiation results as a variety of specialized activities and separate subunits emerge and exert approximately equal amounts of influence or control upon each other. Vertical differentiation, in contrast, appears when these activities and subunits exercise grossly unequal influence or control, producing a power hierarchy.[4] So pervasive are hierarchical authority patterns in modern societies that some social scientists adopt as a working

---

[2] Thirteen broad propositions concerning the effects of size on other aspects of an organization are offered by Paul E. Mott in *The Organization of Society* (Englewood Cliffs, N.J.: Prentice-Hall, 1965). See also John D. Kasarda, "The Structural Implications of Social System Size: A Three-Level Analysis," *American Sociological Review* 39 (February 1974); 19–28; and Richard H. Hall, *Organizations: Structure and Process* (Englewood Cliffs, N.J.: Prentice-Hall, 1972), chap. 5.

[3] Kasarda ("The Structural Implications of Social System Size") substantiates this generalization for formal organizations, as does Michael Aiken for cities ("The Distribution of Community Power: Structural Bases and Social Consequences," in Aiken and Paul E. Mott, *The Structure of Community Power* [New York: Random House, 1970], pp. 487–525). Additional relevant literature is reviewed by Hall (*Organizations: Structure and Process*), p. 133.

[4] Hall, *Organizations: Structure and Process*, chap. 5.

definition of complexity the presence of three or more levels of authority within a social unit. Differentiation and complexity can also occur along a horizontal axis, however. Hierarchical patterning is not necessary for complexity. Indeed, some highly complex social ordering displays a relatively "flat" pattern—as in many professional and special-interest associations.[5] Regardless of the resulting form, however, complexity inevitably increases the importance of communication, control, coordination, and cohesion processes within all collectivities.

In general, increasing size produces greater internal complexity, since the greater the number of actors or relationships involved, the more extensive the opportunities for task specialization and subunit differentiation.[6] Two qualifications must be appended to this generalization. First, many other factors in addition to size affect the degree of complexity occurring in any social ordering.[7] Second, size does not determine whether differentiation will develop horizontally or vertically or along both axes simultaneously; that is a function of the distribution and exercise of power in the unit.[8]

Differentiation has several significant consequences for the distribution and exertion of social power. First, increasing complexity, along with growing size, tends to decrease power centralization and diffuse the exercise of power among numerous actors.[9] The primary reason for this is that task specialization and subunit semi-autonomy give actors independent bases of power, derived from their own resources and activities, thus freeing them from total dependence on and submission to central elites. Second, functional specialization leaves actors and subunits highly dependent on one another, which gives rise to the dependency process of power creation. And since this process generally results in the exercise of compulsion rather than compliance, various kinds of force tend to be prevalent in highly complex patterns of ordering. Third, complexity markedly expands the number and scope of indirect chains of interdependence, which provides countless opportunities for the exercise of functional dominance. Although force is certainly present to some degree in most instances of complex ordering, increasing differentiation and interdependence tend to produce a relative

[5] Eugene Litwak, "Models of Organizations Which Permit Conflict," *American Journal of Sociology* 67 (September 1961): 177–184.
[6] Hall, *Organizations: Structure and Process*, p. 115. Peter M. Blau, "A Formal Theory of Differentiation in Organizations," *American Sociological Review* 35 (April 1970): 201–218. Marshall W. Meyer, "Size and the Structure of Organizations: A Causal Analysis," *American Sociological Review* 37 (August 1972): 434–441.
[7] Hall, *Organizations: Structure and Process*, p. 149.
[8] D. S. Pugh et al., "Dimensions of Organizational Structure," *Administrative Science Quarterly* 13 (June 1968): 72–74, 78–79.
[9] Jerald Hage and Michael Aiken, "Relationship of Centralization to Other Structural Properties," *Administrative Science Quarterly* 12 (June 1967): 71–92.

shift away from the intentional exercise of force toward unintended exertion of dominance. For this reason, as contemporary social ordering becomes steadily more complex, we can expect to find an increasingly greater proportion of all individual and collective actors exerting some amount of dominance derived from their performance of specialized activities on which numerous other actors indirectly depend.

Formality. This third basic dimension of all social ordering pertains to techniques for prescribing how, when, and by whom activities are to be performed. In a relatively formal pattern of social ordering, such as a military unit, many of the interactions among members and subunits are prescribed in advance and routinized. Standard rules and procedures (either written or unwritten) guide the actions and relationships of the participants and often allow them little leeway for autonomy and creativity. In contrast, relatively informal social patterns, such as a friendship group, display considerable variation and fluidity. Social actors have wide latitude to use their own discretion in devising and modifying their actions and interactions. In short, *formality results from specification of guidelines for social action and relationships.*

Established patterns of social ordering not only display wide variations along this continuum, from stringent formality to lax informality, but also often contain various mixtures of both simultaneously. A factory will undoubtedly be more formal than a hobby club in its social ordering, but an elaborate set of informal relationships may exist alongside (and be interwoven with) a highly formalized set of rules and procedures. Considerable research has even suggested that relatively formal social ordering must contain a complementary web of informal relationships among its participants if it is to remain stable and function effectively.[10]

As a general principle, increasing size and complexity are both often associated with greater formality, since a certain amount of standardization and predictability is necessary to maintain a large and complex pattern of ordering and achieve collective goals. But this generalization ignores a crucial distinction between rigid and flexible formality. As usually conceived, formality refers to a relatively rigid set of rules and procedures to which actors are expected to adhere with little or no variation. It is possible, nevertheless, for rules and procedures to be specified quite broadly and flexibly so as to provide only general parameters rather than minute prescriptions for action. This is again a matter of degree, with unlimited variations and combinations occurring in reality, but it can have numerous consequences for both collectivities and individuals. Collectivities that rely on relatively standard rules and procedures often find increased rigidity a

[10]George Homans, *The Human Group* (New York: Harcourt, Brace, 1950).

virtual imperative if they are to preserve their social ordering and functional effectiveness as they grow in size and complexity. In the long run they may pay a severe price for this choice, however, as they find it increasingly difficult to innovate and adjust to changing conditions, which can eventually jeopardize their basic stability. In contrast, collectivities that utilize relatively broad guidelines can often adjust to growth and complexity with a minimal amount of flexible formality. This type of collectivity will normally remain open to innovation and change and thus preserve long-term stability despite day-to-day variability.

Extensive research has also demonstrated that rigid formality can have numerous undesirable consequences for individuals. These include "rule fixation," in which strict adherence to rules overrides all other concerns or responsibilities,[11] personal alienation, or a feeling that one has lost control over one's activities,[12] and development of a "bureaucratic personality," or a learned incapacity to deal with situations that deviate from the standard mold.[13] Lest strict formality appear totally debilitating, we must remember that most individuals learn to cope successfully with considerable formality in numerous spheres of social life, and that many types of rigid formality— such as Robert's Rules of Order or detailed job descriptions—can bring order and predictability into situations that otherwise might become totally chaotic.

More flexible types of formality are especially useful when the individuals involved are highly skilled in the activities they are performing, as in the case of professional workers. Their extensive training has already given them elaborate codes of conduct and performance guidelines, so that they do not normally require detailed rules and regulations to enact their tasks. Such persons usually perform most effectively under conditions of minimal flexible formality,[14] which has led Richard Hall to suggest that formalization (in the customary rigid sense) and professionalization are essentially two alternative ways of accomplishing the same end of instilling regularity and stability into social ordering.[15]

The distinction between rigid and flexible formality is also crucial for understanding relationships between formalization and power exertion. Traditional sociology theory, building on the writings of Max Weber, has long held that standard rules and procedures are an integral aspect of what he termed "rational-legal authority," which has become increasingly evident

---

[11] Michel Crozier, *The Bureaucratic Phenomenon* (Chicago: University of Chicago Press, 1964).
[12] Robert Blauner, *Alienation and Freedom* (Chicago: University of Chicago Press, 1964).
[13] Robert K. Merton, "Bureaucratic Structure and Personality," in his *Social Theory and Social Structure*, rev. ed. (New York: Free Press, 1957), pp. 195–206.
[14] George A. Miller, "Professionals in Bureaucracy: Alienation Among Industrial Scientists and Engineers," *American Sociological Review* 32 (October 1967): 755–768.
[15] Hall, *Organizations: Structure and Process*, pp. 189–191.

in modern societies as patterns of social ordering have grown in size and complexity.[16] We therefore often assume, rather uncritically, that hierarchical formal authority is the most effective type of social power in complexly ordered collectivities. Examples of this assumption surround us at every turn, from schools to businesses to governments. Recent research has demonstrated, however, that if operating rules and procedures are left relatively broad and flexible and if the participants have previously acquired their own professional or other personal guidelines, the need for strict exercise of centralized authority is considerably reduced. In these settings, individuals and subunits acquire legitimacy on the basis of their own demonstrated competence, so that decision making and other forms of power exertion tend to become widely dispersed throughout the entire collectivity.[17] As members of contemporary societies become steadily better educated and more highly trained in their various activities, reliance on hierarchical authority patterns may slowly give way to new forms of "participatory democracy."

SOCIAL STRUCTURE

Social ordering, or the interweaving of social interactions and relationships into recurrent and stable patterns, is a continually flowing process. Describing and analyzing this dynamic process can be quite difficult, however, because of our limited ability to perceive ongoing processes and our learned tendency to conceptualize reality in static rather than dynamic terms. This effort is also hindered by our language, which assumes that objects first exist and then act in some manner, rather than perceiving objects as outgrowths of activities. In other words, from a process perspective the statement "The committee is handling that matter" would be more accurately stated as "Handling that matter creates the committee." To perceive and discuss social ordering, consequently, we commonly transpose this dynamic process into a fixed concept by temporarily "freezing" ongoing social patterns into static structural forms. That is, we abstract from social reality the major features of a flowing pattern of social ordering and perceive them as a motionless configuration, with the result that our accounts and analyses of social ordering typically distort social reality by referring only to isolated instances of what is actually a continual process.

These static portrayals of dynamic social ordering are descriptions of social structure. Thus *social structure is a static representation of the*

---

[16] Max Weber, *The Theory of Social and Economic Organization* (Glencoe, Ill.: Free Press, 1947), pp. 329–340.
[17] Hage and Aiken, "Relationship of Centralization to Other Structural Properties." See also Peter M. Blau, "Decentralization in Bureaucracies," in Mayer N. Zald, ed., *Power in Organizations* (Nashville, Tenn.: Vanderbilt University Press, 1970), pp. 150–174.

patterns that emerge in the process of social ordering.[18] Social structure is patterned social ordering as we observe and describe it. Although we all constantly use motionless structural terminology as a convenient means of describing and analyzing social life, we must not allow this practice to blind us to the fact that any particular representation of social structure is a perceptual and conceptual abstraction from dynamic social reality. This distinction between "real existence" (social ordering) and "perceived conceptions" (social structure) has an ancient philosophical lineage and was embedded in modern science via Kant's ideas of "noumena" and "phenomena," but it is not always recognized by contemporary social scientists.

To clarify the concept of social structure, let us briefly examine two situations in which sociologists might give structural descriptions of social ordering. First, as we observe the activities of a small work group we might discover that one person frequently points out tasks to be done, suggests ways of doing these things, and coordinates the activities of other members. A second person is also quite active in the group, but most of his or her attention is devoted to encouraging and praising others, helping people to understand what others are saying, and resolving interpersonal conflicts. We might then depict the social structure of this group as consisting of two leaders, one of whom we would call the "task leader" and the other the "emotive leader." We might also discover that the task leader is the highest ranking member of the group in terms of power and prestige, while the emotive leader is the best-liked member. With this information, we could draw a simple diagram depicting these two leadership positions and their status in relation to each other and the rest of the group. This static representation of the group's structure would tell us nothing about the ongoing activities occurring within the group, but it would portray the main features of its dominant social pattern at that point in time.

As a second example of social structure, consider a typical sociological description of the pattern of socioeconomic stratification existing in a community. In reality, each individual has several different statuses in the various spheres of his or her daily life, each of which is constantly being reaffirmed or altered as he or she interacts with others. To simplify this extremely complex process involving thousands of people, however, we commonly describe the community stratification structure as consisting of a few relatively discrete social classes ranked in a vertical hierarchy. For instance, we might say that Smithville contains five major social classes: the economic and political elites, an upper middle class of professional and managerial persons, a lower middle class of white-collar employees and small-business people, a working class of skilled and semi-skilled blue-collar

---

[18] Much of the conceptualization of social structure presented in this section is taken from S. F. Nadel's *The Theory of Social Structure* (New York: Free Press, 1957).

workers, and a lower class of unskilled workers and unemployed persons. This five-class stratification structure is clearly a gross oversimplification of ongoing patterns of social inequality, but again it facilitates our analysis of complex dynamic processes—as long as we remember that this depicted structural configuration is a static abstraction from social reality.

As far as possible, social scientists constantly strive to make their structural descriptions congruent with real patterns of social ordering. They do this not only by following the guidelines of scientific methodology, but also by deriving their pictures of social structure from many separate observations of ongoing social processes. Instead of merely observing and recording a single instance of social patterning, the sophisticated sociologist will study several different instances of this process at successive time periods, to ensure that the depicted structural forms are relatively stable through time.

How much regularity or stability must a process of social ordering display before we can identify its structural patterning? There can be no precise answer to this question, for whether we view phenomena in process or structural terms is rather arbitrarily determined by the range of human mental abilities. We think of a stone as having a static structure only because we cannot perceive the constant exchange of atoms between it and the environment as it is slowly worn down by natural forces. Our memories, aided by photographs, do enable us to remember that the oak tree in front of our house was once a tiny seedling, but nevertheless we still tend to think of it as a fixed entity rather than as a dynamic process. Individual personalities are somewhat easier to perceive as changing phenomena, but we nevertheless expect people to remain relatively stable from day to day, and we label as mentally ill those who do not.

On the opposite side of the fence, why do we not perceive hurricanes, light rays, chemical reactions, or atomic explosions as static structures? Sensitive mechanical instruments might be capable of "freezing" and recording these processes as structural configurations, but human minds lack such perceptual and cognitive capabilities. It is possible, however, to train people to increase their awareness of social ordering and hence their ability to perceive social structure. All of us would undoubtedly agree that a marching band or a university classroom or a business corporation evidences enough social ordering to warrant describing its structural configuration. But can we speak of the social structure of a simple conversation, a cocktail party, or a lynch mob? Most of us would probably see these phenomena as too transient to have any observable social structure, yet sociologists have identified structural patterning within each of these situations.

At first glance, this argument that social structure results from social processes, rather than vice versa, may seem highly academic. From a practical perspective, however, conceptualizing social organization as a dynamic outgrowth of ongoing interactions and relationships will directly affect the way in which we approach all social phenomena. The essence of this perspective is that no social ordering—from a friendship clique to the United Nations—is a fixed entity that, once created, continues to operate perpetually until some outside force destroys it. Social reality is quite the opposite. All social ordering must be continually created through the interweaving and stabilizing of social relationships. As a result, organized social life is always undergoing modification, change, and growth or decline. *Social organization is a continual process of becoming.* This fact has two major consequences for human endeavors. On the one hand, we can never rest content in the belief that once we have established some cherished organization we can henceforth reap the benefits of predictable social ordering with only minimal housekeeping efforts. The perpetuation of social ordering and organization demands endless attention and labor. On the other hand, we need never be helplessly and rigidly tied to the practices and traditions of the past. Social ordering and organization can be endlessly flexible, changeable, and open to further improvement.

Both of the theoretical perspectives on social ordering examined in this chapter—coercion theory and ecological theory—have traditionally tended to focus more on social structure than on social processes, but both are fully compatible with a dynamic perspective toward social organization. The fact that only recently have theorists of these persuasions begun writing in process terms does not indicate an inherent bias in the theories, but rather reflects a broad tendency toward static structural analysis that has pervaded much sociological thinking for a long time. In the following discussions these theoretical perspectives are portrayed in dynamic terms whenever possible.

Coercion Theory

MANY writers refer to this theoretical perspective as "conflict theory" because of the frequent linkages between coercion and conflict in social life. The emergence of social ordering through the exercise of coercive power is nevertheless analytically distinct from social conflict, and is seen by coercion theorists as the essence of social organization. Some of these theorists describe their perspective in more general terms as "power theory," since their analyses often incorporate all forms of social power, but the narrower term "coercion theory" is used here for two reasons. First, this theoretical argument is primarily concerned with compulsive power exertion arising from interdependence, rather than with compliant power exertion based on mutual trust. Coercion can take the form of either force or dominance, but should not be equated with violence, which is only one of many means of exerting coercion. Second, most of the other five theoretical perspectives examined in this book also involve the use of social power in some way, which is the main reason for our basic assumption that power pervades all social life and provides the dynamic medium for the entire process of social organization.

Underlying the coercion perspective are three basic assumptions that are not usually articulated by these theorists:

1. One or more actors desire some kind of collective action by other actors. Most commonly this would be oriented toward instrumental goal attainment, but it could also involve expressive activity. Coercion theory does not assume, however, that these goals or needs are shared by all or even a majority of the involved actors. On the contrary, actors are assumed to be acting as autonomous elements concerned primarily with their own interests—which conflict at least as often as they coincide—so that broad consensus on common goals is relatively rare in social life. The goals being sought through collective action are therefore generally held by only a few of the total set of participating actors.

2. The actors who are seeking to create collective action are themselves already involved in some kind of social ordering to some minimal degree. The resulting interdependence and interaction give them a basis for creating compulsive power through the dependency process. Coercion theory, in other words, assumes the existence of potential or active power arising out of previously established social relationships, and is concerned with the use of this power, not its creation. As a consequence, coercion theory cannot account for the initial instigation of social interaction. It must rely on some version of interaction theory (either exchange or symbolic) to explain that first step in the process. But in reality this is not a severe restriction, since all actors are normally involved in many kinds of existing social ordering.

3. This currently existing power, as well as all additional power created through further collective activities, is distributed more or less unequally among the involved actors. The degree of power inequality can vary considerably, but coercion theory always presumes that some of the actors— usually a fairly small proportion of the total—will be capable of exercising more power than the others. These more powerful actors—or elites—are the principal focus of coercion theory, which gives considerable attention to such questions as who the elites are and why they are able to exercise more power than other actors. Without this third assumption, coercion theory reduces to the more general power perspective that sees social power pervading all social organization. As an empirical generalization, the assumption of power inequality is validated by almost all human history. But many coercion theorists (with the notable exception of Marx) have taken

the additional step of assuming that such inequality is either necessary or inevitable in organized social life, thus converting an empirical generalization into a theoretical imperative. Since that latter step is logically unnecessary for coercion theory, however, we shall avoid it and treat power inequality as merely a widely observed fact in social life.

BASIC THESIS

Given the above assumptions, coercion theory is essentially an attempt to answer this fundamental question: In order to create collective action, how can actors' self-interests and -orientations be transcended so as to shift their actions from those of autonomous elements to those of involved parts of a larger collectivity, thus bringing regularity and stability into social relationships? In the previous chapter we saw that interaction theory provides several answers to this question, including eliciting voluntary cooperation based on mutual trust, developing common norms, and awarding selective incentives for participation. Coercion theory argues in rebuttal that (1) cooperation and trust can operate only in quite small groups where people interact on a personal basis, and even in those settings mutual trust can be quite precarious; (2) common norms can help to maintain and strengthen existing patterns of social ordering, but they cannot explain the creation of social ordering, since norms arise out of shared collective experiences; and (3) reliance on selective incentives implicitly assumes an existing power system capable of allocating rewards to participants. Coercion theory's answer to this fundamental question about the creation of social ordering is expressed in the following principle:

> PRINCIPLE 11: To attain desired ends, elites employ their superior power capabilities to coerce other actors into collective action, thereby creating social ordering.

Several aspects of this statement should be noted. First, the ends being sought will likely be based on personal interests of the elites, but they could just as well be aimed at serving others or improving the common welfare. Much social activity is self-interested, but coercion theory is applicable to any goal or need and hence is not biased in any particular direction. Second, this general principle does not specify the relative size of the elite group, who the elites are, or how powerful they are in relation to others. Elites are simply actors who are capable, for one reason or another, of exerting more power than others and who use it to obtain desired ends. Third, as far as possible, elites attempt to coerce others, or control their activities through the exercise of compulsive power that is not dependent on voluntary compliance. Fourth, although elites purposefully exert power to achieve whatever ends they are seeking, they do not necessarily intentionally create social ordering. Social ordering is generally an outgrowth of efforts to control the actions of others. Although purposeful creation of social ordering is not precluded by this principle, and sometimes does occur, this is not presumed to be the usual course of affairs.

The patterns of social ordering that emerge through this process may or may not facilitate the elites' goal-attainment efforts. If the resulting ordering proves to be more of a hindrance than a help, elites will normally attempt to exert more coercion in alternative ways so as to alter these patterns of ordering to more adequately suit their purposes. Their efforts are often restrained, nevertheless, by the fact that as established patterns of social ordering become institutionalized through time, they can become quite resistant to change. Elites therefore sometimes find themselves virtual prisoners of social ordering patterns that they have unwittingly created but that do not serve their initially desired purposes. More commonly, however, the collective action and social ordering that elites succeed in establishing does prove more or less beneficial to them. In these cases, elites will normally attempt, in whatever way possible, to stabilize and maintain the existing social ordering. And the more beneficial it is to them, the more resources and power it will provide them for these efforts.

If they are to succeed in this effort at maintaining beneficial patterns of social ordering, elites must preserve or improve their ability to coerce others. As already suggested, they are aided in this endeavor by the fact the social conditions they have created usually benefit them disproportionately in relation to others, so that their resources for power exertion are protected or enhanced by these conditions. Nevertheless, elites periodically find themselves being challenged by other actors seeking either to usurp their positions of power or change the existing social order. In either case, elites will normally resist these threats to their power to the best of their ability, using a variety of techniques to be described later. The result is either covert or overt conflict, which explains why coercion theorists give so much attention to the process of social conflict. A second basic principle of coercion theory is therefore:

> PRINCIPLE 12: **To the extent that patterns of social ordering prove beneficial to elites, they will utilize power to strengthen and perpetuate this social ordering.**

Coercion theorists have generally agreed that the predominant flow of power throughout all organized social life is from elites to other actors. Hence power-wielding elites can usually affect or shape, if not completely control, most activities and relationships within their spheres of concern. To understand and explain social ordering, therefore, we must focus primarily on the nature and actions of elites. The "masses" of "ordinary" actors are of only minor importance from this theoretical perspective, since they normally exercise relatively little influence on the process of social ordering. The only exceptions to this generalization are situations in which nonelites either (1) have established means of exerting influence on elites, as in democratic elections, or (2) become powerful enough to seriously threaten elites, as in revolts and revolutions.

The following paragraphs examine various arguments given by the major coercion theorists to explain this basic process in greater detail. Three characteristics of these writings should be noted in advance, however. First, beyond the basic propositions given above, there is little agreement among coercion theorists. In fact, large portions of their writings have been devoted to emphasizing the points that divide them rather than any common themes. Nevertheless, insofar as possible, we shall treat coercion theory as a unified perspective on social ordering. Second, all of the major coercion theorists—including Karl Marx, Gaetano Mosca, Vilfredo Pareto, Robert Michels, Ralf Dahrendorf, and T. B. Bottomore—have been Europeans, which is perhaps a reflection of the historical role of coercion in European history. For reasons that sociologists of knowledge might well explore, this perspective on social life has until quite recently been relatively rare in American sociology. Third, coercion theory has been given many diverse ideological overtones by its various proponents, ranging from "radical" demands that the "masses" must organize and overthrow the dominant class that is exploiting them, to "liberal" beliefs that no particular distribution of power is impervious to change, to "conservative" arguments that there will always be powerful elites, to "reactionary" insistence that the existing power structure is inevitable and that the present "ruling class" is inherently superior. The obvious conclusion to be drawn from these contrasting views is that coercion theory does not in itself contain any ideological bias, although it can certainly be used to buttress any shade of political opinion.

POWER BASES

A principal concern of all coercion theorists has been to identify the major bases from which elites draw their power superiority. The six power bases described in the following paragraphs illustrate the wide diversity of thinking within this theoretical school.

1. Personal Superiority.   As argued by Gaetano Mosca, elites tend to be superior individuals in such qualities as intelligence, ambition, drive, tenacity of purpose, strength of will, and self-confidence, although elitist family background is also quite important in giving individuals vital training and resources. "Elites are distinguished from the mass of the governed by qualities that give them a certain material, intellectual, or even moral superiority; or else they are the heirs of individuals who possessed such qualities. In other words, members of a ruling minority regularly have some attribute, real or apparent, which is highly esteemed and very influential in the society in which they live. . . ."[19] Which particular individuals become elites at any particular time is determined through a competitive struggle for preeminence, but to compete at all successfully in this reverse Darwinian social competition one must possess superior personal qualities and family background.

Vilfredo Pareto attempted to systematize this argument by suggesting that elites are superior individuals because of the particular residues that guide their actions. Residues are not personality characteristics, but rather basic nonlogical modes of action. Residues of "group persistence" are particularly crucial for elites, since persons in whom these residues predominate are especially skillful at using force to create social order. Unfortunately, however, they also tend to be rather inflexible and resistant to change, which in time leads to their replacement by new elites who exhibit predominant residues of "combination" and are talented at manipulating others to achieve goals through swift adaptation to changing circumstances.[20]

This type of explanation unfortunately tells us very little, for apart from biological intelligence—which is also greatly affected by social conditions—it is ultimately a tautology. Why are some people elites? Because they have superior personal characteristics. What are these characteristics? Qualities displayed by elites. Moreover, this approach totally ignores all social conditions that contribute to elite formation. Although personal qualities may determine which individuals attain elite status in a particular situation, this argument cannot explain why certain kinds of characteristics provide viable power bases in that situation while others do not.

2. Mass Support. If elites tend to be superior persons, the complementary argument follows that the masses of nonelites are, if not incompetent, at least uninformed and apathetic. They know little and care less about public affairs, collective problems, or organized power exertion. Consequently, they desire and welcome leadership from above that will relieve them of the burdens of collective responsibilities and decision making, and quite willingly submit to the dictates of elites. And even if they did seek leadership positions, most of them would be totally incapable of

[19]Gaetano Mosca, *The Ruling Class*, trans. by Hannah D. Kahn (New York: McGraw-Hill, 1939), p. 53.
[20]Vilfredo Pareto, *The Mind and Society*, trans. by A. Bongiorno and A. Livingston (New York: Harcourt, Brace, 1935), pp. 1512–1527.

effectively wielding power or performing other leadership functions. In the view of Robert Michels, the situation is virtually hopeless: "The incompetence of the masses is almost universal throughout the domains of political life, and this constitutes the most solid foundation of the power of the leaders. The incompetence furnishes the leaders with a practical and, to some extent, with a moral justification. Since the rank and file are incapable of looking after their own interests, it is necessary that they should have experts to attend to their affairs." "Though it grumbles occasionally, the majority is really delighted to find persons who will take the trouble to look after its affairs. In the mass . . . there is an immense need for direction and guidance. This need is accompanied by a genuine cult for the leaders, who are regarded as heroes. . . ."[21] Karl Marx also saw the masses of workers in modern societies as powerless and supportive of existing elites, although he attributed this to ignorance, exploitation, and "false consciousness" rather than to incompetence and apathy. This emphasis was crucial for Marx, since he firmly believed that, with proper awareness of their common plight and adequate organization and leadership, the masses could alter their condition by taking over the dominant power positions in society. Michels, in contrast, saw no hope of escape from the "iron law of oligarchy": "Who says organization, says oligarchy."[22]

Although much historical evidence could easily be marshaled to support the contention that the masses of nonelites are generally less interested, informed, and skilled than elites, this observation nevertheless does not constitute an adequate explanation of elite power. If nonelites display these characteristics, why is this so? Does not the very fact of their relative powerlessness leave them little realistic choice except to be unconcerned about social power and its use? Their attitudes and stances, in other words, are merely reflections of social reality in many cases. But how were these conditions created in the first place? Mass apathy, ignorance, and incompetence certainly act to buttress the power of existing elites, but they cannot explain the original rise of these elites to positions of power.

3. *Control of Societal Resources.* The classical formulation of this thesis is Marxian theory. Marx assumed that all societies (or at least all Western societies) rest on a foundation of economic production. Since people must produce goods and services if they are to survive and attain any other goals, the nature and effectiveness of the productive process will inevitably shape—though not fully determine—all other aspects of social life. Although any society will contain many diverse "modes of production,"

---

[21] Robert Michels, *Political Parties*, trans. by Eden and Cedar Paul (New York: Free Press, 1962), pp. 111–112, 88.
[22] Ibid., p. 365.

for analytical purposes, Marx argued, we need examine only the dominant production mode, such as agriculture in a feudal society or manufacturing in an industrial society. Within a society's dominant mode of production, the "forces of production," or technological aspects of economic activity, are important in determining how effectively surplus resources (that is, wealth) can be produced. But technology does not determine how those resources will be distributed and used in society. Especially crucial for social ordering are the "social relations of production," or the relationships of various segments of the population to the economy, and more specifically, who owns or controls the major means of production. Whoever controls the dominant mode of economic production will determine how existing technology will be utilized and how the resulting benefits will be distributed, and will consequently become the power elites in that society. As expressed by Marx: "It is always the immediate relation of the owners of the conditions of production to the immediate producers—a relation whose specific pattern of course always corresponds to a certain stage in the development of labor and its social force of production—in which we find the final secret, the hidden basis of the whole construction of society, including the political patterns of sovereignty and dependence. . . ."[23]

Mosca attempted to broaden this thesis by proposing that in the long run elites must at least roughly represent the major "interests" or "forces" in a society, whatever they may be. In addition to economic production, these might include political, religious, military, or other significant power resources. He did not specify the factors that determine which interests are dominant in a particular society, however, or otherwise explore this idea in any detail.

Several contemporary writers—including John Kenneth Galbraith[24] and Daniel Bell[25]—have argued that a new kind of resource base is becoming crucial in modern societies. Complex industrial, bureaucratized societies are increasingly dependent on expert knowledge and accompanying skills, including administrative and managerial abilities, scientific and technological expertise, professional competence of many kinds, and educational and mass communication skills. They argue that this growing "knowledge network" is beginning to challenge, if not replace, the economy as the dominant resource base in "post-industrial" societies. Hence individuals and organizations who perform these functions and control the "knowledge system" are emerging as the new elites of tomorrow's societies.

Regardless of whether these knowledge elites replace or merely supplement older economic and political elites, their ability to exercise social

[23] Karl Marx, *Capital*, vol. 3, new ed. (Moscow: Foreign Languages Publishing House, 1954), p. 841.
[24] John Kenneth Galbraith, *The New Industrial State* (Boston: Houghton Mifflin, 1967).
[25] Daniel Bell, *The Coming of Post-Industrial Society* (New York: Basic Books, 1973).

power is clearly based on their control of a vital societal resource. This suggests that classical Marxian theory can be expanded to state that control over major societal resources—whatever their nature—provides a fundamental power basis for elites. To the extent that control of the major mode of economic production—either agriculture or industry—has been the fundamental resource base in most societies throughout human history, this reflects humanity's constant struggle to satisfy its material needs. As economic productivity expands in volume and efficiency, however, humanity is slowly being freed from basic sustenance and related economic concerns, and is able to direct at least a portion of its efforts and attention to other matters. With this trend comes the emergence of many new resource bases for power exertion.

4. *Control of the Means of Violence.* The ability to exercise physical violence—whether through organized police and military units or through isolated acts of terrorism—has been another crucial power base for elites throughout human history. Although we often associate violence with crime and war, it frequently pervades many facets of society. As observed by Thomas Rose: "Violence is omnipresent in American history. From the earliest beginnings of this nation until the present there has been no period without considerable violence. . . . The major feature of American history is that Americans force others to be the way they want them to be: a governing minority has always imposed its will on the majority by force and violence. . . . In the political policies of social control, organized violent control is the might, the cannon, that sanctions and upholds authority and tradition." [26]

Violence plays a central role in Marxian theory, which argues that ruling elites use the political state to control the rest of society through organized violence. In the words of V. I. Lenin: "The state is a special organization of force; it is the organization of violence for the suppression of some class." [27] For Marxists, therefore, this power base is merely an outgrowth of the more basic factor of control of the means of economic production. To the extent that political leaders can acquire alternative sources of economic resources and thus gain autonomy from economic elites, however, they become capable of using violence (or the threat of violence) as an independent power base. History is replete with examples of efforts by kings, emperors, dictators, and presidents to obtain sufficient economic resources through such means as taxation, expropriation, and exploitation to free themselves from direct dependence on economic elites.[28]

[26] Thomas Rose, ed., *Violence in America* (New York: Vintage Books, 1970), p. xx.
[27] V. I. Lenin, *State and Revolution* (New York: International Publishers, 1932), p. 22.
[28] S. N. Eisenstadt, *The Political Systems of Empires* (New York: Free Press, 1969).

And contemporary totalitarian societies illustrate the extent to which political leaders can control a society through the exercise of violence.[29] As control over the means of violence becomes progressively centralized in the hands of professional military and police personnel, however, political leaders often find it difficult to prevent these people from using violence for their own purposes—as witnessed by the numerous military coups and dictatorships around the world today. Control over the means of violence can thus provide a relatively autonomous and significant power base for would-be elites.

These last two power bases—control over major resources and control over the means of violence—both give rise to the organized use of force, or the intentional exertion of compulsive pressures. Coercion theory consequently gives primary attention to force—as opposed to legitimate authority—as the principal means through which social ordering is created by elites. In complexly organized societies, however, functional dominance is steadily emerging as an equally viable means of exerting coercive power and creating social ordering. The next two power bases therefore emphasize dominance derived from the performance of an actor's functions in society.

5. *Occupancy of Official Positions.* In Max Weber's model of the ideal bureaucracy, all power is ultimately concentrated in the hands of a few elites occupying positions at the apex of a hierarchical structure. Regardless of how individuals obtain these positions, occupancy confers on them the legal right to exercise coercive control over all other members. "The organization of offices follows the principle of hierarchy: that is, each lower office is under the control and supervision of a higher one."[30] In this model, therefore, the power base of elites lies in their occupancy of official positions, not from control of economic or other resources. Weber's bureaucratic model has become the prototype structure for instrumentally oriented organizations in all spheres of modern societies because of its functional efficiency. "Experience tends universally to show that the purely bureaucratic type of administrative organization—that is, the monocratic variety of bureaucracy—is, from a purely technical point of view, capable of attaining the highest degree of efficiency and is in this sense formally the most rational known means of carrying out imperative control over human beings."[31] Consequently, occupancy of official positions within bureaucratically structured organizations has become a predominant power base in all contemporary societies.

[29] Carl J. Friedrich, and Zbigniew K. Brzezinski, *Totalitarian Dictatorship and Autocracy,* 2nd ed. (Cambridge, Mass.: Harvard University Press, 1965).
[30] Max Weber, *The Theory of Social and Economic Organization,* trans. by A. M. Henderson and Talcott Parsons (New York: Oxford University Press, 1947), p. 331.
[31] Ibid., p. 337.

Building on Weber's model, Ralf Dahrendorf has developed a "coercion theory of society" which rests on the assumption that "every society is based on the coercion of some of its members by others."[32] The basis of this ability to exert coercion is occupancy of positions of legal authority within bureaucratic structures. "It is not voluntary cooperation or general consensus, but enforced constraint that makes social organization possible. In institutional terms, this means that in every social organization some positions are entrusted with a right to exercise control over other positions in order to ensure effective coercion. . . ."[33] Although Dahrendorf calls this exercise of power "authority," it is clear from the above passage that he is referring to coercive constraint based on occupancy of official positions, not to voluntary compliance based on grants of legitimacy from those governed.

By emphasizing occupancy of official authority positions as the primary source of power in modern societies, Dahrendorf believes that he has corrected a fundamental error in Marxian theory. "Control over the means of production is but a special case of authority, and the connection of control with legal property an incidental phenomenon of the industrializing societies of Europe and the United States. . . . Property is by no means the only form of authority; it is but one of its numerous types. Whoever tries, therefore, to define authority by property defines the general by the particular—an obvious logical fallacy. Wherever there is property there is authority, but not every form of authority implies property. Authority is the more general social relation."[34] Nevertheless, Dahrendorf does accept Marx's thesis that the structure of power in society should be conceptualized as a dichotomy of those who do and those who don't exercise coercion. "With respect to authority . . . , a clear line can at least in theory be drawn between those who participate in this exercise in given associations and those who are subject to the authoritative commands of others. . . . Authority does not permit the construction of a scale. So-called hierarchies of authority . . . are in fact hierarchies of the 'plus-side' of authority, i.e., of the differentiation of domination; but there is, in every association, also a 'minus-side' consisting of those who are subjected to authority rather than participate in its exercise."[35]

Dahrendorf's thesis has been disputed on numerous grounds, the most serious of which is that he fails to explain the creation of hierarchical authority structures, but merely assumes their existence and inquires into how this power base is used to maintain the existing social order. In other words, his theory deals with the consequences of social ordering, not its

[32] Ralf Dahrendorf, *Class and Class Conflict in Industrial Society* (Stanford, Calif.: Stanford University Press, 1959), p. 162.
[33] Ibid., p. 165.
[34] Ibid., pp. 136–137.
[35] Ibid., pp. 146–147.

causes. As noted by Jonathan Turner: "Dahrendorf's inability to explain how conflict and change emerge stems from his inability to address the problem of order seriously: How and why is the organization of imperatively coordinated associations possible?"[36] Nevertheless, Dahrendorf has called widespread attention to the ways in which coercion derived from occupancy of official positions is utilized by elites to preserve and perpetuate social ordering.

6. *Performance of Necessary Functions.* If an actor performs a function or service for others that they need, their dependency gives that actor a basis for exercising control over them. And the more vital and indispensable those services, the greater the power of the actors who provide them. Even though they may not intentionally seek to wield power, actors who perform necessary social functions nevertheless automatically acquire a viable power base and become potential or actual elites. This functional dominance is especially likely to accrue to actors who occupy key functionary positions within an organization. As seen in Chapter 1, key functionaries include gatekeepers who mediate the flow of inputs and outputs between the organization and its environment as well as between subparts of the organization, channelers who provide pathways for the flow of information throughout the organization, switchers who direct the flow of resources and activities among various parts of the organization, and storers who maintain resources and information utilized within the organization. Through the performance or nonperformance of their functions within an organization, these actors can easily become dominant elites.

To explain why oligarchy prevails in all organizations, even when they are ideologically dedicated to member-control and democratic decision making, Robert Michels placed considerable emphasis on the tendency over time for leaders to become functionally dominant and be viewed by others as indispensable. Through occupancy of key (not necessarily official) positions, they acquire control over organizational communications, finances, decision-making processes, resource procurement, and similar necessary functions. Through experience in performing these leadership functions they also develop special abilities and skills not possessed by other members, which adds to their perceived indispensability. Finally, all of this is reinforced by webs of informal obligations and influence that leaders develop through time as they carry out their duties. Speaking of political party leaders, Michels wrote: "Whilst their occupation and the needs of daily life render it impossible for the masses to attain to a profound knowledge of the social machinery, and above all of the working of the political machine, the

[36]Jonathan Turner, *The Structure of Sociological Theory* (Homewood, Ill.: Dorsey Press, 1974), p. 104.

leader . . . is enabled, thanks to his new situation, to make himself intimately familiar with all the technical details of public life, and thus to increase his superiority over the rank and file. . . . Thus the gulf between the leaders and the rest of the party becomes even wider, until the moment arrives in which the leaders lose all true sense of solidarity with the class from which they have sprung, and there ensues a new class-division between ex-proletarian captains and proletarian common soldiers. . . . The democratic masses are thus compelled to submit to a restriction of their own wills when they are forced to give their leaders an authority which is in the long run destructive to the very principle of democracy. The leader's principal source of power is found in his indispensability. One who is indispensable has in his power all the lords and masters of the earth."[37]

A similar argument is made by Piet Thoenes in regard to contemporary welfare societies. As governments have assumed responsibility for providing more and more economic and social services to their citizens, these programs have been redefined as administrative rather than political concerns, and control over them has shifted from politicians to technical experts. As the people become dependent on these welfare services, the technical experts providing them become functionally indispensable and steadily gain power within the government. "What this argument amounts to is that a number of problems have been taken out of the sphere of political debate because . . . they have become problems which, within the system which has been agreed upon, inevitably come to be settled on their technical merits. . . . In other words, the concession of political priorities has become a matter of technical knowledge within the socioeconomic system now in force. To a greater degree than ever, it is not political principles but rather administrative or technico-professional knowledge that can tip the scales."[38] Regardless of the specific context, in short, performance of vitally necessary or indispensable activities gives elites a dominant and stable power base.

The central thrust of all the six diverse bases of power described above is that elites possess or control resources which they can convert into overt force or dominance. All of the factors discussed in the preceding paragraphs—personal capabilities, intelligence, mass support, control of economic production, control of knowledge, control of means of violence, occupancy of official positions, and performance of key functions—provide viable power bases that skillful actors can utilize to exert coercion on others and in the process create social ordering. In summary:

[37] Michels, *Political Parties*, pp. 108–111.
[38] Piet Thoenes, *The Elite in the Welfare State*, trans. by J. E. Bingham (New York: Free Press, 1966), p. 164.

PRINCIPLE 13:   Elites derive their ability to exercise coercive power from possession or control of vital resources that enable them to perform actions which make others dependent on them, which in turn generates compulsive force and dominance.

ELITE STRUCTURES

Assuming an unequal distribution of power in a society or other organization, coercion theorists have given considerable attention to describing prevailing power patterns or structures. For analytical purposes (but not necessarily as descriptions of reality), these theorists frequently conceive of power structures as dichotomies of those who exercise social power (elites) and those who do not (masses)—adding the implicit assumption that the masses are much more numerous than the elites. This dichotomous perspective—as employed by Marx and Dahrendorf, among others—greatly simplifies the analysis of power structures, and also reflects the empirical tendency for conflicting parties to polarize into two opposing factions in many situations.

Other writers have argued, however, that such a perspective grossly oversimplifies and distorts the complex patterning of most power structures. Mosca, for instance, distinguished between "top" or "ruling" elites, who formulate basic policies and wield ultimate power, and "sub" or "supporting" elites, who execute elite decisions and carry out much actual power exertion (thus supporting the top elites in their power positions, as well as providing a constant supply of new personnel for top elite ranks). A similar distinction is often found in contemporary studies of community "leaders" and "subleaders."[39] Moreover, each set of top elites may control several separate sets of subelites operating within specialized spheres of activity. In general, top elites may be thought of as "controllers" who can, if they wish, largely dictate the crucial decisions and policies affecting an organization, while subelites act as "influentials" who affect but do not control the activities of the organization.

A further structural complication introduced by both Mosca and Pareto was the concept of "counterelites," or sets of actors outside the established power structure who have an independent basis of power and seek to overthrow the ruling elites. If these counterelites succeed in gaining control of the power structure, the resulting "circulation of elites" brings new personnel into elite positions but rarely radically changes the basic structure of the established power system. More commonly, however, strong counterelites are brought into the existing power structure through collaboration or co-optation before they can seriously threaten it. Finally, within any power

[39] Robert Dahl, *Who Governs?* (New Haven, Conn.: Yale University Press, 1961), pp. 99–103.

structure there may be one or more sets of "semielites" or "activists" who keep the established patterns of power operating smoothly even though they do not exercise significant amounts of force or dominance.[40]

Despite these efforts to take account of the complexities of power structures in modern societies, all early coercion theorists—from Marx to Michels—shared one basic presumption. They assumed that within any society there was only one power structure and hence just one set of elites— regardless of whether they were called the "ruling class" or the "governing elite" or the "power elite." These theorists observed that some form of centralized government is indispensable in modern societies, which necessarily creates a set of powerful political elites, from which they concluded that these political leaders must invariably also constitute the elites in all other spheres of society. In contrast, most contemporary coercion theorists recognize that all complex societies, communities, and other organizations—even those with totalitarian governments—contain a wide array of power dimensions. In addition to the formal government, there may be more or less distinct power structures within such spheres of activity as industry, commerce, medicine, education, religion, science, law, and communications. Each of these power structures has its own set of elites, subelites, counterelites, and activists, thus creating a highly complex mosaic of multiple sets of elites.[41]

Because each set of elites operates within a relatively specialized area of activity, Suzanne Keller labeled them "strategic elites." Each set of strategic elites typically performs a particular kind of service or function, but no one of them totally dominates the society. Moreover, elites in one area might well be nonelites in another realm, so that there is not likely to be either a single "ruling class" or a vast powerless "mass" of nonelites. And to the extent that all members of a society were active and influential in at least one area of activity, everyone might become a strategic elite or subelite within his or her particular sphere of competence. There might still be a tendency for various sets of strategic elites to share overlapping memberships and to cooperate closely with one another—as illustrated by C. Wright Mills's portrayal of the "power elite" in American society[42]—but they need not necessarily constitute a single dominant "ruling class." This distinction between strategic elites and ruling classes is carefully drawn by Keller:

[40]The concept of "activist" was introduced by Linton Freeman et al., "Locating Leaders in Local Communities: A Comparison of Some Alternative Approaches," *American Sociological Review* 28 (October 1963): 791–798.
[41]This idea of multiple sets of elites has been developed by Raymond Aron, "Social Class, Political Class, Ruling Class," trans. by Reinhard Bendix and Seymour M. Lipset, *European Journal of Sociology* 1 (1960): 260–281; T. B. Bottomore, *Elites and Society* (New York: Basic Books, 1964); and Suzanne Keller, *Beyond the Ruling Class* (New York: Random House, 1963).
[42]C. Wright Mills, *The Power Elite* (New York: Oxford University Press, 1957).

... a ruling class is more diffuse, more permanent, and therefore more difficult to delimit than strategic elites. Its membership is less voluntary, the scope of its activities is wider and less specialized, and its members share not only their occupational and functional positions but also more general habits, customs, and culture. Strategic elites may be thought of as further differentiations of a ruling class, a differentiation necessitated by the growth in size and complexity of advanced industrial societies. In such societies, trained experts are increasingly in demand in all spheres. . . . In principle there can be only one ruling class in a society, but there must be a number of strategic elites. Any single strategic elite is probably numerically smaller than a ruling class as a whole. Because of the differentiation of tasks, strategic elites are less likely to become despotic than a ruling class.[43]

This notion of multiple sets of strategic elites has several theoretical implications, three of which are especially worthy of note. First, as emphasized by Robert Dahl, this pattern permits considerable conflict among different sets of elites, which promotes social flexibility and change while mitigating against extreme power centralization.[44] Second, it underlies Joseph Schumpeter's conception of political democracy as consisting of competition for positions of power among diverse sets of elites, which many political theorists claim is more relevant to modern societies than the classical notion of democracy as popular decision making.[45] And third, it negates the traditional assumption of coercion theory that power must inevitably be unequally distributed among the members of a society. Although in any particular setting some actors will almost invariably exercise more power than others, these roles may be reversed in other settings, so that from a broader perspective it is theoretically possible for all persons to exert some amount of social power, with resulting relative (though not necessarily absolute) power equality throughout the total system.

The essence of this discussion of power structures is summarized in the following principle:

PRINCIPLE 14: **Elites can often be divided into several levels of power exertion, and frequently exercise power only within specialized areas of activity, which gives rise to multiple sets of strategic elites who may or may not coalesce into a single ruling class.**

[43] Keller, *Beyond the Ruling Class*, p. 57.
[44] Dahl, *Who Governs?*
[45] Joseph Schumpeter, *Capitalism, Socialism and Democracy*, 3rd ed. (New York: Harper & Row, 1950).

COERCION STRATEGIES

Given the existence of one or more sets of elites capable of coercing others, how do they use this power to attain their goals and protect their privilages, as well as create social ordering? In short, what strategies do elites employ in utilizing, protecting, and legitimating their power?

Power Utilization. The most obvious and direct manner in which elites promote their own interests and seek to attain their own goals is through the exercise of force. They exert pressures—either positive inducements or negative constraints—to compel other actors, if possible, to obey their dictates. Force can be a highly effective means of obtaining desired ends in particular situations, especially if exercised with subtlety and moderation. Two major problems with this approach, however, are that sooner or later it can exhaust one's resources (unless one is very successful at bluffing), and that the recipients often resent involuntary compulsion and may rebel against it if possible. Consequently, elites usually employ other power strategies as extensively as possible, reserving direct force (and particularly violence) for those situations in which no other approach is applicable.

One common alternative to exerting force is developing functional dominance. As elites perform leadership roles, especially key functionary roles, other actors become dependent on them for these services. The elites thereby make themselves functionally necessary or even indispensable. This enables them, through the routine performance of their roles, to exert dominance over other actors and throughout the entire organization. By performing their roles in particular ways or by threatening to withhold their services, they can compel obedience from others without expending scarce resources to generate force. This process of substituting dominance for force is often quite subtle, with much overlapping, but it brings considerable stability and predictability to coercive power. In large measure it enables elites to exercise determinant control in place of problematic influence.

Another alternative to exerting direct force is creating unbalanced exchange relationships, transforming them from mutual influence transactions into unilateral control situations. To accomplish this transformation, elites must be able to give others more than they take in return, and then prevent the other actors from seeking alternative sources of satisfaction, forming coalitions, or otherwise rebalancing the relationship. This effort is frequently not difficult for elites, given their superior resource supplies. Moreover, if they have already succeeded in establishing strong functional dominance over the other participants, the elites can utilize the control generated through that process to further unbalance their exchange relationships. Both of these techniques of establishing dominance and creating unbalanced exchanges leave other actors dependent on the elites and provide further bases for creating and implementing coercive compulsion.

A third, even more subtle and pervasive strategy for exercising coercion without resorting to overt force is to develop and utilize what Tom Baumgartner and his colleagues call "meta-power."[46] Rather than focusing on specific relationships, elites can use their superior power-wielding abilities to design and control the total social context within which others are acting. They need not be concerned with influencing every particular activity, for they can be certain that the long-run course of events will benefit them. In analytical terms, the elites are exerting systemic control over a total social system. Baumgartner and his colleagues describe meta-power or "relational control" as "attempts to structure or re-structure the social and cultural matrix within which power activities are to be played out. . . . We refer to the exercise of such 'meta-power' as relational control, that is, control over relationships and social structure. . . . The purpose of the exercise of relational control is generally the long-term structuring of social process and its outcomes; the individual and collective actions of those whose social relationships are structured. . . . Among other things, it may be used to encourage cooperative social organization on the one hand, or to produce competition or conflict between actors on the other, and generally to increase power in relation to others." Elites who achieve this degree of control over total social systems are clearly able to wield coercive compulsion with relative ease, for the other actors in the system have little choice but to conform. Indeed, they may even be totally unaware of the degree to which their options have been curtailed and their activities largely predetermined by the controlling elites.

This first set of coercive strategies can be combined as follows:

> **PRINCIPLE 15:   Elites exert coercion in pursuit of their goals through the exercise of overt force, functional dominance, unbalanced exchange control, and overall meta-power or systemic control.**

Power Protection.   In addition to employing coercion to attain goals, elites are usually also concerned to protect their resources and preserve their ability to exert power. The most obvious way of doing this is simply to deprive other actors of all power resources, rendering them incapable of

---

[46] Tom Baumgartner, Walter Buckley, Tom R. Burns, and Peter Schuster, "Meta-Power and the Structuring of Social Hierarchies," in Tom R. Burns and Walter Buckley, eds., *Power and Conflict: Social Structures and Their Transformation* (London: Sage Publications, Ltd., 1976), ch. 10.

challenging the established elites. Even the most ruthless despots normally stop short of total power monopolization, however, for at least three reasons: (1) the effort necessary to acquire all possible resources within an organization is uneconomical if not prohibitive; (2) some resources, such as sheer numbers of people in an angry mob, can never be expropriated by elites; (3) leaving the masses totally powerless renders them incapable of performing any useful activities (and sometimes even incapable of staying alive), so that they are of no use to the elites. Throughout history, consequently, elites have constantly struggled with the problem of how many resources they could effectively expropriate from nonelites, while at the same time leaving them enough so that they remain capable of performing desired activities and are not tempted to rebel against the established order.

Along with resource expropriation, elites have also commonly imposed severe restrictions on entry by nonelites into the established power structure. This can be accomplished in many ways, including appointing only one's friends or relatives to potentially powerful subelite positions, establishing stringent requirements for new personnel and controlling the training or experiences needed to meet these requirements, limiting the number of subordinates who are delegated significant responsibilities and resources, and selecting one's heirs through either personal appointment or family inheritance. Though many such practices are perhaps less flagrant in modern societies than in the past, all elites practice them to some extent in various ways.

Another technique often employed by elites to protect their power is the process of co-optation. If other actors pose threats to the elites that are too strong to be ignored or easily quashed, they can invite these challengers—or at least their leaders—to enter the ranks of the elites within the established order. Instead of opposing their challengers and risking a confrontation they might lose, the elites say in effect: "Come join us and work with us to attain your goals." To be successful, co-optation must be carried out with considerable finesse, for the challengers must be led to believe that they stand to gain more through cooperation than conflict, and also that they are not selling out their cause for personal gain. At the same time, the co-opting elites must exercise care to ensure that their new "partners" are kept in subordinate positions and securely controlled, lest they eventually oust the existing elites through internal power maneuvers. Co-optation is thus always a risky process for elites, but it is nevertheless often less costly than outright confrontation.

As elites become sophisticated in their power-wielding abilities, they frequently come to realize that overexploitation and overcontrol of nonelites can become seriously counterproductive for their own interests in the long run. In addition to the ever-present threat of rebellion by people who feel that they have nothing to lose but their chains, elites may be severely limiting their own power and benefits by depriving others of needed resources and thus limiting the total amount of benefits available within the system. Two "nonexploitative" strategies often employed by more sophisticated elites are "mass pacification" and "system growth." Mass pacification is aimed primarily at keeping nonelites satisfied with and committed to the existing social order. Rather than expropriating all they can from the masses, elites share resources and benefits with them—to a limited extent. When the masses are dissatisfied with their current economic condition, the elites increase their benefits through higher wages, more welfare services, and so on—as long as the elites can retain ultimate control of the economy. When the masses desire more political influence, the elites establish a legislature and give everyone the vote—as long as the elites can ensure that basic decision-making and policy formation processes remain in their hands. These kinds of partial sharing, if done with adequate publicity, will not only keep the masses satisfied, but may fool most of them into believing that they have achieved real equality with the elites. With this kind of mass satisfaction and support, elites can feel quite secure.

Even more sophisticated, however, is the strategy of intentionally promoting overall system growth by "investing" resources in nonelites. Although at any given moment the amount of power being exerted within a social system is finite, so that elites and nonelites are engaged in a zero-sum contest for power, over time the total amount of resources and power within the system can expand as the size, complexity, and functional effectiveness of the entire system grows. By sacrificing immediate benefits in order to invest resources in the system, elites may likely discover that growth has yielded more returns to them than exploitation ever could. For instance, with an exploitative strategy the elites might be able to acquire four of the five "units of power and privileges" within a small system, but that is about as far as they can go without destroying the total system. However, if they invest even two of those four units back into the system (assuming that this is done with some understanding of the workings of the system), the system might in time increase fourfold to a total of twenty units. The two units retained by the elites would then have grown to eight units, and they would be twice as well off as before. These two strategies of growth promotion and mass pacification are mutually reinforcing, since in a growing system the elites can afford to distribute ever-increasing amounts of benefits to the masses without threatening their own welfare or ultimate control of the system. Lest all this appear highly abstract, we might ask if these processes have not been readily apparent in many societies during the past hundred years as they developed from agricultural to industrial economies.

To summarize this second set of coercive strategies, we can state:

> PRINCIPLE 16: **Elites exert coercion to protect their power-wielding capabilities through the strategies of resource expropriation, entry restriction, co-optation, mass pacification, and growth promotion.**

Power Legitimization.   All of the strategies discussed thus far aid elites in stabilizing their power exertion, shifting it from unpredictable influence to predictable control, utilizing it effectively to attain desired goals, and protecting and expanding it. Nevertheless, with all these strategies the elites are still exerting coercion, or compulsive power derived from others' dependency on them. As a further means of securing, stabilizing, and expanding their power-wielding ability, virtually all elites also attempt to legitimate their powers to supplement or replace coercion with command. To the extent that nonelites trust elites and grant them legitimacy, elites can exercise authority and attraction with which nonelites will voluntarily comply. Indeed, if elites fail to gain adequate legitimacy the total system may undergo a serious "crisis of legitimacy."[47]

The simplest way of gaining legitimacy is merely to wield coercive power over a long period of time—preferably several generations—so that a long-standing tradition of rule becomes established. As succeeding generations grow up knowing nothing else but this one structure of power and hearing it described as "the way things have always been," they will likely accept it unquestioningly and voluntarily grant it legitimacy. This is obviously a slow process, however, and not well suited to the modern world.

The most common technique for gaining legitimacy, attempted by almost all elites, is to create and promote ideas, beliefs, and ideologies that justify their exercise of power. History is replete with ideologies such as "the divine right of kings," "the white man's burden," "the inevitable dialectic of history," "inspired by the spirits," "the will of the people," and "manifest destiny." Regardless of the nature or justification of such beliefs, if nonelites accept them as valid they will likely view elites as attractive and authoritative leaders. Compliance then comes voluntarily and enthusiastically, without any need for coercion.

A third, and more subtle, means of gaining legitimacy is to perform vitally needed services for others. In the course of utilizing and protecting their power, elites will often unintentionally perform necessary social functions such as resolving conflicts, stimulating necessary change, facilitating communication, providing scarce resources, coordinating and manag-

---

[47]Alex Inkeles, "Rising Expectations: Revolution, Evolution, or Devolution?" Arden House Conference 1976, *Freedom and Control in a Democratic Society* (New York: American Council of Life Insurance, 1976), pp. 25–37.

ing collective activities, and promoting social cohesion. To the extent that nonelites notice these actions and value them, they will likely grant legitimacy to elites—at least as long as they continue to perform such functions for the system. As elites become increasingly sophisticated, their understanding of this process may develop to the point where they intentionally seek out and perform needed services—especially those with high visibility—so as to appeal to the masses for legitimacy and support.

These arguments are summarized in the following manner:

PRINCIPLE 17: Elites usually seek to gain legitimacy and thus transform coercion into authority through such techniques as establishing long-standing traditions, creating supporting ideologies, and performing socially useful functions.

CREATING SOCIAL ORDERING

Regardless of the intentions of elites—whether they be to attain personal goals, protect current privileges, gain mass legitimacy, or altruistically serve humanity—they create social ordering as they exercise coercion over others. The process of influencing or controlling social interactions and relationships automatically introduces patterning and regularity into those relationships, thus inevitably creating social ordering. Figure 5-1 depicts this process through which coercion exertion produces social ordering, showing it as a simple feedback system. It begins in the left-hand box with elites possessing superior resources of some kind, either personal (such as intelligence, personal characteristics, wealth) or social (such as control over societal resources, means of violence, or vital functions). With skill, they effectively utilize these resources to perform activities that are desired by others, as determined by the needs and goals of those other actors. This in turn leaves the others dependent on the elites, which enables them to exert force to the extent that nonelites do not oppose them. The resulting coercion (both influence and control) creates social ordering, either intentionally or unintentionally. As patterns of ordering become established, two additional processes occur: (1) through the performance of leadership roles, elites come to exercise functional dominance in the organization, which provides them with further bases for coercing nonelites (especially through meta-power control of the total pattern of social ordering); and (2) as they gain legitimacy, elites are able to supplement or replace coercion with voluntary compliance, thereby further strengthening their ability to wield power throughout the entire organization. Finally, as the entire system operates through time—and especially if it grows in functional effectiveness—sophisticated elites can employ all forms of power to constantly replenish

FIGURE 5-1. Creation of Social Ordering through Coercion Exertion

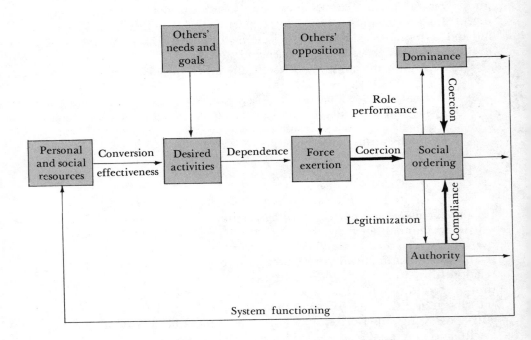

and expand their original resource supply, which perpetuates the cycle through time.

The essence of this thesis is expressed in the following principle:

> PRINCIPLE 18: **Social ordering is created by elites as they exercise various forms of coercion over others in pursuit of their own interests and goals, and the resulting patterns of social ordering enable elites to exert dominance as others become dependent on them and to wield authority as others grant them legitimacy.**

This process of creating social ordering through elite coercion could continue indefinitely if no external factors intruded to alter or upset the cycle. In reality, however, disruptions from the surrounding natural and social environments intrude quite frequently. The ecological theory of social ordering supplements the coercion theory by focusing on several fundamental external pressures acting on all social life.

Ecological Theory

UNLIKE most other theories of social organization, which have intellectual roots in psychology and philosophy, social (or human) ecology grew out of biology. The central concern of both biological and social ecology is the way in which organisms survive in the environment. This theoretical perspective therefore views social organization as an outgrowth of collective efforts by people to adapt to their natural and social environments. Early ecological theory gave heavy emphasis to the problem of meeting basic sustenance needs, but more recently this theory has been broadened to encompass the full range of human activities in contemporary societies. Like coercion theory, the ecological perspective focuses directly on the process of creating social ordering. Social interactions, especially exchange transactions, are assumed to occur, but are not a principal concern. Similarly, cultural norms and values are taken into account as they support and perpetuate patterns of ordering, but are not seen as determinants of social organization. The major contribution of ecology to social theory is its focus on the fundamental role of the environment in shaping social organization, which other theories largely ignore.

The first attempt to develop a general theory of social ecology was by Robert Park, who viewed society as resting on a "sub-social structure" of ecological processes that influence or determine much (though never all) of social life.[48] The most fundamental ecological process, he argued, is competition among organisms (or actors) for scarce resources, with the result that organisms become located in the environment according to their ability to obtain these necessary resources. As unregulated competition moves from the sub-social to the social level of human activities, it becomes transformed into ordered conflict, which in turn gives rise to processes of mutual accommodation and unifying assimilation. Park's distinction between subsocial ecological processes and social ordering has been discarded by contemporary ecologists, who view ecological processes as integral features of social life, although his four concepts of competition, conflict, accommodation, and assimilation are still widely employed. More crucial for later ecologists, however, was his emphasis on space and time as major parameters within which ecological processes occur, which initiated a continuing interest in spatial and temporal aspects of social organization. In recent years most ecological theorists have moved beyond such topics as the "concentric zone" versus "sector" theories of urban spatial patterning, although space and time are still seen as imposing severe limitations on social ordering.

[48] Robert E. Park, *Human Ecology* (Glencoe, Ill.: Free Press, 1952).

Ecological theory makes several basic assumptions about human beings as social actors, the three most important of which are as follows:

1. Every actor must have access—either directly or through other actors—to the environment to obtain resources necessary for survival or other goals. Moreover, actors exert a continual thrust against the environment as they seek to maximize their life conditions and attain desired goals. Because the capability of humans (as opposed to other organisms) to adapt to the environment and obtain needed resources is indeterminant, there are no fixed limits to the size or complexity of social ordering that can result.

2. All actors are inexorably interdependent upon one another for the satisfaction of sustenance and other requirements, so that functional interdependence is the essential foundation of social life. Interdependence takes two basic forms: symbiotic interdependence, based on complementary differences among actors, which produces "corporate" relationships and units (such as a factory); and commensalistic interdependence, based on supplementary similarities, which produces "categoric" relationships and units (such as a social class).

3. In their efforts to satisfy sustenance and other needs, actors must maintain a balance between their collective resource requirements (as determined by their patterns of functional interdependence) and the resource limitations of the natural and social environments. As a result, human beings are inescapably an integral part of the total "web of life" on this planet, which ecologists frequently call the "ecosystem."

SOCIAL ORDERING

Because of their functional interdependence, human beings adapt to the environment through collective activities, rather than through individual behavior. Hence the basic operational unit for all social ordering is a population, or set of individuals engaged in collective activities. Social ordering is therefore an attribute of populations, not of individuals, and the units of analysis for ecological theory are patterns of activities occurring within a population. In their collective efforts to adapt to the environment, populations do two fundamental things: (1) they create patterns of social ordering to regulate and perpetuate their common activities, and (2) they utilize material and social technology (either invented or borrowed from others) to facilitate these collective endeavors. Thus social ordering develops as a population attempts to cope with its environmental conditions by using available technology to obtain necessary resources and attain common goals.

The four major variables of ecological theory are population, ordering (or organization), environment, and technology, which are easily remembered by the acronym "POET." As described by Otis Dudley Duncan and Leo F. Schnore:

> Organization is assumed to be a property of the population that has evolved and is sustained in the process of adaptation of the population to its environment, which may include other populations. Insofar as it is amenable to ecological study, organization tends to be investigated as a ramification of sustenance activities, broadly conceived, which utilize whatever technological apparatus is at the population's disposal or is developed by it. While in its crudest version this framework suggests that organization is to be viewed as the 'dependent variable,' influenced by the other three 'independent variables,' upon a more sophisticated view, organization is seen as reciprocally related to each of the other elements of the ecological complex. In fact, to define any of the elements of this complex adequately, one has to take account of their relationship with organization. [49]

The patterns of social ordering that emerge through this process tend over time to become unified and self-sustaining, with properties of their own that are not dependent on individual members. Because the resulting social organizations are viewed as bounded and integrated whole entities composed of interdependent and interrelated parts, ecological theorists commonly employ the social system model as an analytical framework. In this model, the constituent parts or subsystems are assumed to be functionally differentiated, performing diverse specialized functions for the overall system. Those parts which link the system to its environment and through which it obtains needed resources are called key functionaries. All other parts of the system are dependent on these key functionaries for the resources they need, which gives the key functionaries dominance over them. Key functionaries consequently exercise functional dominance throughout the entire system, influencing or controlling the activities of all other parts that have only indirect links to the environment. Some amount of dominance can also be exerted by many of these other parts, however, in inverse proportion to their distance from the key functionaries. The closer a part is located to the key functionaries, the more likely it is to perform a mediating role as "gatekeeper" or "switcher" within the system, controlling the flow of resources, information, or activities among other system parts. Performance of such a mediating role enables a unit to exert at least limited dominance over other units that depend on it for that function. Power in the form of functional dominance therefore pervades all social systems.

In complex systems, subunits often form along both symbiotic and commensalistic lines. These units in turn become linked into subsystems within the overall system, each of which performs a specialized set of

[49] Otis Dudley Duncan and Leo F. Schnore, "Cultural, Behavioral, and Ecological Perspectives in the Study of Social Organization," *American Journal of Sociology* 65 (September 1959): 132–146.

functions for the system as a whole. In modern societies, argues Paul Mott,[50] the economy is the principal subsystem through which most basic resources are procured from the environment, transformed into needed goods and services, and distributed to the rest of the society. Consequently, the economy becomes the primary key functionary and exercises functional dominance over most other subsystems and subunits in the society. Those actors who control the economy therefore tend to become the "power elites" in contemporary societies, by virtue of their roles within the system and the fact that all other actors are functionally dependent upon them for vital resources. This thesis bears obvious similarities to Marxian theory, providing grounds for convergence between the coercion and ecological theories of social ordering.

A further elaboration of ecological theory proposed by Michael Micklin is the concept of "mechanisms of organizational adaptation."[51] As organizations struggle to cope with impinging population and environmental pressures and to achieve survival and other goals, they tend to develop mechanisms that facilitate those processes. He describes such mechanisms as "organizational structures and processes through which population and/or environmental components are maintained, controlled, or manipulated, resulting in an alteration in survival potential for the system as a whole." Four major classes of adaptive mechanisms are engineering (science and technology), symbolic (ideology and culture), regulatory (political power, policy, and social control), and distributional (mobility of people and resources). Micklin is in effect expanding Mott's thesis, arguing that in complex societies many subsystems in addition to the economy perform crucial specialized functions for the total system. To the extent that the system depends on these functional mechanisms for its survival and operation, the subsystems and actors performing them are each able to exercise functional dominance within their specialized spheres of activity. The patterns of power relationships within the system thus become exceedingly complex. In addition, the concept of adaptive mechanisms also reminds us that social ordering or organization is always a dynamic process consisting of innumerable interrelated activities.

The central theses of ecological theory as an explanation of social ordering can be expressed as a set of three principles:

> **PRINCIPLE 19:** Social ordering emerges as an interdependent population adapts to its environment through the use of technology and other adaptive mechanisms, and survives only as long as it is able to obtain necessary resources from the environment.

[50] Paul E. Mott, *The Organization of Society* (Englewood Cliffs, N.J.: Prentice-Hall, 1965).
[51] Michael Micklin, *Population, Environment, and Social Organization: Current Issues in Human Ecology* (Hinsdale, Ill.: Dryden Press, 1973), pp. 3–19.

PRINCIPLE 20:   Those parts of any social ordering with direct access to the environment become key functionaries capable of exerting dominance over all other parts.

PRINCIPLE 21:   Patterns of social ordering are maintained and enhanced through the use of adaptive mechanisms, the performance of which enables actors to exert dominance within their specialized functional spheres.

SYSTEM CLOSURE

Thus far, ecological theory has said little about the forms or dynamics that patterns of social ordering may display. The concept of closure, or the degree to which system boundaries are open or closed to interchanges with the environment, has provided Amos Hawley with several insights into these phenomena.[52] In a completely open system, all subunits have direct access to the environment in some manner, so that every unit is in effect its own key functionary. (The units must nevertheless still be linked together through relationships of some kind, or else no social ordering would exist.) In a partially closed system, some of the units relate directly to the environment, performing key functionary roles, while others maintain only internal linkages with these key functionaries and are dependent on them for needed resources. In a maximally closed social system, finally, only one subunit interacts with the environment and all other parts are dependent on this single key functionary. (Social systems can never be totally closed to the environment, for they would then have no way of obtaining necessary resources.)

Most real organizations fall somewhere between the extremes of total openness and maximum closure. Hawley postulates, however, that social systems tend to move toward closure as they increase in size and complexity, as a means of achieving unity, stability, and functional effectiveness. He argues that in a relatively closed system

> [o]peration of the several principles mentioned thus far [functional differentiation and interdependence of parts, emergence of key functionaries, exercise of dominance, etc.] moves a system toward a state of closure. This term must be employed here with circumspection, for it cannot have its usual connotation of independence of environment. Closure can only mean that development has terminated in a more or less complete system that is capable of sustaining a given relationship to the environment indefinitely. For closure to be realized, it is required not only that the differentiation of function supportable by the productivity

[52]Amos Hawley, "Human Ecology," in David L. Sills, ed., *The International Encyclopedia of the Social Sciences* (New York: Crowell-Collier and Macmillan, 1968), pp. 328–337.

of the key function has attained its maximum but also that the various functions have been gathered into corporate and categoric subsystems; moreover, the performance of the key function should have been reduced to one unit or to a number of units united in a categoric federation. Then a system is highly selective of its membership and capable of exercising some control over factors that threaten change in the system.[53]

Thus, as a system closes its boundaries and conducts all its transactions with the environment through a few key functionaries, it becomes progressively less vulnerable to external stresses. As a consequence, internal relationships become increasingly crucial for the system.

In a relatively closed system with a limited number of dominant key functionaries—whether they be located in the economy or religion or scientific research or any other sector—the manner in which these actors perform their roles becomes crucial for the welfare of the total system. The more efficiently key functionaries perform their roles, the greater the quantity and quality of resources available to the system. This in turn permits the development of greater functional differentiation among system parts, more adequate overall system coordination, and more effective collective goal attainment. If the key functionaries fail to procure sufficient resources or misuse their dominance, however, the entire system will suffer and may be radically altered or even destroyed. Moreover, even partial boundary closure poses a serious problem of power distribution for all social systems. With closure comes increasing internal functional differentiation of parts, dependence of those parts on one another and the key functionaries, and concentration of dominance in the hands of a small number of parts or actors. A few key functionaries control the entire flow of resources and can wield power throughout the system. At the same time, they become functionally indispensable because of the coordination and regulation they provide for this complex system. The system thus experiences growing power centralization, which may improve its operational effectiveness but simultaneously leaves it highly vulnerable to internal strains and disruptions.

Because the crucial factors of environment, population, and technology are never static, all systems are constantly subject to disruptions and change, either continual or sporadic. Relatively open systems, with many direct ties to the environment, tend to experience frequent and extensive changes, and therefore lack stability. As systems approach closure, they are able to acquire considerable control over the processes of change, but they can never avoid it. In a relatively closed system all changes would be mediated through a few key functionaries and would then affect other parts in successive steps according to their degree of removal from these dominant units. Cumulative change, or growth, of a system in both size and complexity depends on the

[53] Ibid.

ability of its key functionaries to obtain, process, and distribute vital resources. Therefore, the greater the number of efficient key functionaries, the more opportunities a system has for growth. Rapidly expanding systems tend initially to maintain fairly open boundaries, since a relatively closed system has severely limited growth possibilities. Sooner or later, however, the system faces a crucial dilemma. If it is to gain control over its environmental transactions, coordinate its internal activities, and attain unity and stability, it must move in the direction of closure—at the price of continued rapid growth. Hawley views this movement toward closure in developing systems as inevitable, despite the fact that it decreases their possibilities for further growth. Conceivably, however, a system could elect to remain open and growing while sacrificing a certain amount of stability, unity, and perhaps collective goal attainment.

Real social organizations, existing in a constantly shifting environment, rarely, if ever, achieve the state of maximum closure envisioned in Hawley's theory, so that growth need never entirely cease. Ideally, therefore, all social organizations should seek that compromise between openness and closure which best suits the needs and interests of their individual members and the organization as a whole. In the real world of constantly changing environmental, population, and technological pressures, however, this optimum balance point never remains fixed for long. Hence all organizations must continually grapple with the problem of closure in response to both external stresses and internal strains.

The central ideas of Hawley's thesis of system closure are summarized in the following two statements:

> PRINCIPLE 22: As a social system increases in size and complexity, it tends to move toward closure from the environment, giving it more control over its environmental transactions and greater internal unity and stability, while also increasing the functional dominance of the remaining key functionaries.

> PRINCIPLE 23: Growth of a social system requires expanding productivity by key functionaries, which tends to keep the system relatively open, but as the system eventually moves toward closure its rate of change and growth declines while internal problems of coordination become paramount.

Theoretical Convergence

THE coercion and ecological theories of social ordering have radically different intellectual origins in Marx's critique of capitalistic society versus Park's conception of the biological "web of life." Contemporary theorists recognize that these two theories share numerous common themes, while still retaining their separate intellectual identities, so that they complement but do not duplicate each other's central thrusts.[54] Several of these commonalities and complementarities are briefly mentioned in this concluding section.

COMMONALITIES

1. *Social ordering.* Both theories focus directly on social ordering as the core of all social organization, assuming the prior existence of social interaction and treating shared culture as an outgrowth of social ordering.
2. *Social power.* Both theories treat social power exertion as the basic medium through which all social ordering occurs. In both cases, moreover, the emphasis is on compulsive power resulting from interdependence among actors, not compliant power based on shared trust or legitimacy.
3. *Powerful actors.* Both theories view power as unequally distributed, with the more powerful actors—elites and key functionaries—influencing or controlling patterns of social ordering and most activities within them.
4. *Structural hierarchy.* Both theories assume that social ordering normally displays a hierarchical pattern, with elites or key functionaries occupying positions at the apex of the structure and other actors exercising diminishing amounts of power according to their distance from the apex.
5. *Power centers.* Both theories allow for multiple centers or hierarchies of power within complex social ordering. In coercion theory this occurs through the development of specialized strategic elites, while in ecological theory it occurs to the extent that system boundaries remain open.

COMPLEMENTARITIES

1. *Origin of social ordering.* Coercion theory views social ordering as imposed upon people by powerful elites, whereas ecological theory sees social ordering as a collective response by a population of people to their environment. Both processes undoubtedly occur, but under differing circumstances and at different times.
2. *Force versus dominance.* Coercion theory stresses primarily the exercise of force for purposes of direct control, while ecological theory stresses the exertion of dominance in the form of indirect

---

[54] Several of these trends are discussed by various authors in Burns and Buckley, *Power and Control.*

control. Although each theory also takes account of the other form of power, it is assumed to be derived from the more fundamental form stressed by that theory.

3. *Power exertion.* Coercion theory argues that elites create social ordering by purposefully exerting pressures on others in pursuit of their own goals. In contrast, ecological theory proposes that key functionaries shape social ordering by exercising dominance unintentionally through the performance of their normal activities. In reality, both processes undoubtedly transpire simultaneously or in combination.

4. *Analytical model.* Ecological theory makes explicit and extensive use of the social system model for analyzing social ordering. Coercion theory does not explicitly utilize the system model, but rather emphasizes the relative functional and structural autonomy of component units. This difference is easily reconciled, however, by designing a system model in which the parts have considerable (but not total) autonomy to seek their own goals and develop their own patterns of ordering.

5. *Principal tendency.* As a result of their differing analytical models, the two theories postulate the existence of opposing tendencies within social ordering. Whereas ecological theory assumes that social systems tend to move toward increased closure and unity, coercion theory assumes that the units comprising any pattern of social ordering tend to move toward greater divergence and autonomy. Again, however, a system model that allows for partial autonomy of constituent parts can bridge this discrepancy if both tendencies are treated as empirical possibilities rather than theoretical assumptions.

6. *Power bases.* The reasoning underlying ecological theory can become circular, in that closure and unity are assumed to occur as a few key functionaries become more effective in their activities and hence more powerful, while simultaneously attributing the existence and power of these key functionaries to the fact that the system is already relatively closed and therefore by definition contains only a few positions from which dominance can be exerted. This potential circularity can be avoided, however, by taking account of the many other possible bases of power suggested by coercion theory, so that functional dominance is seen as an outgrowth of social ordering created by the exercise of force.

In sum, *coercion and ecological theory converge in the thesis that social ordering is largely created through the exercise of social power by sets of elites or key functionaries.* The resulting patterns of social ordering can then be viewed as partially unified social systems that may move toward either greater divergence or increased unity. Ecological theory, meanwhile, reminds us that social ordering is always a collective process heavily constrained by the natural environment, while coercion theory emphasizes the purposeful use of power by actors in pursuit of their own goals. Both theories also allow for the transformation of force and dominance, based on interdependence, into authority based on trust and legitimacy. For a more thorough explanation of that process we must turn in the next chapter to cultural theories of social organization.

RECOMMENDED READING

Anderson, Charles H. *The Political Economy of Social Class*. Englewood Cliffs, N.J.: Prentice-Hall, 1974.
> A comprehensive presentation of Marxian theory as applied to modern societies.

Bottomore, T. B. *Elites and Society*. New York: Basic Books, 1964, chaps. 1–3.
> Summarizes, contrasts, and compares the main ideas of Marx, the elitist theorists, and C. Wright Mills, and suggests numerous questions for further work in this area.

Dahrendorf, Ralf. *Class and Class Conflict in Industrial Society*. Stanford, Calif.: Stanford University Press, 1959, chap. 5.
> Sketches and then elaborates a "coercion-conflict" model of social organization, centering on the distribution of authority.

Duncan, Otis Dudley. "Social Organization and the Ecosystem." In Robert E. L. Faris, ed., *Handbook of Modern Sociology*. Skokie, Ill.: Rand McNally, 1964, pp. 36–82.
> Extensively discusses the bearing of ecological considerations on the study of social organization, with particular reference to social evolution.

————, and Leo F. Schnore. "Cultural, Behavioral and Ecological Perspectives in the Study of Social Organization." *American Journal of Sociology* 65 (September 1959): 132–146. (Also Bobbs-Merrill reprint S-75.)
> A brief presentation of the fundamental ideas of ecological theory, in comparison with two other theoretical perspectives.

Hall, Richard H. *Organizations: Structure and Process*. Englewood Cliffs, N.J.: Prentice-Hall, 1972, chaps. 4–6.
> Summarizes the existing theoretical and empirical work on the three dimensions of size, complexity, and formalization of social ordering.

Hawley, Amos. "Human Ecology." *The International Encyclopedia of the Social Sciences*, David L. Sills, ed. New York: Crowell-Collier and Macmillan, 1968, pp. 328–337.
> Summarizes the main ideas of ecological theory, and then expands and generalizes this approach to all social organizations.

Klapp, Orrin. *Models of Social Order*. Palo Alto, Calif.: Mayfield, 1973.
> Examines various theoretical perspectives on social order in contemporary sociology.

Michels, Robert. *Political Parties*, trans. by Eden and Cedar Paul. New York: Free Press, 1966, pts. 1, 2, and 6.
> The classic argument for the inevitability of oligarchy in all organizations.

Micklin, Michael. "A Framework for the Study of Human Ecology." In his *Population, Environment, and Social Organization*. Hinsdale, Ill.: Dryden Press, 1973, pp. 3–19.
> An introductory essay to a collection of articles on ecological theory, stressing social processes through which ecological demands are satisfied.

Mosca, Gaetano. *The Ruling Class*, ed. by Arthur Livingston, trans. by Hannah D. Kahn. New York: McGraw-Hill, 1939, chaps. 2, 3, 5, 15.
> The most forthright statement in sociological literature of an elitist theory of social organization.

Mott, Paul. *The Organization of Society*. Englewood Cliffs, N.J.: Prentice-Hall, 1965, chap. 3.
> An introductory explanation of ecological theory, using thirteen basic propositions concerning social organization.

Nadel, S. F. *The Theory of Social Structure*. New York: Free Press, 1957, chaps. 1, 6, 7.
> A theoretical discussion of social structure, as seen from a process viewpoint.

Olsen, Marvin E. *Power in Societies*. New York: Macmillan Co., 1970.
> A series of essays on power as a social process, plus a collection of the major theoretical writings on social power and the coercive theoretical perspective.

Zeitlin, Irving M. *Marxism: A Re-Examination*. Princeton, N.J.: D. Van Nostrand, 1967.
> Reexamines Marx's ideas for their relevance to sociological theory, treating Marxism as an analytical perspective rather than a historical imperative.

6

Cultural Processes and Theories

WE have seen that interaction creates social relationships that through time become patterned into various forms of social ordering. The process of social organization does not end with the creation of social order, however. Unlike most other forms of life, humans are able to construct abstract symbols and ideas, manipulate them through cognitive processes, and communicate them to others. We can therefore assign meanings to our actions and share these meanings with other people. These shared meanings in turn influence and shape all social interaction and social ordering. The emergence of culture—or sets of shared symbolized ideas that give meaning to social life—thus adds a crucial further dimension to human social organization and accounts for many of its unique qualities.

Culture

HUMAN culture is dependent on our ability to symbolize, or create and use abstract symbols to represent more concrete objects, actions, and events. Rather than reacting to stimuli with conditioned responses, we normally create symbols that give meaning to everything happening around us, and then respond to these meanings instead of the immediate stimuli. Similarly, we assign meanings to our own actions and to those of others with whom we interact, so that virtually all social interactions and relationships become infused with symbolized meanings. Participants in collective social activities constantly communicate these meanings to one another, exchanging ideas, expressing attitudes and values, and generating common expectations for relationships. To participate fully in any social organization, therefore, one not only must engage in patterned social relationships but must also learn the symbolized meanings associated with that social ordering. This does not mean that all members of any organization necessarily think alike, but it is highly likely that over time these participants will come to share a body of common ideas, or culture. Each instance of social organization is thus infused with a set of cultural ideas and meanings, some of which are unique to it and some of which are held in common with other organizations. The process of social organization involves both the establishment of social order and the creation of an associated culture.

THE CONCEPT OF CULTURE

Culture is one of the most widely used concepts in the social sciences, and has been defined in many different ways. Originating in anthropological studies of primitive societies, this concept initially referred to the total "way of life" of a society—including everything from weapons to family forms to religious beliefs. Early sociologists borrowed this anthropological conception of culture as a convenient means of describing all nonbiological, or "superorganic," aspects of human life, and rather indiscriminately applied it to behavioral, social, and symbolic phenomena. As a consequence, the terms "social organization," "social order," and "culture" came to be used almost interchangeably in sociological literature.

In recent years, however, most social scientists have begun to differentiate between the social and cultural levels of analysis.[1] The contemporary, more restricted concept of culture refers only to a body of ideas shared by the participants comprising a delineated collectivity. Social ordering and culture are thus distinct but integral aspects of the total process of social organization. Expressed formally, *a culture is a relatively unified set of shared symbolic ideas associated with one or more patterns of social ordering within the process of social organization.* This definition does not specify the kinds of ideas contained within any culture, how consistent they are with one another, or how closely they reflect the accompanying social ordering. These are all problematic questions for empirical investigation.

A subtle but vital distinction must be drawn between cultural ideas and

---

[1]A. L. Kroeber and Talcott Parsons, "The Concepts of Culture and of Social Sytems," *American Sociological Review* 23 (October 1958): 582–583.

specific actions or objects. It is not uncommon for social scientists to mix these usages, as in speaking of the cultural trait of gift giving. Usually they do this merely for convenience of expression, but it confuses the cultural idea that one ought to give gifts on certain occasions with the social interactions through which the gifts are actually exchanged and with the material objects involved. This particular instance of social interaction might be a direct outgrowth of a cultural norm requiring gift giving, and the giver might hope that the gift will serve as a token of concern for the other person, but the cultural idea is not identical with either the interaction or the object that embodies it. Nevertheless, virtually all social actions and many material objects are infused with cultural meanings. If a person kills someone under one set of circumstances, the act is culturally defined as murder and the killer is severely punished. But if the same act is performed under a different set of conditions, the killer is honored as a hero. Similarly, we go to archeological museums to view the artifacts of ancient civilizations (or to museums of science and industry to view our own artifacts), but the beads and pottery (or computers and rockets) we examine there have no meaning to us unless we understand the cultural ideas they represent. In short, social actions and material objects often symbolize shared cultural ideas, while culture gives meaning to both actions and objects.

Cultural ideas tend to be clustered into relatively consistent and unified sets associated with particular patterns of social ordering. Thus each instance of social organization possesses a distinctive culture of its own. To the extent that organizations are overlapping and interrelated, their cultures will contain many shared ideas, so that few cultures are entirely unique. The culture of a particular family, for instance, may incorporate ideas derived from the cultures of its community, its church, various associations to which its members belong, and the total society. Nevertheless, that family's culture will also possess a few ideas peculiar to it, including particular customs, traditions, values, and expectations concerning its members' actions. Consequently, despite many surface similarities among all families in a society, subtle differences in their cultures may produce numerous discrepancies in their daily patterns of living.

Within any given culture it is often possible to identify one or more subcultures, or sets of ideas derived from the encompassing culture but differing from it in various respects. Thus within the culture of the United States as a whole we can identify various community, ethnic, regional, class, and other subcultures. Despite the obvious peculiarities of subcultures, however, they are constantly affected by the encompassing larger culture. On first glance, the values of a juvenile gang practicing car theft might appear to be in direct contradiction to those of the rest of the society. But closer inspection will likely reveal that the gang is stealing as a means of attaining the goals of monetary success and peer prestige that have been acquired from the societal culture. Hence to understand this activity we must discover the ways in which the gang subculture is linked into the broader societal culture and other subcultures. A societal culture normally dominates all subcultures within it, so that smaller organizations have only limited freedom in selecting, modifying, arranging, or rejecting ideas from their encompassing society. Subcultures that become too divergent from the larger societal culture are frequently labeled "deviant," and efforts are made to change, restrict, or destroy them so as to maintain the stability and unity of the total society.

In contrast, societal cultures often differ radically, especially if these societies are relatively isolated from each other. One society's greatest virtue is another society's worst sin. In the United States we look with abhorrence upon parents who coldly murder their own children, but in other societies infanticide and religious sacrifices of children have been praised as the highest tribute that parents could offer to the common welfare or the pleasure of the gods. Any particular cultural idea—but especially basic social values—can be understood and analyzed only in relation to the entire cultural and social setting in which it exists. Ethnocentrism, or judging another culture's ideas by one's own values, is a devastating destroyer of objective sociological analysis.

THE EMERGENCE OF CULTURE

As patterns of social ordering develop from interactions among social actors, they in turn give rise to shared sets of cultural ideas that symbolize, reflect, and give meaning to this social order. Thus *culture emerges from collective social activities*. The growth of capitalism as a form of economic ordering led to the creation of a "business ideology" and laissez-faire philosophies of government; mounting use of automobiles prompted the writing of legal traffic codes; and a widespread shift from rural to urban living has led people to view large families as economic liabilities rather than assets. Although numerous discrepancies often exist between cultural ideas and social practices, these differences cannot become too great without imposing severe strains and conflicts on both the patterns of social ordering and their accompanying cultures. As a consequence of the emergence of cultural ideas from collective social life, patterns of social ordering gain cohesion, stability through time, and operational effectiveness. Moreover, just as emergent patterns of social ordering display properties not inherent in their constituent members and possess a unity greater than the sum of their component parts, so also are emergent sets of cultural ideas real phenomena that can exist apart from the social orders in which they are created and the individual personalities that transmit them.

The partial independence of culture from social ordering is demonstrated in several ways. First, cultural ideas frequently survive, at least in libraries and museums if not in people's memories, long after the society that generated them has ceased to exist. The cultures of ancient Greece and Egypt, for instance, are well known to historians today. Second, cultures may remain virtually unchanged over time, despite drastic alterations in the underlying patterns of social ordering. The ideal of monogamous marriage is as prevalent today as it was two hundred years ago, despite the many changes in family living introduced by industrialization and urbanization. Third, cultural ideas developed in one society may spread to all corners of the globe, as illustrated by Roman legal principles or English and American concepts of democracy. Fourth, and most important, cultural values, beliefs, and other ideas continually influence the social ordering from which they emerged. Patterns of social ordering—as well as the personalities of individual participants—are constantly shaped, constrained, and changed by their associated cultures. A prominent example of this is the current attempt in the United States to resolve the "American dilemma" by bringing interracial practices into accord with the cultural value of human equality. Another example is the translation of the goal of "promoting the general welfare" into specific programs to combat poverty, disease, and ignorance.

Despite this partial autonomy of cultural ideas, patterns of social ordering and their attendant cultures always thoroughly interpenetrate each other. All organized human life has both social and cultural components. Although it is often useful to separate these realms for scientific analysis, this procedure unavoidably distorts the total process of social organization. Cultural ideas divorced from ongoing social relationships—such as the religious beliefs of the ancient Aztecs—are of no direct relevance for existing social life. Similarly, social ordering without associated cultural ideas remains rudimentary, as in the mating and herding patterns of many animals. In short, *all human social organization is infused with cultural ideas, so that social ordering and culture each extensively influence the other.* The process of social organization invariably incorporates both the ordering of social relationships and the creation of associated cultural ideas.

THE COMPONENTS OF CULTURE

Any kind of idea—from knowledge of fire making to existential philosophy—can be included within a culture. Not all cultural ideas are directly incorporated into the process of social organization, however. Although such cultural ideas as language, scientific knowledge, literature, philosophy, and aesthetics may extensively influence social life, they remain external to social organization. In contrast, other types of cultural ideas are integral parts of this process, becoming infused into patterns of social ordering and internalized into the personalities of the participating actors. These cultural components of social organization can be classified into the three categories of postulates, ends, and means. Within each of these categories, some ideas are imbued with moral connotations or imperatives, others are viewed in a relatively neutral or expedient light, and still others are more or less direct guides to action.

Postulates. In all cultures, some ideas are accepted with little or no questioning as "the way things are." These shared assumptions are seen not as ends to be sought or as means to those ends, but rather as given "facts of life." The most fundamental postulate in any culture is its *Weltanschauung,* or "world view," which describes the purpose or nature of life as a whole. For instance, the Weltanschauung of a relatively traditional society might hold that the basic structure of social life is preordained by the gods in a fixed pattern, and that the duty of humanity is to perpetuate this pattern through time as faithfully as possible. A more scientifically oriented society, meanwhile, might see social life as an intricate mosaic of dynamic activities which humanity struggles to control in the pursuit of "progress." A Weltanschauung is thus heavily infused with moral imperatives, of either a sacred (religious) or secular (humanistic) nature.

Whereas a Weltanschauung simply describes the nature of existence, the *social philosophy* prevailing in a culture or subculture explains why things are the way they are. Since a social philosophy is a construct of human intelligence, it is not necessarily viewed as a moral imperative, but neverthe-less it is commonly accepted—at least for a period of time—as a basic postulate of social life. In medieval Europe, the philosophy of scholasticism explained the feudal order as God's divine scheme for coping with "wordly evils" and preparing individuals to enter the paradise of heaven. The industrial era gave birth to the philosophy of social Darwinism, which asserted that life is a constant competitive struggle for survival in which those who are most capable and work the hardest will achieve success and further the cause of social progress. Contemporary "postindustrial" socie-ties, meanwhile, are witnessing the emergence of a social welfare philosophy which juxtaposes the twin ideas that technological and economic growth benefit mankind and that the collective welfare is best served by providing everyone with a minimum standard of living.

Social philosophies rest on, and are justified by, *social beliefs* concern-ing the nature of humanity and social life. A belief is more specific in content than a broad philosophy, but is still viewed by those who hold it as a given postulate of human life. In themselves, social beliefs are morally neutral, although people often assign morality to them and utilize them as guide-lines for social actions that have profound ethical and social consequences.

Of crucial importance in the contemporary world, for instance, are the widely held beliefs that a child's biological parents are normally the persons best suited to rear him or her, that most individuals are capable of judging right from wrong and can be held accountable for their actions, that persons with light skins are superior to those with dark skins, that competition between economic firms keeps prices down, and that individuals' thinking and behavior can be affected by mass media messages. Beliefs such as these may be logical or illogical, scientifically accurate or inaccurate, naive or sophisticated. But in all cases, to the extent that people accept such beliefs as true statements about the nature of humanity and social life, their effects on social organization can be immense.

Ends. All cultures contain numerous ideas about the ends to be sought in organized social life. These collective concerns differ from postulates in that they are not accepted as inherent in the nature of things, but rather are chosen by people as their desired objectives in life. *Social values,* the most basic of these cultural ends, are shared conceptions of what is most desirable in social life. That is, they express collective views of what is good or bad, important or unimportant, and commendable or deplorable in regard to both individual actions and social organization. Shared social values, unlike people's personal values, are held in common by many (but not necessarily all) participants in an organization, are identified with that organization, and become incorporated into the patterns of social ordering comprising that organization. Although values rarely determine the exact nature of any social ordering, they broadly shape patterns of activity occurring in an organization. If industrial growth is highly valued in a society, for instance, we would expect to find strong economic and political pressures for full exploitation of natural resources and little concern with preserving the natural environment against pollution. A more traditionally oriented society, in contrast, might stress the importance of preserving historical landmarks, maintaining folk customs, and living in balance with the natural environment. As these examples suggest, social values are commonly infused with a considerable degree of moral "oughtness."

The central core of any culture consists of a set of basic values that differentiate it from all other cultures. As an illustration, consider James Vander Zanden's suggested list of the principal value configuration in American culture, which he adapted from Robin Williams:

> 1. Materialism. Americans are prone to evaluate things in material and monetary terms. . . . We tend to get quite excited about things as opposed to ideas, people, and aesthetic creations.
> 2. Success. . . . Part of the American faith is that "There is always another chance" and that "If at first you do not succeed, try, try

again." If we ourselves cannot succeed, then we have the prospect for vicarious achievement through our children.

3. Work and Activity. . . . Work and activity are exalted in their own right; they are not merely means by which success may be realized; in and of themselves they are valued as worthwhile.

4. Progress. A belief in the perfectibility of society, man, and the world has been a kind of driving force in American history. . . . Americans tend to equate "the new" with "the best."

5. Rationality. Americans almost universally place faith in the rational approach to life. We continuously search out more "reasonable," "time saving," and "effort-saving" ways of doing things.

6. Democracy. "Democracy" has become almost synonymous with "the American way of life.". . . We extol the Declaration of Independence with its insistence that "all men are created equal" and "governments [derive] their just power from the consent of the governed."

7. Humanitarianism. . . . Philanthropy and voluntary charity have been a characteristic note of America. More recently, more attention has been given to numerous programs for social welfare, with government playing an active role.[2]

Following Karl Mannheim, sociologists frequently categorize values as either ideological or utopian in nature.[3] Ideologies are sets of values that explain, justify, and support existing social arrangements, such as the idea of the separation of church and state, or the American business creed of "rugged individualism." Utopias are sets of values that evaluate, criticize, and change existing social orders, such as the ideas of racial equality or political democracy. Over time, a value that once served as a utopia for social change frequently becomes an established ideology supporting the status quo.

Unlike values, *social interests* carry no implications of morality or oughtness, and are not usually as widely shared among the participants in a social organization. Interests typically express the more immediate, pragmatic concerns of a group of people in regard to a shared social condition. Any organization taken as whole may hold some collective interests, as in the concern of a labor union for the economic welfare of its members, or a family's concern with maintaining its internal harmony. At the same time, however, it is quite common for subgroups and subcultures within an organization to express differing and often contradictory interests. To continue the above examples, the leaders of a union might decide that higher wages would best serve the members's needs, while the workers in a

[2] James W. Vander Zanden, *Sociology: A Systematic Approach* (New York: Ronald Press, 1965), pp. 67–69. Robin Williams, *American Society: A Sociological Interpretation*, 3rd ed. (New York: Alfred A. Knopf, 1970).
[3] Karl Mannheim, *Ideology and Utopia* (New York: Harcourt, Brace & World, 1936).

particular factory might be more concerned with achieving greater job security. In a family, meanwhile, the parents might give highest priority to obedience from children, whereas the children might be interested principally in minimizing their assigned family chores. As suggested by these illustrations, differing interests between organizations and among various parts of an organization often generate social conflict, which in turn leads to the exercise of power as actors seek to defend their particular concerns.

Common interests are frequently expressed in terms of *shared goals* for collective action. The members of a sports team work together to achieve the goal of winning a game; a civil rights association pushes for elimination of discriminatory hiring practices; a business attempts to increase its share of a product market; and proponents of legalized abortion struggle to have their goal enacted into national legislation. When subgroups and subcultures within an organization hold divergent interests, however, they may likely seek different and possibly conflicting goals, with resulting internal competition and strain. Because it is often easier to achieve compromises among specific goals than among more general interests, goal conflicts tend on the whole to be less divisive within and between organizations than are basic conflicts of interest. Within this broad category of cultural ends, moral values are generally the most pervasive and strongly held concerns, pragmatic interests are broad in scope but more adaptable to changing conditions, while action goals apply to specific situations and can shift fairly flexibly. Thus a basic societal value might assert that education is desirable for all, a school system might be interested in educating its pupils in the best manner possible, and a particular high school might hold the goal of sending all its graduates on to college.

Means. This third broad category of cultural ideas with direct relevance for social organization consists of prescriptions and proscriptions concerning the means of attaining cultural ends. These collective standards are shared agreements regarding acceptable and unacceptable social actions to which actors are expected to adhere in their interactions and relationships. Standards that imply some degree of moral "oughtness" and that are observed because they are "the right thing to do" are called *norms.* Compliance with norms is viewed as morally or ethically right, while noncompliance is not merely improper but wrong. The norms of middle-class American society, for example, hold that it is wrong to steal or to directly insult people or to purposefully keep others waiting, and that it is right to thank a person who does something for you, to carry out assigned responsibilities, and to respect private property belonging to others. Norms vary extensively in the importance people attach to them and the rigor with which they are enforced. Sociologists sometimes use the term "folkways" to refer to norms that specify appropriate but not mandatory actions which are enforced interpersonally rather then through organized collective action. Transitory fads and fashions, routine manners, prevailing customs, and established traditions are forms of folkways found in all cultures. In contrast, "mores" are norms that are believed to be vital for the collective welfare of a society or other organization and which are enforced by specially designated agents of that organization. Religious commandments, the incest taboo, military codes of honor, and civil bills of rights are typical examples of strongly held mores.

Standards that carry no moral or ethical connotations are called *rules*. They are more or less purposefully and rationally established as means of coordinating social activities, preventing disruptions in normal patterns of action, or attaining common goals. They are usually followed purely for reasons of expediency, because they facilitate collective social life and enable people to avoid unnecessary problems and conflicts. To play chess, one must abide by the accepted rules of the game; to receive unemployment compensation, one must meet certain criteria set by the state; to keep highway traffic moving smoothly, cars must normally remain on the right-hand side of the road; to graduate from college, one must maintain at least a C average; to vote in elections in the United States, one must be a citizen of the country. Like norms, rules also vary widely in the extent to which conformity is expected and compliance is enforced. Violation of some rules may evoke no more than mild verbal criticism, whereas other violations may lead to a jail sentence. In all cases, however, compliance with social rules is essentially a matter of habit or expedience, not moral compulsion.

The distinction between norms and rules is useful analytically, for it enables an observer to determine why people are observing particular standards and how likely these standards are to change with new circumstances. In reality, however, the distinction can easily become quite blurred, since rules have a tendency to shift into norms over time as people come to accept long-standing rules as "the way things ought to be done." Moreover, both norms and rules can be codified into laws and enforced by the state, although in most societies the majority of folkways never become laws. The norms and rules that people view as crucial to their way of life are most likely to be made into laws, but there is no necessary linkage between the social importance of a standard and its legal status. Adding the legal weight of the state to cultural standards does tend to obliterate the moral-expedient distinction between norms and rules, however. A final complication in this situation arises from the fact that considerable disparity frequently exists between the ideals expressed by both norms and rules and in the ways people actually behave. A basic value may state "Love thy neighbor as thyself;" the accepted norm may be "Treat your neighbor in a polite and civil manner;"

the prevailing rule may be "Respect your neighbor's property and privacy;" but one's daily activities might include throwing stones through his windows because of his race or gossiping about the late hours he keeps.

Also included within this category of cultural means is *social technology*, or knowledge about how to establish, operate, and maintain social organization. By itself, social technology is totally pragmatic with no moral overtones, although the social processes and forms to which it gives rise frequently come to be seen by their participants as the only acceptable way of doing things. Examples of modern social technology include knowledge about managing a monetary system, procedures for operating a mayor-council form of city government, techniques of conducting a jury trial, and the idea of a continuous-flow assembly line. Most of humanity's present store of social technology has been accumulated through a long process of experimentation, although very slowly we are learning to transform the theories and findings of social science into applied social engineering. Technological knowledge about the process of social organization, like material technology relevant to the physical world, tends to accumulate at a continually increasing rate. The more knowledge a society has, the more likely it is to acquire new information through research and innovation. At the present time, nevertheless, numerous social problems are caused by the fact that our stockpile of material technology is growing considerably faster than our social technology. We know how to blow up the world with nuclear weapons, but not how to create international organizations capable of preventing nuclear war.

Among all these diverse cultural components, values and norms have been the principal foci of attention within cultural theories of social organization. Because both values and norms carry strong moral connotations, "cultural consensus" theorists have tended to place much emphasis on moral imperatives, expectations, and obligations as the bases of all social organization. Earlier theorists typically gave principal attention to social norms, while contemporary theorists commonly view shared social values as the source of norms and the foundation of social organization. Hence a useful distinction can be drawn between normative and valuative perspectives on the creation of social organization.

Normative Theory

THIS older theoretical perspective sees social organization as an outgrowth of common norms that constitute moral directives and imperatives for the conduct of collective social life. Patterning, regularity, and predictability in social ordering are the result of an underlying normative consensus concerning proper ways of behaving in various situations. Through a lifelong process of socialization, individuals learn and internalize the norms of their culture and subcultures, so that most of the time they comply voluntarily with these normative expectations. Sometimes, however, it is necessary to apply external pressure or sanctions on people to ensure that their behavior is in line with the prevailing norms. For individuals, this theoretical perspective is relatively deterministic, since most people have only limited room for innovative action. Social stability, unity, and effective collective action are the main concerns of normative theory, not individual autonomy.

The two foremost architects of this theoretical perspective were Émile Durkheim and William Graham Sumner, but it has ancient roots in philosophy and also claims many contemporary adherents. The following discussions of the formation, morality, differentiation, change, and functions of norms are based primarily on the writings of Durkheim and Sumner, although most other normative theorists would probably agree with the majority of these arguments.

FORMATION OF NORMS

In a fundamental sense, this normative perspective rests on an ecological foundation, since the basic requirement of all social life is seen to be survival and the satisfaction of individual and collective needs in a demanding and often hostile environment. To survive, individuals must find ways of collectively meeting their basic needs for food, shelter, protection, and so on, while societies and other organizations must devise procedures for collectively dealing with such problems as increasing population, division of labor, conflict over scarce resources, and stabilization of leadership. In Sumner's words: "The first task of life is to live. Men begin with acts, not thought."[4] Through a long process of trial and error, some kinds of collective activities prove to be beneficial while others do not. As people discover beneficial patterns of acting and solutions to common problems, they tend to repeat them, to symbolize them, and to communicate these ideas to others. Over time, people who continually interact with one another therefore come to share the idea that "these are the ways things should be done." "The operation by which folkways are produced," wrote Sumner, "consists of the frequent repetition of petty acts, often by great numbers acting in concert."[5] Norms are thus symbolic outgrowths of humanity's collective struggle for existence, reflecting common experiences.

This process of norm formation is not usually a purposeful or rational endeavor, but rather emerges spontaneously out of shared social life. Sumner

---

[4] William Graham Sumner, *Folkways* (New York: Ginn, 1940), p. 18.
[5] Ibid.

maintained, in fact, that folkways are never established intentionally, although contemporary normative theorists argue that purposefully created social rules can develop into moral norms through time. Sumner also argued that because people are often unable to think or act rationally, the folkways commonly become infused with magical beliefs, inaccurate ideas, and "false philosophies." As a consequence, the folkways do not always reflect the most effective ways of satisfying either individual or collective needs, which can lead to serious social problems.

The customs, folkways, and other norms that emerge through this process tend to become dissociated from the specific situations in which they first arose, and are slowly generalized to cover broad areas of collective activity. They take on the character of autonomous social forces directing and regulating organized social life, and constitute the core elements of a societal or other culture. As such, norms are seen by those persons subject to them as existing outside of oneself, and as binding on one's actions. They are no longer just useful suggestions of how one might act, but moral directives or imperatives defining how one must act in given situations. Adherence to most norms is not left to individual discretion, but is a social obligation enforced by collective sanctions when necessary. To the extent that norms become internalized within personalities, however, compliance becomes largely voluntary and the necessity for external sanctioning decreases. Consequently, although the origins of norms soon become lost in history, people continue to believe in them and abide by them as a result of lifelong socialization and the weight of tradition.

The crucial theme in this argument is that norm formation results from collective—not individual—responses to a common environment and common problems of living. Cultural norms arise within the process of social organization, but over time come to regulate and direct all organized social life. As expressed by Sumner: "Folkways are . . . the customs of the society, which arise from men's efforts to satisfy their needs. . . . Then they become regulative for succeeding generations and take on the character of a social force."[6] To state this thesis more succinctly:

> PRINCIPLE 24:   Cultural norms emerge as people develop and symbolize ways of collectively coping with common life conditions, but through time the norms become dissociated from their origins and are seen as broad moral imperatives for the conduct of organized social life.

MORALITY OF NORMS

Norms derive their ability to direct social life from the fact that they are imbued with a sense of morality rather than sheer pragmatism, so

---

[6] Ibid., p. v.

that people feel compelled to abide by them. How do norms acquire these moral overtones? This was a crucial question for Durkheim, who believed that shared conceptions of morality constitute the fundamental basis of all social unity. "Durkheim's writings are shot through with a sense of the significance of shared convictions and commitments. The notions of 'collective representations' and the 'collective conscience' recur throughout his work. . . . The social and the moral become inextricably intertwined."[7]

Durkheim's answer to the question of the origin of social morality within a normative framework involves the three concepts of discipline, commitment to the group, and autonomy of choice. As summarized by Everett Wilson, Durkheim's argument proceeds in the following manner:[8] "What is meant by morality, as we see it in practice? Certainly it involves consistency, regularity of conduct. . . . It also invariably involves some sense of authority; we are constrained to act in certain ways. . . . Now, these two features of morality—regularity of conduct and authority—are in fact aspects of a single thing: discipline. . . . Thus the first element of morality is discipline." Discipline should not be interpreted as constraint, however, for it is a liberating force in social life. By making possible social ordering, it frees us from the need to contrive new patterns of acting in each situation we encounter.

If discipline is to be accepted as morally justified, it must be seen as an impersonal force emanating from a group with which we identify, so that it transcends the individual. "Morality involves an impersonal orientation of activity. Behavior dominated by self-interest is never regarded as moral. . . ." Consequently, "the object of moral behavior must be something beyond the individual, or beyond any number of individuals *qua* individuals." For Durkheim, this implied that the object of morality must be social organization of some kind, from a small group to a total society. "Thus, we arrive at the second element of morality, the attachment to, or identification with, the group."

Finally, for the individual to experience socially based discipline as moral, he or she must feel that compliance with it is voluntary rather than coerced. "If strictly self-centered conduct must be regarded as amoral, that which denies the agent's autonomy is equally so; for controlled behavior is not 'good' behavior." This requirement posed a dilemma for Durkheim, since discipline and commitment to the group both imply pervasive coercion. He resolved the dilemma with the notion of "reliable knowledge." "The difference between self-determination and submission lies in the ability to predict accurately the consequences of alternative courses of action.

[7] Everett K. Wilson, Introduction to Émile Durkheim, *Moral Education* (New York: Free Press, 1961), pp. xix–xx.
[8] Ibid., pp. x–xii.

Autonomy involves a personal decision in full knowledge of the inexorable consequences of different courses of action." An autonomous person may therefore choose to ignore or defy prevailing norms and suffer the resulting consequences, or to abide by them and gain a sense of acting morally, again with full knowledge of the likely consequences. A number of contemporary normative theorists part company with Durkheim on this point, arguing that a dichotomous choice between socially defined deviance or morality cannot be a truly free decision. Unless the individual is given two or more options defined as moral, the result becomes social manipulation rather than autonomous choice. They thus reject Durkheim's belief that such choice destroys the imperative character of norms by reducing them to pragmatic guides for serving personal rather than collective interests. Both Durkheim and his critics might be satisfied, however, if we conceptualize this third requirement for morality as adoption of a collective orientation toward the organization with which one identifies. Actors can then voluntarily choose to act as involved parts of that collectivity rather than as independent elements.

Sumner's treatment of this problem of normative morality, meanwhile, was more straightforward and less analytical. He believed that the accumulated weight of custom and tradition is usually sufficient to give the folkways moral justification. After being transmitted through several generations, the folkways spontaneously become infused with conceptions of morality and are viewed as definitive standards of how one ought to act. Because a particular folkway is applicable to a limited set of situations, however, some deviation may be tolerated in socially undefined or novel conditions as long as this action does not threaten the welfare of the larger collectivity.

When people become convinced that a particular folkway is imperative for their collective welfare, it is transformed into a mos (singular of mores) for them. "When the elements of truth and right are developed into doctrines of welfare, the folkways are raised to another plane. Then we call them mores."[9] The mores reflect widespread and deeply held ideas about the nature of social life and actions that are vital for collective survival and the common welfare. People are expected to conform to the mores without question, and violations of them are usually punished severely, for they are seen as threatening the stability and unity of the entire group or society. Many mores are written into laws and sanctioned by the state, although a law tends to apply to a specifically defined domain of action, whereas mores are typically quite broad and undefined in scope.

The morality of folkways and mores can be judged in two different ways, according to Sumner. From the perspective of the involved actor, the

[9] Sumner, *Folkways*, pp. 42–43.

folkways and especially the mores are always right, since the criteria for determining right and wrong are themselves normatively defined and there are no external criteria against which they can be evaluated. "For the people of a time and place, their own mores are always good, or rather . . . for them there can be no question of the goodness or badness of their mores. The reason is because the standards of good and right are in the mores." [10] From the perspective of an outside observer, however, a folkway or a mos is good only if it results in the satisfaction of the interests or needs of those who hold it. Maladaptive or malfunctional norms can be judged as undesirable from this objective perspective. In short, the morality of norms cannot be judged subjectively, but can be evaluated objectively.

Both Durkheim's and Sumner's arguments concerning the morality of norms are combined in the following principle:

> **PRINCIPLE 25:** Norms become imbued with morality when actors voluntarily accept them as traditionally established cultural imperatives of a collectivity with which they identify, toward which they hold collective orientations, and which exert control over their actions.

DIFFERENTIATION OF NORMS

Although all the members of a society or other collectivity will normally share many norms in common, as subgroups form within an organization they tend to develop their own distinctive subcultures. As the struggle for existence continues, Sumner argued, societies become increasingly differentiated internally because it is only through complex social organization that people succeed in their efforts to survive and attain collective goals. The principal dimension of differentiation for Sumner was the division of a society into social classes, each of which develops its own interests and corresponding folkways. His primary concern was the distinction between upper classes of elites and the middle classes or masses. In general, he believed that most folkways originate in the elite classes, who subsequently impose their norms on the rest of the society. Since the masses are the bearers of traditional folkways and mores, however, in the long run they largely determine the nature of society.

The elite classes, meanwhile, constantly endeavor to convince the masses to accept the norms they have originated, thereby supporting elite interests. Because the masses do not readily accept changes in their traditional folkways and mores, however, the elites must often resort to the use of force to coerce the masses into acquiescing to elite norms. In addition, the elites also use force to resist changes in the folkways and mores that threaten their vested interests in existing conditions. For these reasons, coercion

[10] Ibid., p. 65.

becomes a significant factor in the imposition and maintenance of many social norms.

Durkheim, meanwhile, discussed differentiation of norms in a broader theoretical context. His central concern was with the process through which general norms of the "collective conscience" become transmuted into more specific norms regarding particular situations. When this differentiation does not occur, the collective conscience becomes progressively "enfeebled" and anomie—or lack of an adequate set of moral norms—pervades a society.

Contemporary normative theorists identify two interrelated processes through which elites utilize norms to support and perpetuate their privileged social positions. First, because elites frequently occupy key functionary postions in an organization, they perform activities that are crucial for the entire collectivity. Their particular folkways thus become identified with the common welfare and quickly take on the moral imperatives of collective mores. The second of these processes enfolds as elites inculcate their own mores into legal laws, religious dogmas, and social philosophies that are promulgated to the entire population. As the masses come to accept these ideas, elite norms and actions acquire legitimacy which enables the elites to exercise authority rather than coercion in their efforts to control the masses. These two processes were introduced in the previous chapter as the eventual outcomes of the coercion theory of social ordering, so that normative theory is simply adding the idea that these processes are supported and legitimated by moral norms imposed on the participating actors by ruling elites.

Regardless of the validity of Sumner's assertion that most norms originate within elite classes, the central thrust of this argument can be expressed in the following two ideas:

> PRINCIPLE 26: Subgroups within an organization tend to develop distinctive norms which reflect their particular interests, and employ coercion to impose their norms on other subgroups.

> PRINCIPLE 27: Powerful elites are especially successful in the process of normative imposition to the extent that they perform key functions for the larger collectivity and persuade others to accept their norms as legitimate bases for the exercise of authority throughout the organization.

CHANGE OF NORMS

Normative theorists generally agree that folkways and mores usually change rather slowly in comparison with social relationships and patterns of social ordering. People tend to alter their overt actions more easily and more frequently than their conceptions of how they ought to be acting. Nevertheless, as the "life conditions" faced by an organization in its natural and social environments change through time, the norms of this collectivity will also slowly shift in response to the new conditions. As more and more people find the old folkways and mores unacceptable or inadequate, new norms may be created or existing ones may be redefined, modified, or discarded. Because the norms tend to change more slowly than life conditions, however, organizations and individuals often experience strains between the normative expectations of their culture and the problems they currently face. In effect, the prevailing folkways and mores frequently lag behind existing social practices, so that persons pushing for social change are often viewed as deviants who ignore or flout traditional standards and customs. Hence, normative change often becomes widespread only as a new generation replaces those who cling to the old traditions, but it is nevertheless more or less inevitable given enough time.

Sumner suggested that this process of normative change occurs in two different ways, toward greater congruency with existing life conditions and toward greater internal consistency: "The folkways are . . . subject to a strain of improvement towards better adaptation of means to ends. . . . They are also subject to a strain of consistency with each other."[11] Neither of these processes can be deliberately instigated or controlled to any appreciable extent in Sumner's view. Normative change is rather the unforeseen consequence of a great number of minute efforts by actors directed toward fulfilling everyday interests and coping with immediate problems, and Sumner argued vehemently that intentional attempts to alter prevailing folkways and mores will usually produce only harmful social disruptions and conflict. The norms will eventually change to reflect new life conditions, but only in due course of time through natural social processes.

Critics of Sumner and Durkheim have strongly protested the passive laissez-faire political ideology implicit in their skeptical view of deliberate attempts at normative change. If we accept this perspective, the critics argue, all our attempts to purposefully improve society are pointless and should be abandoned—a view that activists and reformers find intolerable. Sumner attempted to offer a way out of this impasse by suggesting that since obsolete folkways and mores can be highly dysfunctional for society, intelligent and rational criticism of existing norms is absolutely necessary for social stability. Social criticism is primarily the responsibility of elite classes, he believed, who presumably can take a more objective viewpoint toward society than can the masses. A critic may often be wrong, and rarely will he or she actually effect significant social change, but nevertheless elites have a moral obligation to criticize. A similar theme has more recently been espoused by Karl Mannheim, who assigned the role of social critic to intellectuals rather than ruling elites, since he believed that elites would

[11] Sumner, *Folkways*, p. 21.

invariably seek to justify the status quo by creating self-serving ideologies and would shun all radical utopian thinking.[12]

To summarize this discussion of normative change, we can state:

> **PRINCIPLE 28: Cultural norms generally change rather slowly, in response to new life conditions, but when the norms do shift they tend to become more relevant to existing life conditions and internally consistent.**

FUNCTIONS OF NORMS

In the discussion of exchange theory we saw that emergent norms such as "distributive justice" and "reciprocity" enable initial transactions to be perpetuated as stable exchange relationships by creating a climate of mutual trust among the actors. Norms are also of crucial importance for the process of symbolic interaction, transforming individuals' interpretations of actions into shared cultural meanings.

On the level of social ordering, normative theorists argue that common norms are the major source of order, stability, and predictability in social life. Without moral norms to guide people's actions, social relationships would quickly disintegrate, collective activities would be impossible to sustain, and anarchy would soon prevail. Because norms regulate and perpetuate the fundamental structure of organized social life, without them there could be no enduring social ordering. In Sumner's words: "The proposition to be maintained is that the folkways are the widest, most fundamental, and most important operation by which the interests of men in groups are served, and that the process by which folkways are made is the chief one to which elementary societal or group phenomena are due. The life of society consists in making folkways and applying them. . . ."[13] Particularly impressive to Sumner was the absolute necessity for "antagonistic cooperation" between competing groups with divergent but interdependent needs and interests. Symbiotic collaboration between such groups, and hence overall social ordering, is possible, he believed, only to the extent that they share common folkways and mores. In short, norms enable actors to achieve collective goals by regulating their actions in the interests of mutual cooperation. When necessary, this process is enforced through the application of external social sanctions, but it becomes much more effective as actors internalize the norms through socialization and comply with them voluntarily. As expressed by Desmond Ellis: "The effectiveness of the normative solution to social ordering is due to the fact that norms and values are not

---

[12] Mannheim, *Ideology and Utopia.*
[13] Sumner, *Folkways,* p. 46.

only shared but also internalized and so become constitutive, rather than merely regulative, of social behavior."[14]

Although all sociologists would undoubtedly agree that cultural norms help to strengthen, maintain, and perpetuate social organization, many theorists contend that normative theory by itself is not adequate to explain the emergence of social ordering. A fundamental criticism frequently aimed at both Durkheim and Sumner is that they did not distinguish between cultural norms and social ordering as separate and often divergent aspects of the overall process of social organization. Durkheim assumed that the essence of any society was its "collective representations" of moral order, while Sumner explicitly defined social structure as the enactment of folkways and mores. From this perspective, all actions that do not conform to the norms are defined as deviant, which leaves little room for social innovation or individual freedom of action. Most contemporary normative theorists avoid this pitfall by recognizing that norms provide only broad guidelines for action, within which many diverse patterns of social ordering may emerge. Nevertheless, this theoretical perspective is still open to the criticism that it does not actually explain how social ordering is created, but deals only with the process by which existing patterns of ordering are maintained. "Normative theorists are primarily interested in identifying the sources of social integration in social systems in which the problem of order has been solved."[15] In addition, the emphasis on moral consensus in normative theory often tends to minimize the frequency and importance of conflict and coercion in organized social life.[16]

One final function commonly attributed to shared moral norms is the provision of a central cultural ethic that gives direction and purpose to collective social life. The classic example of a normative ethic is Max Weber's concept of the "Protestant ethic" as the underlying theme in the rise of modern capitalism.[17] Seeking an explanation of the process through which capitalism replaced feudalism as the prevailing mode of economic organization in Western Europe, he focused on the norms of thrift, self-sacrifice, and dedication to one's worldly calling as preached by the ascetic branches of Protestantism (Calvinism, Methodism, Baptism) in the sixteenth, seventeenth, and eighteenth centuries. Although the leaders of these religious movements were concerned with codes of behavior they believed were necessary for demonstrating or achieving divine grace and salvation,

[14] Desmond P. Ellis, "The Hobbesian Problem of Order: A Critical Appraisal of the Normative Solution," *American Sociological Review* 36 (August 1971): 692–703.

[15] Ibid.

[16] Ralph Dahrendorf, *Class and Class Conflict in Industrial Society* (Stanford, Calif.: Stanford University Press, 1959).

[17] Max Weber, *The Protestant Ethic and the Spirit of Capitalism*, trans. by Talcott Parsons (New York: Scribner's, 1958).

the moral virtues they espoused provided an ideal normative climate, in Weber's view, for the development of acquisitive capitalism. As a consequence, the Protestant ethic became the driving force in promoting and justifying capitalistic economic endeavors. In contemporary "postindustrial" societies, meanwhile, many observers claim that these time-honored virtues are being replaced by a "social ethic" emphasizing social adjustment and interpersonal relations.[18] Regardless of its content, however, the dominant normative ethic of a culture often provides a central theme around which many social activities are organized.

In general terms, these social functions of shared norms can be summarized in the following manner:

> PRINCIPLE 29:   Moral norms generally support and strengthen existing social relationships and patterns of social ordering, giving them continuity, regularity, predictability, and an overall sense of purpose and direction.

Value Theory

CONTEMPORARY theorists within the "cultural consensus" school of thought tend to assign priority to values rather than norms as constituting the core of any culture and hence the basis of social organization. Norms are still crucially important for these writers, however, so that the distinction between value and normative theory is derived only from the priority given to values over norms. Numerous contemporary social theorists—especially in the United States—might reasonably be considered proponents of the value theory of social organization, but Talcott Parsons stands apart from all the others because of his extensive contributions to this school of theoretical thought, and also because most other contemporary value theorists have been students of Parsons or have been heavily influenced by him. For these reasons, our discussion here is confined solely to Parsons's ideas, although we can do no more than briefly sketch the most significant of his thoughts on the structure of social systems and the essence of value theory. This sketch is largely structural rather than dynamic in nature, since most of Parsons's writings on this level of generality deal with analytical categories. There are many dynamic elements in his theorizing, but they typically pertain to more specific social processes such as cohesion and change, which are discussed in later chapters. The following presentation of the general Parsonian theoretical perspective is arranged under four headings: basic value perspective,

---

[18] William H. Whyte, Jr., *The Organization Man* (New York: Simon and Schuster, 1956).

general system model of action, structure of social systems, and implementation of values into social systems.

VALUE PERSPECTIVE

Parsons's most fundamental thesis is that common cultural values shape and control all social organization, as they are expressed in shared norms which are institutionalized into patterns of social ordering and internalized within individual personalities. "That a system of value-orientations held in common by the members of a social system can serve as the main point of reference for analyzing structure and process in the social system itself may be regarded as a major tenet of modern sociological theory."[19]

He quickly points out, however, that no set of basic cultural values is ever fully realized in social life, that the various collectivities comprising a society display these values to widely differing degrees, and that the expression of values in social interaction is always affected by situational constraints and practical interests. "The value system does not 'actualize' itself automatically, but the maintenance of relative control in its terms is dependent on whole series of mechanisms of institutionalization, socialization, and social control. It should be clear that using values as the initial point of reference for the structural analysis of social systems does not imply that they are the sole or even the most important determinants of particular structures and processes in such systems. . . . Beliefs and values are actualized, partially and imperfectly, in realistic situations of social interaction, and the outcomes are always codetermined by the values and the realistic exigencies."[20]

Nevertheless, the ultimate explanation of all social ordering and organization always lies, for Parsons, in common cultural values. In the words of Bennet Berger: "On the whole I think Parsons' solution to the 'Hobbesian Problem' of social order is . . . the sociological answer: social order is possible because men have culture, a set of values which are institutionalized in social structures, 'internalized' in personalities and experienced there as motives and constraints."[21]

SYSTEM MODEL

As a conceptual framework for theoretically explaining all social action, Parsons always employs a system model as a means of preserving "positivism of the observer," as opposed to the voluntaristic

[19]Talcott Parsons, *Structure and Process in Modern Societies* (New York: Free Press, 1960), p. 172.
[20]Ibid., p. 173.
[21]Bennet Berger, "On Talcott Parsons," *Commentary* (December 1962): 507–513.

perspective of participating actors. All systems of action (which together constitute the "action frame of reference") can be analyzed in terms of four basic functional imperatives that all systems must resolve in some manner: (1) latent pattern maintenance (abbreviated L), or "the maintenance of the highest 'government' or controlling patterns of the system"; (2) integration (I), or "the internal integration of the system"; (3) goal attainment (G), or "the attainment of goals in relation to its environment"; and (4) adaptation (A), or a system's "adaptation to the broad conditions of the natural environment."[22] The first two of these functions pertain to internal dynamics within systems, while the latter two pertain to relationships between a system and its environment. For any given system, however, "the integrative function is the focus of its most distinctive properties and processes,"[23] and thus constitutes the core concern of sociological theory.

There are four levels of human action systems, which Parsons distinguishes according to the major function each one performs. Progressing downward, these are cultural systems (centering around latent pattern maintenance), social systems (focusing on integration), personality systems (concerned primarily with goal attainment), and organistic systems (dealing with adaptation). These four types of systems develop through an upward process of emergence, with personalities emerging from organisms, social systems from personalities, and cultural systems from social systems. Systems at each level have distinctive properties of their own and cannot be explained in terms of lower level systems, yet at the same time they thoroughly interpenetrate systems at all other levels. In reference to social systems, he states that: "Though intimately intertwined with the personalities of the interacting individuals and the patterns of the cultural system, the process of social interaction forms a fourth system that is analytically independent of both personal and cultural systems, as well as of the organism."[24] Furthermore, since Parsons believes that the integrative function is always paramount, analysis of social action must always focus principally on social systems.

Below organistic systems lies the natural environment, which is the source of all energy for human activities. Hence there is a continual upward flow of energy (or more broadly, of resources) from the natural environment to higher-level systems, which he refers to as the "hierarchy of conditioning factors." Above cultural systems is the realm of "ultimate reality," which is the final source of all cybernetic control in human activities. Hence there is a

---

[22] Talcott Parsons, "An Outline of the Social System," in Parsons et al., eds., *Theories of Society* (New York: Free Press, 1961), p. 40.
[23] Ibid., p. 41.
[24] Talcott Parsons, *Societies: Evolutionary and Comparative Perspectives* (Englewood Cliffs, N.J.: Prentice-Hall, 1966), p. 7.

continual downward flow of information and decisions from ultimate reality, which he calls the "hierarchy of controlling factors." As a consequence, social systems must always rely on lower levels (the personality and the organism, and ultimately the natural environment) for a constant supply of resources, while at the same time they are always controlled in a cybernetic sense by cultural systems (and more broadly by the nature of "ultimate reality"). "The personality system is ... a system of control over the behavioral organism; the social system, over the personalities of its participating members; and the cultural system, a system of control relative to social systems." [25]

Parsons's use of the system model is summarized in these two principles:

> **PRINCIPLE 30:** All human action falls into four types of emergent systems, each of which centers on one of four basic functions: cultural systems focusing on latent pattern maintenance, social systems focusing on integration, personality systems focusing on goal attainment, and organistic systems focusing on adaptation.

> **PRINCIPLE 31:** All four types of systems are always subject to a downward process of cybernetic control originating in ultimate reality, and to an upward process of resource procurement from the natural environment.

SOCIAL SYSTEMS

Social systems are composed of patterns of interaction that are organized into delineated collectivities. Although any social entity can be analyzed as a system from this perspective, Parsons usually focuses on societies, which he defines as the most inclusive and self-sufficient type of social system. All other organizations within a society are then viewed as societal subsystems, sub-subsystems, and so on. "A complex social system consists of a network of interdependent and interpenetrating subsystems, each of which, seen at the appropriate level of reference, is a social system in its own right, subject to all the functional exigencies of any such system relative to its institutionalized culture and situation." [26] All social systems and their subsystems are open systems, engaging in complicated interactions with other social systems and with cultural, personality, and organistic systems. Yet each social system also maintains boundaries that delineate it from other systems, for without boundaries "it is not possible to identify a set of interdependent phenomena as a system; it is merged in some other, more extensive system." [27]

[25] Parsons, "An Outline of the Social System," p. 38.
[26] Ibid., p. 44.
[27] Ibid., p. 36.

Parsons also uses the LIGA scheme of system functions to differentiate social systems into their major component parts, along both vertical and horizontal dimensions. Vertical differentiation of a social system, first of all, produces four structural components or levels, as follows (in a downward sequence): (1) the latent pattern maintenance or L level, composed of the values from the controlling cultural system that are relevant to this social system and that define its goals and norms; (2) the integrative or I level, composed of clusters of norms (or normative institutions), each of which pertains to a functionally specialized but fairly broad sphere of social activities; (3) the goal-attainment or G level, composed of concrete collectivities, or bounded patterns of relationships among role actors; and (4) the adaptive or A level, composed of social roles (or sets of roles) that individuals enact as they participate in social life. As a result of his overriding concern with integrative functions, however, Parsons gives primary attention to the normative or institutional level of all social systems.

Although the distinctions between these four structural levels of values, normative institutions, collectivities, and roles pervade Parsons's theorizing, he is careful to note that they are analytical, not empirical, in nature, so that any real organization is always a combination of all four components. "We often speak of a role of a collectivity as if it were a concrete entity, but this is, strictly speaking, elliptical. There is no collectivity without member roles and vice-versa, no role which is not part of a collectivity. Nor is there a role or collectivity which is not 'regulated' by norms and characterized by a commitment to value patterns."[28]

The hierarchies of controlling and conditioning factors also operate within social systems, so that Parsons identifies a downward flow of cybernetic control throughout social life. Societal values legitimize, and hence ultimately shape, the clusters of norms constituting various institutional areas. "Values take primacy in the pattern maintenance functioning of a social system."[29] The particular norms of each institution in turn give authority to the collectivities in that area, enabling them to take collective action for the attainment of goals in the public interest. "Norms are primarily integrative; they regulate the great variety of processes that contribute to the implementation of patterned value commitments."[30] Each collectivity then authorizes the incumbents of its component roles to make decisions and otherwise act for the whole collectivity. "The primary functioning of the collectivity concerns actual goal attainment on behalf of the social system. Where individuals perform societally important functions, it is in their capacity as collectivity members."[31] Concurrently, an upward

[28] Parsons, *Societies*, p. 19.
[29] Ibid.
[30] Ibid.
[31] Ibid.

flow of conditioning factors, or resources, moves from roles to collectivities to institutionalized norms to values.

Horizontal differentiation of social systems into functional subsystems, which also follows the LIGA scheme, occurs at each of the four structural levels, but Parsons speaks mainly of the integrative level of normative institutions. The four subsystems of a society at the institutional level are (1) the latent pattern maintenance or L subsystem, composed of all institutions (such as religion, education, and the family) concerned with preserving and perpetuating the basic values of the total social system, as derived from the overriding cultural system; (2) the integrative or I subsystem, composed of the "societal community," which is the bond of shared loyalty or trust, institutionalized in the legal system, which holds the social system together; (3) the goal-attainment or G subsystem, which focuses on the polity as the institution through which actors collectively achieve goals; and (4) the adaptive or A subsystem, which centers on the economy as the institution through which actors obtain necessary resources from the surrounding environment.

In addition to its principal institutional structure, each functional subsystem is also characterized by a "generalized medium of interchange" for conducting internal transactions. For the L subsystem this medium is value commitments, for the I subsystem it is influence (both pressures and suggestions, thus including both compulsion and compliance), for the G subsystem it is power (in the sense of control, both coercion and command, which again encompasses compulsion and compliance), and for the A subsystem it is money. For interchanges between functional subsystems, a given amount of one medium must be translated into an equivalent amount of another medium, as when money is used to buy political power, or when a shared value commitment is invoked to induce loyalty to the societal community. Problems often arise, however, when the participating actors cannot agree on what constitutes an equivalent exchange from one medium to another.

Because the integrative function is always the most crucial function for Parsons, he argues that social theory should focus principally on the societal community subsystem of a society, and secondly on the latent pattern maintenance institutions that uphold the values which legitimize the norms of the societal community. The societal community is not a geographical entity of any kind, but rather the patterned normative order around which a society is organized, and which gives the society integration or unity. "The core of a society, as a system, is the patterned normative order through which the life of a population is collectively organized. As an order, it contains values and differentiated and particularized norms and rules, all of which require cultural references in order to be meaningful and legitimate. As a collectivity, it displays a patterned conception of membership which distinguishes between those individuals who do and do not belong. . . . We will call this one entity of the society, in its collective aspect, the societal community." [32] For analytical purposes, a societal community can also be conceptualized as a system in its own right, and then be further differentiated along both vertical and horizontal axes using the LIGA scheme. Thus a societal community consists, structurally speaking, of a set of general values (derived directly from the values of the encompassing society, and indirectly from a cultural system), clusters of more functionally specialized norms (such as legal codes), certain collectivities (such as courts), and the roles that individuals enact in these collectivities. It can also be divided into its own LIGA functional subsystems (or more properly, sub-subsystems) on a horizontal plane.

In summary, the Parsonian scheme for describing the structure of all social systems is constructed around the two axes of vertical and horizontal differentiation, following the four LIGA functions. In short:

> **PRINCIPLE 32:** Social systems are vertically differentiated into the four levels of values that perform pattern maintenance functions, institutionalized norms that perform integrative functions, collectivities that perform goal-attainment functions, and roles that perform adaptive functions.

> **PRINCIPLE 33:** At the level of institutionalized norms, social systems are horizontally differentiated into the four subsystems of pattern maintenance institutions (religion, education, the family), integrative institutions (the societal community), goal-attainment institutions (the polity), and adaptive institutions (the economy).

VALUE IMPLEMENTATION

Value theory assumes the existence of a set of common values contained within a cultural system, whose basic meanings are shaped by conceptions of ultimate reality. Values can change over time, as a result of both altered environmental conditions (through the "hierarchy of conditioning factors") and new perceptions of ultimate reality (through the "hierarchy of controlling factors"), but these value shifts are normally so slow that for most analytical purposes the existing cultural values can be taken as constants. The principal function that cultural values perform for social systems is to legitimize patterns of social ordering, thereby giving them stability and cohesion—which Parsons calls pattern maintenance. In his words: "The central functional exigency of the interrelations between a society and a cultural system is the legitimation of the society's normative

---

[32] Ibid., p. 10.

order. . . . No normative order is ever self-legitimating in the sense that the approved or prohibited way of life is right or wrong and admits of no questions. Nor is it ever adequately legitimized by necessities imposed at lower levels of the hierarchy of control—e.g., that things must be done in a specific way because the stability or even survival of the system is at stake. . . . A legitimization system is always related to, and meaningfully dependent on, a grounding in ordered relations to ultimate reality. That is, its grounding is always in some sense religious." [33]

The values held in common by the members of a society or other social system are generally quite broad in scope, and are not limited either to specific situations or to specific functions. As actors apply these values to particular organizations or situations, the values become expressed as moral norms and operational rules. "Norms, which . . . are differentiated with reference to function, must be function-specific. They are 'legitimized' by values, but operate at a lower level of generality with respect to expected concrete collective and role performance." [34] These legitimate norms in turn become infused into organized collectivities—a process which Parsons calls "institutionalization"—and function to guide, direct, and control the internal and external activities of these collectivities. To the extent that a collectivity is institutionalized, therefore, it is organized around a set of societal values and norms and performs necessary functions for the society. "In so far as a more inclusive social system comprises many collectivities as subsystems, the behavior of these collectivities is controlled by the institutionalized norms that specify how each type of collectivity must and may behave according to its place within the system." [35]

Finally, as individual actors participate in collectivities by enacting social roles, their actions are largely directed and controlled by societal values and norms that have become internalized within their personalities through the process of socialization. "The major functional problem concerning the social system's relation to the personality system involves learning, developing, and maintaining through the life cycle adequate motivation for participating in socially valued and controlled patterns of action. Reciprocally, a society must also adequately satisfy or reward its members through such patterns of action, if it is continually to draw upon their performances for its functioning as a system. This relationship constitutes 'socialization,' the whole complex of processes by which persons become members of a societal community and maintain their status." [36] Although in modern societies most individuals are able to exercise some

[33] Ibid., p. 11.
[34] Parsons, "An Outline of the Social System," p. 43.
[35] Ibid., p. 44.
[36] Parsons, *Societies*, p. 12.

discretion in selecting roles to enact and in deciding how to carry out these roles, Parsons continually emphasizes the ways in which these role performances contribute to the total social system. "The primary functional relation between adult individuals and their societies concerns the contributions adults make through performing services and the satisfactions or rewards they derive from them."[37] Consequently, he tends to regard all actions that depart significantly from established values and norms as socially deviant, to be dealt with through either social control mechanisms or resocialization.

Detailed evaluation of Parsons's value theory is beyond the scope of this discussion, but we can mention three criticisms frequently made of it. First, what is the source of all values, and how do they change? Postulating the existence of a realm of "ultimate reality" that gives meaning to all values does not answer this question, since we are then left wondering, "What is ultimate reality?" Many critics suggest that Parsons's conception of social life comes close to pure philosophical idealism, in which values emanate downward from a realm of existence that is largely or wholly beyond human control. Second, why must the process of integration be taken as the most important function in any organization or social system? Does this perspective not lead us (either intentionally or unintentionally) to stress a "conservative" ideological view of organized social life, in which conflict and change are seen as unfortunate disruptions of social order that should be prevented or at least corrected if at all possible? Third, and most crucial, is this whole elaborate complex of ideas a theory at all, or is it merely a set of heuristic analytical concepts, which at best orients us toward various features of social organization? That is, has Parsons's work been actual theory construction, or merely "programming for theorizing"?[38]

The following two principles express the essence of Parsons's value theory of social organization:

> PRINCIPLE 34:   Shared cultural values, reflecting conceptions of ultimate reality, largely shape and control all social organization, as they are expressed in norms that are institutionalized into collectivities and their component roles and are internalized within personalities through socialization.

> PRINCIPLE 35:   Values function to legitimate both normative institutions and collective activities, thereby giving them stability and cohesion, while moral norms derived from values function to integrate a social system around its societal community.

---

[37] Ibid., p. 13.
[38] Austin T. Turk, "On the Parsonian Approach to Theory Construction," *Sociological Quarterly* 8 (Winter 1967): 37–50.

Theoretical Convergence

THE task of identifying common and complementary themes in these two versions of cultural theory is not as difficult as in the case of interaction and ordering theories, since the normative and value perspectives both share common intellectual roots and both revolve around the central theme of cultural consensus. The following commonalities and complementarities are nevertheless worth noting.

COMMONALITIES

1. *Cultural emphasis.* Both theories give primary attention to shared culture as the principal component of social organization, which largely shapes and controls social relationships and ordering.
2. *Cultural emergence.* Both theories view culture as initially emerging from collective social activities as actors communicate about their actions and attach common meanings to them.
3. *Cultural externality.* Both theories conceptualize cultural norms and values as existing independently of individual personalities, and hence having properties and reality of their own.
4. *Cultural morality.* Both theories assume that over time values and norms become infused with morality, so that they are experienced as moral imperatives or obligations rather than just pragmatic goals or rules.
5. *Cultural functions.* Both theories argue that the principal functions of culture are to give meaning to social life and stability and cohesion to social ordering.

COMPLEMENTARITIES

1. *Principal focus.* Normative theory deals only with shared norms, and does not explain how they become shared or what gives them coherence (beyond the assumed "strain toward consistency"). Parsons's norms are derived from more general and inclusive values that characterize a total societal culture.
2. *Ecological base.* Normative theory is securely rooted in an ecological base of existing life conditions, which largely determines the prevailing norms through a process of adaptive selection. This notion is implicit in Parsons's idea of the hierarchy of conditioning factors arising from the natural environment, but is not elaborated in any detail.
3. *Normative differentiation.* Normative theory emphasizes differentiation of norms between social classes, but not along any other dimensions. Value theory elaborates this process to include norma-

tive differentiation among various institutional areas, types of collectivities, and component subgroups.

4. *Conception of power.* Normative theory limits power exertion to elite classes, who wield dominance and authority over the masses. In contrast to this conception of "coercion over others," value theory conceptualizes power as the "collective ability to achieve common goals" through the exercise of exchange media such as influence and commitment.

5. *Cultural change.* Normative theory allows for gradual normative change in response to new life conditions. Although this thesis lacks specificity, it can also be applied to value theory to explain historical shifts in basic societal values, which in turn lead to normative change. The tendency of value theory to treat values as constants for analytical purposes is thus at least partially avoided.

6. *System model.* Use of the system model as an analytical tool, with distinctions among types of functions, structural levels, and functional subsystems, is unique to value theory as developed by Parsons. None of the traditional normative theorists employed a system model, since it had not been explicitly formulated at the time they were writing.

In sum, both normative and value theory are variations on the more basic theme of cultural consensus as the core of social organization. Since Parsons explicitly attempted to expand and systematize the work of earlier normative theorists, *value theory is essentially an elaboration of normative theory, placed within a social system model.* Taken together, these two theoretical perspectives might well be blended into a more general cultural theory of social organization—as is done by many contemporary sociologists. It is vital to realize, however, that this substantive theory is logically independent of the social system model. One could propound cultural theory without using that model, while the model can be utilized with almost all theoretical perspectives.

Our overview of the six major schools of theorizing about social organization prevalent in contemporary sociology—exchange and symbolic interaction theories, coercion and ecological ordering theories, and normative and valuative cultural theories—is now complete. Each of these theoretical perspectives offers valuable contributions toward increasing our understanding of the process of social organization, but it is quite evident that none is adequate by itself. The following chapter pulls together the major ideas of all six perspectives into a single theoretical framework that utilizes the social system model (but not Parsons's particular version of it) and treats power exertion as the central dynamic of organized social life.

RECOMMENDED READING

Durkheim, Émile. *Moral Education*, trans. by Everett K. Wilson and Herman Schnurer. New York: Free Press, 1961, chaps. 2–8.
> Presents his conception of society as a normative (moral) reality outside of the individual, and stresses the importance of socialization in perpetuating social organization.

Ellis, Desmond P. "The Hobbesian Problem of Order: A Critical Appraisal of the Normative Solution." *American Sociological Review* 36 (August 1971): 692–703.
> Critically contrasts the "cultural consensus" perspective on social ordering with the exchange and coercive perspectives, and evaluates the ability of normative theory to provide a solution to the problem of world order.

Kluckhohn, Clyde. *Mirror for Man*. New York: McGraw-Hill, 1949, chap. 2.
> The concept of culture is elaborated, illustrated, and analyzed in nontechnical language.

Kroeber, A. L., and Talcott Parsons. "The Concepts of Culture and of Social Systems." *American Sociological Review* 23 (October 1958): 582–583.
> A brief statement clarifying the conceptual distinction between social and cultural phenomena.

Linton, Ralph, The Study of Man. New York: Appleton-Century-Crofts, 1936, chaps. 7, 15, 16, 17.
> Views social organization as a population of individuals who share common normative ideals and pattern their interactions in terms of these ideals.

Parsons, Talcott. "An Outline of the Social System." In Talcott Parsons et al., *Theories of Society*. New York: Free Press, 1961, pp. 30–79.
> The most comprehensive statement of his overall theoretical approach to social organization.

———. *Societies: Evolutionary and Comparative Perspectives*. Englewood Cliffs, N.J.: Prentice-Hall, 1966, chap. 2.
> Relates the major aspects of his social-systems analytical approach to his broader social-action scheme in a brief but inclusive manner.

———. *Structure and Process in Modern Societies*. New York: Free Press, 1960, chap. 5.
> Discusses a number of his fundamental theoretical conceptions in a very straightforward manner, with special reference to the use of authority in society.

Sumner, William Graham. *Folkways*. 2, Boston: Ginn 1940, chaps. 1, 2.
> Contains the main aspects of his conception of social organization as perpetuated patterns of folkways and mores.

Weber, Max. *The Protestant Ethic and the Spirit of Capitalism,* trans. by Talcott Parsons. New York: Charles Scribner's Sons, 1958.

> Sets forth his argument that the "Protestant ethic" provided the normative structure necessary for the rise of modern capitalism in Europe.

Williams, Robin. *American Society: A Sociological Interpretation,* 3rd ed. New York: Alfred A. Knopf, 1970.

> A discussion of the major values in American culture.

Yinger, J. Milton. "Contraculture and Subculture." *American Sociological Review* 25 (October 1960): 625–635.

> The concepts of subculture and contraculture are distinguished and described.

7

A Power Perspective on Social Organization

TO integrate our conceptualization of the total process of social organization, let us pull together the major ideas set forth in the preceding three chapters.

Social Organization

THE creation of social organization occurs within parameters imposed by psychological properties of human beings, demographic characteristics, the natural environment, material technology, and the surrounding social environment. As a result of a wide variety of causal factors, social actors (either individuals or organizations) interact with each other and affect each other's actions. Enduring social relationships arise as these interactions are perpetuated through time. Whereas social actors enter any given social relations as relatively autonomous elements in respect to that relationship, as they become participants in the relationship they must at times act as relatively involved parts of this larger phenomenon. Social actors engaged in social relationships can hold either self orientations (stressing expedient exchange) or collective orientations (stressing moral obligations), but membership in a relationship frequently produces some shift from self to collective orientations. Interactions and relationships can also vary along the dimensions of instrumental—expressive, ascribed—achieved, universal—particular, diffuse—specific, and affective—neutral.

Social ordering emerges as these social interactions and relationships evidence predictable arrangements or regularities. Social ordering thus consists of patterned and recurrent social interactions that maintain their uniformities with some degree of stability through time. These patterns of social ordering display properties of their own that are not inherent in the constituent members, including size, complexity, and formality—all of which profoundly affect the nature and functioning of social ordering. As a result, patterns of social ordering possess a unity greater than the sum of their component parts, which gives them a reality of their own. They are exterior to individual personalities and they constrain or influence the actions of their members. At the same time, individual personalities and patterns of social ordering always interpenetrate each other, so that neither can exist entirely apart from the other. As a means of describing and analyzing social ordering, we are forced by the limitations of our minds to "freeze" these ongoing processes into static pictures. By combining many such observations of social ordering, we are able to abstract perceptions of social structure, or observed patterns of social order.

Shared cultural ideas in turn emerge from social ordering, as the participants communicate with each other about their joint activities and create common ideas of how social life can and should be organized. A unique set of cultural ideas tends to become associated with each instance of social ordering, so that most or all of its participants eventually share a common culture, although subsets of participants may also possess partially distinct subcultures. Of direct relevance for social organization are such cultural components as values, interests, goals, norms, rules, and social technology. Culture, like social ordering, evidences properties that give it existence and reality of its own. The culture of an organization will therefore always influence and shape, as well as reflect, its underlying patterns of social ordering. Nevertheless, culture and social ordering inevitably interpenetrate each other, as do personalities and social ordering, so that all three levels of ordering become fused into the overall process of social organization.

In sum, *social organization is created as social actors interact in ongoing relationships to establish stable patterns of social ordering which become infused with shared cultural ideas and meanings.* The overall process of social organization thus incorporates the three component processes of social interaction, social ordering, and culture sharing. Interaction leads to ordering which generates culture, but each successive process also acts back on preceding ones. Woven together, these three interpenetrating processes create the total process of social organization, as depicted in Figure 7-1.

As also indicated in the figure, each of these three component processes utilizes a different form of power exertion as its principal medium. Social interaction stresses utilitarian power exertion based on the ability of actors to provide things (goods, services, information, meanings) that will meet each other's needs in a balanced relationship. Social ordering emphasizes unbalanced coercive power exertion based on the ability of elites to shape the actions of others by exercising either force (derived from employment of valued resources) or dominance (derived from performance of necessary functions). Culture sharing focuses on unbalanced but justified persuasive

FIGURE 7-1. Three Components of the Total Process of Social Organization

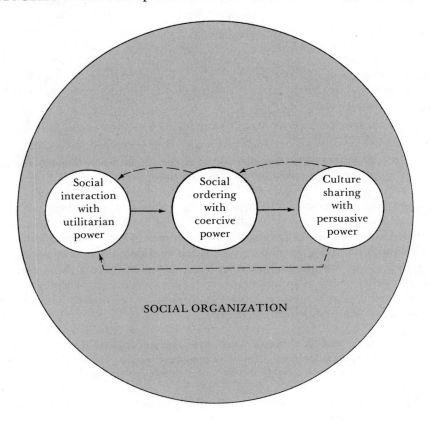

power exertion based on the ability of some actors to convince others to accept their suggestions or commands (by appealing to shared values and norms or to personal considerations).

Theoretical Unification

AS we saw in the preceding chapters, two different theoretical perspectives on the creation of social organization focus on each of the three component processes of social interaction, social ordering, and culture sharing. Each pair of theories, we discovered, shares several commonalities and complementarities. But given the divergent foci of the three pairs, are they compatible with one another? Can these six alternative views on the creation of social organization be combined into at least a roughly unified theoretical perspective? A few preliminary steps toward that goal are explored in this section, although two qualifications must be noted at the outset: (1) this effort incorporates only the most crucial ideas from each perspective and does not attempt to deal with all their details or implications, and (2) the result is merely a crude sketch of a unified theoretical perspective and is far from constituting a completed theory. The following discussion is presented as a series of principles and accompanying explanations, arranged under the three headings of social interaction, social ordering, and culture sharing.

SOCIAL INTERACTION

PRINCIPLE 36: The creation of social organization begins as actors interact in meaningful exchange transactions.

All social interaction is an exchange process of some kind to some degree. These transactions involve either tangible exchanges of goods or actions or intangible exchanges of information or ideas, or a combination of both tangible and intangible items. In these exchanges the actors always respond to the meanings they attach to or infer about others' actions. Consequently, some minimal amount of shared meanings is a prerequisite for successful transactions, but these meanings are continually revised and expanded as the interaction progresses.

PRINCIPLE 37: Actors perpetuate exchange transactions as ongoing social relationships only as long as these interactions are meaningful to them and rewarding to them at acceptable costs.

Interaction that becomes meaningless to an actor is rather quickly abandoned if at all possible, since there is no basis in that situation for meaningful exchange transactions. If it is to be perpetuated, the interaction must also be seen by each actor as rewarding in some way, although the benefits may be intangible (such as clarifying or enlarging shared meanings) or may merely be anticipated in the future. Moreover, the benefits may not necessarily equal or exceed the costs of participating in the interaction, as long as the incurred costs are acceptable to the actors. Social exchanges thus typically utilize a satisfying rather than a maximizing strategy.

> PRINCIPLE 38: **Actors engaged in exchange interactions become dependent on one another for whatever benefits they are receiving, which leads to the creation of social relationships infused with utilitarian power.**

Interdependent interactions commonly become perpetuated as ongoing social relationships. To the extent that one participant depends on another for some kind of needed or desired benefit, either tangible or intangible, the supplier can exercise power over the receiver. This occurs regardless of whether or not the supplier also depends on the receiver for some other benefit in return. The utilitarian power of one actor over another is directly proportional to the dependence of the second actor on the first one within an exchange relationship. Thus utilitarian power pervades all exchange interaction, both unilateral and reciprocal.

> PRINCIPLE 39: **Actors participating in ongoing exchange relationships attempt, insofar as possible, to keep their transactions reciprocal and thus avoid power imbalances that favor other actors.**

Although exchange relationships rarely remain in perfect balance for long, each participating actor will attempt to avoid transactions that give a clear power advantage to another actor. Conversely, actors will frequently— though not always—seek to develop and perpetuate transactions that give them a power advantage over others. The result of these two opposing tendencies is that exchange relationships tend to fluctuate around a point of balance. This balance can be upset, however, if some actors possess or acquire significantly greater resources than others. The relationship then becomes more or less perpetually unbalanced, which leads the weaker actors to take compensatory actions such as withdrawal, coalition formation, goal redefinition, or rebellion. Only if all these efforts fail will a disadvantaged actor typically continue to participate in a seriously unbalanced relationship.

> PRINCIPLE 40: **An exchange relationship that proves rewarding to the participants generates trust and commitment among them that both stabilizes the relationship and provides a basis for the exercise of attractive power.**

By themselves, exchange transactions are inherently uncertain and unstable, since an actor can never be sure that others will reciprocate with needed or desired benefits or not exploit their vulnerability. As these interactions continue to be mutually rewarding over time, however, the actors increasingly trust one another and commit themselves to furthering the relationship. The result of growing interactor trust and commitment is a relatively stable and continuing relationship. In addition, mutual trust and commitment make the actors more attractive to one another and more willing to comply with one another's requests.

SOCIAL ORDERING

PRINCIPLE 41:   As interacting actors benefit from their relationships and become committed to them, they establish patterned social ordering infused with coercive power, within the limitations imposed by prevailing ecological conditions.

Interactions and relationships gain further stability and predictability as they are interwoven into established patterns of social ordering. Consequently, as actors share common interests, benefit from mutual relationships, and feel committed to their collective endeavors, they create increasingly complex and encompassing social ordering. The interwoven relationships that comprise these patterns of social ordering are pervaded by coercive influence and control among participants and collectivities. Possibilities for establishing viable social ordering are always limited, however, by the prevailing ecological conditions of the natural environment, population, and technology.

PRINCIPLE 42:   Creation of social ordering is accomplished primarily through the exercise of force and dominance by more powerful actors over less powerful actors, which is often termed leadership.

Since exchange relationships are rarely perfectly balanced, at any given time some actors will be able to exert disproportionate power over others who are dependent on them in some way. To attain desired goals—either their own or shared—these more powerful actors seek to influence or control existing relationships. To the extent that these efforts are successful because the more powerful actors are able to overcome the resistance of others or perform needed functions for them, patterns of social ordering are created. This process may be intentional, but quite often it is a more or less unintended consequence of goal-seeking actions by powerful actors.

PRINCIPLE 43:   Actors within patterns of social ordering who control valued resources or perform functions needed by the collectivity tend to

become increasingly powerful relative to others, and are often termed elites.

Elites within established collectivities may or may not be the leaders who originally created that social ordering; the power of these elites may extend throughout the entire collectivity or be confined to specific functional areas; and they may be divided into several layers of differing power capabilities. In general, however, the larger and more complex a collectivity the more likely it is to contain numerous sets of diverse elites, whose actions together largely shape the major features and activities of that collectivity. The ability of elites to exercise force or dominance over others is derived from either the valued resources they control (economic, political, military, religious, knowledge, etc.) or the key functionary roles (gatekeeper, communicator, decision maker, etc.) they perform for the collectivity.

> **PRINCIPLE 44: Elites employ a variety of coercive techniques to attain their goals and protect their power wielding capabilities, all of which affect the overall structure and functioning of the collectivity.**

A number of these coercive techniques were described in Chapter 5 and need not be repeated here. The specific techniques used in any particular situation will of course depend on a number of interacting factors, including the resources and sophistication of the elites, the scope of their domain, the nature of the collectivity, and the opposition offered by others. The principal point is that these coercive techniques, though frequently intended to serve elite interests, nevertheless often influence the entire collectivity or significant portions of it. This is especially likely when the elites are capable of exercising meta-power to shape and control fundamental patterns of social ordering within collectivities.

> **PRINCIPLE 45: All aspects of social ordering, from its initial creation through its ongoing functioning and perpetuation through time, are pervaded by coercive power, especially force and dominance.**

This final principle concerning social ordering, implicit in all the preceding ones, asserts that coercive power exertion constitutes the principal dynamic medium through which the process of social ordering occurs. Coercion is not the only form of power exertion occurring in social ordering, since utilitarian power arising from exchange transactions and normative power derived from shared cultural ideas also impinge on all patterns of social ordering to the extent that these three levels of ordering interpenetrate one another. But coercive power exertion—principally force and dominance, ranging from subtle manipulation to overt violence— are inherent in all instances of social ordering. The total amount of power being exercised within and by a collectivity at any given time is distinct, however, from the degree to which power exertion capabilities are distributed equally or unequally among the participants in that collectivity.

CULTURE SHARING

PRINCIPLE 46: As actors interact in social relationships and patterns of social ordering, they symbolize these experiences and communicate them to others as expectations, meanings, values, and other ideas that over time coalesce into a culture.

The process of creating and sharing cultural ideas arises out of and reflects collective actions and experiences, so that culture is always grounded in shared social life. This process occurs through symbolic communication among actors, but as a shared culture emerges it is experienced by the actors as external to themselves and as dissociated from any particular relationships or situations. It therefore exists as a separate reality, partially independent of both the actors who create and perpetuate it and the patterns of social ordering that it reflects.

PRINCIPLE 47: Shared culture, especially common values, imbues norms with a sense of morality and provides a basis for ascribing legitimacy to leaders, both of which infuse culture with normative power.

To the extent that actors experience their culture as external to themselves and as embodying shared beliefs and values, the culture can influence their actions and interactions. In particular, the norms of the culture become infused with morality so that actors voluntarily abide by them out of a sense of "oughtness" or social responsibility. In addition, a shared culture will also tend to legitimize existing patterns of social ordering for their participants, especially leadership positions and decision-making procedures. Culture sharing thus generates normative power founded on mutual trust.

PRINCIPLE 48: Normative power, expressed as both individual self-control and systemic authority, facilitates the stabilization and perpetuation of social organization.

As individuals internalize cultural norms through socialization and trust others to also respect and abide by these norms, they will tend to exercise internal self-control over their own actions. As a consequence, their interactions acquire regularity and predictability, which facilitate the process of social ordering. Mutual trust also enables collectivities to exert systemic power in pursuit of organizational goals, as their leaders exercise legitimized authority both within the organization and in interactions with other organizations. In short, as collectivities become infused with shared culture, the process of social organization incorporates normative as well as utilitarian and coercive power, which tends to stabilize and perpetuate social relationships and patterns of social ordering.

> **PRINCIPLE 49:** **The creation of normative power within organizations increases the power of elites by enabling them to supplement or replace the exertion of force and dominance with legitimate authority.**

Coercive power, especially overt force, frequently becomes unreliable if exercised over a long period of time. As a general rule, therefore, elites seek to gain legitimacy for their actions in order to exercise authority through suggestions and commands as much as possible. This not only protects their positions, but also enhances their ability to wield power in pursuit of whatever goals they seek. To the extent that their actions serve collective interests and facilitate attainment of organizational goals, the collectivity as a whole expands its systemic power capabilities.

> **PRINCIPLE 50:** **With the generation of shared culture that becomes infused into patterns of social ordering arising out of interwoven social relationships, the process of creating social organization is complete.**

This final principle concludes our overall theoretical perspective on the process through which social organization is created. The twin themes pervading this perspective are (1) the blending of social interaction, social ordering, and culture sharing into emergent social organization which exists as a reality apart from its component members, and (2) the pervasive role of social power, in all its various forms and manifestations, as the dynamic medium through which the process of social organization transpires. Out of this ongoing creaive process emerge organizational units of all kinds, which can be analyzed using a social system model.

PART III

Enacting Social Organization

THE units or collectivities formed through the process of social organization—including all the various types of organizations sketched in the previous chapter—can be analyzed as social systems. Although we do not assume that they perfectly resemble an ideal system model, we can nevertheless use this model as an analytical paradigm with which to explore their dynamic activities. System processes, as we noted in Chapter 1, can be divided into the two broad categories of morphostasis, or pattern maintenance, and morphogenesis, or pattern development. The four chapters comprising the third part of this book examine a number of morphostatic processes that pervade all social systems as they are enacted and perpetuated through time. The four chapters comprising the fourth and final part will then focus on several morphogenetic system processes.

Chapter 8 deals with the cooperative processes through which actors participate in organizations as involved parts and contribute to maintaining system stability. These processes are social learning, self-regulation, and social role enactment.

Although cooperation provides a necessary basis for social organization, it is often insufficient to maintain an organization and keep it operating effectively. Various forms of social control are also usually necessary to preserve and perpetuate social organization. As discussed in Chapter 9, control processes are exerted on both individual participants and organizational processes.

With effective implementation of social controls, organizations gain overall cohesion or integration. Chapter 10 examines the nature of social cohesion, the two basic processes of functional and normative cohesion, and the complementarity of cohesion with conflict in social life.

An additional outgrowth of the exercise of power for control purposes within organizations is distribution, or the differential allocation of resources, privileges, and prestige among organizational members and subparts. The result of this process is structured social inequality, or stratification. Chapter 11 explores several dimensions of stratification, some alternative explanations of how it occurs, and the structure of social classes in modern societies.

8

Cooperative Processes

IF people are to successfully maintain and operate the social organizations they create, they must first of all be able to cooperate with one another within social relationships. Social cooperation rests on an underlying foundation of prior and current social learning. When individuals are participating in social relationships, cooperation is enhanced by their ability to exercise self-regulation of their activities. When they are acting as fully involved parts of an organization, cooperation occurs primarily through the process of role enactment. All three of these topics are discussed in this chapter.

Social Learning

TO the extent that individuals behave idiosyncratically as autonomous personalities on the basis of personal motives, goals, and meanings, they do not contribute to any social organization. Whenever people interact with others through time, however, they become participants in the process of social organization. Regardless of whether they create new relationships or join existing collectivities, this process of social participation involves cooperation with others. To be able to cooperate with other actors, the individual must have learned various interaction skills, ordering techniques, and cultural ideas.

Social learning is part of the broader process of socialization, through which individuals both develop personalities and learn to be social actors. Thus socialization can be viewed from two different perspectives, focusing on either the formation of the personality as it matures in childhood and throughout adult life, or on the learning of those capabilities necessary for participation in organized social life. Although in reality these two sides of the socialization process are always inexorably interwoven, it is often useful to distinguish between them for analytical purposes. The personality formation aspects of socialization are studied primarily by psychologists and psychologically oriented social psychologists, while the social learning aspects of socialization are generally of more interest to sociologists and sociologically oriented social psychologists. For our concern with the maintenance of social organization, individual personality characteristics are largely irrelevant, since our interest lies in how people learn to cooperate rather than in how they develop distinct personalities. Hence our discussion here is limited to the social learning side of socialization.

THE SETTING OF SOCIAL LEARNING

The process of social learning—as well as personality formation—is frequently assumed to occur primarily in childhood, but this is a gross oversimplification. Certainly childhood, and especially the first few years, is an especially critical period in a person's life, for it is during this time that he or she acquires basic personality characteristics and learns many fundamental interaction skills—one of the most important of which is language. Nevertheless, the social learning process does not end with adolescence, but continues throughout a person's entire life. Our participation skills are continually developing and changing, and whenever we enter into new social relationships or organizations we must learn appropriate patterns of interaction, ordering techniques, and cultural ideas. In fact, for the student of social organization, adult socialization is often of greater relevance than is childhood socialization. We must therefore keep in mind throughout this discussion that the social learning process applies to all persons at all times.

Crucial problems for sociologists concerned with social learning include acquiring social-interaction skills, becoming familiar with various role expectations and techniques of role acting, learning cultural norms and values, and related phenomena. *Much of one's social learning takes place within "primary groups"* such as the family and peer group, which is why social scientists point to these organizations as the major agents of socialization. During childhood, when the individual is first acquiring social capabilities, almost all of his or her activities center in intimate primary groups. Later in life, social learning also occurs in larger and more complex organizations, but again it is among one's immediate acquaintances within these organizations that most social learning actually transpires.

THE DYNAMICS OF SOCIAL LEARNING

Our present knowledge about the dynamics of social learning is quite fragmentary, although we do know that it occurs primarily through social reinforcement within interaction situations. When we first enter a social situation for which we are totally unprepared—and to some extent whenever we initiate interaction in any situation—we tend to act in a rather random, trial-and-error fashion, trying first one action and then another. If other persons are present, we can imitate their actions, assuming that what is appropriate for them also applies to us—which is frequently open to doubt. Our task is also made easier if someone else tells us what to do, either orally or in writing. In this case, though, we must decide whether or not our instructor is competent, whether this person represents the other participants for whom he or she speaks, and whether the instructions are congruent with what is actually being done at the present time. In short, we necessarily remain in a state of some uncertainty until other persons begin responding to our actions.

Once we receive responses from other actors, however, we gain a basis for evaluating our own actions. Some of the things we do will likely be disapproved by others, and we will be discouraged from doing them again. Other things we do will be accepted by others, giving us some leeway in deciding whether or not to repeat them. Finally, still other things we do will be approved by others, and we will be encouraged to continue them. This learning process is further reinforced as the individual acquires skill at "taking the role of the other," which enables one to anticipate others' probable responses to his or her intended actions before overtly acting. On the basis of this anticipation, one can then modify these intended actions.[1] Many crucial variables are left unexplained in this brief outline, including one's ability to interpret correctly the responses of others, one's receptivity to reactions from others, and the nature and strength of approving and disapproving responses. Nevertheless, it does suggest that *social learning is essentially similar to all other forms of learning, in which the nature and degree of reinforcement received by the individual in response to his or her*

[1] George Herbert Mead, *Mind, Self and Society* (Chicago: University of Chicago Press, 1934).

actions are the crucial factors determining what and how much is learned.
The unique features of social learning are simply that we learn social
capabilities (rather than purely cognitive information, emotional associations, or motor skills) and that the significant respondents are almost always
other social actors with whom we are engaged in ongoing social interaction.

These generalizations about the dynamics of social learning suggest the
following principle:

> **PRINCIPLE 51:** **The social learning necessary for participation in social
> organization is acquired primarily through a process of social
> reinforcement in which we take account of the anticipated or actual
> responses of others to our actions.**

From a broader perspective, viewing socialization as a combination of
both personality formation and social learning suggests that this process has
a dual outcome. Socialization results in the simultaneous development of
both personal autonomy and social responsibility. We often uncritically
think of these two goals as contradictory. After all, if one accepts social
responsibilities does one not surrender at least a portion of personal
autonomy? In some settings, yes, but not always. The assumption of social
responsibility can also lead to greater personality development and hence
increased personal autonomy. To cite a common example, marriage (which
certainly entails numerous responsibilities) sometimes does become an
unbearable prison for an individual, but it can also provide him or her with
opportunities for personal growth and social learning that are not normally
available to a single person. The development of individual maturity and
the creation of social organization are never inherently incompatible—
though they can become so. They can, and frequently do, both increase
together, with each reinforcing the other. The fundamental paradox of
socialization lies in the fact that through this process the individual
simultaneously develops a mature and relatively autonomous personality,
and also learns to become a responsible and involved participant in organized social life.

Self-Regulation

ONCE a person has acquired at least some social learning—the
necessary amount and kind depend on the situation and the individual—
he or she becomes capable of exercising self-regulation in social interaction.
To the extent that all the participants in a relationship or organization

regulate their own actions to mesh with the actions of others, successful cooperation becomes increasingly possible. The process of self-regulation occurs in three principal ways, which we shall call internalization, identification, and compliance.[2]

INTERNALIZATION

Internalization occurs as social norms are accepted by the individual as his or her own personal standards of action. These norms are not just learned, but are incorporated by individuals into their personalities. They abide by the norms because of external forces or rational decisions, but because their own minds and total personality compel them to. If one should violate a deeply internalized norm, he or she would feel guilty regardless of whether or not anyone else knew of these actions, and would likely punish oneself in some manner.

Norm internalization is largely an unconscious process. We are not usually aware of doing it and hence rarely realize the extent to which our "own" standards are actually learned from the cultures in which we participate. Most people would probably be surprised, if not shocked, to discover the degree to which their "self-discipline" is actually a reflection and expression of deeply internalized social norms. For instance, many of us probably believe quite strongly that killing is morally wrong, and thus find it difficult to realize that we would have no scruples against it if we lived in a society that encouraged killing. However, the fact that our moral inhibition is actually an internalized social norm can be easily demonstrated. If an individual is placed in an organization whose culture encourages killing under certain conditions—such as an army in battle—he or she will then very likely come to feel that killing is permissible or even desirable in this situation.

Social scientists presently know very little about how the process of internalization occurs, although many speculative theories have been suggested. One of the most fascinating events in the history of social thought was the convergence of the work of Émile Durkheim, George Herbert Mead, and Sigmund Freud upon the crucial importance of internalization for social life. Durkheim, a sociologist, Mead, a social philosopher, and Freud, a physician, came from different intellectual backgrounds, worked independently, and had little or no knowledge of one another. Yet at approximately the same time (the early years of the twentieth century) each of them

---

[2] The latter two terms are not wholly standardized in sociology, and various synonyms are frequently employed, but the underlying concepts are widely accepted. These particular terms are adapted from Herbert C. Kelman, "Compliance, Indentification, and Internalization: Three Processes of Attitude Change," *Journal of Conflict Resolution* 2 (March 1958): 51–60. See also his "Process of Opinion Change," *Public Opinion Quarterly* 25 (Spring 1961): 57–78.

developed theoretical viewpoints that emphasized norm internalization.[3] They used different terminology—Durkheim spoke of the "collective conscience" becoming manifest within individuals, Mead discussed the incorporation of "the generalized other" within the self, and Freud examined the effects of the "superego" upon the personality—and their resulting theories differed in numerous substantive respects. But to a remarkable extent they all saw social life as resting primarily on voluntary conformity by individuals to social standards that had been incorporated into their personalities.

Since we are already familiar with some of the thinking of George Herbert Mead, let us examine briefly his idea of "the generalized other." As an individual temporarily "takes the role of the other" and sees oneself through another person's eyes, one develops conceptions of what this person expects of one. At first, these conceptions are closely tied to particular individuals, as the young child becomes aware of "what mother expects of me," "what brother expects of me," and "what teacher expects of me." Mead called this the "play" stage, since the child is largely "playing" at the roles of specific others as they relate to himself or herself. Over time, though, the expectations of all those persons with whom one interacts in a given situation become fused into a single conception of what is expected of one in this social setting. Mead referred to this as the "game" stage, since the child is now learning to participate in organized games or group activities. Eventually, as the individual matures, these various situationally relevant standards of action tend to merge into a single generalized conception of what all other people—an amorphous "they"—expect one to do. Mead used the term "the generalized other" to describe this third stage. At each stage of this process, the individual not only learns the expectations of others, but also incorporates them into the self-conceptions one forms of oneself, so that they become not just what others—another person, other participants in a game, or "they"—expect of me, but what I expect of myself, because of my own self-images and self-identity. In this way, social norms become internalized within the individual.

IDENTIFICATION

A second form of self-regulation occurs as an individual identifies himself or herself with a particular social organization—usually one to which he or she belongs or would like to belong. *Identification often leads the individual to accept the norms or rules of an organization in order to participate in it.* In this case, the social standards of the organization are not

---

[3]For discussions of this convergence, see Talcott Parsons, "The Superego and the Theory of Social Systems," in Parsons et al., *Working Papers in the Theory of Action* (New York: Free Press, 1953), chap. 1; and Guy E. Swanson, "Mead and Freud: Their Relevance for Social Psychology," *Sociometry* 24 (December 1961): 319-339.

internalized, but the individual nevertheless willingly accepts and abides by them because they are part of the culture of the organization with which he or she identifies. Once a person has identified with a social organization, no external pressures are necessary to induce him or her to conform to its standard of actions. The college freshman who modifies his appearance and behavior in an attempt to emulate the upper-class fraternity men whom he admires is exercising this kind of self-regulation. So is the store proprietor who becomes more conservative in her political opinions and votes a straight Republican ticket because of her identification with "the business community." A third example would be the recent immigrant to a society who conspicuously adopts all the customs and traditions of his or her neighbors because "this is the way we do things in my new country." Over time, strong identification with an organization can lead to internalization of its norms, but these two processes are analytically distinct.

Self-regulation resulting from identification can occur regardless of whether or not the individual actually belongs to the organization. In fact, this phenomenon is especially common among nonmembers who are seeking membership by demonstrating their acceptance of organizational norms and rules. Sociologists frequently apply the concept of "reference group" to an organization whose standards an individual accepts as a result of identification, regardless of whether or not he or she is actually a member of that organization.[4] Studies have discovered, for instance, that the manual worker who accepts the "middle class" as a reference group will often conform more rigorously to "middle-class" norms than will business and professional persons.

COMPLIANCE

Self-regulation also takes the form of compliance resulting from expedient or utilitarian considerations. *Compliance occurs when an individual abides by the social standards of an organization in hopes of benefiting from this conformity.* That is, he or she expects to gain rewards or escape punishments because of his or her actions. One does not internalize the organizational standards, nor does one accept them because they are part of an organization with which one identifies. In this case, self-regulation is based on more or less rational calculations of expediency. The individual decides that, for one reason or another, it is in one's interests to regulate one's own actions. A motorist follows posted speed limits to avoid the possibility of receiving a speeding ticket, an employee takes on extra duties

[4]Robert K. Merton and Alice S. Rossi, "Contributions to the Theory of Reference Group Behavior," in Merton's *Social Theory and Social Structure*, rev. ed. (New York: Free Press, 1957), chap. 8; Tamotsu Shibutani, "Reference Groups and Social Control," in Arnold Rose, ed., *Human Behavior and Social Processes* (Boston: Houghton Mifflin, 1962), pp. 128–147.

and works overtime in hopes of being promoted, and some college students study only to attain satisfactory grades.

This phenomenon of compliance is clearly related to social sanctioning (directly applying rewards and punishments), which is discussed in the next chapter. The distinction between compliance and sanctioning lies in the fact that rewards and punishments are not actually necessary for compliance. The individual's actions are regulated by his or her anticipation of rewards or punishments, regardless of whether or not one ever receives them. Compliance based on calculated expediency is particularly important in producing conformity to rules, in comparison with norms, since rules are not internalized and are not always accepted as a result of identification.

The foregoing discussions of internalization, identification, and compliance as three forms of self-regulation lead to the following generalization:

> PRINCIPLE 52:   Cooperation among the participants in a social organization is greatly facilitated by the processes of internalization, identification, and compliance, which lead actors to regulate their own actions as they interact with others.

Role Enactment

AS individuals participate in a social organization they begin to change at least some of their actions from those of relatively autonomous social elements to those of relatively involved social parts. The greater this shift in their actions, the more deeply involved they become in that organization and the more extensively they enact social roles within the organization. This process of role enactment in turn promotes more effective cooperation among organizational members.

NATURE OF ROLES

For social roles to exist there must first be some amount of social organization, since roles are component parts of organizations and cannot exist apart from patterns of social ordering and cultures. *Roles are the smallest subunits of all social organizations.* Individuals enact roles and thereby become involved in social ordering, but the individual is not a subunit of any organization. A given person is often a member of numerous different organizations, so that he or she cannot simultaneously be a structural subunit of all of them. But the roles one enacts within an organization belong exclusively to that collectivity and hence constitute its smallest subunits. To fill a social role, therefore, a person must at least temporarily act as an integral part of some social organization. Whether or not one is considered a member of the organization while acting in this manner depends on the prevailing criteria for membership.

Role enactment necessitates involvement in organized social life, but participation does not necessarily entail role enactment. It is safe to say that the participants in an organization must frequently fulfill organizational roles if that organization is to attain goals or even survive. But any individual might, at any given time, interact with others as either an element or a part. As a relatively autonomous element, his or her actions would be determined largely by his or her own motivations, interests, and goals. As a relatively involved part, these actions would be shaped to some extent by expectations and demands of the larger organization. Only in the latter situation would one be enacting a social role in the organization. One might well retain membership in the organization while acting as an element—so long as he or she did nothing that would lead others to deprive him or her of membership—but one would not then be fulfilling an organizational role.

Social roles exist within all types of social organizations, from the smallest and most informal group to the largest and most complex society. For example: a friendship clique might include the role of initiator, who suggests activities for the group; a family usually provides for such roles as disciplinarian, cook, and income-producer; an association may contain a wide variety of roles, from chief executive to foreman to janitor; a mob frequently follows its leaders; social classes sometimes create the role of spokesperson to present and defend their interests; community roles vary from those of the mayor to the "town gossip"; social networks rely upon the fulfillment of communication and coordination roles to keep their interrelated activities operating smoothly; and societal roles are as important as those of a prime minister or member of Congress, as demanding as that of a soldier in combat, or as nebulous as that of a voter or taxpayer.

We have thus far conceived of social roles as dynamic processes, but they can also be viewed from a more static or structural perspective. *Any location within a social structure, or observed pattern of social ordering, can be termed a social position.* Associated with each position is a set (often more than one) of related roles that the incumbent of the position is expected to enact. The concepts of roles and positions thus provide complementary means of analyzing what is essentially the same phenomenon, as viewed from either a process or a structural perspective.

A process view of social life suggests that to identify a given social position we must perceptually and conceptually "freeze" ongoing role activities and single out the structural point at which a set of roles being enacted by an individual converges.[5] For example, the position of "store

[5] J. Eugene Haas, "Role, Position, and Social Organization: A Conceptual Formulation," *The Midwest Sociologist* 19 (December 1956): 34.

manager" represents the juncture of such roles as "direct supervisor of department heads," "second-line supervisor of store clerks," "coordinator of store activities," and "representative of the store in community affairs." The position of "chairperson of the entertainment committee" is derived from the convergence of the roles of "coordinator of committee activities," "member of the executive council," and "subordinate of the association president." The position of "state governor" is identified by such roles as "chief administrator of the state government," "chief executive of the state," "employer of all state employees," and so on. Both dynamic roles and structural positions are real social phenomena; they are simply different aspects of the process of participation in social organization.

There are two significant differences between roles and positions, however. First, because a social position is an identified location within a social structure, it is seen as existing whether or not anyone is presently occupying it. This is not always true of roles. The positions of store manager, chairperson of the entertainment committee, and state governor will all be recognized by members of their respective organizations during the interim period after one incumbent leaves and before another is selected. Some roles, in contrast, are not anticipated and must be enacted by an individual before they will be recognized as existing. Such unformalized and transient roles as "confidant to the president," "sparkplug of the athletic team," or "mediator of family quarrels" do not constitute social positions. Another distinction between positions and roles is that positions are often more institutionalized, so that they may be governed by a wider range of social norms and may be perpetuated for long periods of time.[6]

To summarize these concepts of roles and positions:

> PRINCIPLE 53: Dynamic social roles are the smallest subunits of all social organizations, and are enacted as individuals participate in organizations, while structural social positions are identified and institutionalized locations within organizations that exist regardless of whether or not they are currently occupied.

THE COMPONENTS OF ROLES

Just as social organization always consists of both social ordering and culture, so social roles—as subunits of organizations—always contain the twin components of overt action patterns and cognitive expectations. *Cognitive expectations prescribe and proscribe actions and attitudes for the persons enacting a given role.* These role expectations are of three different

---

[6] William J. Goode, "Norm Commitment and Conformity to Role-Status Obligation," *American Journal of Sociology* 66 (November 1960): 246–258.

types: cultural, situational, and personal.[7] Cultural expectations are contained in the culture of the organization of which the role is a part. They are the social norms and rules that apply specifically to this role. Situational expectations are held by the other people, or role partners, with whom the role is enacted in a given situation. These role partners (such as a physician's nurses and patients, the lawyers and defendants in a judge's court, or one's spouse and children) derive some of their expectations for the role from their common culture, but they also create some of them especially for the situations in which they encounter the role. (Situational role expectations are similar to "definitions of the situation," except that the latter concept can apply to several different roles simultaneously if they all occur in one social situation.) Personal expectations are those which the actor holds for himself or herself in this role. Again, some of these personal expectations are learned from one's culture and some from one's immediate role partners, but others may be uniquely one's own.

The more encompassing, precise, and rigid the cultural expectations pertaining to a role, the less opportunity the individual has to shape the role to fit the immediate situation and his or her own personal expectations. Thus, for instance, the Roman Catholic Church minutely defines almost everything a priest does when celebrating a Mass. In contrast, the doctrine of academic freedom grants the university professor great leeway—though not unrestricted license—to say whatever he or she wants in the classroom. An organization loses some immediate control over the way its roles are enacted if its cultural expectations provide only broad outlines and general guidelines, so that role actors and their partners are given wide latitude to shape the details of each role to fit the demands of the immediate situation and their own expectations. Both the organization and the individual can benefit from such an arrangement, however. Because role actors can then alter their actions to deal with the various contingencies that arise in different situations and at different times, the organization as a whole gains flexibility, adaptability, and stability. At the same time, these individuals are encouraged to become creative in their social actions, to be concerned for the expectations and desires of others, and to assume responsible orientations toward the social organizations in which they participate.

Cognitive expectations tell a person what he or she should and should not do in a role, but *a social role is actually fulfilled when individuals express these expectations in overt patterns of action and interaction.* Role enactment should not be viewed as a mere exercise in behavioral conformity to preordained expectations, however. Role acting is a creative social

---

[7] This categorization scheme is derived from S. Stanley Sargent, "Conceptions of Role and Ego in Contemporary Psychology," in Muzafer Sherif and John H. Roherer, eds., *Social Psychology at the Crossroads* (New York: Harper & Row, 1951), pp. 355–370.

process, in the course of which existing expectations are often altered and new ones established. It is through role acting that roles are actually created. No matter how minutely cognitive expectations may be defined, they can never anticipate and specify actions for every contingency. Hence every role enactment is a creative performance. Some roles give the individual much more room for social creativity than do others, of course. But considerable skill in social interaction is necessary to bring any role to life. A role actor is always devising a performance on the basis of his or her own goals, role partners' expectations, cultural norms and rules, and the demands of the immediate situation.[8] As Shakespeare noted long ago: "All the world's a stage, / And all the men and women merely players."

Unfortunately, considerable terminological ambiguity has crept into sociology concerning the process of role enactment. There are at least three distinct forms of this phenomenon.[9] Role *acting* is the basic process of assuming a social role, accepting expectations for it, and shaping one's actions in terms of it. A role actor seriously fulfills a social role in interaction with others. Role *playing*, on the other hand, is not "for real." It occurs when children "play at" being firemen or mothers, and also when adults pretend to assume roles that do not normally occupy. Sometimes, of course, it is hard to tell whether a person is seriously acting a role or only pretending to play it, and fraudulent role acting is not a rare occurrence. Role *taking*, finally, is the mental activity of temporarily putting oneself in another person's role so as to better understand and predict that person's attitudes and actions. Empathetic skill in mentally "taking the role of the other" is an extremely valuable asset to anyone engaging in social interaction, and we all do it in many of our daily encounters.

We can now formulate a more precise conceptualization of social roles that takes into account both their cognitive and behavioral components:

> PRINCIPLE 54: A social role is an interrelated set of expectations and actions that is an integral part of a social organization.

THE ACQUISITION OF ROLES

The various social roles that individuals enact as they participate in organized social life are acquired in one of two ways: by ascription or by achievement. *Ascribed roles are assigned to individuals because of one or*

---

[8] The most provocative analyst of this process is Erving Goffman. See his *The Presentation of Self in Everyday Life* (Garden City, N.Y.: Doubleday Anchor, 1959), and numerous other writings.
[9] The following three concepts are taken from Walter Coutu, although the terms used here are not his: "Role-Playing versus Role Taking: An Appeal for Clarification," *American Sociological Review* 16 (April 1951): 180–187.

more social characteristics they possess. The most fundamental of these ascriptive criteria are age and sex, although factors such as race, religion, family background, and socioeconomic status are also often used as bases for assigning roles to individuals. Under most circumstances it is extremely difficult, if not impossible, for a person to acquire an ascribed role without possessing the requisite social characteristics. Our society does not allow persons below a specified age to vote as citizens no matter how mature they may be, and it will not sanction a "marriage" between persons of the same sex. On the other hand, if one possesses a certain characteristic, the accompanying role (or roles) cannot easily be escaped. The son of a peasant in a feudal society does not have much freedom of choice in selecting most of his social roles, but neither does the son of the reigning king. In the contemporary United States, essentially the same process often occurs in the assignment of many occupational and related roles. The social fate of the child of an unskilled black welfare recipient is broadly (though not fully) predetermined, but so is the future career of the child of an affluent, college-educated white business executive.

Achieved roles are gained by individuals on the basis of demonstrated capability or performance. In this case, the person must satisfy certain socially prescribed criteria before being awarded the role, and will likely lose the role if its requirements are not fulfilled. Sometimes the criteria for achieving a certain role are precisely defined. To become a United States senator, one must receive a plurality of all votes cast in a senatorial election, and to become a lawyer, one must pass a state bar examination. Quite often, though, such criteria are specified only vaguely, if at all. What does one do to achieve the roles of "top influential" in a community or "office wit" at one's job? As a broad generalization, it is noteworthy that the number and variety of achieved roles are constantly expanding in modern societies as organized social life becomes increasingly complex. Illustrations of achieved roles abound in contemporary societies: member of a football team, vice-president of a business corporation, bridge partner, chairperson of a committee, city attorney, foreman of a construction crew, deacon of a church, commander of a military unit, or college student.

The more important roles in most societies throughout human history have normally been ascribed rather than achieved. This practice assured that these vital roles were always filled, while open conflict for the roles was kept to a minimum and the society remained stable. A monarchy does not face the succession crises that periodically occur in societies with elected governments. Open competition for those societal roles which carry considerable amounts of social power is a relatively recent development—and even today it is still quite rare in many traditional societies. The shifting of socially vital roles from ascription to achievement places unprecedented demands on an organization for collective social sophistication and maturity, and can produce serious social problems—as many modernizing societies in today's world are discovering. In the long run, though, open role achievement not only increases individual freedom by allowing persons to acquire and enact those roles for which they are most qualified and which they personally desire, but it can also benefit the larger organization by channeling the most competent persons available into crucial roles and by encouraging them to perform to the best of their abilities.

In actual social life, the processes of role ascription and achievement are often combined. Many social roles occur in sets, so that if a person fulfills one role he or she is also expected to enact other associated roles. Many businesses expect their executives to participate in community civic activities and to display certain status symbols; the holder of a military commission is expected to act as a "gentleman" as well as an officer; a minister's wife might also be required to head the Women's Alliance of her husband's church; a person convicted of a felony is commonly denied the citizen's right to vote; and professors are normally expected to engage in research as well as teaching. In all of these examples the original role is achieved, but the other roles comprising the total set are ascribed to the person on the basis of the original role.

As individuals participate in numerous different social activities and organizations, they commonly acquire and learn to enact many diverse social roles. A person often possesses a "repertoire" of several dozen ascribed or achieved roles, which he or she enacts at different occasions and in different settings. Quite obviously, one cannot fulfill all of these roles simultaneously. As a person enters each new social situation, one selects (either consciously or unconsciously) from one's repertoire the role that is most appropriate. As the situation changes, the person may later discard this role and shift to another. Meanwhile, most or all of the other social roles he or she might potentially be enacting will remain temporarily dormant. In short, *at any given time only a few of an individual's entire repertoire of possible roles are salient for him or her.*

This phenomenon of differential role saliency enables individuals to fulfill many diverse roles in various types of organizations at different times, even though these roles may not be fully compatible with each other. To the extent that such incompatible roles are kept segregated from each other, they will not come into conflict. The man who arranges to spend Monday, Wednesday, and Friday evenings with his wife and Tuesday, Thursday, and Saturday evenings with his lover has turned a potentially explosive situation into one that is relatively peaceful and rewarding—at least for him. In addition, the greater the number of diverse roles that an individual can accumulate, the more benefits he or she is likely to acquire from role enactment. These positive benefits of multiple role accumulation include (1) increased rights and privileges associated with these roles; (2) enhanced overall role security, since if a person fails in one role he or she has others to fall back on; (3) acquisition of additional resources that can be transferred from one role to another when needed; and (4) enrichment of one's personality, such as learning flexibility in adjusting to the expectations of various role partners, as well as the ego gratification that may result from a sense of being appreciated or needed by a number of different role partners.[10]

Differential saliency of one's various roles also provides opportunities for individuals to act at least occasionally as relatively autonomous personalities. If a person enters a social situation for which no existing roles are relevant or salient, he or she is free to act "on one's own" as a social element—and perhaps to initiate the creation of new social organizations. In contrast, a member of a tightly controlled traditional or totalitarian society is constantly confronted with a few rigidly prescribed roles that pervade his or her entire life, so that he or she has much less opportunity for autonomous action. The existence of a large number of competing and limited social roles, from which a person can pick and choose, is therefore one means of providing for freedom of action in social life.

In sum, the process of role acquisition occurs in two different ways:

> **PRINCIPLE 55: All individuals possess an extensive repertoire of both ascribed roles that have been socially assigned to them and achieved roles that they have acquired through their own actions.**

ROLE CONFLICT

As social organizations grow in size, scope, and complexity, individual participants are called upon to enact an ever widening and increasingly diversified repertoire of social roles. A direct outgrowth of these demands is role conflict, which almost all members of contemporary societies experience at one time or another. Most role conflicts can be classified as one of two basic types. *Interrole conflict, or role incompatibility, occurs when a person is called upon to enact two or more incompatible roles simultaneously.* A common example is the plight of the educated woman who experiences social pressures to have a career and also be a wife and mother. *Intrarole conflict, or role inconsistency, occurs when an individual and one or more of his or her role partners hold incompatible expectations for a single role.* The student who does not believe in cheating but is pressured by friends to use a "crib sheet" on a forthcoming examination

---

[10] Sam D. Sieber, "Toward a Theory of Role Accumulation," *American Sociological Review* 39 (August 1974): 567–578.

experiences this kind of role conflict. One type of role conflict can, and often does, lead to the other type, either sequentially or in combination.

Role conflict is produced by any number of different social situations, of which the following are only a few illustrations: (1) membership in two or more organizations that make incompatible role demands on an individual—such as a club that encourages drinking and a church that discourages it; (2) convergence over time of two or more roles that were originally separated and enacted by different people, but which are now expected of the same person—as in the situation of competing wife and career roles; (3) inconsistency among the major values of an organization's culture, or between its values and its expectations for certain roles—as when the norms hold that killing is wrong but the soldier is told to shoot the enemy; (4) the necessity of enacting the same role to different sets of role partners who hold conflicting expectations for the role—such as the social worker who must deal with clients seeking help ranging from money to psychotherapy; and (5) cultural expectations for a role that have not kept abreast of changing demands being made upon that role—as in the case of a university president who is nominally a scholar but actually mainly a fund raiser.

If role conflict is so prevalent in our lives, why are we not all "nervous wrecks" from trying to deal with overdemanding and impossible role expectations? The apparent answer is that most people learn to utilize a wide variety of "coping mechanisms," or social and psychological techniques for managing or resolving role conflicts. An examination of these various social-psychological processes is outside the purview of this book, but several excellent analyses are available for the interested reader.[11]

THE CONSEQUENCES OF ROLES

We encounter social roles—both our own and those of other actors—whenever we participate in social organization. Roles vary considerably, as we have already seen, in the manner in which they are acquired, in the nature and content of their expectations, in the ways in which they are enacted, in their relative saliency at any given time, and in the degree to which they conflict with one another. But as a general phenomenon, roles pervade all organized social life. What, then, are the major consequences of social roles for both individuals and organizations?

Social roles have two main consequences for individuals. First, *roles*

---

[11]See the following: J. W. Getzels and E. G. Guba, "Role, Role Conflict, and Effectiveness," *American Sociological Review* 19 (April 1954): 164–175; Neal C. Gross, Ward S. Mason, and Alexander W. McEachern, *Explorations in Role Analysis* (New York: John Wiley & Sons, 1958), chaps. 15–17; Robert K. Merton, *Social Theory and Social Structure*, rev. ed. (New York: Free Press, 1957), pp. 368–384; and Jackson Toby, "Some Variables in Role Conflict Analysis," *Social Forces* 30 (1952): pp. 323–327.

provide guidelines for our social actions. If one is acquainted with the main expectations for a certain role, he or she can fairly easily "step into" this role, as into a suit of clothing, and enact it. Much fruitless and possibly embarrassing trial-and-error searching for appropriate actions is thereby avoided. Although you have never before eaten in a particular restaurant, you are able to walk in, order a meal, eat it, pay your bill, leave a tip, and walk out, all without the slightest hesitancy or worry about what to do next. The setting is novel, but the role is not; you have enacted this role of a restaurant customer many times before, and you are thoroughly familiar with its expectations and actions.

Second, *roles give regularity and predictability to our social interactions.* In addition to telling us how to act, social roles aid us in anticipating and predicting the actions of others with whom we interact. Once we determine the role another person is enacting, presuming that we already know something about this role, we then can predict with a fair amount of accuracy (though never total certainty) what the other person will do and how he or she will react to our actions. On the bases of these anticipations, we then modify our own actions to take account of what we expect the other person to do. The salesperson in a clothing store is a total stranger to the customer who comes in to buy a new suit, but even before any communication takes place between them, the customer will have a rather detailed idea of what the salesperson will do and say. From the salesperson's point of view, the role of the customer is only slightly less predictable, and with experience he or she will learn to categorize most customers into one of a few standard roles. For all participants, then, social interaction through role enactment becomes a continual process of interweaving one's own role expectations and actions with one's anticipations of others' expectations and actions.

The enactment of social roles also has several consequences for the organizations in which these roles occur. *To the extent that the roles comprising a social organization are adequately fulfilled, that organization will gain in overall stability and cohesion.* Its patterns of social ordering will be predictable, interrelated, and perpetuated over time. In addition, *adequate enactment of vital organizational roles contributes to the satisfaction of that organization's functional requirements.* If the membership chairperson of an association adequately performs his or her duties, for instance, recruitment of new members will not become a serious problem for the organization. Not all activities within an organization—and hence not all roles—will necessarily contribute to the satisfaction of organizational requirements. Some roles (such as that of a gangster in the community) can even have serious detrimental consequences for social organization. But the survival and operational requirements of an organization are much more likely to be satisfied through the enactment of socially responsible roles than through the disparate actions of relatively autonomous individuals. From the perspective of social systems analysis, therefore, we can say that adequate role enactment by system members will help to ensure that boundaries are maintained, necessary resources are procured from the environment, key functions are satisfactorily carried out, sufficient cooperation will prevail among system parts, and system goals are attained. In short:

> PRINCIPLE 56:   Role enactment is the primary means through which the members of a social organization cooperate in carrying out and perpetuating the social relationships and patterns of social ordering comprising that organization.

In brief summary, both dynamic social roles and structural social positions are parts of larger, established social organizations. It is through the enactment of roles and the filling of positions that individuals actively participate in social organizations. The expectations and actions that comprise a social role provide guidelines and predictability for one's social interactions. At the same time, role enactment contributes to the process of social organization. Organizations could not exist if necessary roles were not adequately fulfilled by individuals acting as responsible parts of those larger entities. Role enactment can create problems, however, since total involvement in minutely predefined roles leaves the person with few opportunities for individual creativity, and ultimately produces social organization that is rigid and incapable of change. A fundamental challenge inherent in social life, therefore, is to create social organization that provides opportunities for meaningful individual action within social roles whose enactment is rewarding to both the actor and the total organization.

RECOMMENDED READING

Bales, Robert F. "Task Roles and Social Roles in Problem-Solving Groups." In Eleanor E. Maccoby, Theodore M. Newcomb, and Eugene L. Hartley, eds., *Readings in Social Psychology*, 3rd ed. New York: Holt, Rinehart and Winston, 1958, pp. 437–477.
> This classic study distinguishes two basic types of leadership roles that tend to develop in many organizations.

Berger, Peter. *Invitation to Sociology*, Garden City, N.Y.: Doubleday Anchor, 1963, chaps. 4–5.
> The processes of self-regulation and role enactment are presented and illustrated in a highly readable manner.

Goffman, Erving. *The Presentation of Self in Everyday Life*. Garden City, N.Y.: Doubleday Anchor, 1963.
>An analysis of the various processes and problems involved in role enactment.

Gross, Neal, Alexander W. McEachern, and Ward S. Mason. "Role Conflict and Its Resolution." In Eleanor E. Maccoby et al., *Readings in Social Psychology*, 3rd ed. New York: Holt, Rinehart and Winston, 1958, pp. 447–459.
>A field study of alternative ways in which persons subject to role conflict tend to resolve it.

Mead, George Herbert. *Mind, Self and Society*. Chicago: University of Chicago Press, 1934, pt. 3, secs. 20, 22, 27, and pt. 4, sec. 33.
>Highlights of Mead's theory of social organization through social learning and self-regulation based on the internalization of the "generalized other" into the "me" of the self.

Sieber, Sam D. "Toward a Theory of Role Accumulation," *American Sociological Review* 39 (August 1974): 567–568.
>An exploration of the benefits that accrue to actors as they accumulate and enact multiple compatible roles.

Shibutani, Tamotsu. "Reference Groups and Social Control." In Arnold Rose, ed., *Human Behavior and Social Processes*. Boston: Houghton Mifflin, 1962, pp. 128–147.
>A discussion of the concept of reference groups and the ways in which this phenomenon produces self-regulation.

Turner, Ralph H. "Role Taking: Process versus Conformity. In Arnold Rose, ed., *Human Behavior and Social Processes*, Boston: Houghton Mifflin, 1962, pp. 20–40.
>Argues that role enactment is a dynamic and continual process of creation, not just behavioral conformity to pre-existing expectations.

9

Control Processes

THE process of enacting social organization would be considerably simplified if individuals willingly and adequately fulfilled all necessary organizational roles, if actors never experienced role conflict or engaged in "deviant" actions, if organizational units interacted smoothly with one another and never tried to influence each other's actions, and if collective decisions arose spontaneously when required. In actual social life, however, these conditions are never realized—and perhaps fortunately so, since a perfectly ordered utopian world might be a very dull place in which to reside.[1]

Given the dynamic and imperfectly ordered nature of social life, the enactment and perpetuation of social organization remains a continual problematic concern for all social actors. The cooperative process discussed in the previous chapter—social learning, self-regulation, and role enactment—bring individuals together into collectivities and enable them to

---

[1] This theme has been elaborated by Ralf Dahrendorf in "Out of Utopia: Toward a Reorientation of Sociological Analysis," *American Journal of Sociology* 64 (September 1958): pp. 115–127.

relate to one another in patterned and meaningful ways. Nevertheless, these processes merely provide necessary conditions for the enactment of social organization; they are not sufficient to ensure its preservation through time or any degree of functional effectiveness. Although all of the processes discussed in the following chapters contribute to the ongoing enactment of social organization, the central key to understanding the dynamics of social ordering is the process of social control.

The Nature of Social Control

THE idea of social control is one of the most fundamental concepts in sociological thought, and was a principal concern of most classical theorists. As emphasized by Morris Janowitz, social control has traditionally referred to a perspective on social organization that "focuses on the capacity of a social organization to regulate itself."[2] He goes on to point out that many contemporary sociologists tend to ignore this original systemic conceptualization of social control, defining the process instead as the social psychology of individual conformity, with the result that analyses of control processes often focus on the level of individual behavior rather than organizational dynamics. In this chapter we take a comprehensive view of social control, examining the social regulation of both individual organizational participants and collective organizational activities and subunits. Our concern is with the crucial question of how patterns of social ordering and shared cultural ideas are enacted and maintained through time despite a continual flow of personnel, constant variations and alterations in role expectations and actions, frequent conflicts among social actors, and the ever-present need for collective regulation of social action.

THE MEANING OF CONTROL

All social actors—both individuals and organizational units—are constantly subjected to various forms of social control, so that this process is inherent in organized social life. Without it, even the best-intentioned efforts at cooperative endeavors would fairly quickly dissolve into uncoordinated separate pursuits by the various actors. In the terminology introduced earlier in this book, the participants would sooner or later revert to acting principally as autonomous elements rather than as involved parts of a larger organizational whole. And should this occur, social organization would no longer exist among them.

As a basic conceptualization, we shall adopt Janowitz's notion that

[2] Morris Janowitz, "Sociological Theory and Social Control," *American Journal of Sociology* 81 (July 1975): 82–108.

social control is the process through which a social organization regulates and perpetuates itself. By exercising control over its participants and its activities, an organization is able to achieve stability (or morphostasis) through time and to function more or less effectively. Once again, the idea of organizational stability does not mean static inactivity, but rather continual dynamic action. In addition, when we speak of an organization regulating itself, this does not imply that the collectivity per se, apart from its constituent members, is taking action. Social controls are always exerted in the name of the organization by one or more of its elites, key functionaries, or agents acting for them. The control efforts of these actors may likely reflect norms, rules, laws, and role expectations contained in the common culture of the organization. These shared cultural ideas provide prescriptive and proscriptive standards for participation in the organization, as well as criteria by which social actions are to be judged. But the actual enforcement of social control occurs through social interaction and patterned social ordering.

CONTROL AND CONFORMITY

The absolute necessity of social control in all organizations does not suggest that the process of social organization demands absolute and total conformity to arbitrarily imposed standards by all participating individuals or subunits. Some organizations—such as concentration camps, highly traditional communities, or totalitarian societies—might attempt to enforce total conformity, but the vast majority of organizations do not. *Effective social control can provide for considerable freedom of individual action*, for several reasons.

In the first place, the norms, rules, laws, and role expectations of the organization need not be arbitrarily imposed. To the extent that rationality is applied to the process of social organization, the standards of action that evolve may greatly facilitate the attainment of the goals the members of the organization are seeking through their collective activities. Similarly, these standards can be modified, changed, or totally rejected by the members if democratic decision-making procedures have been established, if individuals and subunits possess some degree of functional autonomy, and if the standards are viewed as secular (or man-made) guidelines rather than as sacred (or divinely inspired) imperatives.

Second, total conformity of all actions to established social standards is never necessary for the enactment or maintenance of social organization. In fact, despite the predictions of George Orwell's *1984* and Aldous Huxley's *Brave New World*, it is highly doubtful if total conformity could ever be achieved in any real organization. Most organizations normally attempt to control only those activities that are vital to their welfare, so that these demands commonly pertain to only a limited portion of any person's whole life. Various types of organizations usually seek to control different kinds of actions, so that an activity that is extensively controlled in one orga- nization—such as personal friendships among members—is often left to individual discretion in another organization. In the long run, total social control is almost always destructive of social organization. Existing organi- zations can never be changed or new ones developed if people are not sometimes free to innovate and create novel patterns of social ordering or new cultural ideas.

Third, standards for social action need not be rigidly prescribed. As we saw in the case of role expectations, many organizational standards provide only broad outlines and general guidelines, leaving considerable latitude for individual and situational modification and elaboration. In addition, orga- nizations frequently provide alternative standards for a given activity or situation, from which actors are free to select the ones most appropriate to their activities.

Fourth, the word "control" unfortunately carries many invidious connotations for some people, which lead them to protest against "confor- mity." As an aid to maintaining analytical neutrality, these people might prefer a term with a more neutral image, such as "social regulation." Although in practice some social control is unquestionably aimed at achieving behavioral conformity as an end in itself, this is not inevitable and does not explain the whole process of social control. In a broader sense, the purpose of social control is to encourage individuals and subunits to act as responsible participants in social organization, so that these collectivities will be perpetuated and will be able to function effectively. From this perspective, social control is only a necessary means to a more fundamental end. If, in any given organization, social controls do promote socially responsible actions by participants, the resulting social organization can provide these actors with opportunities and benefits—and hence freedom— that would be unattainable outside of organized social life. Social control in some areas of life—such as the enforcement of public health measures or the prevention of crime—can increase the total amount of freedom available to all individuals in a society.

Finally, the specific techniques through which social control is effected need not include overt coercion. Indeed, coercion is a relatively inadequate technique, and often is invoked only as a last resort when the actor is unwilling (or unable) to respond to any other form of control. Although coercion can produce beneficial results for an organization, especially if applied carefully and sparingly, it is perhaps the least effective means of achieving social responsibility in most situations over any period of time.

CONTROL AS POWER SYSTEMIZATION

A central thesis of this book is that the process of social organization can be viewed as the exercise of power to bring order into social life, with the result that organizational entities come to approximate social systems. These twin themes of power and systemization are perhaps most evident in the process of social control, since *control is accomplished through the exertion of one or more forms of social power for the purpose of melding actors into functioning units with systemic properties.*

.In modern societies, social control is most commonly experienced as the exercise of legitimate authority by organizational leaders or elites over the actions of members and subunits. Since authority is usually the most effective and least costly form of power exertion—as long as it rests on a secure foundation of widespread legitimacy—elites will typically seek to control organizational activities and members through authoritative commands whenever possible. In addition, to the extent that elites perform vital functions for the organization, they become key functionaries and can also exercise control through functional dominance.

Almost inevitably, however, situations will arise—often of a novel or unusual nature—that fall outside the elites' sphere of legitimate authority or functional dominance. To exercise control in these situations, elites frequently resort to exerting force through either pressures or coercion. Because the exertion of force necessitates expending resources (either personal or organizationl) that are often limited or nonrenewable, this form of control cannot in most cases be used indefinitely. But it can be quite effective in particular situations for short periods of time. Alternatively, elites can sometimes draw on feelings of attraction or indebtedness which members feel toward them to exert control through suggestions and requests. As emphasized by Peter Blau, attraction can provide a rather effective basis for social control, especially in relatively small groups.[3]

Regardless of the manner in which control is exercised in an organization, it may serve either or both of two purposes: to secure personal benefits for the controlling actors (or their friends, colleagues, and others) and/or to facilitate the functioning of the total organization (or one or more of its parts). Although the pursuit of personal benefits is a common occurrence in all organizations, when actors do this they are acting as autonomous elements, not as involved parts of the organization. Only when individuals or subunits exercise social power as agents of a collectivity does the process of social control contribute to organizational systemization.

As we saw in Chapter 1, organizations approximate social systems to the extent that they maintain effective boundaries, regulate internal activities,

[3] Peter Blau, *Exchange and Power in Social Life* (New York: John Wiley & Sons, 1964), chap. 1.

perform key functions, and perpetuate stable patterns of social ordering—all of which are outcomes of social control processes.

Boundary Maintenance. Social systems are always open to their natural and social environments to one degree or another. Hence they must continually engage in input and output transactions with external conditions and with other actors, which occur through gateways in their boundaries. Although vitally necessary for system functioning, these transactions nevertheless frequently generate tensions for the system and threaten the viability of its boundaries. One crucial function for the exercise of power as social control in organizations is therefore to protect and maintain system boundaries and critical gateways.

Internal Regulation. Regulatory activities within social systems can take numerous forms, including feedback and feedforward, collective decision making, and coordination of subunit interactions. Successful performance of all such activities requires the exertion of social power in one or more of its various forms, since regulation always involves promoting or restricting at least some of the actions of system components. A second crucial function of social control in organizations is thus to regulate the actions of members and subunits in the interests of the collectivity.

Key Function Performance. A key function within a social system is any activity that contributes to the systemic processes of either morphostasis or morphogenesis. In addition to gatekeeping, communication channeling, decision making, and interaction coordinating, these functions can include socializing new members, defining social norms and role expectations, sanctioning deviant actions, preserving basic values, allocating collective resources and benefits, resolving conflicts, promoting system cohesion, and representing the system in the external environment. Hence, a third crucial function for the exercise of power as social control in organizations is to ensure that all necessary operational functions of the organization are adequately performed.

Social-Ordering Perpetuation. The most fundamental feature of any social system is its overall interrelatedness and unity. Although it is not necessary for each system part to be related directly to every other part, all of the parts are bound together as a single functioning entity that preserves stable—not static—patterns of social ordering through time. We need not reiterate here all of the processes that contribute to social ordering, except to emphasize again the importance of power exertion as the dynamic medium through which all social ordering occurs. A fourth crucial function of social control in organizations is therefore to provide for the perpetuation of stable patterns of social ordering.

In summary, the conceptualization of social control presented here can be stated thus:

> PRINCIPLE 57:   Social control, in the form of effective but not necessarily oppressive power exertion, is the principal process through which social organizations acquire systemic properties by maintaining their boundaries, regulating internal activities, performing key functions, and perpetuating patterns of stable social ordering.

Control of Organizational Participants

THE basic prerequisite for the existence of any kind of social organization is that its members or participants act as involved parts of that collectivity at least some of the time. As a result of the social learning, self-regulation, and role enactment processes discussed in the previous chapter, most individuals most of the time fulfill their social responsibilities as parts of various collectivities on their own initiative. Nevertheless, all social organizations also utilize—to widely varying degrees—control processes of one kind or another to encourage desired actions by participants and to discourage or prevent actions that are seen as harmful to the organization. To the extent that this process of controlling the actions of individual participants is successful, it contributes to the systemization of organizations by facilitating boundary maintenance (defining who belongs to the organization and who does not), internal regulation (promoting collectively oriented actions), key function performance (encouraging members to enact these vital roles in an adequate manner), and overall social ordering (preventing "deviant actions").

DEVIANT ACTIONS AND SOCIAL DISORGANIZATION

In a general sense, much social control over the actions of individuals within organizations can be viewed as an effort to discourage or prevent undesired or "deviant" actions and thus maintain the organization as a viable entity. But what constitutes deviant action? Are there definite criteria by which all such actions can be identified or classified? The answer is unequivocally no. Any action by any actor might in some situation be considered deviant. *Deviancy is always socially defined,* so that actions which the members of one organization condemn and seek to prevent might be praised and rewarded by the members of another organization.

The greatest variations in definitions of deviancy usually occur among societies with widely divergent cultures. In the United States we would react with horror if someone butchered a stranger from another community and then called in his neighbors for a ritual meal. Yet there are still tribes in New Guinea that consider such actions highly praiseworthy. Differing definitions of deviancy can also be found within societies. Gambling is a crime in most parts of the United States, but not in Nevada. A man who deserts his family is severely criticized by most "middle-class" persons, but this action is commonly tolerated among many "lower-class" people. And the relaxed standards for sexual behavior that are accepted by an increasing number of young people today still dismay their elders. The point to be stressed is that whatever constitutes deviant action within any given social organization is determined by its prevailing culture, not by any absolute criteria.

Whether or not the particular actions that a given organization defines as deviant and attempts to control are actually detrimental to the welfare of that organization is a problematic question open to investigation. But the fact that a particular action has no objectively harmful consequences for an organization will not prevent its becoming the object of social control measures if the culture of that organization defines it as deviant. In other words, no matter how effectively an organization controls its members, the exercise of social control never automatically guarantees the preservation of social organization. The crucial factor is whether or not social control operates to encourage those actions which benefit the organization and to prevent those actions which actually do have harmful consequences.

As a consequence, *deviant actions cannot be equated with the broader process of social disorganization, or the breakdown of the total process of social organization.* Deviant activity can destroy social organization only under the following kinds of conditions: (1) such actions are practiced by large numbers of people over a considerable time, rather than being sporadic actions by isolated individuals; (2) actions defined as deviant are actually detrimental in some way to existing patterns of social ordering or cultural ideas; (3) these actions are not effectively controlled by the organization; and (4) the organization is already so weakly unified that it cannot absorb or manage whatever conflicts arise as a result of the actions.

In short, social disorganization is a considerably broader and more complex process than is deviant action by individuals. Furthermore, uncontrolled deviant activity is only one possible cause of social disorganization. Patterns of social ordering and cultural ideas can also be destroyed by such phenomena as conquest by another organization, drastic changes in the natural environment, rapid decline or growth of population, unmanageable technological innovations, unresolved conflicts among the various subunits of the organization, breakdown of internal communications, sharp differences in basic values among organizational subunits, or failure to satisfy any of the other requirements necessary for organizational survival. In fact, deviant actions are often not so much a cause of social disorganization as a consequence of this process.

All organizations—from the smallest groups to total societies—at least occasionally exert pressures directly on individual participants as a means of controlling their actions. Although we commonly associate such efforts with the prevention or punishment of deviant action, social control is also often used to promote or sustain socially desired actions by members.

Social pressures exerted upon individuals by organizations in the process of social control are termed sanctions. *Social sanctioning is the process of directly administering rewards and punishments to individuals to ensure that they adhere to organizational standards.* An endless variety of sanctions is employed in organized social life, from the simplest and most informal compliments and criticisms to the most formal and elaborate rituals of bestowing knighthood or executing a death sentence. Social sanctioning may be interpersonal, such as praising or ostracizing a person; it may be organizational, as in promotions or demotions to new positions; it may be economic, as in levying fines or giving bonuses; it may be symbolic, as in awarding a citation or censuring an individual; or it may be physical, as when a person is placed in jail or given a key to the executive lunchroom. In general the more immediate and personal a sanction, the more effective it will be in producing social control.

Despite the widespread use of all kinds of sanctions throughout social life, social sanctioning—especially the administration of relatively formal rewards and punishments—is not a particularly effective means of achieving social control. Three problems inherent in this process can be briefly mentioned. One is that of surveillance. How can an organization possibly watch all of its members all the time, so as to detect every instance in which sanctioning is necessary or appropriate? A second problem is that of administration. Punishments tend to produce only minimally acceptable behavior, never total commitment, while rewards can be used only sparingly if they are not to lose all effectiveness by becoming "rights" rather than "privileges." Third is the problem of reinforcement. No matter how severely a person is sanctioned, it will have little ultimate effect on his or her actions if the larger social environment does not support and reinforce the intent of the sanction. If a person emerges from jail as a local hero, it is doubtful that the confinement will influence his or her future actions in the desired direction. For these reasons, most organizations rely primarily on means of control other than formal sanctioning, and reserve formal sanctions for only the more seriously beneficial or disruptive types of actions, using them either as supplements or as last resorts when other methods fail.

SOCIAL MANAGEMENT

Since virtually all social action is affected to one degree or another by the setting in which it occurs, social control can also be exerted in a more indirect and subtle manner by managing or manipulating that broader setting without bringing any pressures to bear directly on individuals. That is, *social management is the process of controlling individuals' actions indirectly by constructing or altering the social settings in which they act.* Broad patterns of social ordering and cultural norms and rules are shaped in such a way that some potential actions are possible or probable, while others are precluded or discouraged from occurring.

As an example, it is extremely unlikely that an individual will become a professional criminal if he or she has no contacts with criminals and hence encounters no opportunities to become acquainted with their way of life or occupational skills. Conversely, attending the "right" college and knowing the "right" people can be extremely helpful in furthering a business, political, or professional career. Finally, one of the principal reasons why so many black Americans are poor, uneducated, unskilled, live in slums, and have a "lower-class" life style is that the white community has for generations denied them the opportunities to gain an adequate education, secure better jobs, earn enough income, live in desirable neighborhoods, or learn "middle-class" values and norms.

Besides the opening and closing of "doors" to possible social activities, social management can also be accomplished by changes in the structure of an existing organization. A clear example of this type of social control occurred in a sociological experiment dealing with resistance to change.[4] The purpose of the study was to discover how new production techniques might be introduced into a small factory without arousing hostility and resistance among the workers. The employees were divided into a number of small groups, some of which were allowed to discuss (under the direction of a management representative) the various work problems they were encountering and possible ways of resolving these difficulties. Discussion continued in these groups until all the members arrived at a solution that was acceptable to management—until they "voluntarily" decided to make the changes that management desired. Other groups of workers were simply informed of the changes to be made, without any opportunity for discussion. Measurements taken after the changes had been introduced revealed that productivity was considerably higher (and dissatisfaction lower) in the groups that had "participated" in the process of decision making.

---

[4] Lester Coch and John R. P. French, Jr., "Overcoming Resistance to Change," in Eleanor Maccoby et al., eds., *Readings in Social Psychology*, 3rd ed. (New York: Holt, Rinehart and Winston, 1958), pp. 233–250.

Another important technique of social management involves purposeful structuring of the socialization process through which individuals learn organizational norms and rules. The final effect of this procedure is to determine the social bases of self-regulation, but it must begin with modifications in external social conditions. By bringing "socially and culturally deprived" children into a Head Start Program, we hope to prepare them to benefit more fully from later schooling. The U.S. Army teaches its norms of military discipline to new recruits by temporarily isolating them from virtually all outside social relationships and subjecting them to constant demands and duties. On a more extensive plane, twentieth-century totalitarian nations have experimented with controlled socialization techniques such as state-operated nurseries, political propaganda combined with educational instruction, and official youth organizations for children of all ages.

When this process of social management occurs at the level of the total society—either intentionally or unintentionally—it is sometimes referred to as "meta-control." By shaping and directing the basic structure and functioning of a society, national elites can exercise far-reaching control over the actions of all citizens. As described by Baumgartner and his associates: "As societies evolved and became larger and more complex, their structures of control and regulation evolved also—both the intended and unintended structures. These social regulatory processes, involving structures of power, authority, and influence evolved what we call a *meta-level of power or control*. Structures and processes (both planned and unplanned) concerned with the development, preservation, or change of the codes and structures themselves became central to the regulatory process." [5]

The preceding discussions of social sanctioning and social management can be summarized in this manner:

> PRINCIPLE 58: Social control of activities by individuals in organizations—both to promote desired actions and to prevent socially defined deviant actions—is accomplished primarily through the two processes of social sanctioning, or administering rewards and punishments to individuals, and social management, or shaping the encompassing social settings in which people act.

BUREAUCRATIZATION AS AN EXAMPLE OF SOCIAL CONTROL

One of the most distinctive features of modern societies is the extent to which formal organizations pervade most realms of social life.

[5] Tom Baumgartner, Walter Buckley, and Tom R. Burns, "Multi-Level, Dialectical Social Action: An Open Systems Theory Perspective," paper presented at the 1975 annual meeting of the American Sociological Association. See also Tom Baumgartner et al., "Meta-Power and the Structuring of Social Hierarchies," in Tom R. Burns and Walter Buckley, eds., *Power and Control: Social Structures and Their Transformation* (London: Sage Studies in International Sociology, 1976), chap. 10.

Such organizations are characterized by elaborate procedures for controlling the actions of large numbers of people for the purposeful attainment of desired goals as efficiently and effectively as possible. Instead of doing things "the way they've always been done," we are asking "What do we want to accomplish through collective action, and what is the most expedient means of achieving this goal?" As we purposefully set goals for collective action, establish organizations to attain these goals, and attempt to operate such organizations as efficiently as possible, we are bureaucratizing social life. As observed by Max Weber, the process of bureaucratization involves two key features: rationalizing the process of social organization, and effectively controlling the actions of individuals to ensure that their activities contribute to collective goal attainment.[6] In more formal terms, *bureaucratization is the process of rationalizing and controlling social action, so as to improve operating efficiency and more effectively achieve common goals.* In this section we shall examine the process of bureaucratization as an example of the pervasiveness of social control of individual actions in contemporary formal organizations.

Several aspects of our conception of bureaucratization require elaboration. First, bureaucratization is an ongoing social process, not a particular kind of organization, although we often apply the term "bureaucracy" to organizations that clearly manifest this trend. Second, "rationalization" is used here in a sociological, not a psychological, context. It refers to such activities as purposeful goal setting, collection and utilization of all relevant information, objective evaluation and decision making, and social planning. Third, the criterion of rationality applies only to the ordered means employed by an organization to achieve its goals, not to the ends themselves. The ends or goals of collective social activities remain valuative in nature, while bureaucratization provides an efficient and effective organized means of achieving these goals. Fourth, the process of bureaucratization occurs most frequently within relatively formal associations, such as businesses, governments, universities, military units, labor unions, political parties, and special-interest organizations of all kinds, as well as in the social networks uniting such associations. To the extent that any other type of organization—from a family to a community to an entire society—attempts to rationalize its activities for the attainment of specific goals, however, it may also evidence bureaucratic characteristics. Fifth, bureaucratization normally involves extensive application of both forms of social control discussed above—social sanctioning and social management—to all individuals who participate in an organization.

In popular speech, "bureaucracy" is commonly equated with strict

---

[6] Max Weber, *The Theory of Social and Economic Organization*, trans. by A. M. Henderson and Talcott Parsons (New York: Free Press, 1947).

rigidity, "red tape," and general inefficiency, but sociology discards these connotations. All kinds of operational problems can and do arise in bureaucratic organizations, but they are normally due to inadequate or misdirected bureaucratization, not to its excess. In a more sophisticated but still imprecise sense, "bureaucratization" is sometimes used to mean simply the growth of numerous large and complex organizations throughout a society. To repeat, bureaucratization technically refers to the rationalization and control of the process of social organization for effective goal attainment. "Bureaucratic administration is, other things being equal, always, from a formal, technical point of view, the most rational type. For the needs of mass administration today, it is indispensable."[7] Four organizational factors are particularly critical in producing bureaucratization: growth in the size of social organizations, formalization of social ordering, secularization of values, norms, and goals, and developments in techniques of social control.[8]

As long as organizations are relatively small, there is little need for bureaucratization. Families, friendship groups, artisan workshops, village communities, and similar small and intimate organizations can usually function fairly well without purposefully attempting to rationalize and extensively control their activities. Whatever difficulties arise can be handled through face-to-face interaction. Larger organizations, in contrast, often find the establishment of formal operating and administrative procedures to be mandatory if collective goals are to be realized. A certain amount of standardization and routinization is thus a functional imperative in all large organizations that seek to attain goals as effectively as possible.

It is difficult, if not impossible, to rationalize and control the activities of an organization unless its social ordering is relatively formalized. The structure of an organization is formalized to the extent that it meets such criteria as these: existence of clearly defined social positions and subunits; extensive task specialization, or division of labor, among positions and subunits within the organization; channeling of social interactions and communications among position incumbents and subunits into certain prescribed patterns; institutionalization of power within the organization as authority, which is located in certain specific positions and subunits; and overall coordination and regulation of organizational activities. Extensive formalization of patterns of social ordering does not obviate more personal or informal social relations among organizational members, however. Indeed, the reverse is often true; the more formal the social structure, the more extensive and viable the web of informal friendships is likely to be, as a

[7] Ibid., p. 337.
[8] These factors are identified in Peter M. Blau, *Bureaucracy in Modern Society* (New York: Random House, 1956).

"counterbalance" to excessive formality. But only as relationships within an organization become relatively formalized is there a basis or need for rationalization and extensive control of organizational activities.

No matter how large and formal an organization, *rationality will not be thoroughly applied to collective activities until the prevailing values and norms, as well as goal-setting procedures, become secularized.* As long as patterns of social life are viewed as divinely inspired and impervious to human desires, people will make no attempt to change or improve existing activities or organizations. Only as goals for collective action become both purposefully formulated and realistically attainable will people seek to bureaucratize their social organizations. In addition, normative criteria of functional effectiveness and efficiency must predominate over traditional customs and folkways before individuals will willingly adhere to rationally derived procedural rules and social controls.

The social control techniques involved in bureaucratization are illustrated by Max Weber's list of the major characteristics of bureaucratic organizations. To answer the question "What would an organization be like if its operations were fully rationalized?" Weber constructed an "ideal type" of completely bureaucratized organization. That is, he attempted to specify all of the ways in which an organization might be rationalized, and then extended these features to their logical extremes. No real organization will necessarily ever correspond to an ideal type in all its details, but Weber's sketch gives a picture of several of the major characteristics of totally rationalized organization. His bureaucratic ideal type contained the following ten features, all of which can be viewed as techniques of rational social control:[9]

1. Each role and position has clearly defined duties and responsibilities.
2. All positions are arranged in a vertical hierarchy of authority relationships.
3. All activities are guided by formally prescribed rules and regulations.
4. All decisions are made on the basis of technical knowledge, not personal considerations.
5. All activities are recorded on written documents, which are preserved in permanent files.
6. Relationships among role incumbents are impersonal and limited to role obligations.

[9] Weber, *The Theory of Social and Economic Organization, From Max Weber: Essays in Sociology,* trans. and ed. by H. H. Gerth and C. Wright Mills (New York: Oxford University Press, 1946), chap. 8.

7. Positions are filled on a contractual basis, with selection determined by fixed criteria of merit (training and/or experience).
8. Role incumbents are judged solely on the basis of proficiency, and discipline is impartially enforced.
9. An individual's work is one's sole or primary occupation, and constitutes a career with opportunities for advancement.
10. Individuals are given job security, in the form of fixed salaries, tenure, and retirement pensions.

Many contemporary organizations have adopted numerous other control practices aimed at furthering the rationalization of their activities. The more common of these include: cost accounting, inventory control, personnel training programs, information feedback, work simplification, flow process analysis, work inspection, management/worker conferences, and planning based on future projections.[10] These examples underscore the basic point that a bureaucracy is not a certain type of organization that meets fixed criteria. Rather:

> **PRINCIPLE 59:** **Bureaucratization is a process through which any social organization can seek to rationalize and control its functioning so as to achieve more efficiently and effectively whatever goals it seeks.**

In this discussion of bureaucratization we have not yet considered social power, especially as it is used to control activities and maintain order within organizations. Weber believed that power relations within a rationalized organization must be based primarily on authority derived from grants of legitimacy. He further maintained that such authority must be rational-legal in nature. Several writers have pointed out that Weber's conception of rational-legal authority actually contains two separate dimensions: expert (rational) and official (legal) authority.[11] *Expert authority rests on technical knowledge and experience*; an actor is granted the legitimate right to exercise power within a defined set of activities because of recognized

[10] For a more extensive discussion of contemporary techniques of social rationalization, see Robert A. Dahl and Charles E. Lindbloom, *Politics, Economics, and Welfare* (New York: Harper & Row, 1953).

[11] This distinction was first made by Talcott Parsons in his introduction to Weber's *Theory of Social and Economic Organization*, pp. 58–60. It has been extensively discussed by Alvin W. Gouldner, "Organizational Analysis," in Robert K. Merton, Leonard Broom, and Leonard S. Cottell, Jr., eds., *Sociology Today* (New York: Basic Books, 1959), pp. 402–403 and 413–417; and by Victor Thompson, *Modern Organization* (New York: Alfred A. Knopf, 1961), chaps. 1–5. For two empirical studies of this phenomenon, see Stanley H. Udy, Jr., "'Bureaucracy' and 'Rationality' in Weber's Organization Theory: An Empirical Study," *American Sociological Review* 24 (December 1959): 791–795; and William M. Evan and Morris Zelditch, Jr., "A Laboratory Experiment on Bureaucratic Authority," *American Sociological Review* 26 (December 1961): 883–893.

competence and expertise. *Official authority inheres in organizational positions;* whoever occupies such a position in the structure of the organization is granted the legal or official right to exert power, by virtue of office. Weber assumed that in a fully bureaucratized organization these two dimensions of expert and official authority would be identical, since according to his scheme officeholders were selected strictly according to technical merit. Both logically and empirically, however, these dimensions do not necessarily coincide. There can be either "knowledge without office," as in the case of the staff specialist who advises but never commands, or "office without knowledge," as in the case of a figurehead board chairperson who wields no real power. Strains and conflict often inhere in such situations, which thus become the foci of numerous organizational problems. Nevertheless, both of these dimensions of authority in bureaucratized organizations are used extensively by organizational leaders to control the actions of members in the interests of collective goal attainment.

In conclusion, we reiterate the fundamental idea that social control need never be a purely repressive process designed to enforce behavioral conformity for its own sake. Rather, it is through the process of social control that individual participants in social organizations are encouraged to act in socially responsible ways so as to perpetuate these organizations and contribute to the achievement of common goals. Through such organized social activities individuals can gain opportunities and benefits that are unattainable by individual action. Meaningful personal autonomy ultimately results from the assumption of collective responsibilities in organized social life.[12]

Control of Organizational Activities

ALTHOUGH most recent sociological writing on social control has focused on actions of individuals, the original conception of control—as developed by all the classical nineteenth-century sociological theorists— dealt with the means by which organizations regulate and perpetuate their collective activities. In this section, we shift our analysis of social control from individual actors to organizational dynamics, examining three critical functions performed by control processes which facilitate the systemization of organizations. This discussion of organizational control activities is most directly relevant to formal associations, but in a broader sense is applicable to all social organizations.

[12] For further discussion of this general thesis, see Marvin E. Olsen, "The Mature Society: Personal Autonomy and Social Responsibility," *Michigan Quarterly Review* 3 (July 1964): 148-159.

The first of these macrolevel functions of social control is to ensure that vital organizational requirements are adequately satisfied. The process of social organization, we have seen, begins with individual needs, goals, and actions, but as organizational entities develop they acquire a reality of their own with numerous functional requirements. *These organizational requirements are activities which collectivities must perform in some manner if they are to survive through time and attain their goals.*

The term "organizational needs" is a frequently used synonym for this same idea, although for some sociologists it conveys too many biological overtones. These requirements are not inherent in the organization in any anthropomorphic sense, but neither are they inherent in any particular individual members—except insofar as the members act as responsible parts of the organization and thus recognize the existence of these requirements. Organizational requirements are located in the interactions between an organization and its natural and social environments, and in the relationships among its component subunits. They must therefore be satisfied through various kinds of organizational activities.

A number of social theorists have suggested lists of basic organizational requirements, among which the following are common themes:[13]

1. Maintenance of the population, through either reproduction or recruitment.
2. Provision for the training and/or socialization of members of the organization.
3. Promotion of communication and interaction among members and parts of the organization.
4. Establishment of a division of labor through specialization of tasks, activities, duties, and responsibilities.
5. Assignment of social actors to necessary roles, or tasks, activities, duties, and responsibilities.
6. Sharing of common social values among the members, including agreement on organizational goals.

[13]These items are summarized from the following works: David F. Aberle et al., "The Functional Prerequisites of a Society," *Ethics* 60 (January 1950): 110-111; John Bennett and Melvin M. Tumin, *Social Life: Structure and Function* (New York: Alfred A. Knopf, 1948), p. 168; Theodore Caplow, *Principles of Organization* (New York: Harcourt, Brace & World, 1964), pp. 121-124; Kingsley Davis, *Human Society* (New York: Macmillan Co., 1948), pp. 28-31; and Talcott Parsons, Robert F. Bales, and Edward A. Shils, *Working Papers in the Theory of Action* (New York: Free Press, 1953), chaps. 3-5. Parsons and his collaborators have suggested that all of these functional requirements can be classified into four categories, which they call "adaptation," "goal attainment," "integration," and "latency." For an introductory discussion of this scheme, see Edward C. Devereaux, Jr., "Parsons' Sociological Theory," in Max Black, ed., *The Social Theories of Talcott Parsons* (Englewood Cliffs, N.J.: Prentice-Hall, 1961), pp. 53-63.

7. Establishment of a common, consistent, and adequate set of social norms and rules.
8. Procurement of necessary resources from the natural and social environments.
9. Control of deviant and disruptive actions by organizational members.
10. Coordination of organizational activities so as to achieve collective goals.
11. Provision for the allocation to members of the benefits of organizational activities.
12. Protection of the organization against external threats and stresses.
13. Creation of procedures for managing or resolving conflicts within the organization.
14. Promotion of organizational unity or cohesion.
15. Development of procedures for changing the organization.

Undoubtedly this list is far from complete, but it does illustrate the range of requirements that all social organizations face at one time or another.

Organizational requirements can be divided analytically into two broad categories, although in practice the two types merge imperceptibly. *Survival requirements,* or functional imperatives, must be satisfied by all organizations if they are to exist for any length of time. They are basic to the process of social organization. *Operational requirements,* or functional requisites, must be satisfied if an organization is to operate effectively and attain its goals. Some operational requirements are common to all social organizations, while others are determined by the actions and goals of specific organizations at particular times.[14]

Many, if not all, organizational requirements can normally be met in more than one way, through different courses of organizational action. As an illustration, a society can procure new members through the birth of children to present members, through immigration of persons from other societies, or by waging war to conquer additional people. Sociologists speak of these diverse means of satisfying a given requirement as "functional alternatives," "functional equivalents," or "functional substitutes."[15] This fact tends to give an organization considerable flexibility, so that in most cases survival and operational requirements do not rigidly determine either the actions or the structure of the organization—though they often influence and limit organizational forms and activities.

[14] For a discussion of the distinction between survival and operational requirements of organizations, see Amitai Etzioni, "Two Approaches to Organizational Analysis: A Critique and a Suggestion," *Administrative Science Quarterly* 5 (September 1960): 257–278.
[15] Robert K. Merton, *Social Theory and Social Structure,* rev. ed. (New York: Free Press, 1957), chap. 1.

If the survival and operational requirements of an organization are not met, it will experience either partial or total disorganization. This process need not occur immediately, however. The organization may be able temporarily to weather problems or obstacles, and many requirements can be dealt with rather intermittently. Once an adequate set of norms and rules has been adopted or devised, for instance, the organization may be able to rely on these standards of action for some time, with only occasional minor modifications. Over a period of time, nevertheless, unsatisfied requirements will begin to generate tensions and to disrupt the organization. The resulting process of social disorganization is essentially the reverse of the process of social organization. Social relationships will not be perpetuated, patterns of social ordering will break down, common cultural ideas will be rejected, boundaries will be destroyed, and the organization will lose stability and unity. Eventually the organization as an entity will cease to exist. To prevent this process of disorganization from occurring, all social organizations attempt to exercise social control over their activities to ensure that their survival and operational requirements are adequately met. Consequently:

> **PRINCIPLE 60:** Social control on the organizational level involves the establishment of procedures for the satisfactory fulfillment of necessary organizational survival and operational requirements.

INTERNAL COORDINATION

The second of these macrolevel functions of social control is to coordinate the interactions occurring among the component subunits of an organization, thus enabling the organization to cope with functional uncertainty. Since social organizations always approximate open rather than closed systems, they are constantly beset with numerous functional uncertainties caused by lack of information about future events, so that alternatives and their outcomes are unpredictable.[16] Yet if an organization is to adequately perform any tasks or achieve any goals, it must operate with at least some degree of certainty concerning the outcomes of its activities. Consequently, in the words of James Thompson, "the central problem for complex organizations is one of coping with uncertainty."[17] Although many of these functional uncertainties are created by actions of other actors

---

[16] This definition of uncertainty is taken from D. J. Hickson et al., "A Strategic Contingencies' Theory of Intraorganizational Power," *Administrative Science Quarterly* 16 (June 1971): 219–229. Although the concept of uncertainty was developed in conjunction with task-oriented complex organizations, it is quite applicable to all types of organizations. The two major theoretical writings on organizational uncertainty are Michel Crozier, *The Bureaucratic Phenomenon* (London: Tavistock Institute, 1964), and James D. Thompson, *Organizations in Action* (New York: McGraw-Hill, 1967).

[17] Thompson, *Organizations in Action*, p. 13.

in the external social environment, they also frequently arise from indeterminacies in the interactions among the component subunits of an organization.

As organizational subunits interact with one another and affect one another's activities, they become interdependent. As a result, they control vital contingencies for each other's task performances. To the extent that this occurs, each subunit is faced with uncertainties about the actions of other subunits which control vital contingencies for it. For instance, the production department of a manufacturing company may have to contend with uncertainties concerning the ability of the procurement department to have raw materials available when needed, of the personnel department to provide qualified workers, of the maintenance department to keep the machinery operating, and of the sales department to market the products. As these patterns of functional uncertainties are multiplied throughout the organization, the overall capability of the organization to operate smoothly and achieve its goals can become quite problematic.

As long as subunits retain any degree of functional autonomy, these functional uncertainties cannot be totally eliminated within the organization. Hence *organizations generally strive not to avoid uncertainty, but to establish means of coping with it.* These procedures typically include standardized operating routines, detailed functional rules, specified spheres of responsibility, and extensive channels of intraunit communication. If these techniques function effectively, they enable each subunit to carry out its activities with relative—though never absolute—certainty by minimizing what would otherwise be unpredictable contingencies. In other words, they enable subunits to cope with uncertainty in a more or less adequate fashion.

The various units in an organization often differ considerably in their coping ability. This depends on the degree to which their vital contingencies are controlled by other units and the adequacy with which the coping procedures existing in the organization meet their particular requirements. In general, therefore, the power of any unit in relation to other units within the organization will be determined by (1) the degree to which it is able to cope with its own functional uncertainties by ensuring that other units on which it depends will act in predictable ways, (2) the extent to which it controls vital contingencies of other interdependent units, and (3) its ability to affect the coping capabilities and hence functional certainties of those other units.[18]

The larger and more complex an organization, the more likely it is to face pressing problems of providing elaborate coping procedures for its subunits and preventing serious power imbalances among them. As a

---

[18] These arguments are elaborated more fully in Hickson et al., "A Strategic Contingencies' Theory."

consequence, *organizations often find it necessary to create a special subunit with responsibility for overall coordination of internal organizational activities.* This coordinating unit is given authority to establish and enforce organizationwide procedures for coping with intraunit uncertainties, and to regulate interactions among subunits. In short, it exercises control over the other units to ensure that their activities are adequately coordinated so that the goals of the total organization can be achieved.

Depending on the manner in which the parts of an organization are interrelated and interdependent, different coordination strategies may be employed. James Thompson has identified three forms of sub-unit interdependence and described a method of coordination which he suggests is best suited to each form.[19] (1) In *pooled interdependence* each part is not directly dependent on all the other parts, but "each part renders a discrete contribution to the whole and each is supported by the whole," so that "unless each performs adequately the total organization is jeopardized." The most appropriate means of coordination in this case is *standardization,* or the creation of routines and rules which constrain the action of each unit into paths that are consistent with those taken by other units. (2) In *sequential interdependence* the parts are linked together in serial fashion, so that the output of one provides input for a second, whose output is in turn input for a third, and so on. In this case, coordination is best achieved through *planning,* or the establishment of schedules governing the actions of the interdependent parts. "Coordination by plan does not require the same high degree of stability and routinization that are required for coordination by standardization, and therefore is more appropriate for more dynamic situations." (3) In *reciprocal interdependence,* the output of each part is a necessary input for all other parts, so that the parts all interpenetrate each other. This condition is most effectively coordinated through mutual *adjustment* (or feedback), in which new information is transmitted throughout the organization in the process of collective action. "The more variable and unpredictable the situation, . . . the greater the reliance on coordination by mutual adjustment."

Regardless of the specific means of coordination used by an organization, the central point here is that subunit interdependence generates numerous functional uncertainties with which the units must cope. This process is greatly facilitated by the creation of special units and procedures which exert social control throughout the organization to coordinate its internal activities. In short:

> **PRINCIPLE 61:** Social control on the organizational level involves the creation of coordinating units and procedures to facilitate intraunit

---

[19] Thompson, *Organizations in Action,* pp. 54–56.

interaction by providing coping mechanisms with which to reduce functional uncertainty.

DECISION MAKING

A third macrolevel function of social control is to facilitate making and enforcing decisions for the organization. To the extent that any organization functions as a collectivity, it must continually make decisions concerning its goals, actions to be taken in pursuit of those goals, the distribution of tasks and responsibilities among component units, its relationships with other organizations, and countless additional matters. Any member or subunit of the organization could make such decisions, of course, but if these decisions are to be binding on the organization as a whole they must be backed by either general acceptance or enforcement capability—or more commonly by both. In short, *organizational decision making is effective only to the extent that it is linked with the exercise of social control.*

Decisions that are accepted and complied with by the members of an organization are grounded in what Guy Swanson calls its "constitutional order."[20] This sphere of collective jurisdiction is characterized by three features: (1) "It alone applies to actions of the collectivity as a whole and to actions of members when they relate to one another as members of the whole." (2) "It specifies original and independent powers of control that can legitimately be exercised over actions of the collectivity." (3) "Within the collectivity, there is no higher authority to which appeal can be made." Although we commonly associate the notion of a constitutional order with government, Swanson argues that all organizations—even the simplest friendship groups—contain at least a minimal set of rules and procedures for making and carrying out collective decisions. In some organizations, this constitutional order may be strong and pervasive enough to legitimate all collective decisions, but in most cases it must be supplemented with at least occasional exertions of force or dominance by decision makers to compel others to abide by their decisions.

The process of organizational decision making, regardless of whether it rests on the exercise of legitimate authority or on the exertion of force and dominance, may be enacted by a single actor (individual or subunit) or by any number of actors within the organization. Max Weber's ideal type bureaucracy assumed that full rationality and control of organizational functioning could only be attained with a unitary decision-making structure in the form of a hierarchy. Numerous contemporary writers have suggested, however, that effective operational rationality and control can be achieved or

[20]Guy E. Swanson, "An Organizational Analysis of Collectivities," *American Sociological Review* 36 (August 1971): 607–624.

even enhanced with a more diverse decision-making structure.[21] These two contrasting organizational forms are described in more detail in the following paragraphs.

In a unitary organization, emphasis is placed on official authority that is exercised downward through a hierarchical pyramid of successively broader structural levels. Legitimacy is granted to the organization as a whole, not to any individual incumbents or subunits, and hence ultimately focuses on the single position at the apex of the structural hierarchy. (This position may be occupied by either one individual or a small group, but it must always speak with a single voice.) Authority is then delegated downward from the top position through a graded hierarchy of subordinate units and offices. Each position in the hierarchy derives its authority from the one immediately above it and is always responsible to this superior office. As a consequence, any given position normally exercises less power than those above it in the hierarchy, but more power than those below it. Furthermore, as we proceed down the hierarchy of authority, each successive structural layer usually contains more positions than does the level above it, giving the entire organization a pyramidal appearance. Overall, the subunits of the organization tend to have relatively little functional autonomy.

Two major arguments are frequently given for the necessity of unitary decision making if organizational rationality and control are to be achieved. The first argument begins with the observation that many goal-oriented organizations are held together mainly through functional interdependencies rather than shared norms and values. It is imperative, therefore, that a complex web of complementary exchange relationships be maintained among the specialized and mutually interdependent organizational units. This in turn requires unitary decision making to ensure overall communication, coordination, regulation, and planning. The second argument is based on the assumption that in most organizations operational rationality must be imposed upon the majority of the members and subparts. This argument assumes that if they are left on their own, individuals will tend to give more emphasis to interpersonal relationships than to impersonal rules, while subunits will tend to place their own requirements and goals above those of the larger organization. Discipline need not be harsh or autocratic—this is the main argument of "human relations management"—but it must originate from those positions at the top of the authority hierarchy which presumably represent the best interests of the entire organization.

---

[21] For a sampling of this literature, see the following: Rensis Likert, *New Patterns of Management* (New York: McGraw-Hill, 1961), chap. 8; Eugene Litwak, "Models of Bureaucracy Which Permit Conflict," *American Journal of Sociology* 67 (September 1961): 177–184; and Clagett Smith and Arnold Tannenbaum, "Organizational Control Structure," *Human Relations* 16 (1963): pp. 299–316.

Unitary decision making tends to produce many serious operational problems for an organization, however. Three of these are stifling of initiative and creativity, organizational rigidity, and ineffective supervision. Individuals and groups at lower levels of the hierarchy are expected to perform their roles in accordance with the established rules and dictates of their superiors. Innovation is actively discouraged, unless it is first approved by higher authority. This procedure can work fairly well, despite the frustration and apathy it produces among workers, as long as tasks are uniform, routine, or repetitive. But it eliminates many opportunities for functional improvements, and it becomes totally inadequate when members are required to deal with tasks that are diverse, unique, or highly technical. A direct outgrowth of the stifling of initiative and creativity is organizational rigidity. The organization becomes incapable of continually and flexibly adjusting to changing external or internal situations. Over time, it will experience constantly declining functional efficiency and effectiveness, and it may eventually be overcome by conditions with which it cannot cope. Finally, adequate supervision becomes extremely difficult in a unitary organization as role requirements demand increased technical knowledge and skill. A supervisor cannot acquire or retain proficiency in all the intricate, technical aspects of his subordinates' work. He or she thus loses the ability to evaluate them, solve their problems, or promote coordination among them.

In a relatively diverse organization, emphasis is placed on expert authority that is exercised in all directions throughout a horizontal structure according to functional requirements. Authority is vested in role incumbents according to their technical knowledge, experience, and ability, rather than in formally defined offices. A comptroller is given full responsibility for handling all organizational finances, for instance, but only after he or she has mastered extensive technical knowledge and skills, acquired many years of practical experience, and demonstrated his or her capabilities in less demanding positions. Each member or unit of the organization must earn authority; it is never simply delegated to the incumbent of a position. Structurally, the organization is divided into a number of semi-autonomous units, each of which performs certain special activities for the entire organization. These functional subunits are arranged horizontally, not vertically, so that all units exercise relatively equal power, while each unit's authority is limited to its particular sphere of competence. Consequently, subunits of the organization retain considerable functional autonomy.

The two main arguments for unitary decision making—the necessity for functional coordination and for discipline—are met in a diverse organization through different procedures. Ensuring adequate communication, coordination, regulation, and planning, which are critical problems in an organization with many semi-autonomous specialized units, are accomplished by establishing a specialized administrative staff. Instead of occupying the upper levels of a hierarchical pyramid, the administration is simply another equally authoritative functional unit of the organization. Administrators are technical experts in their particular field of coordination and planning, but they exercise no authority outside their sphere of competence. They are relieved of the tasks of making and enforcing decisions for the entire organization, and can devote full attention to purely administrative responsibilities.

Discipline over individuals and subunits within a diverse organization, meanwhile, can be effectively maintained through professionalization. Within each functional area a code of professional ethics and norms is formulated, stressing the individual's responsibilities to his clients, his colleagues, and the total organization—all of which take precedence over his own self-interests. These standards are internalized by each member as part of his or her technical or professional training and socialization in the organization, so that most of the person's actions are self-regulated. If external enforcement should become necessary, appropriate sanctions are applied by colleagues, not by administrators.

A diverse organization also faces distinctive functional problems. On the one hand, because administrators have close access to informational flows, resource procurement, and other organizationwide activities, there is always a possibility that their power will slowly expand beyond their prescribed area of authority. However, it is possible to build into an organization various safeguards against this tendency, as seen in the role of a hospital administrator who is prohibited from making any decisions pertaining to the medical care of patients. On the other hand, there is always the possibility that professionals will begin to place the interests of their particular discipline above those of the total organization. Such conflicts of interest can also be controlled through appropriate procedural techniques, however, and can even be transformed into creative inducements for higher standards of performance.

As described here, both unitary and diffuse organizations are solely analytical types. Almost all real organizations possess various combinations of features from both types. Nevertheless, for analytical purposes we can describe most organizations as relatively unified or diverse in their decision-making structures. Historically, unitary decision making has tended to predominate in many organizations, possibly because official authority is somewhat easier to establish and maintain than is expert authority, at least in the short run. Diffuse decision making is steadily gaining more adherents, however, as its long-range benefits become apparent. Research laboratories and hospitals are examples of organizations that are currently moving toward extensive diffusion of decision making based on expert authority and professionalization. And even such traditionally unitary organizations as business corporations and military units are now experimenting with more diverse decision-making structures. The ultimate goal for both social scientists and applied practitioners in this regard will be to discover the unique combination of unified and diverse decision making which is best suited for achieving effective rationalization, control, and goal attainment in each type of social organization. In summary:

> **PRINCIPLE 62:** Social control on the organizational level involves establishing decision-making procedures and some combination of unitary versus diverse structure that will enable the organization to reach and enforce binding collective decisions.

CENTRALIZATION AS AN EXAMPLE OF SOCIAL CONTROL

As organizations become increasingly large and complex, and as problems of macrolevel social control become correspondingly demanding, there is a general tendency for the exercise of power and control—as well as many other organizational activities—to become steadily more centralized. In this final section we therefore examine organizational centralization as an example of a pervasive trend in modern societies to strengthen macrolevel social controls.

The process of centralization within organizations refers to the convergence of social power, and hence control over all collective activities, in a relatively small number of dominant elite positions. Centralization can and does occur in all kinds of organizations, although it is perhaps most evident in associations, networks, communities, and especially societies. We have spoken of unitary decision making as a major characteristic of many organizations, but in a broader sense centralization is a dynamic social process that pervades most large and complex organizations in today's world. Thus we can identify trends toward increased centralization within any organization, regardless of its present social structure or distribution of power. Highly centralized power is by definition authoritarian, in that it is exercised downward through an organizational hierarchy from the ruling elites. These elites might be chosen by the rest of the members, so that centralization is not incompatible with representative democracy, but it does prohibit classical democracy in the sense of popular decision making on all substantive issues. Authoritarian power must not be confused with autocracy, however. Centralized authority becomes autocratic only if it is used by elites solely for their own benefit, without any concern for the welfare of the whole organization—which need not occur. There is no inherent relationship between centralization and autocracy.

Centralized power within an organization frequently becomes focused within a formal ruling unit whose primary functions are making decisions for the organization and controlling organizational activities. Such a unit might be referred to as "the executive committee," "top management," "the power elite," "central command," "the inner circle," "national headquarters," or "the federal government," but in any case it constitutes a fairly unified subunit that exerts influence and control throughout the entire organization. This centralization of power within a ruling unit does not always occur in simpler types of societies. Under feudalism, for instance, power is highly diffused among all land-owning nobles, so that the formal government is quite weak. During the early stages of industrialization, dominant power usually shifts to the owners and managers of industries, who frequently "employ" the societal government to protect their private interests. With growing centralization of power, however, official authority transcends force and dominance based on economic or related activities. Hence, *the specialized wielder of official authority in an organization—its "government"—normally comes to predominate over all other subparts.*

Notice, however, that the convergence of official authority in a governmental unit is only the most obvious aspect of the much broader process of centralization. In addition, control over economic resources often becomes centralized in a few functionally dominant units within the organization, whether it is a community, a voluntary association, a large corporation, an interrelated network, or a total society. The wielding of physical coercion is likely to become the special prerogative of highly centralized police and military units—either public or private. And given modern technology, the flow of information and cultural ideas throughout the organization also tends to be directed largely by centralized communication media. In short, *the process of centralization may extend into all the activities occurring within an organization.*

What factors produce this trend in a society? The impetus toward centralization, if not the exact degree or forms it takes, is largely provided by the three trends of industrialization, urbanization, and bureaucratization. First, the high levels of economic productivity generated by industrialization in turn create enormous amounts of new resosrces in a society, and enable people to attain goals that were once unimaginable. As a consequence, the exercise of power becomes an increasingly crucial social phenomenon. Furthermore, industrialization tends to concentrate economic power to an extent undreamed of in the days of skilled artisans in a handicraft economy. In a modern factory, incumbents of a few positions effectively control the work of hundreds or thousands of people, as well as the economic resources of the entire organization. Hence industrialization both increases the total amount of power being exerted in a society and tends to centralize it in the hands of a few functionally dominant elites.

Second, urbanization brings together in a small area large numbers of people, and forces them to seek new, collective solutions to common problems. Activities that were once carried out primarily in the family or local neighborhood—such as fire and police protection, public transportation, food distribution, social welfare, education, public health measures, or determination of land usage—must now, for purely functional reasons, be turned over to specialized but also centralized agencies. Hence urbanization carries centralization beyond the economic sphere into numerous other areas of social life.

Third, the process of bureaucratization usually results in the growth of large, hierarchically structured, and predominantly centralized organizations. As we have already seen, the trend within organizations toward increased efficiency and effectiveness of goal attainment does not necessarily require the creation of centralized power hierarchies, but in practice this has usually been the outcome of bureaucratization. Until quite recently, we have tended to assume that rationalization of organizational functioning demanded power concentration, so that most highly bureaucratized organizations in all realms of social life have been structured in hierarchical patterns and operated in a centralized manner.

It is commonplace to think of organizational centralization and decentralization as opposing tendencies. But are they? If it is true that in the United States the national polity and other societywide networks are becoming increasingly centralized, while at the same time many smaller associations are experimenting with diffuse decision-making arrangements, these trends would appear to be contradictory. From a broader perspective, though, the real negation of power centralization is anarchy, not decentralization. As random social actions become ordered into stable social organizations, it is perhaps inevitable that social power not only will be created but will be focused in dominant units or roles. The process of social organization creates centralized social power in the place of powerless anarchy. To take one simple example, eleven isolated individuals standing on a football field would be no match for any organized team. But as interactions among these individuals become patterned and recurrent in the form of a unified football team, the group as a whole gains the ability to do what no player could accomplish by himself—exert organizational power to score touchdowns. There can be only one signal caller on the team if chaos is to be avoided, so that the power of the entire team is centralized in the authoritative position of quarterback. He then delegates responsibilities for specific plays to the other members as he (or his coach) sees fit.

Decentralization of power in an organization can occur only after some minimal amount of centralized power has been created through the process of social organization. Decentralization does not destroy the overall organization or its social power, but only distributes it among many subunits, each of which thus becomes capable of partially autonomous action. The presumed benefits of decentralization, despite its attendant problems of coordination, are stimulation of creativity, greater flexibility, functional efficiency, new opportunities for growth, and more effective goal attainment. Moreover, as various subunits acquire some latitude to develop their own special capabilities, the total power of the organization can be tremendously increased. To continue our football example, decentralization can occur only after the team has been organized to the point where it can be split into offensive and defensive units, each of which is given partial autonomy to perform certain specialized tasks and each of which now has a signal caller.

One resolution of the apparent paradox of centralization on a national scale versus decentralization in smaller organizations is that these two organizational levels are currently at different developmental stages. The process of creating associations with limited size, complexity, and goals has been carried on successfully in this society for numerous generations, so that many of these organizations are now well enough established and unified to be capable of experimenting with decentralization without threatening their existence. In contrast, only recently have we begun to create social networks—most notably in the political and economic spheres, but to some extent in several other areas also—that are truly societywide in size and scope, that are fantastically complex, and whose goals are undefined except for vague conceptions of "public welfare." At this level of national organization, functional activities and social power may not yet be fully enough developed and centrally unified to allow extensive decentralization, especially when local organizations are frequently reluctant to assume responsibility for initiating new programs of collective social action. Societywide centralization of power might thus represent not so much a loss of power by local organizational units as the creation of new social activities and power on the societal level where none previously existed.

As an empirical fact, the United States appears to be currently undergoing a noticeable trend toward increased centralization. C. Wright Mills has amassed considerable evidence that suggests growing power centralization within the executive branch of the federal government, gigantic business complexes, and the military, which he claims are the dominant spheres of organized power in today's society.[22] This trend can also be seen in labor unions, professional associations, mass communication and transportation, and several other areas. Mills then goes on to assert that the federal government, big business, and the military are not only becoming internally centralized, but concurrently are growing together to form a unified national "power elite" which increasingly dominates all major societal activities. His

[22]C. Wright Mills, *The Power Elite* (New York: Oxford University Press, 1956).

empirical evidence for this second thesis is not fully convincing to many critics, although even the most casual observation of American society suggests that the federal government, big industry, and the military are indeed becoming increasingly interwoven and functionally interdependent.[23] At the same time, we must also avoid the fallacy—which Mills fell into—of assuming that as the power of the polity or the economy expands, other organizations such as local communities must necessarily lose power. The creation of power through time is a positive-sum, not a zero-sum, phenomenon. For instance, if the federal government begins providing funds to cities for urban renewal, this also stimulates considerable community growth. Although the community may have only partial control over federally financed housing developments, it still gains many forms of new power that previously did not even exist.

As a final aspect of this discussion of centralization, we note Robert Michels's insightful theory concerning an inherent tendency in all organizations toward oligarchical rule.[24] He argued that *oligarchy—the monopolizing of power by a small, self-perpetuating, elite group—is sooner or later inevitable in every organization.* He gave many reasons for this, including the following:

1. Large size and an elaborate division of labor necessitate centralized coordination and regulation for effective action.
2. Collective decisions on complex organizational matters can be made speedily and efficiently only by a few elites.
3. Incumbents of leadership positions become indispensable as they develop special skills and experience in running the organization, so that other members cannot afford to deprive them of power.
4. Over time, leaders build up a legitimate right to high office, as well as an extensive web of personal influence, which further increases their power.
5. Leaders acquire dominant control over organizational finances, communications, disciplinary agencies, and so on, all of which they can use to their own advantage.
6. Leaders are normally more unified than other members, and hence they can effectively thwart or absorb (co-opt) potential challengers.
7. Most rank-and-file members tend to be indifferent and apathetic toward the organization and its problems, and are only too happy to leave the problems of leadership to those who are willing to assume them.

[23] See Fred J. Cook, *The Warfare State* (New York: Macmillan Co., 1962); and Marc Pilisuk and Thomas Hayden, "Is There a Military Industrial Complex Which Prevents Peace?" *Journal of Social Issues* 21 (July 1956): 67–117.
[24] Robert Michels, *Political Parties*, trans. by Eden and Cedar Paul (New York: Free Press, 1966).

Michels sought to test his thesis by studying European socialist political parties at the beginning of the twentieth century. He reasoned that if oligarchy existed in these associations, which were dedicated to democracy, both internally and throughout society, then it must indeed be inevitable in social organization. He concluded that his research fully substantiated his predictions, from which he reasoned that "Who says organizations, says oligarchy." [25]

This "iron law of oligarchy" may not be as inescapable as Michels presumed, but it is a serious problem with which all organizations must contend if they wish to preserve any aspects of democracy. It is perhaps most critical in highly centralized organizations, but it also plagues those with decentralized authority structures if the power of administrators is not strictly limited. We are therefore left with the fundamental question of how to provide for necessary centralized leadership and overall functional effectiveness in social organizations, while maintaining democratic decision making and ultimate control. As yet we have no adequate solution to this problem. As a general principle, however, we can say that:

> **PRINCIPLE 63:** Centralization of power and control is a pervasive tendency in all large organizations, but oligarchy is not inevitable if power and control are distributed among semi-autonomous organizational subunits.

RECOMMENDED READING

Aberle, D. F., A. K. Cohen, A. K. Davis, M. J. Levy, Jr., and F. X. Sutton. "The Functional Prerequisites of a Society." *Ethics* 60 (January 1950): 100–111. (Also Bobbs-Merrill reprint S-1.)
> The original presentation of the idea of organizational requirements.

Asch, S. E. "Effects of Group Pressure upon the Modification and Distortion of Judgments." In Eleanor E. Maccoby, Theodore M. Newcomb, and Eugene L. Hartley, eds., *Readings in Social Psychology*, 3rd ed. New York: Holt, Rinehart and Winston, 1958; pp. 174–183.
> A laboratory example of the ability of group pressures to influence an individual's thoughts and actions.

Bendix, Reinhard. "Bureaucracy: The Problem and Its Setting." *American Sociological Review* 12 (October 1947): 493–507. (Also Bobbs-Merrill reprint S-16.)
> Bureaucratization is seen as a process involving both rationalization and human relations, and containing both authoritarian and democratic power structures.

[25]Ibid., p. 365.

Coch, Lester, and John R. P. French, Jr. "Overcoming Resistance to Change." In Eleanor E. Maccoby et al., *Readings in Social Psychology*, 3rd ed. New York: Holt, Rinehart and Winston, 1958, pp. 233–250. (Also Bobbs-Merrill reprint S-45.)

> An experimental study of the use of organizational management as a means of social control.

Evan, William M., and Morris Zelditch, Jr. "A Laboratory Experiment on Bureaucratic Authority." *American Sociological Review*, 26 (December 1961): 883–893.

> Differentiates between official and expert authority, and attempts to measure experimentally the separate effects of each type.

Hickson, D. J., C. R. Hinings, C. A. Lee, R. E. Schneck, and J. M. Pennings. "A Strategic Contingencies' Theory of Intraorganizational Power," *Administrative Science Quarterly* 16 (June 1971): 219–229.

> Uses the process of coping with uncertainty through control processes to explain the structure of power within organizations.

Janowitz, Morris. "Sociological Theory and Social Control." *American Journal of Sociology* 81 (July 1975): 82–108.

> Traces changes that have occurred in the concept of social control, and argues for a return to its original meaning of organizational self-regulation.

Michels, Robert. *Political Parties*, trans. by Eden and Cedar Paul. New York: Free Press, 1966, pt. 1A, chaps. 1 and 2; pt. 1B, chaps. 1 and 2; pt. 2, chap. 1; and pt. 6, chaps. 1, 2, and 4.

> Michels's famous argument for the inevitability of oligarchy in social organization.

Morse, Nancy C., and Everett Reimer. "The Experimental Change of a Major Organizational Variable." *Journal of Abnormal and Social Psychology* 52 (January 1956): 120–129. (Also Bobbs-Merrill reprint S-206.)

> Reports the results of a field experiment in which control within an organization was decentralized to the worker level.

Ross, Edward A. *Social Control: A Survey of the Foundations of Order*. Cleveland, Ohio: The Press of Case Western Reserve University, 1969. (Originally published in 1901 by the Macmillan Co.).

> A classic discussion of social control as a societal process in relation to the dynamics of social change.

Weber, Max. *From Max Weber: Essays in Sociology*. Trans. and ed. by H. H. Gerth and C. Wright Mills. New York: Oxford University Press, 1946, chap. 8.

> Weber's classic description of the major features of a bureaucracy.

10

Cohesion Processes

AS social organizations exercise effective social control, they gain operational strength, stability, and effectiveness. If this crucial aspect of social ordering is not adequately enacted, no organization will survive for long. Conversely, with adequate control procedures, an organization possesses the minimally necessary requirements for survival and action. But this does not guarantee that an organization will realize its full potential for operational viability, flexibility, or goal attainment.

The Nature of Social Cohesion

TO develop those latter capabilities to their fullest—and hence maximize the degree to which it approximates a dynamic social system—an organization must acquire and maintain at least some degree of cohesion or solidarity. Social cohesion is not, however, a direct outgrowth of social ordering. Rather, it is a result of activities within the social-interaction and culture-sharing components of the overall process of social organization. In other words, although social ordering constitutes the central core of social organization, the cohesive processes that most strongly solidify organizations occur within the spheres of interaction and culture. Nevertheless, cohesion acquired within either of these two realms will further strengthen patterns of social ordering.

THE MEANING OF COHESION

As an organization gains cohesiveness, its component parts become bound together so that the organization gains overall solidarity. A relatively cohesive collectivity ceases to be a mere collection of diverse activities or units, and increasingly acquires a wholeness that is greater than the sum of its separate parts and that enables it to act as a unified entity. Expressed more precisely, *social cohesion is the process through which the component parts of an organization become united so as to give solidarity to the total organization.* Virtually all organizations possess some degree of cohesion, but its quality and quantity vary extensively among organizations and through time within any particular organization.

A frequently used synonym for cohesion is social integration, although this term may convey unwarranted implications of homogenity. In other words, "integration" may imply that an organization is a monolithic entity whose component parts retain no functional autonomy and which exhibits no internal conflicts or deviant actions. The concept of cohesiveness, in contrast, suggests solidarity without denying the pervasiveness of internal dynamics among semi-autonomous constituent parts. Cohesiveness enables an organization to function as a whole at least part of the time and gives it characteristics of its own that are not inherent in any of its parts, while also allowing those parts to retain some degree of autonomy to act on their own as partially distinct entities.

The conception of social cohesion proposed here is summarized in the following principle:

> **PRINCIPLE 64:** Social cohesion, which gives an organization solidarity and a wholeness that is greater than the sum of its component parts while also allowing them some degree of functional autonomy, occurs in the realms of social interaction and culture sharing, which in turn strengthens patterns of social ordering so that the organization increasingly approximates a unified social system.

RELATED CONCEPTS

It is important to avoid confusing social cohesion with the broader concept of social organization, especially since the two forms of cohesion discussed in the following section are frequently treated by sociologists as general theories of the total process of social organization. Cohesive processes occur within and contribute to the enactment of social organization, but do not by themselves completely explain the overall organizational process. Social relationships, patterns of social ordering, and shared cultural ideas can be established and perpetuated even though the resulting collectivities display little solidarity. This is particularly evident in the case of organizations whose existence depends on the exercise of overt force or direct coercive control, such as prisons. Although such an organization may be able to continue functioning as long as extensive controls are constantly and rigorously applied, it will lack inner solidarity and stability and its existence will always be precarious. Once again, control processes are vital aspects of social ordering, but an organization gains overall solidarity only to the extent that it incorporates effective cohesive processes.

The concept of cohesion must also be distinguished from the idea of individual assimilation into organizations. Cohesion is always a property of an organization as a whole, not of its individual members. Assimilation, in contrast, refers to the process through which individuals become linked or bound into organizations. Organizational members commonly vary considerably in the strength of their ties to the collectivity. One person might be intensely involved, while for another person the organization might be of marginal significance. These variations in the degree of member assimilation do not necessarily determine the cohesiveness of the total organization, however. Member assimilation and organizational cohesiveness are usually interrelated, in that it is virtually impossible for an organization to be highly unified if its members are only weakly assimilated. But failure to distinguish between these two concepts can produce much analytical confusion. Too often, for instance, we speak first of a community as being highly cohesive, and then of the strong ties that residents feel toward the community, without considering the possibility that individuals may be closely bound to their community even if it lacks viable cohesion. For analytical clarity, therefore, it is necessary to treat assimilation and cohesion as separate processes. Our concern in this chapter is solely with organizational cohesion.

Theories of Cohesion

TWO fundamental theories of social cohesion have pervaded social thought since ancient times. These twin explanations of how all organizations achieve and maintain solidarity/cohesion/integration are usually termed functional and normative cohesion, although other terms are also used. These include "symbiotic" and "consensual" cohesion, Émile Durkheim's phrases "organic" and "mechanical" solidarity, and Robert

Angell's "interdependence" and "common orientation" concepts.[1] The classical presentation of both these theories is Émile Durkheim's analysis of the bases of social solidarity in primitive and modern societies,[2] although each theoretical perspective claims numerous proponents among contemporary theorists.

FUNCTIONAL THEORY

The theory of functional cohesion has roots in both utilitarian philosophy and classical economic theory. Its contemporary version, meanwhile, is strongly emphasized by Amos Hawley and other social ecologists.[3] This thesis, which focuses on the realm of social interactions and relationships, begins with the initial assumption that some task specialization or division of labor exists among the members and component parts of an organization. As these functionally differentiated members and parts become specialized in their activities, they grow increasingly interdependent. This interdependence in turn necessitates the formation of numerous complementary exchange transactions. The resulting functionally interdependent relationships bind the members and subunits together and give the total organization cohesion and wholeness. To promote and maintain these relationships, moreover, the organization must formulate operational rules and establish some kind of administrative unit to regulate and coordinate the exchange processes. In short:

> **PRINCIPLE 65: A social organization gains functional cohesion as complementary exchange relationships are established among its interdependent members and subparts and are regulated by standardized procedural rules and overall coordination.**

[1] For a more extensive discussion of both classical thought and contemporary theorizing on the topic of social cohesion, see Robert C. Angell, "Social Integration," in David L. Sills, ed., *The International Encyclopedia of the Social Sciences* (New York: Crowell-Collier and Macmillan, 1968), pp. 380–386. Angell also identifies a third type of social cohesion based on interpersonal attraction, which he terms the "interpersonal theory" of integration. It is based on personal attraction, friendship, and other emotional ties among all the members of a group. Shared affectivity is obviously extremely important in holding together families and some small groups, but it cannot have significant effects for larger organizations in which the members do not know each other personally. Because of its limited applicability, interpersonal integration is not included in the present discussion. Werner Landecker ("Types of Integration and Their Measurement," *American Journal of Sociology* 56 [January 1951]: 332–340) once proposed a fourth type of social integration, based on the extent and effectiveness of the communications within an organization. As Angell points out, however, adequate communication is a necessary requirement for any kind of social cohesion, rather than being a distinct type itself. Many of the ideas presented in the following discussion of cohesion theories were originally sketched in Marvin E. Olsen, "Durkheim's Two Concepts of Anomie," *Sociological Quarterly* 6 (April 1965): 37–44.

[2] Émile Durkheim, *The Division of Labor in Society*, trans. by George Simpson (New York: Free Press, 1951).

[3] See especially Amos Hawley, "Human Ecology," in Sills, ed., *The International Encyclopedia of the Social Sciences*, pp. 328–337.

The degree of functional cohesion existing in any social organization is thus determined by such factors as (1) the extent of specialization or division of labor among its components, (2) the establishment and maintenance of complementary exchange relationships among these interdependent parts, (3) the presence of adequate and internally consistent procedural rules to guide these relationships (that is, lack of discordance[4]), (4) the effectiveness of the overall coordinating unit, and (5) the operation of communication channels to make rules known and to report back problems to the administrative unit.

NORMATIVE THEORY

The theory of normative cohesion can be traced back to ancient social thought and is evident in the political writings of the Enlightenment. Today it is closely associated with Talcott Parsons and his colleagues.[5] This explanation of the cohesive process, which focuses on the realm of shared culture, begins with the assumption that a number of basic values are held in common among the members and subunits of an organization as a result of a common cultural heritage. These values are applied to specific social situations through sets of moral norms. As people create various kinds of organizations to attain collective goals, these units become infused with the shared values and operate in accordance with the prevailing norms—a process that is sometimes called "institutionalization." These organizations in turn shape individuals, through norm internalization and role acting, into social actors who cherish the fundamental common values and seek to perpetuate and realize them through their actions as responsible members of the organization. In short:

> **PRINCIPLE 66:** **A social organization gains normative cohesion as moral norms based on common values become imbedded within it and internalized by its members.**

The degree of normative cohesion in any social organization thus depends on such factors as (1) the extent of consensus on basic values and absence of any antithetical values, (2) the development of an adequate and internally consistent set of norms (that is, lack of anomie),[6] (3) the relative

---

[4]Discordance is a condition within social organizations in which the existing procedural rules are inadequate to regulate complementary relationships among interdependent subparts in the interests of the total organization. See Olsen, "Durkheim's Two Concepts of Anomie."

[5]See especially Parsons's "An Outline of the Social System," in Talcott Parsons et al., eds., *Theories of Society* (New York: Free Press, 1961), pp. 30–79.

[6]Anomie is a condition within social organizations in which the social norms are inadequate to guide and direct the actions of individuals and subparts in the interests of the total organization. See Émile Durkheim, *Suicide*, trans. by John Spaulding and George Simpson (New York: Free Press, 1951), pp. 246–258.

congruence between values and norms, so that adherence to norms leads to realization of the values, (4) the degree to which common norms are infused into organizations, so as to keep organizational activities in line with basic values, and (5) the effectiveness of role training and norm internalization procedures for individuals.

EVALUATION OF THE THEORIES

Both of these theories of social cohesion contain several weaknesses. Functional theory does not explain how—in the absence of shared norms or an encompassing organization capable of assuring adequate social order and stability—the members and components parts of a developing organization come to trust each other enough to surrender self-sufficiency and become dependent on each other in symbiotic relationships. Nor does it explain why the subunits of an organization adhere to common procedural rules instead of seeking to exploit each other for their own self-interests—unless one also includes in the theory either an assumption of total rationality or an ultimate reliance on the use of force. In short, what is the "invisible hand" that turns self orientations into collectivity orientations, if it is not shared social values and norms?

Normative theory leaves unanswered the question of how consensus initially arises on a set of common values. Shared cultural values normally emerge from shared social experiences, not vice versa. Hence a certain amount of unified social organization must already exist before the process of normative cohesion can begin. To carry this line of reasoning further, the two requirements comprising the core of the theory—normative consistency and infusion of norms into organizations—also cannot occur until social organizations have already been created and partially solidified. In short, it can be argued that a certain amount of functional cohesion must exist before effective normative unification can begin.

The limitations inherent in both these perspectives suggest that neither theory is adequate by itself to explain social cohesion, so that neither process can operate effectively without the other. In combination, however, the weaknesses of each process of cohesion are nicely complemented by the strengths of the other.

COMPLEMENTARITY OF THE THEORIES

The complementarity of functional and normative cohesion was recognized and explored by Durkheim in his discussion of the effects of growing division of labor in society.[7] He argued that "mechanical solidarity" (normative cohesion) tends to predominate in small, primitive, homogeneous societies, because of their strong common values and norms and

---

[7]Durkheim, *The Divison of Labor in Society.*

relative lack of division of labor. As societies grow in size and density of interaction, however, division of labor increases and "organic solidarity" (functional cohesion) becomes progressively dominant. He carefully pointed out that a certain amount of consensus on norms and rules is still vital in these societies to ensure the establishment and fulfillment of contractual relationships—which he referred to as "the moral basis of social contracts." But the primary source of unification in complex modern societies is functional interdependence. Durkheim's evolutionary thesis, as an attempt to explain the effects of growing size and complexity of social organization on the process of cohesion, has proved stimulating to two generations of sociologists. Today, consequently, many social theorists argue that *both functional and normative cohesion occur together as complementary processes in virtually all organizations.*

No theorist has yet succeeded in explaining both functional and normative solidarity in a single composite theory of social cohesion.[8] Two possible starting points for such an effort can be identified, however. One is that the climate of mutual trust necessary to initiate complementary exchange transactions before a common set of values and norms has emerged might be provided by what Alvin Gouldner calls "the norm of reciprocity."[9] The essence of this norm is that social actors are obligated to return benefits to those from whom they have previously received some benefits—although the norm does not necessarily require perfect equity in these exchanges. If this single norm is shared by actors starting an exchange relationship, it provides some minimal grounds for confidence and thus promotes a willingness to initiate action. Gouldner points out that to the best of our knowledge this moral norm of reciprocity is universal (although that fact does not explain its ultimate origin), so that a potential foundation exists among all peoples on which to base complementary relationships and begin the process of creating cohesive social organization. Peter Blau has argued, meanwhile, that even this minimal norm of reciprocity is not necessary, and that simple exchange transactions can be initiated through a cumulative series of conditional reciprocated actions that slowly generate mutual trust among the participants.[10]

A second potential starting point for interrelating functional and normative cohesion lies in the fact that both processes incorporate the

---

[8]An effort in this direction has been made by Talcott Parsons, but it strongly reflects his own emphasis on normative phenomena: "Durkheim's Contribution to the Theory of Integration of Social Systems," in Kurt H. Wolfe, ed., *Émile Durkheim, 1858–1917* (Columbus, Ohio: Ohio State University Press, 1966), pp. 118–153.
[9]Alvin W. Gouldner, "The Norm of Reciprocity," *American Sociological Review* 25 (April 1960): 161–178.
[10]Peter Blau, *Exchange and Power in Social Life* (New York: John Wiley & Sons, 1964), pp. 92–95.

exercise of social power, even though neither is solely a power phenomenon. Functional theory emphasizes interdependent relationships among organizational parts, which assumes that each part is capable of performing activities that benefit other parts. To carry out such activities, each part must possess resources on which it can draw for the exertion of power. Hence the greater the number and types of resources available to an organization, the more likely its component parts are to become functionally interdependent and the less likely it is that any one part will monopolize most or all organizational resources. As a result, the extent of an organization's resources base indicates its capability for viable functional cohesion as well as the exercise of force among its component parts. Normative theory, in contrast, emphasizes broadly shared values and norms, which assumes that they are generally viewed as legitimate. If the values and norms of an organization were not accepted as legitimate by its members, they would not likely be widely shared. Hence the extent to which legitimacy is attributed to organizational values and norms indicates its capability for viable normative cohesion as well as the exercise of authority among its component parts. These observations suggest, therefore, that both functional and normative cohesion are outgrowths—though not direct results—of an organization's ability to effectively utilize social power in a constructive manner.

Lest this discussion of functional and normative cohesion appear solely academic and of no practical use, let us briefly apply these two theories to the process of creating viable international organization. Throughout the twentieth century humanity has been attempting to erect some kind of international organization to prevent war. To our dismay, neither the League of Nations nor the United Nations has proved capable of meeting this challenge. Perhaps the underlying reason for the failure of these organizations to unify the world is that both of them have relied primarily on normative cohesion. More specifically, both the League and the UN were founded on the assumption that all participating nations shared a common set of basic values, which were elaborately spelled out in a covenant and a charter. It is readily apparent at this point in history that the assumption of shared values was not valid in either case. In marked contrast, the European Economic Community (the "Common Market") has achieved spectacular success in unifying the economies of its member nations, despite several sharp value conflicts. Perhaps the crucial difference here is that the EEC is based largely on functional cohesion. It has sought to create mutual interdependence and solidarity among its members through the gradual establishment of complementary exchange relationships. Value consensus, especially in politics, is expected as an outgrowth of these mutually beneficial relationships, rather than being a necessary precondition for unity. As value consensus develops through time, however, it should further strengthen the ties among the Common Market nations. Whether or not this experiment in economic functional integration will eventually lead to political and other forms of international unification remains to be seen.

This example suggests the following general principle:

> PRINCIPLE 67: Social cohesion is most effectively established when it begins with mutually interdependent relationships, which through time give rise to shared cultural values, but functional and normative cohesion are complementary processes and both occur to some extent in most organizations.

Social Cohesion in Complex Societies

LARGE, complex, modern societies cannot achieve strong functional or normative cohesion unless several additional supporting social conditions also exist within them. The following paragraphs mention a few of these considerations.

FUNCTIONAL COHESION

Viable functional cohesion is not likely to develop in small, homogeneous, simply organized collectivities. Although even the most rudimentary group often exhibits some task specialization (on the basis of age or sex, if nothing else), such a group lacks the elaborate division of labor necessary for full functional cohesion. This process operates most effectively in complexly structured organizations with large populations and high levels of material and social technology. Extensive division of labor does not automatically ensure functional solidarity, however. The achievement of functional cohesion also requires such factors as a vast web of complementary exchange relationships, procedural rules (such as contract laws and a money economy) for carrying out these relationships, a communication network, overall regulation and coordination of exchange relationships to prevent disruptions and resolve operational problems, and control procedures to discourage extreme dominance of one subpart over the others or exploitation of a particularly vulnerable participant.

All of these requirements tend to push an organization in the direction of centralized administration. Quite frequently, one or more administrative units are established to provide these overall communicative, regulative, coordinative, and control services, since none of the more specialized parts has a broad enough scope of power to deal with all activities throughout the entire organization. If this administrative unit also assumes the task of making and implementing decisions for the total organization, as often happens, it becomes a centralized government. The tendency toward increased centralization of administration and decision making in all modern societies is so marked that social theorists sometimes state as a fundamental social "law" the proposition that growing functional specialization within an organization demands increased centralized control if the organization is to remain functionally cohesive.

This requirement for overall regulation and coordination within complex societies does not imply any necessity for totalitarianism, however—although totalitarianism is one means of achieving it. More specifically, the necessity for centralized administration in modern societies does not dictate whether decisions are to be made democratically or autocratically, whether the society will be operated for the benefit of all members or just the controlling elite, whether governmental positions will be filled through open achievement or closed ascription, the extent to which specialized subparts can influence collective decision making and control societal activities, or whether regulation and coordination are to be exercised through voluntary compliance, overt coercion, or some other procedure. Most important, this demand for centralized administration does not indicate the degree of overall control required for adequate functional cohesion. In fact, the most effective situation is perhaps one of less than total power centralization, since completely centralized control often tends to make a society extremely rigid and incapable of adjusting to changing social conditions. In short, *a partially segmented society in which the component parts retain considerable autonomy can maintain functional cohesion as long as adequate procedures are present for societywide regulation and coordination.*

NORMATIVE COHESION

Strong normative cohesion, in contrast to functional cohesion, is most effectively developed in relatively small, homogeneous, simply organized groups. Common values and norms are easily shared and maintained, they can become deeply imbedded within the organization, and they are always imminent in the lives of individual members. Within contemporary complex nations these social conditions may occur in small groups and other component collectivities, but they are not met by the total society itself. For normative cohesion to occur in such societies, therefore, a series of social links must exist between the individual and the society, in the form of multitudinous groups, associations, communities, and other types of "intermediate" organizations. These "mediating" organizations provide the setting in which normative cohesion of the total society actually occurs. To the extent that these organizations act as responsible parts of the larger society, they will embody basic societal values, support societal norms, and provide roles for individuals that benefit the whole society.

The mere existence of intermediate organizations within a society does not guarantee normative cohesion, however, since they usually retain some degree of functional autonomy and can at times act counter to the interests of the larger society. Moreover, subcultures usually differ somewhat from the culture of the entire society and often directly conflict with it. Thus individuals frequently find themselves caught between the values, norms, activities, and demands of their society and those of other organizations to which they belong. Because these latter organizations are usually more immediate and important in most people's lives than is the total society, persons caught in such a dilemma will commonly give their first allegiance to the local community groups and associations to which they belong. As a result, the society lacks normative cohesion. This condition can be at least partially overcome, however, if the society possesses an extensive web of mass communications that expose the total population to common values, norms, and social expectations.[11]

In a totalitarian nation, adequate normative cohesion is achieved by establishing a proliferation of intermediate organizations throughout the society, all of which are directly controlled by the government or the official party. In this way the elites can be sure that the only values and norms being expressed in the society are those which they provide. Nevertheless, *it is fully possible to obtain a high level of societal normative cohesion while at the same time maintaining a considerable amount of functional and cultural autonomy among component subunits.* Partially autonomous intermediate organizations can perform the mediating actions necessary for normative cohesion if they are themselves normatively cohesive, if they present their particular values and norms as supplements to the societal culture rather than as alternatives to it, if they have overlapping memberships (especially of leaders) that tie them together, if they interact with each other and in the process influence and limit each other's activities, if there is a common socialization or educational process for the entire society that cuts across all subunits and subcultures, and if the society possesses extensive mass communications.

Functional and normative cohesion are sometimes described as antithetical processes for solidifying complex contemporary societies, since the demand of normative cohesion for networks of intermediate associations seems to oppose the demand of functional cohesion for centralized administration. But the underlying social conditions required by these two forms of social solidarity are not incompatible. Both functional and normative cohesion depend upon the creation of viable relationships among partially autonomous subunits, as well as procedures for overall organizational

[11] Irving Lewis Allen, "Social Integration as an Organizing Principle," in George Gerbner, ed., *Mass Media Policies in Changing Cultures* (New York: John Wiley & Sons, 1977), chap. 21.

coordination. Furthermore, neither form of cohesion necessitates complete absorption of all subunits. Extreme segmentation among the component parts can destroy the cohesion of any social organization, but total submersion of all component parts to the overriding interests of the total society often provokes social consequences that are equally disastrous for the society in the long run.

Complementarity of Conflict and Cohesion

AT first glance, conflict and cohesion appear to be contradictory processes. Conflict often seems to disrupt social organizations, while cohesion solidifies them. In fact, however, this need not occur. Under certain conditions the two processes not only coexist, but can directly complement and reinforce each other. Let us explore this possibility further.

The basic thesis underlying this reinforcement argument can be stated thus:

> PRINCIPLE 68: The amounts of conflict and cohesion existing in any social organization are mutually interrelated, so that the greater the cohesion of an organization, the more conflict it can tolerate and utilize without being destroyed.

Although extensive conflict may severely weaken or even destroy an organization with little cohesion, it can greatly benefit a highly solidified organization. Cohesion thus enables an organization to encourage conflict as long as it can be adequately managed, thereby increasing its flexibility, stability, and potential for change. Extensive conflict throughout an organization does not necessarily indicate lack of cohesion, nor does absence of conflict indicate strong cohesion. In reality, the situation may in fact be just the opposite of what it appears to be.[12]

If an organization exhibits only weak cohesion and lacks adequate procedures for managing conflict, it cannot tolerate recurrent or extensive disruptions without being torn apart by them. Hence it must seek to resist and suppress conflict if it is to survive and retain at least short-run stability. It thus becomes extremely rigid. On the other hand, if an organization displays strong cohesion and has established procedures for effectively managing disruptions, it can reap the benefits of ordered social conflict. Indeed, it can actively encourage and promote a considerable amount of intentional conflict. We are therefore led to conclude that *an optimum*

---

[12] Lewis Coser, *The Functions of Social Conflict* (Glencoe, Ill.: Free Press, 1956), chap. 4.

condition for social organization is not some sort of balance or compromise between conflict and cohesion, but rather simultaneous growth in both areas.

To the extent that many social organizations throughout human history have tended to discourage conflict, the reason may be that they have lacked viable functional and normative cohesion. Their only recourse has been to suppress conflict, maintain order through the overt or covert use of force, and resist pressures for social change until they became too strong to be contained, at which point abrupt, far-reaching, and often violent conflict has frequently erupted. Perhaps, though, if social organizations can slowly increase both their functional and normative cohesion and also develop effective procedures for conflict management, they can then expand their capacity to tolerate conflict and benefit from it. The result would be greater flexibility in social organization, continuous instead of sporadic change, and long-term social stability.

In summary, this chapter has examined the phenomena of functional and normative cohesion, viewing them as both theoretical explanations of organizational solidarity and dynamic processes occurring in all social organizations. The point has been stressed that these two types of cohesion not only occur together in virtually every organization but are in fact highly interdependent. Each process supplements and reinforces the other. High levels of both functional and normative cohesion can be achieved in complex societies, provided that their subunits possess some degree of functional autonomy and that effective procedures for overall administration have been developed. Finally, a highly cohesive organization can frequently tolerate, encourage, and benefit from extensive social conflict without being destroyed.

RECOMMENDED READING

Aberle, David. "Shared Values in Complex Societies." *American Sociological Review* 15 (1950): 495–502.

>   Examines the phenomenon of "cultural unity within diversity," or normative cohesion in societies containing diverse subcultures.

Angell, Robert C. "Social Integration." In David L. Sills, ed., *The International Encyclopedia of the Social Sciences.* New York: Crowell-Collier and Macmillan, 1968, pp. 380–386.

>   Summarizes and evaluates existing theoretical and empirical work on the phenomenon of social cohesion.

Back, Kurt W. "Influence through Social Communication." In Eleanor Maccoby, Theodore M. Newcomb, and Eugene L. Hartley, eds., *Readings in Social Psychology*, 3rd ed. New York: Holt, Rinehart, and Winston, 1958, pp. 183–197.

> A report of one of the major laboratory studies of social cohesion in small groups.

Coser, Lewis. *The Functions of Social Conflict*. Glencoe, Ill.: Free Press, 1956, chap. 4.

> Develops the thesis that conflict and cohesion can be mutually supportive.

Durkheim, Émile. *The Division of Labor in Society*, trans. by George Simpson. New York: Free Press, 1951, Book 1, chaps. 2, 3, 7, and Book 2, chap. 2.

> The classic discussion of the ideas of mechanical solidarity (normative cohesion) and organic solidarity (functional cohesion).

Gouldner, Alvin. "The Norm of Reciprocity." *American Sociological Review* 25 (April 1960): 161–178.

> A suggestive discussion of the phenomenon of reciprocity as a common link between functional and normative cohesion.

Gross, Edward. "Symbiosis and Consensus as Integrative Factors in Small Groups." *American Sociological Review* 21 (April 1956): 174–179.

> Studies of several natural groups indicated that functional cohesion tended to produce greater group unity than did normative cohesion.

Landecker, Werner S. "Types of Integration and Their Measurement." *American Journal of Sociology* 55 (January 1951): 332–340.

> Discusses four different types of cohesion and suggests procedures for measuring each type.

11

Distributive Processes

AS the process of social organization is maintained through cooperation, control, and cohesion, various collective benefits—such as useful resources for power exertion, valued material and nonmaterial privileges, and desired social prestige—commonly accrue to the members of organizations. In one way or another, these benefits of collective action—power resources, privileges, and prestige—are then distributed among the component subunits and individual members of the organization. In other words, the distribution of social benefits is an outgrowth of the successful enactment of the process of social organization and the exertion of social power to attain collective goals. The specific manner in which this distributive process is accomplished—whether through coercion, exchange, legislation, or some other technique—depends on the way a particular organization functions. In general terms, however, social distribution is the process through which the benefits of organizational activities are allocated to the parts and members of that organization.

Theoretically, all collective benefits could be distributed equally among the parts and members of an organization, so that no inequality would result. Outside of some small friendship groups, though, this situation rarely occurs. Almost invariably, some subunits and individuals acquire more power, privileges, and prestige than do others, so that the resulting distribution of collective benefits becomes ordered in unequal patterns. The polar opposite of total equality would be complete concentration of all power, privileges, and prestige in the hands of one or a very few elites. Within most organizations, however, patterns of distribution fall somewhere between these two extremes of total equality and complete inequality. The various actors within an organization normally hold differing amounts of power, privilege, and prestige, and hence can be ranked on one or more vertical status dimensions. As these differences are perpetuated through time, social stratification develops. In this chapter we examine the nature of social stratification and social classes, two competing theories of the origins of social inequality, contrasting views of the class structure in modern societies, and a few broad consequences of social stratification.

Social Stratification

TO note that individuals differ widely in the power they wield, the privileges they enjoy, and the prestige they receive is to state the obvious. But to observe that these various types of social inequality are largely shaped by established social organizations, and are themselves patterns of social ordering, is to view stratification as a dynamic social process. Virtually all organizations, from friendship cliques to modern nations, exhibit some amount of social stratification, and this pervasive phenomenon has been observed as far back in human history as written records exist. Yet, paradoxically, there is no imperative theoretical reason why stratification must exist within social life, in the same sense that cooperation, control, and cohesion are inherent in the process of social organization. Social stratification, in other words, is a result of people's more or less purposeful strivings to gain social power, privilege, and prestige in relation to others.

THE MEANING OF SOCIAL STRATIFICATION

Formally defined, *social stratification is the process through which power, privilege, and prestige are unequally distributed, patterned, and perpetuated within social organizations.*[1] Social power has already been described as the ability to shape social organization, but the ideas of privilege and prestige require elaboration.

Social privilege is access to desired goods, services, activities, or posi-

---

[1] This conceptualization of social stratification is derived from Gerhard E. Lenski, *Power and Privilege: A Theory of Social Stratification* (New York: McGraw-Hill, 1966), chaps. 3–4.

tions that is granted to an actor by others. Privileges can take unlimited specific forms, according to what is deemed desirable in a given situation—which is in turn largely shaped by cultural values. The most obvious privilege in contemporary societies is money, which in turn allows the holder to acquire a wide variety of other benefits. In addition, privileges often include selective participation in certain social activities or organizations, prerogatives to act in distinctive ways or to receive services from others, and special rights to enact specific activities.

Social prestige is favorable evaluation that an actor receives from others. Whereas privileges are relatively tangible benefits or rewards, prestige is always an intangible evaluation. It also takes numerous forms, including recognition, esteem, honor, and fame. Prestige is usually expressed through deference on the part of others, ranging from casual remarks (such as compliments and praises) to symbolic gestures (differential modes of speech) to overt actions (saluting or remaining standing) to formal awards and honors (citations and memorials).

Power, privilege, and prestige are distinct social phenomena, but they usually become highly interrelated with the process of social stratification. In fact, it is often possible for an actor to transform one of these phenomena into another, as when a person uses his or her "good name" to acquire special privileges or to influence a decision, or when membership on the executive committee of an organization brings a person both honor and control over organizational policy. And money can serve simultaneously as a prestige symbol (when it is given or displayed), as a means of gaining privileges (when it is spent for goods and services), and as a resource for power (when it is used to influence actions or decisions).

Privilege and prestige, like power, are created through the process of social organization, and are meaningful only within social relationships. Privilege and prestige differ from power in one important respect, however. They must be granted to the actor by others, whereas social power (especially force and dominance) can often be wielded regardless of the wishes of others. Furthermore, privilege and prestige are normally sought as ends in themselves, because of the benefits or satisfactions they give to their recipients. Power is sometimes sought as an end in itself, but more commonly it is exercised as a means for shaping social organization or for acquiring privilege and prestige.

The basic units of social stratification, as of all social organization, are social roles. In the most fundamental sense, it is the various roles within an organization that acquire differential amounts of power, privilege, and prestige. Most roles are rather closely associated with the individuals who enact them at any given time, however, so that studies of social stratification have usually taken individuals rather than roles as their units of analysis. In many social settings, moreover, it is possible to focus on the nuclear family as a single unit within a pattern of stratification, since both spouses (as well as minor children) tend to share similar power, privileges, and prestige in the community. Although it has not frequently been done, there is no theoretical reason why even larger social bodies could not be taken as the primary units of social stratification, as long as these organizations did in fact act as single entities. It should be possible, for instance, to investigate the differential power, privilege, and prestige of associations within a functional network, or communities within a society. Our discussion in this chapter will focus largely on roles and individuals as units of stratification—but we reiterate that social stratification occurs whenever social actors of any kind enjoy differential amounts of the benefits of organizational operations.

Closely related to this topic of units of stratification is the question of the organizational setting in which stratification takes place. Social stratification always occurs within some encompassing organization, as a result of unequal allocation of power, privilege, and prestige among the component units or members of that organization. Thus there could be a pattern of stratification within a small committee, which might or might not resemble the stratification structure of the larger "parent" association, which might or might not correspond to the distribution of power, privilege, and prestige in the entire community, which in turn might or might not reflect the national stratification pattern. The various patterns of stratification existing within different organizations commonly exhibit considerable similarity, but they are rarely identical. For example, as a lawyer employed by a large business corporation, Mr. Smith might be the junior member of the executive policy committee, even though he rated VIP treatment in the company as a whole. Concurrently, his status in the community might be relatively low because of his short period of residency and his particular ethnic background, even though he enjoyed a national reputation within his profession. It is therefore a gross oversimplification to speak of social stratification in general terms, without specifying both the social units involved and the relevent organizational setting.

THE DIMENSIONS OF STRATIFICATION

The larger and more complex a given social organization, the more extensive will be its distributive process, and the greater the likelihood that its patterns of stratification will be multidimensional rather than unidimensional. In other words, *an organization can contain a number of different stratification hierarchies or dimensions.* Although these various dimensions might in fact be highly interrelated, the sociologist must attempt to distinguish them analytically and to determine the degree of congruence among them. A given stratification dimension, in turn, can often be measured in terms of several empirical variables, which may be only partially intercorrelated.

In the contemporary United States, for instance, the major stratification dimensions and their empirical indicators include the following: (1) socio-economic, as indicated by one's occupation, educational credentials, or income; (2) public influence, as measured by one's activities in party politics, community decision making, or mass communications; (3) reputation, as shown by the recognition, esteem, or deference granted one by others; (4) ethnicity, as determined by one's race, religion, or national origin; (5) style of life, as demonstrated by one's neighborhood, housing, or other material possessions; and (6) intellectual level, as seen in one's social attitudes, values, preferences, or intellectual attainments.[2] Of all the empirical measures of stratification, a person's occupation is the single indicator most commonly employed in sociological studies, because of the crucial importance of one's occupational role in all industrial societies, because occupational status serves as a general measure of power, privilege, and prestige, and because occupation is highly correlated with many other objective indicators.

The phenomena of power, privilege, and prestige cut across all of these stratification dimensions and variables, and probably enter into each of them to some extent, although obviously some dimensions give more weight to power, others stress privileges, and still others are primarily expressions of prestige. As a general rule, the various dimensions and indicators of stratification within an organization are never totally unrelated, but in modern societies wide divergences commonly occur among them.

Each of the stratification hierarchies within an organization normally consists of numerous gradations, or statuses. That is, *a social status is a specific level or structural position on a stratification dimension or indicator.* The number of identifiable statuses contained within a given hierarchy depends partially upon the complexity of the organization, but also on the concerns and sophistication of the observer who designates them. For example, one study might lump together all persons with incomes between $10,000 and $20,000 as a "middle income level," while another study might separate these same people into several income categories. The distance from the top to the bottom statuses of any such stratification hierarchy is sometimes spoken of as the "range" of that dimension or variable.

Most social actors normally hold several social statuses, according to the number of separate stratification hierarchies on which they are located and

---

[2] This conceptualization of social stratification as a multidimensional phenomenon is an expansion of ideas first suggested by Max Weber, "Class, Status, and Party," *From Max Weber: Essays in Sociology,* trans. and ed. by H. H. Gerth and C. Wright Mills (New York: Oxford University Press, 1958), pp. 180–195.

the number of different social settings in which they act. A given social status, in other words, is specific to a particular dimension and to a particular organization. Mr. Wilson might reside in a more desirable neighborhood of the community than Mr. Baker, even though Mr. Baker might be Mr. Wilson's supervisor at work. Some amount of congruence normally exists among an actor's various social statuses, since power, privilege, or prestige gained in one area can often be transferred into other related activities. But considerable disparity can develop among an actor's various statuses, at least in the short run. A high income, for instance, does not automatically bring one either public esteem or intellectual sophistication. The terms *status consistency* or *status crystallization* (they are synonymous) are used by sociologists to describe the degree to which the diverse statuses of a given actor are equivalent.[3]

In general, the more complex the stratification process within an organization (in terms of the number of different status dimensions, plus the variety of subunits with dissimilar stratification patterns) and the faster the prevailing rate of social change, the more likely it is that many actors in the organization will experience status inconsistency. As a consequence, widespread status inconsistency is considerably more common in modern industrial societies than in primitive agricultural societies, and more common in large metropolises than in small towns. Several empirical studies have suggested that marked inconsistency among an actor's various statuses may cause him or her to hold liberal political orientations, presumably in hopes of redressing disparate social conditions through political change.[4]

Patterns of inequality in power, privilege, and prestige vary widely in their stability through time. If we are to observe and describe social stratification, ordered inequality must persist for some minimal period. Random fluctuations in the distributive process are not usually spoken of as social stratification. But how long a given pattern of stratification will endure is always a problematic question. Historically, broad societal patterns of social stratification have commonly persisted through at least several generations, changing only slowly and gradually. Children have tended to assume approximately the same statuses in the society and the community as their parents, and to pass on these same statuses to their offspring. To the extent that social roles and their accompanying social statuses are ascribed rather than achieved, an existing pattern of stratification is especially likely to continue with only minor changes for a long time.

[3] The term "status crystallization" was first suggested by Gerhard E. Lenski, "Status Crystallization: A Non-Vertical Dimension of Social Status," *American Sociological Review* 19 (August 1954): 405–413.
[4] Phillip A. Salopek and Christopher K. Vanderpool, "Status Inconsistency and Democratic Party Preference: A Replication and Critique," *Journal of Political and Military Sociology* 4 (Spring 1976): 29–38.

One of the most striking characteristics of modern societies, however, is the opening of more and more roles to competition. There are many reasons for this trend, including the existence of more wealth to be distributed among all the members of the society, rapidly expanding public education facilities, and slowly emerging norms of rational efficiency and social equality. No existing society even approaches the ideal of total role achievement and completely open role competition—if that were ever possible—so that considerable grounds for the perpetuation of patterned stratification still exist everywhere. Nevertheless, social stratification in many contemporary societies is tending to become considerably more fluid than ever before.

SOCIAL STRATA AND CLASSES

Although it is conceivable that a set of social actors might be distributed evenly along the stratification dimensions in an organization, in reality this rarely occurs. Instead, they tend to cluster to one degree or another at various points along these dimensions. These clusterings of actors with similar statuses on one or more stratification dimensions are called either social strata or social classes. Both strata and classes are outcomes of the process of social stratification, but there is a crucial difference between them. Social strata are merely analytical clusterings, whereas social classes are real organizational entities.

Expressed more precisely, *social strata are arbitrarily defined categories imposed upon one or more status hierarchies by social scientists for analytical purposes.* The boundaries separating one stratum from another are therefore only artificial lines, and the members of any given stratum constitute only a population without any necessary social ordering. There can be as many different social strata in an organization as a social scientist wishes to designate. In some cases the analyst might be content to work with a simple dichotomy such as "manual" and "nonmanual" occupations, while at other times he or she might decide to split the organization into a large number of much smaller strata. The point is that social strata are delineated only for theoretical or research purposes, as a means of temporarily simplifying—for analytical convenience—the patterns of clustering along one or more status hierarchies.

In many social settings, though, differences in social status among actors give rise to the existence of real social entities, or classes. Social classes emerge as actors who share roughly similar statuses on one or more of the major stratification dimensions within a larger organization become delineated by identifiable boundaries and ordered as social units. The members of a class interact to create at least minimal patterns of social ordering and common cultural ideas, although the degree to which they are thus organized is always problematic. In short, *social classes are bounded, discrete social organizations composed of actors with approximately similar amounts of power, privilege, and prestige on one or more status dimensions.* Because the various stratification dimensions are rarely perfectly correlated, sociologists frequently describe a separate set of classes for each dimension, so that "socioeconomic classes" are distinct from "public influence classes" or "ethnicity classes." In reality, however, most classes cut across several, if not all, status dimensions, and hence constitute multidimensional phenomena. By definition, classes always exist within more encompassing organizations—such as associations, communities, or societies—and hence can be looked upon as subunits of these larger bodies. To the extent that a class possesses some degree of functional autonomy, however, it also constitutes an organization in its own right. The essential point is that social classes, in contrast to strata, are never arbitrarily defined by an outside observer; they are real social objects existing in social life.

Class organization frequently develops around common concerns and living conditions that actors share as a result of their similar amounts of power, privilege, and prestige. As a class becomes delineated and acquires organizational unity, stability, and effective power, it tends to come into conflict with other classes and organizations. We must remember, though, that the degree of class organization, as well as conflict, existing in any given situation is always a problematic question, not a theoretical imperative. The occurrence of this process of class organization is commonly affected by such factors as the degree of status homogeneity among class members, strength of the class boundaries, and extensiveness of communication within the class. Nevertheless, whenever class organization does occur it usually involves the creation of class consciousness, or awareness among the actors of their common social situation, as well as the emergence of patterns of social ordering among class members and the creation of a shared class culture.

As classes develop, they commonly seek to maximize their power, privileges, and prestige by restricting membership to a limited circle of eligible actors, which Frank Parkin describes as the process of *social closure*.[5] Depending on the location of a particular class on a stratification hierarchy, its closure process will normally take one of two different forms, based on either strategies of exclusion or strategies of solidarity. Relatively advantaged classes tend to seek closure by excluding "outsiders" and subordinating them to inferior classes. In contrast, relatively disadvantaged classes are forced to seek closure as a means of avoiding exploitation by promoting a sense of solidarity against external threats. "The crucial distinction between these two modes of closure is that techniques of

[5] Frank Parkin, "Strategies of Social Closure in Class Formation," paper presented at the 1976 annual meeting of the Pacific Sociological Association.

exclusion exert political pressure downwards, as it were, in that [class] advantages are secured at the expense of collectivities which can successfully be defined as inferior; whereas strategies of solidarism direct pressure upwards in so far as [their] claims upon resources threaten to diminish the share of more privileged [classes]. Thus whereas exclusion is a form of closure which stabilizes the stratification order, solidarism is one which contains a potential challenge to the prevailing system of distribution through the threat of usurpation. All this indicates the ease with which the language of closure can be translated into the language of power. Modes of closure can be thought of as a different means of mobilizing power for purposes of staking claims to resources and opportunities.''[6]

This conceptualization of social stratification can be summarized in the following manner:

> PRINCIPLE 69: Patterns of social stratification, displaying multiple dimensions of hierarchical status ordering and clustering of actors with similar statuses into bounded social classes, develop as power, privilege, and prestige become unequally distributed among the members of an organization.

SOCIAL MOBILITY

Although patterns of social stratification commonly display considerable stability through time, in most organizations at least some of the actors can alter their statuses by gaining or losing power, privileges, and prestige. That is, they can be socially mobile, in either an upward or downward direction. *Social mobility occurs whenever a social actor changes one or more statuses within a pattern of stratification.* The rate, extent, and forms of social mobility are all empirical questions to be investigated in particular social settings, but the general processes of both upward and downward social mobility occur quite frequently within almost all organizations. Social mobility can be experienced by any social actor, but most theory and research on this topic has focused on individual mobility processes.

Some amount of social mobility is virtually inevitable in any organization, as old members leave and others move in to fill their places. Several other social processes also contribute to the promotion of both upward and downward mobility, however. First, as the practice of role achievement (in contrast to role ascription) becomes increasingly prevalent in an organization, opportunities for mobility expand. Open competition for roles and positions enables actors to be upwardly mobile to the limit of their abilities

[6] Ibid.

and interests, forcing other, less competent actors to move downward. Second, broad changes in overall stratification processes and patterns normally produce considerable social mobility. If the major resource for power in a society shifts from control of money to possession of technical knowledge, for instance, many individuals will find themselves either gaining or losing both privileges and prestige. And third, extensive expansion or contraction in the size of an organization or its activities often leads to widespread mobility. If the organization is growing in size or activities, new roles and positions are continually being created, thus allowing many members to be upwardly mobile. In contrast, if the organization is declining in size or activities, numerous members may be pushed downward.

For any actor, social mobility is always relative to other actors; he or she moves upward or downward by comparison with them. From the perspective of the larger organizational setting, though, *social mobility can be either relative or absolute*. If the size and activities of the organization remain essentially unchanged through a given period, then any upward mobility that occurs must be balanced at least roughly by a corresponding amount of either downward mobility or withdrawal from the organization. There is normally only a limited amount of power and privileges to be allocated within the organization, so that if one member gains, another must lose. This is a condition of relative mobility. However, if the encompassing organization as a whole is growing in size and activities, then the amount of power and privileges to be allocated among the members will increase through time. Consequently, many members can be upwardly mobile without denying status to others. All gain in the long run, and at no one else's expense, though likely at somewhat different rates. Conversely, if the total organization were contracting, there would be much more downward than upward mobility. This is a condition of absolute mobility.

The process of absolute upward mobility on a vast scale is a significant feature of most contemporary industrial nations. Whereas some amount of relative mobility has undoubtedly always occurred in all societies, extensive absolute mobility is a new phenomenon in social life. As long as agriculture forms the primary economic base of a society, the amount of surplus resources and benefits available for distribution to members will remain relatively limited. Inequalities in power, privilege, and prestige will normally be quite marked, and most upward mobility (to the extent that any occurs) must be matched by corresponding downward mobility or withdrawal (through death or emigration). Although social reformers since antiquity have called for a more equitable distribution of power and wealth in society, their demands have largely gone unheeded—for a very simple reason. They were essentially calling for a redistribution of the existing benefits among the people, which would have required elites to relinquish some of their power and wealth. In other words, elites would have to be downwardly mobile so that others might move upward. Elites have not usually taken kindly to such suggestions, and for the most part have successfully resisted all attempts to promote greater equality in preindustrial societies.

The situation is entirely different, though, if the primary economic base of the society is expanding rapidly through industrialization. Under these conditions of growth, the total volume of resources, power, and privileges in a society will be constantly increasing, so that large numbers of people can be upwardly mobile without denying benefits to others. In the simplest of terms, almost everyone becomes at least a little better off, in comparison with the past. Most significantly, elites are not forced to relinquish their superior statuses, and hence are not so likely to resist change. Absolute upward mobility by many or even all members of an organization does not necessarily eliminate social inequality, however. If everyone gains at the same proportional rate, patterns of inequality will remain unchanged, though they may become more tolerable to those at the bottom. If elites gain benefits at a faster rate than others, social inequality will actually increase. But if a reverse process occurs, so that those persons with lower statuses gain proportionately more than those with higher statuses, then overall patterns of inequality will tend to decrease. Everyone will be moving upward, but those with farther to go will be moving somewhat faster, thus decreasing the distance from the top to the bottom of the stratification pattern. In very broad terms, this is what has been happening in recent years in many industrial nations throughout the world.

In more specific terms, as a society industrializes and thus expands its available resources, several interrelated trends begin to occur, all of which tend to promote considerable amounts of absolute upward mobility. These social trends include: (1) a shift in the occupational distribution resulting from a decline in the number of unskilled manual jobs and a growth in the number of skilled and nonmanual jobs available, which forces many people to be upwardly mobile in order to find work; (2) an expansion in the number of goods and services available to all persons, as a consequence of continually rising economic productivity; (3) expanding educational opportunities of all kinds, which provide routes for upward mobility to many people; (4) declining birth rates, especially among higher-status families, which necessitates recruitment from below for many higher positions; and (5) creation of organizations such as labor unions through which less privileged persons can exert pressures upon elites to share the expanding benefits more equally among all persons. None of these trends is an imperative consequence of industrialization, but to the extent that they do occur, they make possible more extensive opportunities for social mobility than have existed in the past.

As social mobility occurs in an organization, it can take one of two basic forms: (1) career mobility, in which a person significantly changes one or more statuses during his or her own lifetime; and (2) generational mobility, in which a person's major statuses are noticeably different from those of his or her parents. Both kinds of mobility occur often in relatively "open" societies such as the United States, but generational mobility appears to be more frequent. It is not that individuals rarely change statuses during their lives, but rather that a person's occupational role is increasingly being determined by the amount and nature of one's education, so that the most extensive shifts in status tend to occur between generations through formal education instead of during a person's occupational career.

It is interesting to note, finally, that most individual cases of mobility involve relatively short movements, whether upward or downward. Most persons, that is, tend to hold social statuses not too dissimilar from those of their parents, and to make only relatively minor shifts during their lifetimes. The Horatio Alger dream of "rags to riches in a lifetime" has always been more of a myth than a reality. Nevertheless, the cumulative effects of thousands of small individual status changes upon a society's stratification pattern can become exceedingy significant. In short:

> **PRINCIPLE 70:** **Upward and downward social mobility occur as actors gain and lose power, privilege, and prestige, either in an absolute sense or in relation to others, both within their own lifetimes and across generations.**

Theories of Social Inequality

TWO general theories of the causes of social inequality are predominant in current sociological thinking. One of these, the "functional theory" of inequality, has been extensively debated in the literature for over thirty years but still lacks adequate supporting proof. The other, which might be called the "power theory" of inequality, represents an ancient idea that has only recently been formulated as a general thesis. Let us examine and evaluate each of these theories.

POWER THEORY

In essence, *the power theory of social inequality argues that stratification results from the differential exercise of power in social life.* As formulated by Marx and elaborated by Gerhard Lenski, the major ideas of this thesis are that:[7]

---

[7] These propositions are derived from *Power and Privilege* and from personal conversations with Professor Lenski. The most complete compilation available of Marx's original formula-

1. Power determines the distribution of nearly all surpluses existing in any society beyond the bare subsistence level. Hence privilege is largely an outcome of the exercise of social power, and is only slightly a product of altruism.

2. In turn, prestige is largely, though not solely, a resultant of the exertion of power and the enjoyment of privileges in all postsubsistence societies.

3. In general, both privilege and prestige are ultimately derived from the exercise of social power. Privileges and prestige accrue to those who wield power in social life.

4. Although power is sometimes sought as an end in itself, more commonly it is used to gain various forms of privilege and prestige valued by the actors. Hence social actors usually seek to exercise as much power as possible, and then to transform this power into privileges and prestige.

5. Once the use of power has resulted in the acquisition of some forms of privilege and prestige, these benefits can in turn be utilized as resources for gaining additional power, privileges, and prestige. In other words, the phenomena of power, privilege, and prestige are all highly interrelated in social life, so that any one of these factors can eventually produce either of the other two in a circular process.

6. Although it is conceivable that power, privilege, and prestige might be evenly distributed among all the members of an organization, in reality this rarely happens. Power, and hence privilege and prestige, tends to become unequally distributed among social actors for a variety of psychological, social, and cultural reasons, including inequalities in resources and ability to utilize them, operational advantages inherent in certain positions, intentional power-seeking efforts by some actors, and passive acceptance of power exertion by others.

7. Patterns of stratification are perpetuated through time because most forms of privilege and prestige are highly valued. Consequently, social actors normally attempt to retain whatever privileges and prestige they presently enjoy, to acquire more privileges or prestige through increased utilization of power, and to pass their power, privileges, and prestige on to their children or other heirs.

8. As they employ power to attain and protect privileges and prestige, actors frequently come into conflict with each other. Such conflicts can be either distributive or developmental in nature—that is, aimed at either redistributing existing benefits or creating additional resources or benefits.

tion of power theory is given by Ralf Dahrendorf in *Class and Class Conflict in Industrial Society* (Stanford, Calif.: Stanford University Press, 1959), chap. 1.

9. Conflict and competition will lead social actors to devise and use whatever techniques they can to protect, increase, and perpetuate the social power, privileges, and prestige they presently enjoy. Such devices include restricting the ability of others to exercise power or to gain access to privileges, employing one's present resouces to acquire additional power, creating ideologies to justify one's privileges and prestige, supporting traditional customs such as inheritance and nepotism, and using overt force to oppose competing actors.

10. Of the three factors of power, privilege, and prestige, power is the most immediately dependent upon ongoing social relationships, and hence is the most fluid, while prestige is the most detachable from a given social context and hence is the most stable over time. At any given time, therefore, many discrepancies can exist among an actor's power, privileges, and prestige. In the long run, though, these three factors will tend to remain in approximate balance, so that a change in any one of them will eventually result in changes in the other two also.

Taken by itself, the power theory of social inequality is open to numerous criticisms. For instance, how are organizational requirements satisfied according to this theory, except by pure chance, since presumably every social actor is basically self-oriented and without serious concern for larger collectivities? Or how is the process of functional cohesion to be explained if all actors continually strive to maximize their autonomy? Furthermore, the theory gives little consideration to normative influences on stratification patterns, as seen in contemporary ideals of social equality, "protection of the inept," and public responsibility for promoting the welfare of all persons.[8] On a more empirical level, power theory has considerable trouble explaining why powerful actors such as leaders of political "machines," who may virtually dominate a community, nevertheless do not often enjoy public esteem and honor. Nor can it adequately account for such people as Albert Schweitzer or Eleanor Roosevelt, who exercised little social power and yet were revered by others. Perhaps the weakest feature of this theory, however, is its failure to specify the precise mechanisms through which the exercise of power is transformed into privilege and prestige in various settings.

These limitations to the power theory of inequality raise doubts concerning its broader theoretical implications, but they do not deny its usefulness for explaining many facets of social stratification. And despite

---

[8] The growing importance of these phenomena has been stressed by William J. Goode, "The Protection of the Inept," *American Sociological Review* (February 1967): 5–19.

these criticisms, the theory is at least partially supported by the empirical observation that in virtually all societies those actors who exercise significant amounts of social power also tend to receive considerable privilege and prestige.[9]

In formal terms, the power theory of social inequality states:

> **PRINCIPLE 71:** **Patterned social stratification is primarily a result of inequities in the distribution of social power, the exercise of which leads to unequal distributions of privilege and prestige which are perpetuated through numerous techniques of power preservation and social conflict.**

FUNCTIONAL THEORY

In an entirely different vein, *the functional theory of social inequality argues that stratification exists because it is beneficial for social organization.* This thesis was originally proposed by Kingsley Davis and Wilbert Moore, although it has subsequently been modified and elaborated by several other writers.[10] The main ideas of this theory can be expressed thus:

1. All organizations must satisfy numerous functional requirements if they are to survive or attain goals.
2. The various roles in an organization contribute differentially to the fulfillment of these functional requirements. The roles that contribute most directly to the satisfaction of crucial organizational requirements are of the greatest functional importance to that organization.
3. If the organization is to survive or attain goals, these functionally important roles must be enacted by qualified persons in an adequate manner.
4. In general, however, these functionally crucial roles require higher qualifications and more extensive training than do other roles in the organization, and are also frequently quite demanding in terms of duties and responsibilities. Consequently, the supply of actors to fill these roles is normally limited in any organization.

---

[9] Lenski (*Power and Privilege*) has amassed much data from many types of societies to support this generalization.

[10] Kingsley Davis and Wilbert E. Moore, "Some Principles of Stratification," *American Sociological Review* 10 (1945): 242–249. See also Talcott Parsons, "A Revised Analytical Approach to the Theory of Social Stratification," in his *Essays in Sociological Theory,* rev. ed. (Glencoe, Ill.: Free Press, 1954); Richard Simpson, "A Modification of the Functional Theory of Stratification," *Social Forces* (December 1956), pp. 132–137; Dennis H. Wrong, "The Functional Theory of Stratification: Some Neglected Considerations," *American Sociological Review* 24 (1959): pp. 772–782; and Wilbert E. Moore, "But Some Are More Equal Than Others," *American Sociological Review* 28 (February 1963): 13–18.

5. All organizations are thus faced, in varying degrees, with the twin functional problems of filling functionally important roles with qualified actors and of encouraging these actors to enact their roles to the best of their abilities.

6. These problems are resolved by the organization through the differential awarding of privileges and prestige to various actors. That is, valued forms of privilege and prestige become incorporated into functionally necessary roles, as a means of inducing actors to acquire necessary training and adequately enact these roles.

7. These inducements or rewards need not be directly proportional to the functional importance of each role, as long as they are sufficient to ensure that the role will be filled and performed by qualified actors. Nor do the functionally most important roles in an organization have to be performed by the most qualified people, as long as the incumbents are capable of adequately enacting these roles.

8. Thus social privileges and prestige tend to accrue to those positions who perform necessary functions for an organization, in rough proportion to the difficulty of inducing actors to adequately fulfill these roles. "Social inequality is thus an unconsciously evolved device by which societies insure that the more important positions are conscientiously filled by the most qualified persons."

9. In general, some degree of unequal privileges and prestige is a functional necessity if an organization is to survive and attain goals. The actual amount of inequality required in any situation depends on such factors as the nature of the organization's functional requirements, the supply of qualified actors, and the demands of the crucial roles to be enacted.

10. The process of allocating differential awards to role actors is sometimes purposefully performed by organizational leaders, but more commonly it is an indirect result of the balancing of supply and demand in the labor market. In either case, though, the unequal distributions of privilege and prestige within an organization that result from this process constitute patterned social stratification.

The functional theory of social inequality has been criticized on several grounds, only the most significant of which are noted here.[11] First, how do

---

[11] These criticisms are drawn from several sources: Melvin Tumin, "Some Principles of Stratification: A Critical Review," *American Sociological Review* 18 (1953): 387–394; Simpson, "A Modification of the Functional Theory of Stratification"; Walter Buckley, "Social Stratification and the Functional Theory of Social Differentiation," *American Sociological Review* 23 (August 1958): 369–375; and George Huaco, "A Logical Analysis of the Davis-Moore Theory of Stratification," *American Sociological Review* 28 (October 1963): 801–804.

the members of an organization discover what its crucial survival or operational requirements are, or determine which roles satisfy these requirements? And on what grounds do they rank these roles into hierarchies of social importance, or decide how many and what kinds of privileges and prestige are necessary to induce individuals to train for and enact them? All of these tasks are largely beyond the capability of contemporary social science, and obviously they could not be accomplished in most organizations except through mere happenstance or shrewd guessing. Second, the theory assumes that all roles are acquired through open achievement, when in fact the majority of functionally necessary roles in most societies have historically been filled through closed ascription. (Davis and Moore note that under conditions of closed role ascription their theory explains only role performance, not recruitment or training.) Third, to what extent do roles that carry heavy public responsibilities require "external" inducements to attract capable individuals or to encourage maximum performance? Do not most such roles carry their own "intrinsic" rewards, such as a sense of accomplishment or creativity, so that in many cases they would be filled regardless of whatever privilege or prestige was attached to them? In other words, cannot there be functional alternatives to inequality that would also ensure the satisfaction of necessary requirements?

Fourth, the functional theory entirely ignores classes as established social organizations, as well as the perpetuation of patterned stratification through time. It attempts to show that status inequality is functionally necessary, but it does not apply this argument to organized, perpetuated social classes. In this light, the theory is perhaps more accurately an explanation of the division of labor in society than of social stratification. Fifth, social inequality can have many dysfunctional consequences for an organization as well as the beneficial effects described by the theory. Under various conditions it can impede vital communications and coordination, promote unnecessary social conflict, restrict social change, and weaken the cohesion of an organization. Sixth, this theory at times anthropomorphizes social organization, when it claims that "society unconsciously ensures" that socially important roles will be carried out. Individuals within organizations may sometime purposefully take such a course of action—as when an employer decides to offer a high salary for a job in order to attract "the best man available"—but society has no mind and cannot engage in this kind of teleological action. And seventh, on a more empirical level, functional theory is contradicted by persons such as professional athletes and entertainers who presumably are not fulfilling functionally crucial roles, but who nevertheless reap fame and fortune. Nor does it explain why people such as teachers, who supposedly are performing vital roles for society, receive relatively small incomes and little public honor.

We are thus led to the conclusion that although the functional theory of social inequality may be applicable within specific social settings—such as the compensation offered for various jobs in the occupational marketplace— it does not provide a complete explanation of the total process of social stratification. Nevertheless, the theory is at least partially confirmed by the repeatedly demonstrated fact that a substantial correspondence exists in most societies between the perceived functional importance of an occupation and the privileges and prestige afforded to those who perform it.[12]

Stated formally, the functional theory of social inequality says that:

> **PRINCIPLE 72:** **Patterned social stratification is primarily a result of the differential awarding of privilege and prestige to individuals to ensure that functionally necessary roles are adequately filled and enacted by qualified people, so that the organization will be able to survive and attain its goals.**

COMPLEMENTARITY OF THE THEORIES

Although neither the power nor the functional theory appears to be adequate by itself to explain all social inequality in most societies, the existing empirical data do suggest that each theory is relevant to some aspects of this process. Perhaps, then, *these theories can be viewed as complementary rather than competing explanations of stratification.*

One basis for this conclusion lies in the fact, recently noted by Theodore Kemper, that both theories acknowledge that the distribution of privilege and prestige is affected by both social power and role requirements. "Both theories recognize that differential social power can determine the distribution of rewards in society, although they seriously disagree on the extent to which power determines the actual distribution. In addition, both theories recognize a basis for unequal rewards on grounds other than power, although according to somewhat different criteria. The crucial question, as it affects both social policy and sociological theory, is the degree to which the differential distribution of rewards is determined by power as against any other basis."[13] Thus it is not a question of power versus role requirements

---

[12]Alex Inkeles and Peter A. Rossi, "National Comparisons of Occupational Prestige," *American Journal of Sociology* 56 (January 1956): 329–339. See also Archibald O. Haller and David M. Lewis, "The Hypothesis of Intersocietal Similarity in Occupational Prestige Hierarchies," *American Journal of Sociology* 72 (September 1966): 210–216. A more recent study of over 700 of the largest companies in the United States discovered limited evidence of a relationship between the functional importance of executive roles (measured by the magnitude of their responsibility) and the salaries paid to the incumbents of these roles, but no relationship between several measures of overall company performance and executive compensation: Leonard Broom and Robert Cushing, "A Modest Test of an Immodest Theory: The Functional Theory of Stratification," *American Sociological Review* 42 (February 1977): 157–169.

[13]Theodore D. Kemper, "Marxist and Functionalist Theories in the Study of Stratification: Common Elements That Lead to a Test," *Social Forces* 54 (March 1976): 559–578.

that divides these two theories, but rather the differential emphasis that each places on these contrasting causal factors.

A second basis for concluding that the two theories are complementary lies in the relationship between conflict and cohesion in society. Power theory clearly emphasizes conflict as a dominant social process, whereas functional theory emphasizes cohesion. As we have already noted, however, conflict and cohesion are often mutually reinforcing. Hence it would seem that these two theories of social inequality are also mutually supportive. Each theory simply explains a different facet of stratification, both of which occur in most organizations. Functional theory is most relevant for explaining role acquisition and performance, as mediated by the occupational marketplace, while power theory is most relevant for explaining class formation and the perpetuation of inequality through time. Moreover, power theory assumes adequate role enactment as a basis for organizational activities that generate and legitimate social power, while functional theory assumes that power is exerted in organizations to ensure that privilege and prestige accrue to the occupants of functionally vital roles.

A complete theory of patterned social inequality will therefore undoubtedly incorporate at least portions of both the power and functional theses. Such a theory might make the following arguments:

1. Social actors tend to seek power, privilege, and prestige because of the benefits these phenomena give them. Although power may not be sought as an end in itself, under most conditions actors must first gain the use of social power if they are to acquire valued privileges and prestige.
2. One means of acquiring power—though not the only means—is to become qualified for, or otherwise gain access to, social roles that control resources. Adequate enactment of such roles will then enable the actor to exercise power for the attainment of privileges and prestige.
3. Considerable power inheres in the enactment of functionally necessary roles. To the extent that a role contributes to the satisfaction of organizational requirements, its incumbent will wield dominance over other related roles and actors. Functionally important roles are also likely to provide additional types of power, including access to resources with which to exercise force, a basis for gaining legitimacy and hence authority, and even attraction through public visibility.
4. Hence the power-wielding roles that actors seek and enact, as a means of gaining desired privileges and prestige, are also quite likely to contribute to the fulfillment of organizational requirements. However, the fact that an actor's roles may be functionally

important for some larger social organization is often unknown to him or her, or if known, is usually incidental to his or her interests. An exception is the special case of social altruism. Thus the satisfaction of organizational survival and operational requirements is largely an unintended, or at least secondary, consequence of the enactment of power-wielding roles by actors seeking privileges and prestige.

5. Elites who occupy powerful organizational roles frequently reward other less powerful role actors in proportion to the services they render to these elites. That is, differential distribution of privilege and prestige is utilized by elites to promote role enactment that is functional for them in the attainment of their particular goals. Some of these roles may also have beneficial consequences for the total organization; others will not.

6. Actors who occupy power-wielding roles will normally attempt to protect and enhance their power, privileges, and prestige through such techniques as limiting the access of others to the roles, making themselves functionally indispensable, using their roles to gain additional power, and legitimizing their activities in the eyes of others.

7. Because these powerful roles frequently do have functional consequences for other actors and for organizations, pressures will be exerted on the incumbents to perform the roles in an adequate and responsible manner. If these pressures do not produce minimally acceptable role performance, the incumbent is likely to lose the role sooner or later, unless he or she can marshal enough power to resist all such pressures.

8. The patterns of social inequality that emerge and are perpetuated through this process constitute social stratification. The fundamental causal factor in this process is the seeking by social actors of power, privilege, and prestige, but as a consequence of their role activities, organizational functional requirements do tend to be satisfied, at least in the long run.

9. In general, the more complex an organization, the greater the number of its roles possessing some functional importance, and hence dominance and other types of power. As a result, growing complexity of social organization provides a basis for—though does not guarantee—increased diversification in the distribution of power, privilege, and prestige among all participants.

10. As the overall functional effectiveness of an organization increases, there is also a tendency for a norm of equality to develop, since enough resources and power are now being generated to give all

participants at least minimally acceptable privileges and prestige. As this norm gains support, the organization will tend to create various procedures for more equitable distribution of privileges (if not always prestige) and for protection of the incapable and inept.

The essence of this proposed synthesis of the power and functional theories of social inequality is as follows:

> **PRINCIPLE 73:**   **Patterned social stratification results primarily from the exertion of social power by actors in pursuit of desired social benefits, but in the process of exercising power, elites often perform necessary social roles that intentionally or unintentionally satisfy organizational functional requirements.**

Classes in Modern Societies

IT is often difficult for Americans to conceive of social classes as discrete entities, since most class boundaries in this society are vague, weak, blurred, and transitory. The United States shows a considerable amount of social stratification, but for the most part it takes the form of relatively continuous hierarchies of power, privilege, and prestige, all containing innumerable status gradations. Yet even a brief glance into history or around the world at other contemporary societies reveals that discrete social classes are common phenomena. In fact, class boundaries sometimes become so strong—as in the caste structure of India—that a person cannot normally change social classes during his or her lifetime no matter what he or she does. Nor should we too quickly conclude that class lines are absent in the United States, simply because they are vague. A number of writers have in fact pointed to the emergence of several new class boundaries in this society, which could in time become quite marked.[14] The most provocative model of the social class structure in modern industrialized societies nevertheless remains Karl Marx's conceptualization of the bourgeoisie and proletarian classes within capitalistic nations.

MARX'S MODEL OF SOCIAL CLASSES

Besides being a revolutionary polemicist, Karl Marx was also a profound social theorist who devoted his life to describing and analyzing the

---

[14]Three such works are James Burnham, *The Managerial Revolution* (Bloomington, Ind.: Indiana University Press, 1960); Ralf Dahrendorf, *Class and Class Conflict in Industrial Society*; and William H. Whyte, Jr., *The Organization Man* (New York: Simon and Schuster, 1956).

effects of industrialization on society.[15] Although Marx defies easy categorization, the single phrase most descriptive of his overriding concern might be "secular humanitarianism." Observing Europe at the middle of the nineteenth century, he was struck by the existence of a profound paradox. On the one hand, growing industrialization was creating more wealth than ever before experienced in any society. But on the other hand, he saw everywhere exploitation of workers, atrocious working conditions, pitifully low wages, extreme poverty, vast slums, and general human misery. What was wrong with the organization of a society that produced so much inequality and misery in the midst of hitherto undreamed of wealth? And how must society be changed to correct these evils and enable everyone to benefit from the productivity of industrialization? These were the questions his theory attempted to answer.

Marx's general theory of social organization in modern societies has three major components: a sociological perspective—economic-political dominance; a philosophy of history—dialectic social change; and a connecting thesis—social classes in continual conflict. To understand his model of social classes, we must first briefly examine his underlying sociological perspective and his dynamic philosophy of history.

Pervading all of Marx's thought was the sociological thesis that *society rests on an economic foundation, so that whoever controls economic production can exert tremendous influence throughout organized social life.* He did not claim that all other sectors of a society—such as government, religion, education, or the family—are totally determined by the economy, but he did believe that they are highly shaped and constrained by more basic economic forces. Not all aspects of the economy are equally important for social organization, however. The fundamental factor in his theory was control over the major means of economic production within a society. Whoever controls the basic sources of wealth will determine how much wealth is produced and how it is distributed and used, and hence will exercise controlling power in the society. Under feudalism these economic elites are the landed nobility; with industrialization they become the owners of factories and related business concerns. Relationship to (or control over) the means of production, which is as much a political as an economic phenomenon, is thus the fundamental factor in all social organization.

---

[15] The following discussion of Marx is based on several sources: Charles H. Anderson, *The Political Economy of Social Class* (Englewood Cliffs, N.J.: Prentice-Hall, 1974); T. B. Bottomore and Maximilien Rubel, *Karl Marx: Selected Writings in Sociology and Social Philosophy* (London: C. A. Watts & Co., 1956); Ralf Dahrendorf, *Class and Class Conflict in Industrial Society* (Stanford, Calif.: Stanford University Press, 1959); C. Wright Mills, *The Marxists* (New York: Dell, 1962); Joseph Schumpeter, *Capitalism, Socialism, and Democracy* (New York: Harper & Row, 1962); and Irving M. Zeitlin, *Marxism: A Re-Interpretation* (Princeton, N.J.: Van Nostrand, 1967).

This theoretical perspective was for Marx a key to understanding the dynamics of all societies, but his overall view of human history was shaped by the idea of dialectic social change. *Marx applied Hegel's philosophical dialectic of thesis, antithesis, and synthesis to European history as an analytical tool with which to explain societal change.* In a broad sense, feudalism was taken as the original thesis, capitalism was seen as its antithesis, and socialism became the emerging synthesis of these two previous societal forms. Capitalism was necessary to destroy feudalism, but sooner or later would give way to socialism.

Because the various subunits in a society are in continual conflict for control over the means of economic production, all societies contain with themselves potential seeds of change. Whether these seeds actually blossom into radical social change remains a problematic question in any given society, however. Marx used the dialectic as a heuristic analytical tool, not as an imperative blueprint for all history. Although theoretically all societies should develop from feudalism through capitalism to socialism, empirically this process is contingent on many interrelated factors, including the strength of the existing elites, the degree of organization among the masses, and the effectiveness of the class leaders advocating social change. To the extent that the broad sweep of history does follow a dialectic pattern, however, societies will inexorably move toward socialism, or the "classless society."

To merge his sociological perspective with his philosophy of history, Marx formulated his well-known thesis of conflicting social classes. By defining social classes in terms of their relationship to the major means of production, and assuming that less powerful classes will inevitably be exploited by the dominant class that controls the means of economic production and hence rules the society, Marx neatly joined his sociological and historical interpretations into a single theory. In brief, he argued that *all societies past the simple folk type are composed of two or more social classes, which are identified on the basis of their relationship to the means of production and which are locked in continual power conflicts.* A population of people who share similar relationships to the means of production in a society comprise a potential social class, or a "class-in-itself." For such an aggregate to constitute an organized social entity, or "class-for-itself," however, several additional conditions must occur. As specified by Charles Anderson, these are (1) a "separate way of life and cultural existence"; (2) "conflicting and hostile interests vis-á-vis another class"; (3) social relationships and social community extending across local and regional lines"; (4) "a societywide class consciousness"; and (5) "political organization."[16]

For analytical purposes, industrial society can be described in terms of

[16]Charles H. Anderson, *The Political Economy of Social Class.*

two major social classes: the bourgeoisie who own the factories, and the proletariat who are forced to sell their labor to the industrialists. (Marx recognized the existence of other classes, such as peasants, small merchants, and intellectuals, but felt that they were not theoretically important because they were either rapidly disappearing or being incorporated into the proletariat.) The dominant bourgeoisie, Marx insisted, are not necessarily evil persons, but they are forced by the intrinsic laws of capitalism to exploit their workers in order to make a profit. If they do not exploit, they soon go out of business. Hence the inherent economic injustice of industrial capitalism. To support his criticisms of capitalism, Marx drew on the prevailing nineteenth-century labor theory of economic value, much of which has since been rejected by most economists. Nevertheless, there is abundant historical evidence that early industrialists did in fact severely exploit their workers, whatever the underlying reasons.

The proletariat in industrial society is a social class with boundaries determined by its subordinate relation to the means of economic production, but the members of the proletariat often remain largely unaware of their common interests. Before this population can take collective action, its members must develop class consciousness, or become aware of their common social fate, and must become strongly organized. The bourgeoisie make their fatal mistake, Marx contended, when they drive the small middle class, especially intellectuals, into the industrial proletariat. These intellectuals provide the leadership the industrial workers had lacked, promote proletarian class consciousness and class organization, and set the stage for revolutionary social change.

Theoretically, societal change might be gradual and continual, but in practice this rarely happens, according to Marx. Rather, the dialectical process of social change usually occurs through the vehicle of class conflict. Drawing on his observations of feudalism, Marx concluded that powerful elite classes will never voluntarily surrender or share power, but instead will use whatever means are available to retain power as long as possible. The most important tool at the disposal of the bourgeoisie is the state and its military forces, which they control. Hence, if the proletariat is ever to gain power and give birth to socialism, it must organize and forcibly take control of the means of production from the bourgeoisie. Socialism can be created only through revolution. "The proletarians have nothing to lose but their chains. They have a world to win."[17]

After the inevitable proletarian revolution the bourgeois class will be destroyed, but the "classless society" will not yet exist. Still remaining is the staggering task of completely reordering society by putting all means of

[17]Karl Marx and Friedrich Engels, *The Communist Manifesto* (New York: International Publishers, 1948), p. 44.

production under public ownership and control, as well as teaching the people to assume the social responsibilities now being thrust upon them. To achieve these goals, it is necessary to create a temporary "dictatorship of the proletariat," during which time the revolutionary leaders act as agents of the people to prepare them and society for the future. Marx feverently hoped, nevertheless, that eventually complete communism could be achieved, the "classless society" would become a reality, and the full possibilities of human life would finally be realized by all persons. Because society would then be morally organized and all individuals would be socially responsible, the state as an enforcer of external social control would no longer be necessary, and would largely wither away. Under communism, control over the means of economic production would be shared by everyone, hence by definition there would be no more social classes, hence no more exploitation and human misery, hence no more class conflict, and hence no more dialectic social change. A morally perfect society will then have been attained on earth, in which all people participate and benefit on an equal basis. True social equality will prevail, while individual and collective social responsibility, not power and exploitation, will form the foundation of organized social life.

As a theory of social organization, Marx's ideas have been criticized on many grounds. For instance, the following theoretical weaknesses are frequently cited by sociologists: First, he saw most social change as originating in internal strains, and minimized external forces and stresses such as international trade, war, or cultural diffusion. Second, he drew too heavily from the history of feudalism in assuming that class conflict is inevitable and that all social change must be revolutionary in nature. Third, he failed to realize that public ownership of industry requires larger and more complex governmental organization than does private ownership, which invariably leads to differences in power, privilege, and prestige, and hence makes a "classless society" impossible. Fourth, he did not offer an adequate theory of social cohesion to explain the unification and persistence of social ordering, beyond the use of force and exploitation.

More devastating to Marx's predictions than any amount of academic criticism, however, have been the economic and political developments of the twentieth century in the United States and Western Europe. Neither Marx nor anyone else in the nineteenth century could have begun to imagine the fantastic growth in productivity and wealth that would eventually result from full-scale industrialization. Manufacturing has become more efficient, profits more dependable, markets broader, personal incomes higher, and goods and services more readily available than could possibly have been foreseen a hundred years ago. As a consequence, owners and managers of industry have been willing (either voluntarily or under relatively mild pressure) to pass more and more of the profits of industrialization on to their workers. They could do this without feeling threatened or deprived because they themselves were also profiting so greatly from continued economic growth. As Henry Ford argued, the more you pay your workers, the more they can buy from you, and the greater your profits. Conversely, if the bourgeoisie totally exploited the proletariat, there would soon be no markets for most industrial products and the entire economy would collapse. At the same time, industrial workers have come to value the existing economic order because of the benefits it gives them. They still seek improvements in wages and working conditions, but they have no desire to destroy the entire economy. They have too much to lose and not much to gain through class revolution.

Along with these purely economic developments have come a host of related social and political changes that have further negated Marx's predictions: (1) the creation, public acceptance, and successful accomplishments of labor unions that are economically rather than politically oriented, and which therefore attempt to gain benefits for workers by operating within the established economic order rather than by destroying it; (2) steadily rising levels of mass education, which give people more opportunities for improving their social statuses through individual mobility rather than class revolution; (3) extension of the franchise to all citizens rather than just property owners, which gives workers an advantage because of their larger numbers; (4) adoption of graduated income and inheritance taxes (as proposed by Marx) to curb the upper extremes of the income distribution; (5) intervention of government into private business as a regulator, coordinator, and spokesman for the public interest, but not necessarily as an outright owner or controller; and (6) development of public welfare programs designed to aid those individuals who are socially disadvantaged in one way or another.

The cumulative results of all these trends have been so extensive that Marx's original model of bourgeoisie and proletarian classes locked in inexorable conflict for control of society now appears gravely oversimplified. Nevertheless, many of his insights into the dynamics of social classes are relevant for modern societies, and they continue to inspire both social theorists and political leaders around the world.[18] This is especially evident in societies that have not yet attained the full fruits of industrialization or that are encountering severe difficulties in even initiating that process. For these people, the doctrine that economic and political power must be taken from traditional elites and used by new leaders for the benefit of the total society has immediate relevance and appeal.

---

[18] Perhaps the most comprehensive attempt to apply Marxian theory to the contemporary world is Charles Anderson's *The Political Economy of Social Class.*

SOCIOECONOMIC CLASSES IN MODERN SOCIETIES

As the Marxian model of two conflicting social classes has increasingly proved to be inapplicable to highly industrialized societies such as the United States, sociologists have constructed a number of alternative models to describe the class structure in modern societies. A complete review of all these theoretical and empirical writings would lead us far beyond the scope of this book, but we can sketch one model containing four relatively identifiable socioeconomic classes that illustrates this current thinking. It deals only with the dimension of socioeconomic inequality, but it is not incompatible with the fact that a total societal stratification system will likely also incorporate political, legal, prestige, intellectual, and ethnic dimensions. And although this model has been developed largely in reference to American society, it may well become increasingly evident in all highly industrialized societies—unless drastic social changes lead to the emergence of radically different conditions in these societies in the future.

The basic contention of this model is that socioeconomic classes in contemporary societies are delineated primarily by qualitative differences in people's ability to exercise socioeconomic influence. The boundaries separating these classes are fairly pervasive—though not impermeable—throughout the society. As convenient names for the four classes comprising this model, let us call them the influentials, the affluents, the workers, and the dispossessed. Within each of these classes there is considerable variation in people's power, privileges, and prestige, so that they are far from being homogeneous groups of status equals, but this intraclass inequality is status, not class, stratification. Each of the four classes in this model is described in more detail in the following paragraphs.

The *influentials* are those people who are able to exercise significant amounts of socioeconomic influence within such realms as business and industry, government, labor unions, professional associations, the mass media, and retailing and mass consumption. Members of this influential class derive their influence largely from occupancy of crucial—but not necessarily top policy-making—positions within formal organizations, which enables them to affect the courses of action taken by those organizations. Control of manipulable financial resources is another source of influence for many of these people, while possession of expert knowledge and skills is rapidly becoming a third important resource for wielding social influence. Individually, most of these people are not extraordinarily powerful, but collectively they shape and direct the major socioeconomic activities within a society, and hence affect the lives of all other members of that society.

There is no formal requirement for admission to the influential class, beyond the ability to wield social influence, and entrance routes include climbing an organizational hierarchy, inheriting disposable wealth, or acquiring a professional skill. It is worth noting, however, that many commentators on "postindustrial" societies point to the rapidly growing importance of expert knowledge as the key to social influence in the future.[19] And since possession of such knowledge is usually certified by a higher degree or license of some kind, entry into the influential class may increasingly come to depend on possession of a requisite certificate.

Occupationally, members of the influential class are usually classified as executives, officials, or professionals. In terms of income, most are well above the national median, with salaries between $20,000 and $40,000 being quite common. In regard to education, an undergraduate degree is rapidly becoming the expected minimum, and graduate or professional degrees are widespread. Again, however, it is not occupation or income or education alone that makes one a member of the influential class, but rather the ability to exercise significant socioeconomic influence. In any given setting it may also be meaningful to distinguish two or more subclasses of influentials—such as the demarcation between elites and subelites that is often made in community power studies.[20] But these categories are usually specific to a particular setting or activity, so that a subelite in one area might well be a key influential or top elite in another area or at a different time.

The majority of the population in industrial societies such as the United States falls within either the affluent or working classes, however. Some observers of the current American stratification scene have argued that the distance between these two classes has been rapidly closing, and hence prefer to speak of a single "middle mass."[21] They point to the facts that the distinction between "white-collar" and "blue-collar" jobs is being eradicated by automation, that skilled craftsmen often earn more than white-collar workers, and that the majority of workers now have at least a high school education. Depending on one's ideological bent, this trend is described as either "embourgeoisement of the proletariat," emphasizing the continually rising standard of living of the working class, or as "proletarianization of the middle class," stressing the inability of most white-collar workers to exercise significant amounts of socioeconomic influence outside their private lives.

Nevertheless, considerable empirical evidence suggests that the traditional class boundary between the affluent and working classes has not yet disappeared. Studies examining occupational mobility and residential

---

[19] Daniel Bell, *The Coming of Post-Industrial Society* (New York: Basic Books, 1973).
[20] Robert A. Dahl, *Who Governs?* (New Haven, Conn.: Yale University Press, 1961).
[21] Harold L. Wilensky, "Mass Society and Mass Culture: Interdependence or Independence?" *American Sociological Review* 29 (April 1964): 173-197.

segregation patterns,[22] friendship networks,[23] and social, economic, and political attitudes[24] have all concluded that these two classes are still quite distinct in contemporary society.

The most fundamental feature of the *affluents* is that these people benefit comfortably—sometimes even lavishly—from the outputs of the socioeconomic system in modern societies. (The term "middle class" is often applied to these people, but in reality most of them hold socioeconomic statuses above the median of the socioeconomic stratification dimension. "Upper middle class" is a more appropriate but rather cumbersome term.) They occupy responsible occupational positions and enact functionally vital roles within the socioeconomic system, so that the functional theory of stratification is perhaps most applicable to them. They do not, however, exercise significant amounts of influence over the operation of that system. In their personal lives—including their neighborhood, work group, voluntary associations, church, and similar activities—they often do exert notable amounts of social influence, but this power does not extend to major organizational actions of the overall socioeconomic system. The main criterion for entry into the affluent class, consequently, is not the exercise of influence, but rather receiving a substantial income that allows one to enjoy a relatively affluent standard of living.

The affluents typically occupy fairly prestigious "white-collar" positions as lower-level professionals and semiprofessionals, technicians, managers, independent proprietors, or salespersons. (Clerical workers are also frequently included in this category, but recent evidence suggests that their social and economic ties are closer to the working class.[25]) Their incomes commonly range between $15,000 and $30,000, although some families (especially when both the wife and the husband are employed) enjoy even higher incomes. Most of them have completed at least some postsecondary or higher education, and college graduation is rapidly becoming the mode within this class. In combination, the education, occupations, and income of these people enable them to experience a life style that incorporates both an affluent standard of living and a set of "sophisticated" social attitudes and values that is perhaps their most distinctive characteristic.

The *workers* in modern societies are also increasingly achieving a relatively comfortable material standard of living, although it does not

[22] Reeve Vanneman, "The Occupational Composition of American Classes: Results from Cluster Analysis," *American Journal of Sociology* 82 (January 1977): 783–807.
[23] Edward O. Laumann, *Bonds of Pluralism: The Form and Substance of Urban Social Networks* (New York: John Wiley & Sons, 1973).
[24] John H. Goldthorpe et al., *The Affluent Worker and the Class Structure*, (Cambridge, England: Cambridge University Press, 1969); and James DeFronzo, "Embourgeoisement in Indianapolis," *Social Problems* 21 (Fall 1973): 269–283.
[25] Vanneman, "The Occupational Composition of American Classes."

include the many luxuries that more affluent people enjoy. More significant than any differences in income, however, is the status of workers in the occupational marketplace. Whereas members of the affluent class commonly have higher education or skills that enable them to pursue a "career" and hence give them a fair amount of employment flexibility, most members of the working class simply hold a "job" that requires at most a few weeks or months of training, so that they are much more dependent on the current exigencies of prevailing employment conditions. (This generalization is not applicable to highly skilled craftsmen, but it can be argued that many of these people are currently gaining the occupational status and income of technicians, which moves them into the lower rungs of the affluent class.) Symbolic of the differing relationships of these two classes to the occupational marketplace is the fact that affluents usually receive a fixed salary (or fees or commissions) and are not normally laid off during economic slowdowns, whereas most workers are paid on an hourly basis only for the time they actually spend on the job and are always subject to layoffs. The resulting differences in both economic security and occupational status between members of the affluent and working classes affect many aspects of their life styles.

The working class is composed of all manual or "blue-collar" workers (with the possible exception of some highly skilled craftsmen), most clerical workers, and all service workers. Their family incomes typically range between $10,000 and $20,000, although again if both spouses are employed this figure may be somewhat higher. Most of these people have completed at least some secondary education, and increasingly high school graduation is becoming the expected educational standard. In short, they live adequately within the existing socioeconomic system of society, but do not exercise any influence on it, so that in practice they are essentially relatively easily replaceable parts of that system.

The *dispossessed*, finally, are those people who cannot, for one reason or another, function effectively within the existing socioeconomic system. Because they cannot adequately cope with the system, they live largely at its mercy as marginals or outcasts of an industrialized society, exercising little or no influence over even the course of their own lives. The major characteristic of the dispossessed is that they are not regularly employed, so that they live on the edge or outside the occupational marketplace. Some of them are totally unemployed because of handicaps or lack of marketable skills; some work irregularly as manual laborers but frequently experience long periods of forced unemployment; some are migrant farm laborers who drift with the crops; some are retired people living on small fixed pensions; and a few have voluntarily chosen this status by rejecting involvement in the normal occupational world for ideological or personal reasons.

Economically, most of the dispossessed are below or not far above the poverty line, depending on their eligibility for various public benefits, but their poverty is a result, not a cause, of their low socioeconomic status. Many of them are also very poorly educated, and this handicap not only limits their ability to find regular employment but will also make it increasingly difficult in the future for them to escape the dispossessed class, as education becomes the main route of upward socioeconomic mobility. In addition, many—though far from all—members of this class also suffer from racial or ethnic discrimination, which further restricts their employability and hinders upward mobility. Whatever the reasons for their relegation to the ranks of the dispossessed, however, all members of this class share the common fate of total socioeconomic powerlessness.

In summary, the essence of these descriptions of the class structure in modern society—whether the Marxian model or the more contemporary model sketched here—is that class boundaries and placement in industrial society are determined primarily by one's ability to exercise social influence upon or within the societal socioeconomic system, as suggested long ago by Max Weber.[26] That is:

> PRINCIPLE 74: Socioeconomic classes in modern societies are largely outgrowths of differential exercise of social power in relation to the economic system, the occupational structure, and the consumption marketplace.

The Consequences of Social Stratification

TO emphasize the significance of stratification for social life, let us in this final section briefly examine a few of the innumerable consequences of this process for both individuals and organizations.

The social statuses that an individual occupies in various stratification dimensions have been shown by many studies to affect a wide range of one's actions and attitudes. Strictly speaking, these relationships are only statistical correlations, not statements of causation, but they do indicate that much of what a person thinks and does is directly associated with his or her social statuses.

In the area of health and welfare, the higher an individual's socioeconomic and other statuses, the longer one's life expectancy, the less likely one is to become psychotic, and the better the medical care one receives. In regard to participation in organized social life, the higher a person's statuses, the more likely he or she will be to have several close personal friends, to belong

---

[26] Max Weber, "Class, Status, and Party."

to one or more special-interest voluntary associations, to vote in elections, to take part in civic activities, and to attend a house of worship fairly regularly. In reference to sociopolitical attitudes, higher-status people are more prone to hold "conservative" opinions on many economic questions and to vote Republican, but at the same time they tend to give much stronger support than do lower-status people to "liberal" positions on civil liberties, civil rights, and international cooperation. As stated here, these extremely crude generalizations gloss over the many qualifications and exceptions that researchers have carefully specified, but they do illustrate the pervasive effects of social stratification upon all individuals.

On a broader scale, the extent and nature of social stratification occurring within an organization can also have numerous consequences for that entire collectivity. Notwithstanding the debate over the functional benefits of stratification in satisfying organizational requirements, it is clear that gross inequalities in the distributions of power, privilege, and prestige have underlaid a considerable proportion of all social strife and conflict throughout human history. This is particularly true when the process of stratification gives rise to relatively delineated and closed social classes. Privileged classes have traditionally sought to protect and expand their benefits, while relatively deprived classes have periodically—though often not too successfully—sought to gain more for themselves. Whether the immediate issue is a local zoning ordinance, industrial wages, control of the national government, or the present worldwide "revolution of rising expectations," some kind of inequality will almost inevitably be a crucial, if not the basic, factor in any social dispute.

The most critical problems for social organizations arising from the existence of social stratification center on the use of power by elites. To the extent that power in a society or other organization is centralized within a closed elite class (or classes), it becomes increasingly difficult for other members to affect or limit the ways in which these elites exercise their power. If an elite class chooses to wield power primarily for its own benefit rather than for the welfare of the whole organization—as has frequently occurred throughout history—other classes may be incapable of exerting enough pressures on the elites to make them act in socially responsible ways. Under such conditions, unless some external agent forces the elites to alter their actions, the organization may experience serious operational problems if not total destruction.

This chapter completes our survey of the basic social processes through which social organization is maintained. As a general conclusion, it may be well to reemphasize that all these social processes occur only within patterned social ordering and shared cultures, and hence must be viewed as aspects of the broader process of social organization. Although they are distinct social phenomena, these processes are thoroughly intertwined in actual social life. Hence no one of them can be thoroughly understood unless all the others are also taken into account.

RECOMMENDED READING

Anderson, Charles H. *The Political Economy of Social Class.* Englewood Cliffs, N.J.: Prentice-Hall, 1974.
> A comprehensive presentation of the full scope of Marxian theory applied to modern societies.

Dahrendorf, Ralf. *Class and Class Conflict in Industrial Society.* Stanford, Calif.: Stanford University Press, 1959, chap. 1.
> The most complete compilation available of Marx's formulation of the power theory of social stratification.

Davis, Kingsley, and Wilbert E. Moore. "Some Principles of Stratification." *American Sociological Review* 10 (1945): 242–249. Melvin Tumin. "Some Principles of Stratification: A Critical Review." *American Sociological Review* 18 (1953): 387–394. (These two articles are bound together in Bobbs-Merrill reprint S-69.) George Huaco. "A Logical Analysis of the Davis-Moore Theory of Stratification." *American Sociological Review* 28 (October 1963): 801–804.
> The major presentation and two critiques of the functional theory of social stratification.

Inkeles, Alex, and Peter A. Rossi. "National Comparisons of Occupational Prestige." *American Journal of Sociology* 56 (January 1956): 329–339. (Also Bobbs-Merrill reprint S-425.)
> Summarizes and compares occupational prestige rankings in six different industrialized societies, pointing out the high degree of similarity existing among all these societies.

Kemper, Theodore D. "Marxist and Functionalist Theories in the Study of Stratification: Common Elements That Lead to a Test." *Social Forces* 54 (March 1976): 559–578.
> Explores several common themes in the power and functional theories of stratification.

Landecker, Werner. "Class Boundaries." *American Sociological Review* 25 (December 1960): 868–877.
> Reviews the distinction between discrete social classes and continuous social strata, and suggests a procedure for objectively delineating class boundaries.

Lenski, Gerhard E. *Power and Privilege: A Theory of Social Stratification.* New York: McGraw-Hill, 1966, chaps. 3, 4.
> The major presentation of contemporary power theory of stratification.

Vanneman, Reeve. "The Occupational Composition of American Classes: Results from Cluster Analysis." *American Journal of Sociology* 82 (January 1977): 783–807.
>   Analyzes recent national survey data to determine current occupational class boundaries.

Weber, Max. "Class, Status, and Party." *From Max Weber: Essays in Sociology*, trans. and ed. by H. H. Gerth and C. Wright Mills. New York: Oxford University Press, 1958, pp. 180–195.
>   The classic statement of the multidimensionality of social stratification.

PART IV

Transforming Social Organization

VIEWED as a continual dynamic proess, social organization is constantly being altered or modified in countless ways. At the same time, stability and persistence are fundamental characteristics of social ordering. The resolution of this apparent paradox lies in the realization that as organizations approximate social systems they display relatively stable processes of transformation. In system terminology, morphostasis shades into morphogenesis as pattern maintenance provides a basis for pattern development through time. The four chapters comprising this final part of the book examine the process of morphogenesis, or organizational transformation, from contrasting but interrelated perspectives.

Social conflict is explored in Chapter 12 as a social process that occurs throughout all social organization. The conflict theories of Karl Marx, Georg Simmel, Ralf Dahrendorf, and Lewis Coser are each sketched, followed by an overview of an integrated theory of social conflict.

Social change is treated in Chapter 13 as a generic social process that pervades all social organization. Following discussions of the nature and sources of social change, two metatheoretical views of change and a number of more specific growth-oriented theories of change are presented.

Chapter 14 treats organizational transformation as a developmental process leading toward social evolution or systemic growth. The two major modernization trends of industrialization and urbanization are first discussed, after which four models of possible postmodern societies are briefly sketched.

Chapter 15 then approaches organizational transformation as an intentional process of social guidance. Involved in this process are the activities of selecting goals to maximize the quality of social life, social planning to devise means of achieving those goals, and social activization to maximize the potential for successfully attaining our goals.

12

Social Conflict *

VIRTUALLY all social relationships evidence conflict at one time or another, so that conflict is ubiquitous in organized social life. This is true at all levels of analysis, from the simplest and most informal small groups to the most highly complex and formalized associations or societies. Cooperative processes bring actors together and establish a foundation for collective action. Effective control processes ensure that their actions contribute to the common endeavor and that the organization functions relatively smoothly and effectively. The process of social cohesion binds organizations into unified entities. Nevertheless, almost inevitably some actors will come into conflict with others, and the manner in which this conflict is enacted and resolved will have numerous consequences for social organizations and social change.

The Nature of Social Conflict

SOCIAL conflict can arise when two or more actors seek the same goal or mutually incompatible goals, when actors are dissatisfied with

*This chapter was written in collaboration with Leonard Beeghley.

existing social conditions such as an equitable distribution of scarce resources and benefits, or when one actor seeks to influence or change another.
The participants in a conflict process may be individuals, subparts of a larger
collectivity, or total organizations. Hence conflicts are commonly divided
into the two categories of "intraorganizational" and "interorganizational,"
although this distinction depends entirely upon the perspective of the
observer. A political campaign, for example, might be described as either an
internal conflict within the political system of a society or as an external
conflict between competing political parties.

THE MEANING OF CONFLICT

Definitional disagreements concerning the meaning of social
conflict have been so pervasive among sociologists that, as one review of the
literature noted, "conflict is . . . a rubber concept, being stretched and
moulded for the purposes at hand."[1] Nevertheless, the generic meaning of
the concept can easily be identified. *Social conflict is social interaction in
which the actors oppose one another in some manner.* This definition is
deliberately broad and inclusive, and many qualifications must be noted
depending on one's specific focus. For example, conflict may be threatened or
overt, violent or nonviolent. It may take the form of competition (orderly
pursuit by actors of a prescribed goal), aggression (attempts by one actor to
harm or destroy another), or cleavage (a split between factions of an
organization). It can be precisely regulated by norms, as in a trial, or it can be
largely unregulated, as in a riot. In all cases, however, conflict is a form of
social interaction. While psychological states of actors (for example, their
feelings of hatred or relative deprivation) are obviously important factors in
the study of social conflict, they do not constitute this process. "Social
conflict is not synonymous with opposition of interests, nor with psychological incompatibilities, dissonances, incongruities, or disagreements."[2]

THE DIMENSIONS OF CONFLICT

Viewed in a more systematic manner, most instances of social
conflict can be classified along several theoretical dimensions that have been
identified by various writers:[3]

1. *Instrumental versus expressive conflict.* Instrumental conflict is
   marked by opposing practices or goals, whereas expressive conflict
   results from desires for tension release, from hostile feelings, or from

[1] Raymond W. Mack and Richard C. Snyder, "The Analysis of Social Conflict—Toward an
Overview and Synthesis," *Journal of Conflict Resolution* (June 1957): 212-248.
[2] Robin M. Williams, "Social Order and Social Conflict," *Proceedings of the American
Philosophical Society* 114 (June 1970): 217-225.
[3] Mack and Snyder, "The Analysis of Social Conflict."

ignorance and error. In other words, instrumental conflict is a means to some other end, whereas expressive conflict is an end in itself.

2. *Ideological versus operational conflict.* When a conflict concerns basic values it tends to become ideological in nature, or a question of "right" and "wrong." When a conflict is over operational procedures for obtaining common goals, it is a practical question of "effectiveness" and "ineffectiveness."

3. *Direct versus indirect conflict.* Direct conflict involves immediate confrontation among the contesting actors, as in a debate, whereas indirect conflict is mediated through one or more third parties, as in many court cases.

4. *Regulated versus unregulated conflict.* The former end of this continuum is characterized by explicit rules and control procedures designed to keep the conflict within limits and of some benefit to all those involved. The latter end of the continuum is random, unpredictable, and uncontrolled by any larger organizational unit.

Social conflict also normally varies along several different empirical dimensions, the more common of which include: frequency (how often does it occur?), scope (how many actors or what parts of an organization are involved?), intensity (how committed are the participants to the conflict?), duration (how long does it last?), and expression (through what specific activities does it occur?). Any instance of social conflict can be described in terms of all of these variables, but over time such characteristics often change.

Although there is a common tendency to equate conflict with the breakdown of social organization, *conflict is neither identical to nor indicative of social disorganization.* This generalization is supported by two significant observations. First, social conflict frequently exhibits considerable patterning or ordering (especially when it is relatively instrumental and regulated), and thus constitutes an established social relationship. In other words, conflict is itself a form of social ordering within the process of social organization. One researcher, for instance, has identified several distinct stages through which most community controversies pass before they are resolved.[4] Second, under certain conditions, conflict can increase the cohesion of an organization. We shall explore this idea more extensively in the following section.

By way of summarizing the essential nature of social conflict, we paraphrase five propositions that Raymond Mack and Richard Snyder suggest as the fundamental properties of all conflict phenomena and situations.[5]

[4] James Coleman, *Community Conflict* (New York: Free Press, 1957), pp. 10–14.
[5] Mack and Snyder, "The Analysis of Social Conflict."

1. Conflict requires at least two actors (individuals or organizations), since it is by definition an interaction relationship.
2. Conflict arises from some kind of "scarcity," or desired but limited resources, activities, positions, or goals.
3. Conflict actions are designed to limit, thwart, destroy, control, or otherwise influence another actor, and a conflict relationship is one in which the actors can gain only at each other's relative expense.
4. Conflict requires interaction among actors in which their actions and counteractions are mutually opposed.
5. Conflict relations always involve attempts to acquire or exercise social power.

More succinctly, conflict can be conceptualized in this way:

> PRINCIPLE 75: Social conflict occurs when two or more actors oppose one another in social interaction, reciprocally exerting social power in an effort to attain scarce or incompatible goals and prevent the opponent(s) from attaining them.

Theories of Social Conflict

RATHER than seeing conflict as a patterned social process about which theories must be developed, many sociologists have treated social conflict in "metatheoretical" terms. Thus, in recent years "conflict theory" has often referreed to a set of assumptions about the nature of society, rather than to a set of propositions about the conflict process. In this form, it has been cast in opposition to "consensus theory" as an alternative way of viewing society. The ensuing "conflict versus consensus" debate has not been directed at theory construction, but at justifying or synthesizing alternative assumptions about the nature of social organization.[6] To avoid that fruitless exercise, we shall focus in this section on the main ideas of the four most important conflict theorists: Karl Marx, Georg Simmel, Ralf Dahrendorf, and Lewis Coser. The final section will then sketch a framework for a more encompassing theory of social conflict.

KARL MARX

Marx was both a revolutionary activist and a social scientist. He was a participant, organizer, and often a leader of radical political groups

---

[6] Several writers have attempted to synthesize the contradictory assumptions of "conflict theory" and "consensus theory," but these efforts have generally been scientifically futile since the assumptions being synthesized have no empirical referents. See Pierre L. van den Berghe,

during the nineteenth century.[7] At the same time, the goal of all his scholarly writings was to construct a theoretical foundation for revolutionary conflict.[8] That foundation is commonly called *dialectical materialism*, despite the fact that Marx himself never used the term. Nevertheless, it serves as a convenient rubric under which to summarize his theoretical perspective and his contributions to a theory of social conflict. We will first discuss Marx's materialist emphasis and his application of the Hegelian dialectic to the study of social organization, and then turn to his theory of conflict.

Marx's Materialism. Marx drew two conclusions from his extensive study of history, both of which placed him in opposition to the prevailing philosophical ideas of Hegel.[9] First, social theory must be empirically based, or grounded in "the existence of living human individuals." Second, compared to other animals, human beings are unique in that only they alter and manipulate the environment while obtaining sustenance. These conclusions led Marx to believe that the most important theoretical task of social science is to discover how people have organized themselves throughout history, both socially and in relation to the natural environment. Marx is called a materialist, therefore, because the cornerstone of his theoretical thinking was the practical human problem of cooperating and organizing to obtain sustenance from the environment.

Marx's Use of the Dialectic. Although Marx rejected much of Hegel's abstract philosophy, he did find the Hegelian dialectic a useful analytical tool with which to view human history. In his hands, dialectical materialism has four characteristics:[10] (1) Society can be viewed as a system, the parts of which are joined by what Bertell Ollman calls "internal relations." For example, wage labor cannot be understood apart from capital, for they are

"Dialectic and Functionalism: Toward a Theoretical Synthesis," *American Sociological Review* 28 (October 1963): 695–704.

[7] See Isaiah Berlin, *Karl Marx: His Life and Environment* (New York: Oxford University Press, 1963).

[8] This discussion of Marx's ideas is drawn from the following writings: Karl Marx, *Capital*, 3 vols. (New York: International Publishers, 1967); Karl Marx, *A Contribution to the Critique of Political Economy* (New York: International Publishers, 1970); Karl Marx and Friedrich Engels, *The German Ideology* (New York: International Publishers, 1947); and Karl Marx and Friedrich Engels, *The Communist Manifesto* (New York: International Publishers, 1948). Although Marx and Engels were close collaborators for more than forty years, in this discussion we follow the usual practice of referring only to Marx.

[9] The two main presentations by Marx of his analytical methods are part 1 of *The German Ideology* and the posthumous Introduction to the *Critique of Political Economy*. The major source on the dialectic is Friedrich Engels, *Anti-Duhring*, (New York: International Publishers, 1972). The best illustration of Marx's use of the dialectic is in his *Capital*.

[10] Bertell Ollman, *Alienation: Marx's Conception of Man in Capitalist Society* (New York: Oxford University Press, 1971), p. 55.

logically and empirically interdependent. (2) Change is inherent in social life and immanent in all social systems. This is because production, consumption, and reproduction reciprocally influence each other in a historically cumulative fashion. (3) Social change has both direction and continuity, in an evolutionary form. That is, history generally proceeds from less complex to more complex forms of social organization. (4) The vehicle of historical social change is conflict among the parts of the social system. Marx saw conflict and change as normal and inevitable processes in all societies, and the problem of accounting for these historical processes was central to his analyses.

Marx's Theory of Social Conflict.   Dialectical materialism was Marx's way of explaining why social "structures giving advantages to one group are destroyed and replaced by structures giving advantages to other groups."[11] *By applying the dialectic to the study of history, Marx believed that he could show why revolutionary conflict was inevitable.* Briefly, his reasoning was as follows. All human societies have productive forces, consisting of both what is produced (through the use of technology) and how it is produced (through the division of labor). In all societies the productive forces are controlled by those who own property. The system of property rights—whether referring to land, capital, or labor—is called the "relations of production." Inequality characterizes all societies in that only a small minority of the people—those with property rights—obtain most of the material benefits of the productive process. This state of affairs is legally and religiously sanctioned, and hence is usually viewed as right and proper. What is not often recognized is that those persons who control the forces of production have a stake in maintaining them in their present form, and through the use of force, fraud, or threat are usually successful in this endeavor. Over time, however, new forces of production are constantly being developed which better satisfy old needs and stimulate new ones, and which are inappropriate to existing social conditions. In Marx's words: "At a certain stage of their development, the material forces of production come into conflict with the existing relations of production, or—what is but a legal expression for the same thing—with the property relations within which they had been at work."[12]

As new forces of production are increasingly adopted, the relations of production must inevitably change in a cumulative manner. Marx used this interpretation to describe the stages of history. For example, in *The Communist Manifesto* Marx and Engels described the process through which ownership of capital replaced ownership of land as the principal basis of

[11] Arthus L. Stinchcombe, *Constructing Social Theories* (New York: Harcourt, Brace & World, 1968), p. 93.
[12] Karl Marx, Preface to his *Contribution to the Critique of Political Economy.*

social power in Europe. This occurred as the feudal nobility encouraged the rise of a merchant class to provide for its increasing consumptive desires. Through new applications of technology and division of labor, the members of this emerging bourgeois class gradually gained control over new and more effective productive forces. In turn, they substituted their own forms of family, government, religion, and—most crucially—economic organization, for those of the landed nobility. A similar process was occurring in the nineteenth century, Marx believed, as the bourgeoisie created a new proletarian class of wage laborers who would eventually seize control of the economic system and usher in a new society.

To elaborate this thesis, Marx attempted to specify the conditions under which a subordinate class will shift from a mere aggregate of people with common interests (a class "in itself") to an organized revolutionary class (a class "for itself"). In general, *the more the members of a subordinate class communicate with each other, become aware of their common interests, and develop a unifying ideology, then the greater their class cohesion and the greater the rate of conflict between them and the dominant class.* In more detail, Marx argued that (1) the more the subordinates obtain educational opportunities, become urbanized, and experience common life experiences, then the greater their communication; (2) the more the subordinates become alienated, suffer inequality, and experience disruptions in their social relations caused by the dominants, then the greater their awareness of common interests; and (3) the more the subordinates develop ideological leaders, and the less the dominants can regulate socialization practices or communication networks among the subordinates, then the more the subordinates will develop a unifying ideology. All of these factors together lead to increasing class cohesion and conflict of all kinds, but not necessarily revolutionary conflict. Marx tended to minimize nonrevolutionary conflict because he attached little importance to such phenomena as citizenship, nationalism, religion, ethnicity, and language—all of which can bind disparate and conflicting groups together and make truly revolutionary conflict quite rare.[13]

In sum, the central thrust of Marx's argument was that throughout human history the major source of conflict in society has been the efforts of subordinate classes to organize themselves and challenge established dominant classes in an attempt to alter the balance of social power, to gain a greater share of the benefits of material production, and to promote dialectical social change. Marx's analysis of social conflict provides a brilliant historical perspective that has served as an ideological touchstone for mass movements all over the world during the twentieth century. As a theoretical

[13]Reinhard Bendix, "Inequality and Social Structure: A Comparison of Marx and Weber," *American Sociological Review* 39 (April 1974): 149–161.

explanation of the conflict process, however, his work is important not so much for his historical details as for the key questions it raises: Who exercises controlling power in a society, and what is the basis of this power? Who benefits from the use of this power, and in what manner? Who has an interest in promoting social change, and who seeks to prevent it? What are the conditions under which subordinates (those without power, who do not benefit, and who desire change) organize themselves and engage in social conflict?

GEORG SIMMEL

Simmel believed that sociology could become a scientific discipline oriented toward the "discovery of timelessly valid laws," and his seminal essay on conflict was an attempt to illustrate that possibility.[14] He began by observing that all social relations are characterized by some degree of conflict: "There probably exists no social unit in which convergent and divergent currents . . . are not inseparably interwoven."[15] Conflict is important not only because it is an aspect of all social interaction, but also because it constitutes a "form of association." That is, *there are numerous regularities or patterns of ordering to social conflict that exist independently of people's motives or purposes.* Furthermore, as will be elaborated below, Simmel argued that the process of conflict itself influences the goals of conflicting groups.

The Study of Social Conflict.   There are two major thrusts to Simmel's essay on conflict. First, he indicates the extent to which the conflict process is patterned and makes a number of crucial conceptual distinctions regarding this patterning. Second, he suggests that conflict has significant consequences for "the inner structure of each party." Unlike Marx, Simmel located the cause of conflict in individuals rather than social structure. "Dissociating factors—hate, envy, need, desire—are the causes of conflict."[16] The consequences of conflict, however, have a "positive sociological character" in that they help to establish or maintain the social structure of an organization. Also in contrast to Marx, Simmel did not try to interpret the stages of human history through conflict. He was neither an evolutionary thinker nor a general theorist. Rather, he simply tried to explain the

---

[14] Georg Simmel, *Conflict and the Web of Group Affiliations*, Kurt H. Wolff and Reinhard Bendix, eds. and trans. (New York: Free Press, 1955). See also his *The Sociology of Georg Simmel*, Kurt H. Wolff, ed. and trans. (New York: Free Press, 1950), and *On Individuality and Social Forms*, D. L. Levine, ed. (Chicago: University of Chicago Press, 1971). The best secondary treatments of Simmel's analysis of conflict are Lewis Coser, *The Functions of Social Conflict* (New York: Free Press, 1956) and Jonathan H. Turner, *The Structure of Sociological Theory* (New York: Dorsey Press, 1974).
[15] Georg Simmel, *Conflict and the Web of Group Affiliations*, p. 15.
[16] Ibid., p. 13.

patterning and consequences of social conflict using a set of basic concepts which serve to classify and organize conflict as an empirical social process.

The Patterning of Intraorganizational Conflict. According to Simmel, conflict within organizations can usually be described as patterned competition. "Groups are distinguished in their sociological characteristics [by] the extent and kind of competition they admit."[17] The foremost characteristics of competition as a form of conflict are that it is indirect and regulated. Rather than try to get rid of opponents, competing persons or groups seek similar goals within a normative context. Most conflicts, he maintained, are normatively regulated to varying degrees. This insight led Simmel to an important conclusion: *the more conflict is normatively regulated, then the more resolute it is and the less likely it is to be violent.* To illustrate his point, Simmel selected "antagonistic games" and "legal conflicts" as examples. In both cases, "one unites in order to fight, and one fights under the mutually recognized control of norms and rules."[18] In such a context, competition can be "extreme and unconditional," or resolute, yet remain nonviolent.

Underlying this analysis is the factor of social cohesion, which exists at both ends of a complex process. That is, *the greater the social cohesion of an organization, then the more highly regulated is conflict.* At the same time, *the more conflict occurs in a highly regulated and resolute, yet nonviolent, context, then the greater the resulting social cohesion.* This is what Simmel meant when he stated that conflict has "positive sociological consequences." Conversely, the more conflict is perceived as a threat to social cohesion, the less regulated it is and the more likely it is to be violent. Similarly, the more violent conflict is, then the more it threatens social cohesion.

The Consequences of Interorganizational Conflict. Social conflict between organizational units can have important consequences for both the internal dynamics of these units and the relationships between them. Internally, conflict tends to unify an organization. That is, *the greater the rate of conflict with other units, then the greater the centralization within an organization, the greater its cohesion, and the less tolerance it has for deviant actions by members.* Simmel argued by analogy that just as a fighter must "pull himself together," so must an organization solidify itself when it engages in conflict with another collectivity. This tendency toward increasing centralization, cohesion, and intolerance of deviance is especially useful for small groups, he noted, but occurs to some degree in virtually all organizations.

[17] Ibid., p. 64.
[18] Ibid., p. 35.

Externally, conflict will often bring disparate organizations closer together. In fact, conflict is often "the basis of group formation" because it generates relatively intense interaction between individuals or organizations that would otherwise have little or nothing to do with each other. Simmel therefore proposed that *the greater the rate of conflict between organizations, then the more likely alliances are to be formed among some of the participants and the greater the solidarity of these allies.*

In sum, Simmel's main thesis was that social conflict is a form of patterned social interaction that is inherent in organized social life. Conflict is not an absence of social organization, but rather an integral aspect of this process. Moreover, most social conflict is normatively regulated in the form of ordered and nonviolent competition, especially in relatively cohesive organizations. And conflict can have beneficial consequences for social life by increasing an organization's internal unity and establishing ongoing relationships among organizations. Because Simmel did not deal with the social causes or dynamics of conflict, he did not give us a complete theory of social conflict. But he did place conflict squarely within the process of social organization.

RALF DAHRENDORF

In a series of publications, Dahrendorf has tried to reorient sociological theory away from what he believes is the "utopian" vision of society embodied in currently prevailing consensual perspectives on social organization.[19] His alternative perspective, called the "constraint approach" to the study of social organization, is an argument for the primacy of inequality, authority, coercion, conflict, and change in social life. He argues that these factors, to which Marx gave so much attention, have been largely ignored by contemporary sociologists until quite recently, with the result that much current theorizing fails to give an accurate picture of the true nature of social organization.

Dahrendorf's Model of Society. Dahrendorf begins with three assumptions about the nature of society. The first is that "authority is a characteristic of social organizations as general as society itself."[20] This is because the roles that comprise any organization are inherently unequal,

---

[19]Ralf Dahrendorf, "Out of Utopia: Toward a Reorientation of Sociological Analysis," *American Journal of Sociology* 64 (September 1958): 115–127; "Toward a Sociology of Conflict," *Journal of Conflict Resolution* 2 (June 1958): 170–183; *Class and Class Conflict in Industrial Society* (Stanford, Calif.: Stanford University Press, 1959); *Conflict After Class* (New York: Humanities Press, 1967); and *Essays in the Theory of Society* (Stanford, Calif.: Stanford University Press, 1968). For an overview of his work, see Turner, *The Structure of Sociological Theory.*

[20]Dahrendorf, *Class and Class Conflict*, p. 168.

with the result that their interrelationships always involve the exercise of social power which is commonly legitimized into authority. The second assumption is that authority is inextricably related to conflict. Authority "pervades the structure of all industrial societies and provides both the determinant and substance of most conflicts."[21] Underlying this assertion is the third assumption that the various roles and positions in any organization can be dichotomized into two "quasi-groups" whose members have totally contradictory interests. Those actors who wield authority desire to preserve the status quo, while those who do not exercise any authority desire to change it—at least to the extent of gaining authority for themselves. These two "quasi-groups" are potential antagonists in that their members share common roles and interests, whether or not they are aware of them.

Dahrendorf's Theory of Conflict. The theory of conflict developed by Dahrendorf centers on three major questions that grow out of, but are not answered by, the above assumptions. First, how do conflicting collectivities arise within the process of social organization? Here—and throughout his work—Dahrendorf deals with issues first raised by Marx, attempting to demonstrate their relevance for contemporary sociology. He answers this first question with a proposition drawn directly from Marx: *the more a "quasi-group" becomes organized as a subordinate collectivity, then the more likely it is to conflict with a dominant unit or collectivity.* This process of transition from a potential "quasi-group" to an organized "conflict group" occurs as the members develop a leadership cadre, a consistent ideology, an awareness of their common interests, a communication network, and interact frequently with one another.

The second question is what forms can the struggles among such "conflict groups" assume? Rather than answering the question directly, Dahrendorf distinguishes between the intensity and violence of conflict. By intensity, he means the emotional involvement and animosity felt by the participants. He proposes that *the greater the organization of "conflict groups," the more their disparate conflicts overlap, the greater the polarization between them, and the lower the rate of mobility between them, then the more intense their conflict.* In regard to violence, Dahrendorf suggests that *the more organized the "conflict groups" and the more regulated their conflict, then the less violent the conflict will be.*

The final question asks how does conflict cause changes in social organization? Dahrendorf argues that *the more intense the conflict, then the greater the amount of social change.* In addition, *the more violent the conflict, then the greater the rate of change.* Both of these propositions are quite suggestive theoretically, but unfortunately Dahrendorf does not pro-

---

[21]Ibid., p. 71.

vide any further details about how the processes occur, such as the conditions under which the intensity or violence of conflict affect the degree and rate of social change.

In conclusion, Dahrendorf's theorizing constitutes an effort to emphasize the pervasiveness and importance of social conflict as a basic social process arising out of authority relationships within organizations. His major contributions are his emphasis on the exercise of authority as the principal basis of social conflict, his attention to the two dimensions of conflict intensity and violence, and his linkage of conflict with social change. Nevertheless, he leaves largely unanswered the questions of (1) what are the social sources of the authority relationships underlying conflict, and (2) how does conflict give rise to social change? Dahrendorf's theory of conflict is far from complete, but has succeeded in generating extensive interest in the conflict process among contemporary sociologists.

LEWIS COSER

Like Dahrendorf, Coser has been exceptionally influential in rekindling contemporary interest in the sociology of conflict, although in a different direction.[22] Whereas Dahrendorf tries to build upon Marx, Coser attempts to explain and elaborate on Simmel. In addition, Coser has been decisively influenced by the prevailing emphasis on functional analysis in American sociology, as seen in his use of "function" as a causal explanation of conflict.[23]

The Functional Analysis of Conflict. Coser has been primarily concerned with "the functions, rather than the dysfunctions, of social conflict."[24] This is a useful task because Coser, like Simmel, believes that under certain conditions conflict can have positive sociological consequences for social organization and is not merely a negative or destructive force in human affairs. He also argues that such positive functions are often latent or unanticipated, so that identifying them greatly increases our sociological knowledge of the conflict process. A major problem with this mode of analysis, however, is that phrasing statements in functional terms often blurs rather than clarifies causal relationships.[25] For

[22] Lewis A. Coser, *The Functions of Social Conflict* (New York: Free Press, 1956), and *Continuities in the Study of Social Conflict* (New York: Free Press, 1967). For a codification of Coser's ideas and a comparison of his work to Dahrendorf, see Turner, *The Structure of Sociological Theory.*
[23] The principal elaboration of functionalism as a form of sociological analysis is Robert K. Merton, *Social Theory and Social Structure,* rev. ed. (New York: Free Press, 1949), chaps. 1 and 2.
[24] Coser, *The Functions of Social Conflict,* p. 8.
[25] William J. Goode, *Explorations in Social Theory* (New York: Oxford University Press, 1973), pp. 64–96.

example, Coser argues that "internal social conflicts which concern goals, values, or interests that do not contradict the basic assumptions upon which the relationship is founded tend to be positively functional for the social structure."[26] This statement is vague because it does not specify how the identified factors affect one another. Use of the concept of "function" in this context is a way of suggesting a causal relation without specifying it in causal terms. Nevertheless, the above proposition does add an important element to Simmel's thesis that organized cohesion can result from highly regulated conflict—provided it does not threaten core values.

Coser's Theory of Conflict. Coser's work contains such a plethora of propositions and distinctions that only a few of the more crucial ones can be identified here. He clearly distinguishes among the causes, the sequence, and the consequences of social conflict. In respect to causes, his emphasis is on the sources of conflict within organizations, not between them. His main argument is that *the more frequently deprived individuals withdraw legitimacy from existing patterns of resource distribution, the greater the relative deprivation they experience, and the more rigid their organization, then the more likely conflict is to occur and the more likely it is to be violent.* In this case, Coser goes far beyond Simmel, who did not speculate about the social causes of conflict. In fact, like Marx, Coser sees dissatisfaction with the unequal distribution of scarce resources as a major contributor to the generation of conflict. Unlike Marx, however, Coser does not identify conditions under which the subordinate members of a collectivity will become organized.

In his analysis of the conflict sequence, Coser carefully distinguishes between its duration and the resoluteness with which it is pursued. He first suggests some of the conditions which might shorten conflict. *The more limited are each unit's goals, the greater the agreement between opposing units on the specific goal of the conflict, the more knowledge each side has of the other, the less both sets of leaders strive for complete success, and the greater their influence over their followers, then the less prolonged the ensuing conflict.* He does not, however, go on to suggest any factors that might prolong conflict, such as its rate, its level of violence, or whether it concerns core values. Coser than identifies a number of factors affecting the intensity of a conflict, or the determination with which people pursue it—which Simmel termed its resoluteness. In this context, Coser adds several more propositions, two of which are as follows. *The more conflicts are objectified apart from individual self-interests, and the greater the emotional involement of the participants, then the more resolute the conflict.* At the

[26]Coser, *The Functions of Social Conflict*, p. 151.

same time, *the more conflict occurs over core values, the less regulated and the more resolute it is.*

The consequences of social conflict discussed by Coser can be divided into the three areas of (1) the internal consequences of intraorganizational conflict for that organization, (2) the internal consequences of interorganizational conflict for a participating organization, and (3) the external consequences of interorganizational conflict for the relationship between the involved organizations. To illustrate the theoretical continuity between Simmel and Coser, let us focus primarily on the second area, which was Simmel's main concern. Simmel proposed that interorganizational conflict was related to greater centralization, more cohesion, and less tolerance for deviance within the organization. Coser elaborates on each of the factors in this generalization. He first suggests that *the less the social differentiation within an organization prior to nonviolent conflict with another organization, then the less the resulting centralization.* Violent conflict is much more likely to produce centralization in all cases, however. He next argues that *conflict with another organization will increase a unit's cohesion only if it was relatively strong prior to the conflict, or if the unit's existence is directly threatened.* Finally, Coser maintains that *the larger the organization, the greater its rate of conflict with other organizations, and the less its members are emotionally involved in the conflict, then the greater the tolerance for deviance.* This is because larger organizations typically allow a wider range of permissible behavior and provide more possibilities for anonymity.

Very briefly, some of the other beneficial consequences of conflict for organizations that Coser identifies include the following: (1) establishing and maintaining organizational boundaries, (2) creating awareness of organizational stresses, strains, and problems, (3) stimulating activity to deal with those situations, (4) promoting the formation or clarification of organizational norms and rules, (5) breaking down old rituals and routines and thus encouraging innovative actions, and (6) fostering organizational change.

Limitations to Beneficial Conflict. Because of Coser's functional perspective on social organization, he maintains that *not all conflicts produce beneficial consequences (or positive functions) for an organization.* If conflict is to provide useful social consequences for an organization, according to Coser, a number of conditions must prevail: (1) the conflict must be practical, centering on operational issues rather than ideological positions; (2) it must be instrumental rather than expressive in nature, so that it is not valued for its own sake; (3) it must be limited to specific areas and manifested through prescribed channels; (4) it must be managed or resolved within a reasonable length of time, so that it does not become too prolonged or overly disruptive; (5) it must be sequential and intermittent, so that several related conflicts do not occur at the same time; (6) conflicts must be crosscutting rather than cumulative or superimposed, so that various disruptions will cut across the organization in different ways rather than all reinforcing the same entrenched cleavages; (7) conflict must not threaten to destroy the basic values of the organization; and (8) the culture of the organization must contain a certain amount of normative diversity, as well as a norm of tolerance for social and cultural differences. We can summarize all of these requirements by saying that the organization must possess established social procedures for effectively managing—that is, limiting, directing, controlling, and resolving—social conflicts.

In essence, Coser's principal contribution to developing a theory of social conflict has been to emphasize, explain, and elaborate Simmel's original analysis—which is no small accomplishment. In particular, we have noted his thesis that social conflict is particularly likely to arise from dissatisfaction with inequality in the distribution of scarce resources; his examination of factors that contribute to the duration and intensity of conflict; his elaboration of the consequences of conflict for an organization's centralization, cohesion, and tolerance of deviant actions; and his specification of the conditions under which conflict will have beneficial social consequences for an organization. Perhaps the major weakness in Coser's approach to conflict is his tendency to emphasize its positive but not its negative social consequences, although this focus has stimulated much sociological interest in the functions of social conflict.

Toward a Theory of Social Conflict

THE four theorists dicussed in the previous section—Marx, Simmel, Dahrendorf, and Coser—have each contributed many valuable insights into the process of social conflict. But none of them has constructed a comprehensive, integrated theory of social conflict. That demanding task cannot be accomplished here, but we can at least juxtapose their major ideas into a single framework that will provide a guideline for further theoretical development concerning the conflict process. This overview, which is divided into the three categories of the causes, dynamics, and consequences of conflict, consists of a series of general principles drawn from the writings of the four theorists.

THE CAUSES OF CONFLICT

PRINCIPLE 76: **The greater the inequality of resources and benefits in an organization, and the more disadvantaged actors experience this**

inequality as unacceptable relative deprivation, the greater the rate of social conflict within that organization.

The fundamental thesis here is that structured inequality in the distribution of desired resources and benefits (material, social, and symbolic) among the members of an organization is the principal underlying source of internal social conflict. Nevertheless, inequality will not normally produce conflict unless disadvantaged individuals or subunits experience it as relative deprivation which they find unacceptable, which they desire to rectify, and which cannot be altered through social mobility or other achievement efforts. Under these conditions, disadvantaged actors will often instigate conflict—either threatened or overt, and either nonviolent or violent—with relatively advantaged actors in an effort to eradicate or reduce the inequality.

> PRINCIPLE 77: **The greater the intensity with which two or more organizations seek goals which are in some way incompatible, and the less willing they are to resolve their differences through mutual compromise, the greater the extent of conflict between these organizations.**

Interorganizational conflict, that is, typically arises when organizational units seek to attain similar or interrelated goals that are limited in some manner so that a gain by one unit would result in a loss by another. Expressed differently, conflict between organizations often occurs in zero-sum situations which preclude all the participants from fully attaining their goals. Conversely, if these goals are not incompatible or are not in limited supply, or if the involved units are able to achieve at least partial success in attaining what they desire through compromise, then conflict is not likely to occur.

The distinction drawn here between intraorganizational and interorganizational conflict is of course entirely relative, depending on the perspective of the analyst. For example, a dispute over wages between a labor union and the management of a business concern could be analyzed as either conflict between two parts of a single organization or between two separate units, depending on the purposes of the analysis. Consequently, "relative inequality" and "incompatible goals" are often simply alternative ways of describing the same situation. These two causal conditions underlying social conflict can have different implications for the conduct and outcome of the conflict process, however, so that the distinction between them is analytically useful.

THE DYNAMICS OF CONFLICT

> PRINCIPLE 78: **The greater the cohesion among the members of a conflicting unit, as determined by their communication, awareness of**

common interests, and possession of a unifying ideology, the more effectively that unit can engage in conflict without experiencing disorganization.

Although a loosely organized aggregate of actors may become a participant in a conflict process, the relative lack of internal ordering and a shared culture among these actors will make it difficult for them to act collectively in a unified manner. The more cohesive an organizational unit, the more adequately it will be able to marshal its resources, formulate its goals, exert power, and sustain a conflict against opposition. In short, effective conduct of social conflict requires viable social organization within each of the involved units.

> PRINCIPLE 79: The greater the emotional involvement of individuals participating in a conflict, the more directly the conflict touches on basic values of the participants, and the more extensively the conflict is normatively regulated, the more resolute the conflict is likely to be.

The resoluteness, or firmness and determination, with which a conflict is conducted depends heavily on the importance that the individual participants attach to the issues at stake. As with all interaction processes, the more crucial a conflict is to the participants, the more likely they are to persevere in maintaining it until their goals are satisfied. In addition, resoluteness is also increased by the presence of regulatory norms which guide the participants in the conduct of the conflict process.

> PRINCIPLE 80: The more extensively and effectively a conflict is normatively regulated, the less violent it is likely to become and the greater the likelihood that a mutually satisfactory resolution will be achieved.

Beyond facilitating the resoluteness of a conflict, normative regulation is a vital requirement for peaceful and mutually acceptable conflict resolution. Without the guidelines provided by a set of regulatory norms, a conflict can easily become violent and destructive for the participants, and will likely continue until one or all of them are totally destroyed. Conversely, shared normative guidelines enable the conflicting parties to negotiate with each other in a nonviolent manner toward the goal of achieving a solution to the conflict that is at least minimally satisfactory to all involved parties.

THE CONSEQUENCES OF CONFLICT

> PRINCIPLE 81: The greater the extent of regulated conflict within an organization, the more likely this process is to promote release of tensions and necessary adjustments among its members and subparts, to

revitalize existing norms and generate new ones, and to provide organizational stability.

Over time, strains and tensions will almost invariably develop among the members and component parts of any organization. If these difficulties are not adequately resolved, they may continue to build up until they explode in a violent eruption that can easily destroy the entire organization. However, if they are expressed and resolved through periodic conflicts— especially regulated nonviolent ones—the strains and tensions can be dissipated before they do irreparable harm to the organization. A frequent outgrowth of this process, moreover, is the revitalization or generation of common norms that will aid the organization in coping with such difficulties in the future, should they arise again. As a consequence, the organization gains increased stability through time.

PRINCIPLE 82:   The greater the extent of conflict with other organizations, the more likely an organizational unit is to strengthen its boundaries, centralize and enhance its ability to exert social power, increase its internal cohesion, and establish viable relationships with its opponents.

If it is to engage effectively in conflict with other organizations, a collectivity must be able to act in a concerted and unified manner. External conflict is therefore an extremely effective means of drawing together and solidifying the members and subparts of an organization, delineating its boundaries in relation to other units, centralizing its power structure, and stimulating its ability to exercise power in pursuit of its goals. An external threat, in short, will commonly force an organization to "tighten up" and realize its maximum potential for collective action—or else suffer possible disintegration or total disorganization. An additional result of this process, moreover, is that the organization will often establish new relationships with its opponents that may likely endure long after the immediate conflict is resolved and that may eventually develop into mutually beneficial cooperative arrangements.

PRINCIPLE 83:   The greater the extent of regulated conflict, either internal or external, the more likely an organization is to experience beneficial social change and hence remain flexible and viable.

Conflict can provide a dynamic stimulus to social change in an organization by identifying potential weaknesses and dysfunctional processes, by challenging established modes of action, by bringing new and more capable leaders to the forefront, and by suggesting alternative and more effective means of dealing with organizational problems. Conflict does not always produce change, of course, and not all changes are beneficial to an organization. If conflict is continually suppressed by an organization, however, it will unquestionably lose the ability to remain flexible and viable in the face of continuously emerging internal challenges and a constantly shifting external environment.

This last principle emphasizes one of the most crucial aspects of the conflict process for all organizations: promoting dynamic flexibility through effective conflict management. As organizations experience either internal or external conflict, they can respond to it in several different ways. Some organizations view conflict as essentially undesirable because of the resulting disruptions or alterations in established social practices, and hence seek to prevent or suppress this process whenever possible. Other organizations remain basically neutral in their responses to conflict, neither discouraging nor encouraging it, but simply accepting it as it occurs and letting it resolve itself. Still other organizations view conflict as essentially desirable as long as it can be kept within broad limits and can be constructively utilized, which necessitates developing procedures for effectively managing this process. What we are here describing is a continuum along which all social organizations can be classified, depending on the degree to which they purposefully promote, manage, and utilize social conflict in a creative manner.

As an ongoing social process, conflict frequently becomes ordered, so that it follows fairly regular and predictable patterns. To accomplish this, however, organizations must establish numerous means of effectively managing and resolving conflict whenever it occurs. Typical management techniques include procedures for bringing together opposing sides of conflict, for promoting full communication among them, for achieving mutually satisfactory compromises or other solutions to conflicts, and for providing compensatory mechanisms to deal with losses suffered as a result of conflict. Labor-management negotiations, as currently practiced in many industries, provide an example of the application of such management techniques to one type of conflict. They constitute an organized means whereby the contending parties can peacefully resolve their differences and achieve solutions to the conflict that often benefit all parties involved.

The extent and success of these management procedures largely determine the form that conflict will manifest in an organization. For analytical purposes, social conflict can be described as either sporadic or continuous, although there are innumerable intermediate combinations. *If an organization resists and suppresses conflict, it will occur only sporadically.* Conflict can never be totally eliminated, however, since external stresses and internal strains never cease acting upon an organization. If the pressures they generate are not brought into the open in some manner, tensions will continue to build up within the organization. Eventually they may become uncontainable and erupt into sharp and potentially violent conflicts which can seriously disrupt, alter, or even destroy the entire organization. Divorces, strikes, race riots, and political revolutions are common manifestations of this kind of drastic conflict.

In contrast, *if an organization encourages the expression of conflict through established procedures as fully as possible, it will occur relatively continuously.* No single conflict will become very disruptive or extensive, but over time the cumulative effects of many minor conflicts may produce extensive social change and continued organizational stability. Such organizations are spared the throes of violent and disintegrative conflicts because stresses and strains are resolved as they arise rather than being allowed to mount up over time.

Organizations falling at the former end of this analytical continuum are frequently described as rigid, whereas those at the latter end are flexible.[27] *A rigid organization resists and suppresses conflict as much as possible.* Such tactics will frequently enable it to survive for some time. But because it cannot resolve stresses and strains and adjust to new conditions, these disruptive forces are likely sooner or later to overcome their bonds and explode in rapid and often violent social conflict and change. Nevertheless, in some organizations at some times, relative rigidity may be the most effective means of preserving crucial values or other organizational characteristics.

In contrast, *a flexible organization promotes and encourages conflict that follows established procedures.* Because of ceaseless activity, such an organization appears at any given time to be rather unstable. But because it resolves stresses and strains as they arise and is capable of continually adjusting to new conditions, the resulting regulated and managed conflict may give this organization great stability in the long run. In some cases, though, flexibility may purchase organizational stability at the price of sacrificing traditional practices and beliefs.

In summary, the main point of this concluding discussion has been that conflict is ubiquitous throughout organized social life, as a result of numerous stresses and strains that perpetually act upon all organizations. Conflict is an inherent aspect of social organization and does not negate this overall process, though it often disrupts or alters it. Conflict frequently displays considerable patterning, and hence can be studied as an ordered social process. The ways in which an organization responds to and manages conflict nevertheless have broad consequences for the overall functioning

[27] For a more extensive discussion of these concepts, see Lewis A. Coser, "Social Conflict and the Theory of Social Change," *British Journal of Sociology* 8 (September 1957): 197–207.

and structure of that organization, and especially for the process of social change.

RECOMMENDED READING

Coleman, James. *Community Conflict*. New York: Free Press, 1957.
>An exploration and analysis of the process of social conflict as it occurs in communities.

Coser, Lewis A. *The Functions of Social Conflict*. New York: Free Press, 1956.
>Elaborates and interprets Simmel's ideas on conflict, emphasizing its positive consequences for social organization.

————. "Social Conflict and the Theory of Social Change." *British Journal of Sociology* 8 (September 1956): 197–207. (Also Bobbs-Merrill reprint S-51.)
>Discusses the relationship between social conflict and change, suggests several beneficial consequences of conflict, presents the concepts of rigid and flexible organizations, and emphasizes the relationship between conflict and cohesion.

Dahrendorf, Ralf. *Class and Class Conflict in Industrial Society*. Stanford, Calif.: Stanford University Press, 1959.
>First expands and interprets Marx's writings on conflict, and then elaborates his own perspective on social conflict as originating in authority relationships within organizations.

————. "Toward a Theory of Social Conflict." *Journal of Conflict Resolution* 2 (1958): 170–183.
>Presents a view of social organization that stresses ubiquitous social conflict and the importance of power exertion in conflict processes.

Marx, Karl, and Friedrich Engels. *The Communist Manifesto*. New York: International Publishers, 1948.
>The classic statement of Marx's theory of social conflict in relation to broad historical processes of change.

Simmel, Georg. *Conflict and the Web of Group Affiliations*, ed. and trans. by Kurt H. Wolff and Reinhard Bendix. New York: Free Press, 1955.
>The most complete presentation of Simmel's theory of social conflict as an inherent aspect of organized social life.

Thompson, James D. "Organizational Management of Conflict." *Administrative Science Quarterly* 4 (March 1960): 389–409. (Also Bobbs-Merrill reprint PS-282.)
>Outlines several ways in which organizations seek to manage and control social conflict.

Williams, Robin M. "Social Order and Social Conflict." *Proceedings of the American Philosophical Society* 114 (June 1970): 217–225.
>Examines the manner in which conflict as a social process contributes to the creation of social ordering.

13

Social Change

AT first glance, a process perspective on social organization seems to imply that social life is constantly fluctuating and varying, so that change is inherent in organization. From a broad perspective, this is true. New and different events are always occurring, and no two instances of social interaction are ever identical. Hence social change is part of the general process of social organization, and not merely an accidental disruption of otherwise static social conditions. Because of the dynamic nature of all social life, social organization is continually being created and enacted. At the same time, social actors strive to bring stability and predictability into their lives by forming relatively enduring patterns of social ordering and shared cultural meanings. Although social ordering and culture are rarely static, they often endure with considerable stability for long periods of time, precisely because they are being constantly modified in many small ways to take account of new conditions.

The Nature of Change

NEVERTHELESS, at times existing patterns of social ordering or cultural meanings are noticeably and permanently altered in some manner.

328

These critical turning points in organized social life—which may occur either gradually or suddenly—can be identified as significant social changes. They are not shifting fluctuations or minor modifications in the course of social life, but constitute crucial alterations in the substance of existing social organization. In other words, *social change is an identifiable, extensive, and enduring reordering or redefinition of the process of social organization.*

THE IDENTIFICATION OF CHANGE

When does a ceaseless process of variation in social life become an identifiable instance of significant social change? Quite obviously there is no sharp dividing line, so that what we call "social change" is actually an arbitrary decision made by a participant or an outside observer. An alteration in social life becomes a social change when it is identified as relatively extensive and enduring in comparison to what has previously been occurring. To identify a particular social change, we must compare the social conditions existing at two or more points in time and decide whether or not the differences between them are great enough to warrant the label "change." This decision will be affected by one's focus of concern, the encompassing social setting, and one's personal orientations. Hence observers will frequently disagree over whether or not a "change" has actually occurred in a given situation, and also over the rate and magnitude of change.

Consequently, *any identified instance of social change is a conceptual abstraction from social reality, derived from empirical observations but defined by subjective judgments of the observers.* Social changes are real historical phenomena, but to identify and understand them we must treat them as mental constructs. That is, any specified instance of change is an arbitrary abstraction from history, although this need not prevent us—either as social scientists or as participants in social life—from treating it as a real event.

CONFLICT AND CHANGE

Some changes enter social life so slowly and imperceptibly that we remain unaware of them until after they have fully transpired. This is not the usual case, however, since *most social changes are preceded by conflicts within an organization, and are in turn resisted by conflicting forces seeking to prevent change.* An outbreak of open conflict is not imperative for social change, but conflict frequently does promote change. Once people have created workable social organizations within the ongoing processes of social life, they understandably wish to perpetuate these existing patterns of social ordering and shared cultural ideas. Established social organization can be preserved without keeping it rigid and unchanging, but quite frequently this is what does occur. Although Newton's law of inertia is not inherent in organized social life, people frequently act as if it were. In such situations, conflict is necessary to upset or disrupt established practices before extensive change can take place.

Although conflict often promotes social change, it never automatically results in permanent changes in social life. Whether or not the disruptions in patterns of social ordering and shared culture produced by a conflict have lasting consequences for an organization depends on the nature, intensity, resolution, and other features of the conflict situation. For example, a community conflict over the construction of a new city park will result in community change only if the park is actually built and the public recreation program is significantly altered to make use of the park. On the national level, a political battle over whether or not to lower income taxes is not itself a societal change (though it might be a novel activity for the legislature), but the effects of this decision could have untold ramifications throughout the economy and ultimately the entire society.

This problematic linkage between conflict and change results from the fact that permanent social change is only one of a number of possible consequences of disruptive conflicts. Other frequent outcomes of conflict are avoidance or suppression of the conflict situation, standing "agreements to disagree" that quiet the conflict but do not resolve it, compromise solutions that effectively maintain the status quo, individual deviant actions, random fluctuations that have no cumulative effect on the organization, or temporary social adjustments that are discarded after the conflict abates. Only if there is some kind of relatively permanent and extensive alteration in the organization as a result of this conflict can we say that social change has occurred.

A proposed or attempted alteration in social ordering or culture will in turn often generate additional conflict. Resistance to social change is extremely common in social life. Such factors as vested interests in the status quo, opposing values and goals, apparent deficiencies and inadequacies in the proposed alteration, perceived intolerable consequences, and sheer human inertia commonly give rise to opposing forces that may succeed in limiting or blocking social change. And even well-established changes are often resisted for long periods of time. Thus conflict is a consequence as well as a cause of social change. The ultimate fate of any social change may be said to hang in the balance between the forces producing it and those opposing it.

Resistance to change is sometimes explained in terms of psychological phenomena such as fear of the unknown, reluctance to try something new, or a "closed mind." From an organizational perspective, though, resistance can be seen as an outgrowth of social processes rather than as individual perversity. Members of an organization normally value the social ordering and shared culture they have created and maintained, because of the benefits derived from these collective activities. It is not surprising, therefore, that at least some of them will see any given change as destruction of beneficial organization, not improvement of it. For instance, opposition to new programs of the federal government and advocacy of increased power for communities and states within the United States are often explained as "conservative reluctance to change." This political position can also be interpreted, however, as a defense of traditional American governmental principles. We tend to forget that two hundred years ago this same position was described as liberal, not conservative, because of its insistence on local self-determination.

Another factor affecting the degree to which social change is resisted is the extent to which the values and norms of an organization have become secularized. In many "premodern" societies the dominant cultural values and norms are viewed as more or less sacred commandments, either given to humanity by some extrahuman power or else sanctified by countless generations of belief and practice. People in these societies commonly find it unthinkable even to question their cultural values or social practices, let alone change them. Needless to say, such conditions obstruct all attempts to "modernize" these societies. Sacred outlooks and beliefs are by no means absent in contemporary "modern" societies, but they are slowly giving way to secular perspectives on social life. Social values and norms are increasingly seen as man-made, heuristic guides to organized social living, and hence open to change whenever necessary or desirable.

THE RAMIFICATIONS OF CHANGE

Once a change is introduced into one part of an organization, the further question remains of how extensively it will influence other parts. On the one hand, *to the extent that the various subunits of the organization are interrelated, a change in any one part will tend to have ramifications throughout other parts or the whole organization.* An initial alteration, that is, can set off a chain reaction, or snowballing, of further changes. For example, the introduction of new production procedures into a factory may alter existing work groups, which in turn leads to worker demands for union control over job assignments, which causes the union to grow in size and strength, which forces management to revise many of its policies and programs, which ultimately changes the structure and functioning of the whole organization. On the other hand, *to the extent that the various subunits of the organization are functionally autonomous, a change in any one part remains isolated in that part.* It will produce few or no corresponding changes in other parts of the organization. Sometimes this situation will create no difficulties for the overall organization. At other times, though, as this one changing part becomes increasingly divergent from the rest of the organization, serious social problems erupt. An illustration of this phenomenon is seen in many developing nations, in which military officers become better educated, more "Westernized," and more politically sophisticated than the rest of the people in the society. The frequent outcome of such disparity is a military coup d'état.

Another important factor determining the spread of change from one subunit throughout an entire organization is the amount of social power exercised by the part that first changes. In general, *the more powerful the subunit of an organization that initiates a change, the greater will be the effects of this alteration on other parts of the organization.* In contemporary societies, for example, social changes introduced by the national government or by dominant economic concerns (such as major industries or banks) normally produce many more derivative changes throughout the entire society than do alterations initiated by churches or by special-interest associations. From a broader perspective, sociologists often argue that the fundamental processes of industrialization, urbanization, and bureaucratization are drastically affecting all other realms of contemporary societies, including the family, education, religion, race relations, mass communications, and social stratification.

The concept of social change presented here can be summarized in the following manner:

> PRINCIPLE 84: Social change is a relatively extensive and enduring alteration of social organization that is identified as significant by an observer, that is often highly interwoven with social conflict, and that frequently has ramifications for many other interrelated features of organized social life.

The Sources of Change

ANY particular social change is a unique historical event, and can be fully explained only in terms of other specific events and activities that precede or accompany it. Nevertheless, all sources of change affecting social organization can be categorized as either *stresses* originating in the external natural or social environments, or as *strains* originating within an organization.[1] Stresses and strains impinging on an organization produce social tensions that must be dealt with in some manner. Many such tensions are

---

[1] Much of the following discussion of sources of social change is adapted from Wilbert Moore, "A Reconsideration of Theories of Social Change," *American Sociological Review* 25 (December 1960): 810–818. See also his *Social Change* (Englewood Cliffs, N.J.: Prentice-Hall, 1963), chaps. 1 and 4.

relieved or resolved or repressed without altering the organization in any critical way. Others are just ignored and eventually disappear in the normal course of events. In some cases, however, social tensions produced by stresses and strains acting on an organization push the participants to change the organization in an effort to eliminate the tensions. This process may be quite deliberate, but more commonly social change occurs unintentionally from the culmination of a series of small actions that are not purposefully designed to alter the organization in any significant manner. In either case, however, social change can be viewed as a process of social tension reduction.

SOCIAL STRESSES

Because stresses originate outside the process of social organization, they do not automatically produce social tensions within organizations. Stresses affect organized social life only to the extent that they actually influence it in some manner. A famine in Indonesia, for instance, would probably have no immediate effects upon the United States. However, if as a result of this famine Indonesia should seek to purchase large shipments of grain from the United States, a widespread controversy might be set off in this country, and some of our trade laws might be changed. Other types of stresses, meanwhile, have more direct effects upon social organization, producing immediate tensions which in turn often lead to social changes. Rapid population growth provides an example. The addition of thirty million people to the population of the United States every ten years (which has been the approximate rate for the past several decades) creates countless problems for this society, since communities, schools, transportation and communication networks, governmental programs, business concerns, and many other social activities must all constantly expand.

The major sources of external stresses are the four factors comprising the parameters of all social organization—the natural environment, population, human characteristics, and material and social technology—plus the social environment within which an organization exists. Stresses from all five of these sources are constantly impinging upon virtually every social organization.

Any major change in the natural environment will have consequences for almost all forms of social organization. Climatic alterations, depletion of vital natural resources, natural disasters, disease epidemics, and even a heat spell or a heavy snowfall all exert countless pressures upon organized social life. Apart from such "crisis" situations, stresses also arise from the fact that most natural phenomena (including space and time) are necessarily limited in availability and hence must be rationed in use. Scientific discoveries have given us partial control over many natural forces, but ultimately the natural environment affects all social organization.

The effects of variations in population size and composition upon social organization have already been illustrated in chapter 1 and need not be repeated here. Nevertheless, one specific kind of population stress—the "demographic transition"—deserves special mention because of its increasing seriousness for many societies throughout the world. Until quite recently, all societies have experienced both high death and high birth rates, which combined to keep their populations stable. With the introduction of better diets, public sanitation practices, and modern medicine, however, the death rate invariably declines—often quite drastically. For some time after that, the birth rate often remains high, because of traditional beliefs and values regarding childbearing and ignorance concerning methods of birth control. The result is a population "explosion," as more and more people are born but fewer and fewer die. When and if the birth rate also declines, the population will again be stabilized. Until that happens, however, the society is faced with a multitude of social pressures and problems that can become virtually unresolvable. The best efforts of such a society to raise its standard of living through industrialization may go to naught, as population increase far exceeds economic development.

Personality variations among individuals normally do not directly affect social organizations, unless these individuals occupy positions of extreme power or strategic functional importance. In a collective sense, though, *characteristics of the human being that are vital for the creation of social organization—such as basic needs, intelligence, symbolization ability, and motivations for survival and goal attainment—do vary among populations, and hence can place stresses upon any organization.* Of these basic human characteristics, level of intellectual development has perhaps the broadest consequences for social change. Alterations in the overall level of intellectual development of the members of an organization, including amount of knowledge possessed, critical reasoning abilities, and intellectual sophistication, can induce manifold tensions and disruptions. Amount of formal education—which is the best single indicator of intellectual development—is related to a vast range of social and cultural phenomena, and any marked shifts in the educational attainments of the members of an organization will have consequences for many aspects of their collective activities.

The most readily apparent source of external stresses upon social organization is material technology. Every major advance in material technology, from fire making to atomic fission, has disrupted established patterns of social life in some way. A prominent example is the automobile, which has altered vast portions of American society in the past two generations, including suburbanization trends, courtship practices, friendship ties, recreation activities, economic markets, and governmental jurisdictions. Electronic communications have had equally far-reaching consequences for contemporary societies. One sociologist has compiled a list of 150 social changes in American society resulting from the invention of the radio,[2] and a similar list for television might be much longer.

No organization—except for the most isolated of primitive tribes—creates most of the material technology it uses. Diffusion, or the spreading of ideas and objects from one organization to another, has occurred throughout human history, although the rate and extent of diffusion is greater today than ever before. As a consequence, most social organizations are constantly bombarded with new technology. These ideas and objects may be ignored, rejected, altered, or adopted, but in any case they place stresses upon an organization and hence often produce change. A family quarrels over whether or not to buy a color television set, a school reorganizes its curriculum to incorporate teaching machines, and a small nation suddenly finds itself listened to in the United Nations after it has acquired atomic weapons from its allies. In short, as material technology is created and then diffused throughout the world, few organizations can escape the stresses that it introduces.

Just as changes in material technology often disrupt organizations, so innovation or diffusion of social technology will commonly introduce social stresses. One well-known illustration makes this point evident: Henry Ford pioneered industrial mass-production techniques as a means of building cars inexpensively, but the rapid diffusion of his idea throughout most other industries also introduced such far-reaching consequences as loss of meaning in work, elimination of small handicraft producers, creation of complex and highly centralized business concerns, growth of industrial labor unions, and governmental programs to regulate mass production.

The social environment of any organization includes all other organizations with which it comes into contact. *As an organization acts to perpetuate itself and achieve its goals, it must continually take account of limits, demands, and restrictions imposed by its social environment.* An organization will often compete with other organizations for members or resources, it must deal with their demands and activities, and it frequently depends upon them for the attainment of whatever goals it seeks. All of these forces act as stresses upon the organization, creating numerous tensions which often lead to change. Moreover, modern communication and transportation are continually increasing the scope of social interdependence and hence the size and complexity of the social environment with which any organization must contend.

Consider, for example, a small, "independent" retail store. This busi-

[2] William F. Ogburn, *Recent Social Trends* (New York: McGraw-Hill, 1933), pp. 153–156.

ness relies upon several wholesalers for the goods it sells. It must abide by numerous federal, state, and local laws. It may be pressured by labor unions to handle only union-made items, by churches to remain closed on Sunday, or by ethnic associations to hire clerks with certain ethnic characteristics. It utilizes newspapers and other communication media for advertising. And it will remain in business only as long as members of the community patronize it. Any of these external stresses, if serious enough, could compel the store to change the way it operates.

SOCIAL STRAINS

Internal strains constitute the second category of sources of social change. Because strains originate within the process of social organization, they will inevitably produce social tensions. They represent disjunctions, fissures, and ruptures occurring inside organizations, and hence cannot be ignored or escaped. All organizations, consequently, experience many diverse kinds of internal strains. For this reason social theorists often speak of social change as imminent and universal within social organization.[3] Perhaps the best known application of this perspective to social life is Karl Marx's theory that social change is primarily a result of dialectic conflict between modes of economic production. We do not have to assume that the dialectic process is inherent in human history—which many theorists reject as turning an empirical question into a postulate of theoretical faith—to appreciate the supreme importance Marx attached to dynamic change within organized social life. The major types of internal strains can be described as interpersonal, cultural, or functional disjunctions.

Disjunctions between individual actions and established patterns of social ordering take many forms, all of which frequently result in organizational strains. First of all, most individuals at least sometimes act as relatively independent elements seeking their own personal goals, rather than as responsible parts of social organizations. As long as the other persons with whom this individual interacts do not expect him or her to act as a member of a common organization, no strains need arise. But if these interaction partners are acting as members of an organization and also expect the individual to responsibly carry out a role as part of that organization, numerous strains may be generated.

Deviant actions—from simple violations of customs to serious crimes— are another source of social strain arising from interpersonal disjunctions. Sociologists commonly attribute such actions to weak or ineffectual social control procedures. Lack of adequate social sanctions within an organization, for instance, unquestionably gives rise to numerous strains, as when a

---

[3] Pitirim A. Sorokin, *Social and Cultural Dynamics* (Boston: Porter Sargent, 1957), chap. 38.

police force is unable to control a riot or a factory cannot prevent substandard work. Nevertheless, we must avoid carrying this thinking to its extreme by assuming that all "social problems" and "deviant actions" are due simply to poor techniques of social control. Most organizations make no attempt to impose total social conformity upon their members—if that were even possible. Limited social control can have many beneficial consequences for social organization, despite attendant strains, by allowing members to exercise a certain amount of initiative and creativity in their actions, thus keeping the organization flexible.

The benefits for organizations of limited demands upon individual members are especially evident in the process of role enactment. As we have already seen, open competition for roles, a wide range of available roles, and nonspecific role expectations all tend to promote organizational flexibility and operational effectiveness as well as freedom of individual action. Beyond these features of role enactment, some organizations are more or less purposefully arranged to promote individual choice and variation in role actions, as in political elections and economic markets within Western societies. But to gain these benefits an organization must bear the price of a certain amount of internal social strain.

Disjunctions between cultural ideas and patterns of social ordering are caused by discrepancies or modifications within the culture of an organization, which then produce strains throughout the organization. Two or more sets of sharply disparate social values, for example, might be contained within the same culture. Examples would be religious demand for moral virtues versus secular concerns with "having a good time," or traditional ideas of thrift, hard work, and self-reliance versus contemporary emphasis on cooperation as a "member of the team." To the extent that such sets of values are irreconcilable, social strains are bound to occur.

Social strains can also erupt within an organization if the norms and rules being observed are not congruent with basic values. As an illustration, the values of a community might unequivocally hold that drinking, gambling, and other such "vices" are morally wrong, while at the same time many residents might covertly accept the norm that these activities are perfectly acceptable as long as they are done in private. Similarly, the government of a community might loudly deplore "creeping influences" of the national government, but simultaneously argue that participation in a federally sponsored urban renewal program is in keeping with long-standing traditions of community improvement.

The norms and rules of an organization also frequently contain internal inconsistencies that place strains on the organization. The bylaws of a labor union, for example, might state that no discrimination will be practiced against members because of race, religion, or nationality, but also stipulate that all new applicants must be personally recommended by a present member, almost all of whom are white Anglo-Saxon Protestants. Or consider a family whose norms simultaneously prescribe joint decision making on all major issues but proscribe the wife from having any say about what job her husband takes.

Finally, it hardly needs to be pointed out that actual social practices in all organizations at best only approximate cultural ideals, and often diverge widely from them. The Soviet Union expounds ideals of economic equality for all, but actually evidences at least as much economic stratification as other industrial societies, while the United States believes in full political democracy but systematically prohibits several million people from voting because of overt residency and covert racial restrictions. On the local level, there is in most communities a marked correlation between a family's economic status and the quality of education its children receive, despite our insistence on the importance of free and equal education for all. To a degree, "imperfections" such as these are probably inevitable in social life. Nevertheless, such disparities between cultural ideals and actual social practices invariably create strains within social organization and frequently result in extensive social changes.

Functional strains in social organization arise within patterns of social ordering, as a consequence of their structures and modes of operation. Most of these strains center around one or more of four situations that occur in all organizations: incomplete fulfillment of organizational requirements, differences in activities and power of partially autonomous subunits, allocation of organizational benefits, and demands for centralized coordination and control.

A brief review of the list of typical social requirements facing all organizations should convince us that these requirements can become overwhelming. No social organization can simultaneously satisfy all of its survival and operational requirements. It must assign some kind of priority ranking to its functional requirements, focusing its activities on the critical ones and at least temporarily deemphasizing or ignoring others. Laboratory studies of small groups, for instance, have indicated that they tend to progress through a fairly predictable series of phases or stages, each of which emphasizes one specific type of functional requirement.[4] The point here is that priority ranking of organizational requirements and phase movements among various types of requirements will invariably introduce strains into social organization. And we must add that organizations often fail to satisfy functional requirements even when they are receiving priority attention.

The component subunits of any social entity will usually have some

---

[4]R. F. Bales and F. L. Strodtbeck, "Phases in Group Problem-Solving," *Journal of Abnormal and Social Psychology* 46 (1951): 485–495.

degree of functional autonomy apart from the total organization. The very fact that they can act at times as relatively autonomous social elements is enough to ensure that strains will emerge within the organization. To the extent that subunits do act to gain their own self-oriented goals and hence compete with each other in their activities, rather than work for the welfare of the organization as a whole, tensions will multiply. This type of social strain becomes particularly acute when power differentials develop among the various component units as a result of unequal resources, size, control over communication, or operational effectiveness. Power differentials often lead to such phenomena as domination, exploitation, coalition formation, and open "warfare," all of which further disrupt the encompassing organization.

Another related process is the distribution of the benefits of organizational activities among subunits. Leaving aside the strains engendered when one or a few dominant parts commandeer most of the benefits for themselves, there is the inevitable dispute between "fair" and "equal" distribution. The parts that are larger or that contribute more toward organizational operations will often demand "fair" distribution of benefits (rewards based on size or activities performed), while smaller or less involved parts will commonly demand "equal" distribution (rewards the same to all parts). Furthermore, whenever some parts of the organization feel that they are being systematically deprived of their just rewards, they are likely to demand alterations in the distributive process, either through peaceful changes (the "haves" share more with the "have-nots") or through violence (the "have-nots" forcibly take from the "haves"). The process of distributing organizational benefits to subunits will thus almost unavoidably create numerous social strains.

The last of these functional problems within all organizations stems from the operational necessity for some degree of overall direction, coordination, and control. To the extent that the subunits of an organization are functionally specialized, they tend to become interdependent upon each other and hence interact within complex exchange networks. To promote and maintain these interdependent relationships, the organization must exercise some centralized control if it is not to disintegrate. Pressures will mount for it to establish procedural rules and laws, enforce them, and settle problems among subunits. Nevertheless, development of centralized coordination and control procedures necessarily imposes restrictions upon the subunits and requires them to surrender at least some power and functional autonomy to the larger organization. They may vigorously resist such moves toward increased centralization, especially when these appear to be in excess of what is functionally imperative for the survival of the total organization. Such a situation clearly invites the appearance of strains and changes within an organization.

In summary, the various sources of social stresses and strains discussed in this section are listed in Table 13-1. We note again that social tensions are ubiquitous throughout all organized social life, as the result of both constant external stresses and inevitable internal strains. And from these tensions arise continual pressures for social change. In short:

PRINCIPLE 85: Social change is an outgrowth of efforts to cope with social tensions produced within the process of social organization by external stresses and internal strains.

TABLE 13-1: Sources of Social Change

I. *External Stresses*
  1. The natural environment
  2. Population changes and imbalances
  3. Human characteristics, especially level of intellectual development
  4. Innovation and diffusion of material and social technology
  5. The social environment surrounding an organization

II. *Internal Strains*
  1. Interactional disjunctions
      a. Individuals acting as elements when expected to act as parts
      b. Individual deviant behavior
      c. Assignment and enactment of social roles
  2. Cultural disjunctions
      a. Sets of disparate social values
      b. Incongruencies between basic values and norms and rules
      c. Inconsistencies among norms and rules
      d. Discrepancies between cultural ideals and actual social practices
  3. Functional disjunctions
      a. Disregard or inadequate fulfillment of organizational needs
      b. Differences in activities and power among partially autonomous subunits
      c. Distribution of the benefits of organizational activities
      d. Necessity for centralized coordination and control

Metatheoretical Perspectives on Change

GIVEN ever-present stresses and strains impinging on all social organizations to produce disruptive social tensions, our next concern is to construct a theoretical explanation of the process through which these stresses and strains lead to relatively extensive and enduring social changes. Unfortunately, sociology does not yet have a general theory of social change. Pervading much of the current literature on social change, however, are two basic metatheoretical perspectives on the nature of change. They are essentially ways of viewing the change process rather than explanations of it, but they do offer several valuable insights. There are no commonly accepted names for these two viewpoints, so let us call them the "adjustment" and "power" perspectives on social change.

THE ADJUSTMENT PERSPECTIVE

The adjustment perspective stresses the functional requirements that all organizations must satisfy if they are to persist through time and attain collective goals. Of particular importance, for both survival and operational reasons, are certain "key features" that determine the basic nature of an organization and influence or shape most of its activities. These key features vary among organizations and over time within an organization, but they frequently include such characteristics as organizational boundaries, internal patterns of social ordering, overall organizational cohesion, centralized decision-making procedures, or major cultural values. The key features of an organization need not remain static, and in fact are often dynamic factors that shift through time, but whatever happens to them will have manifold consequences for the entire organization.

Beginning with this empirical observation, the adjustment perspective goes on to suggest that whenever stresses or strains seriously threaten the key features of an organization—whatever they might be—the organization will very likely initiate compensatory actions to counter these disruptions, in an attempt to preserve its key features. These compensatory activities sometimes successfully nullify or resolve the stresses and strains before they affect the organization's key features, while at other times they fail in this task. In either case, considerable social tension is almost invariably created within the organization or between it and its environment, and widespread changes are likely to occur throughout the organization. If these compensatory activities successfully defend the threatened key features, then whatever changes do occur will be confined to other, less crucial organizational characteristics or activities. In other words, the major outlines and key features of the organization are protected against disruptive stresses and strains, but as a direct consequence of continual changes *within* the organization. To the extent that the organization successfully practices such adjustive maneuvers, it survives through time as a relatively stable social entity and functions effectively to obtain whatever goals it seeks.

There are limits, however, beyond which adjustive or counterbalancing activities and changes cannot go if the organization as a whole is to be maintained in its present form. When disruptive stresses and strains or their resulting social tensions are so severe and prolonged that compensatory mechanisms cannot cope with them, the key organizational features being protected will themselves be altered or destroyed. The entire organization then changes, so that there is change *of* the organization rather than just within the organization. The nature and extent of this total organizational change will depend on numerous factors, such as the strength of the disruptive forces, the particular key features affected, the degree to which various organizational subunits are institutionalized, and the previously existing overall cohesion and stability of the organization.

This distinction between change "within" and "of" organizations is admittedly arbitrary, depending on which features of the organization are taken to be crucial and which merely peripheral, and on how much variation can occur in a key feature before it is considered to have changed, but the distinction is useful for certain analytical purposes. In either situation, *social change results from constant adjustments by an organization to disruptive stresses and strains that threaten its key features.* From this perspective, social change represents a perpetual process of social reorganization.[5]

THE POWER PERSPECTIVE

A radically different conception of social change is held by theorists who stress the crucial importance of power in social organization. This perspective also begins with an empirical observation concerning the activities of all organizations, and then proceeds to explain change as a consequence of these activities. The component subunits of an organization almost always possess some amount of functional autonomy, or ability to act independently of the larger organization. At times, therefore, they will tend to act as self-oriented elements, rather than as collectively oriented parts. They will temporarily seek to deal with their own internal problems and to achieve their own goals, rather than contribute to the functioning of the encompassing organization.

At this point the power perspective steps in to explain the creation of social change. To the extent that organizational subunits act as elements rather than as parts, their activities will necessarily create social tension within the organization—for two reasons. First, they will remain interdependent upon, and interrelated with, many other organizational subunits, with whom they must contend. These other subunits will therefore obstruct and limit any unit attempting to act independently, at least partially thwarting its activities. Second, the larger organization usually expects this subunit to continue acting as a responsible part rather than as an autono-

[5] For a sophisticated elaboration and defense of this theoretical perspective, see Francesca Cancian, "Functional Analysis of Change," *American Sociological Review* 25 (December 1960): 818–827. See also Talcott Parsons, "Some Considerations on the Theory of Social Change," *Rural Sociology* 26 (1961): 219–239.

mous element. Consequently, it will exert various forms of social power upon the subunit, thus generating additional social tensions. Not all such tensions necessarily produce social change, but change is one frequent outcome. More specifically, relatively permanent change in or of the larger organization results from the use of social power by subunits attempting to gain their own goals. Partially autonomous subunits must exercise power in relation to other subunits and the larger organization if they are to succeed in these endeavors. Necessary resources must be procured, existing relationships with other subunits must be altered and new ones created, and the encompassing organization must be induced to meet the demands of these self-acting units. As power is successfully employed by subunits in these directions, both they and the larger organization are very likely to change.

The power explanation of change places special emphasis on the actions of those subunits that wield predominant amounts of power over all other subunits and even the whole organization. The exercise of power by such elites will often result in alterations throughout the entire organization. In effect, social change in organizations is frequently a consequence of actions and activities by powerful elite subunits. Regardless of whether or not such elites purposefully attempt to influence other subunits or the larger organization, their activities will necessarily have ramifications throughout the entire organization of which they are a part. In sum, *social change results from the exercise of social power by subunits of an organization acting as partially independent elements in pursuit of their own goals.* From this perspective, social change represents a perpetual process of social disruption.[6]

COMPLEMENTARITY OF THE PERSPECTIVES

At first glance, the adjustment and power perspectives on social change may appear totally contradictory. Further examination reveals, however, that although they do offer quite divergent explanations of how and why change occurs, they are in fact largely complementary. Each simply orients the observer to different aspects of the total process of social change. The fundamental distinction lies in the focus of one's analysis. The adjustment perspective focuses on a given organization as a single entity, assumes that its subunits are at least temporarily acting as committed parts, and attempts to explain how this organization reacts to external stresses and internal strains. The power perspective focuses on the various organizational subunits, assumes that they are at least temporarily acting as functionally autonomous elements, and attempts to explain how their actions influence the rest of the organization.

---

[6]The major source of this perspective are the writings of Karl Marx. A leading contemporary spokesman for this position is Ralf Dahrendorf, *Class and Class Conflict in Industrial Society* (Stanford, Calif.: Stanford University Press, 1959), chap. 5.

Partial convergence of the two perspectives is readily apparent once we remember that any given organization can be viewed and analyzed either as a separate entity or as a subunit of a larger whole. The threatening stresses and strains that the adjustment perspective takes as given phenomena are frequently power demands of other related organizations, more encompassing entities, or component subunits. And the independent goal-seeking actions of subunits that the power perspective takes as given phenomena are frequently these units' attempts to protect their own key features through adjustive measures.

Moreover, this realization that the two perspectives are merely focusing on different levels of organization suggests that both are fully compatible with the use of a social system model. As elaborated by Pierre van den Berghe (who refers to the two perspectives as "functionalism" and "dialectic"), conceptualizing social organizations as systems enables us to deal simultaneously with both homeostatic and conflict tendencies within organized social life.[7] Critics of the system model often argue that it is useful only for analyzing the consequences of social change, not its causes, and also that it emphasizes order at the expense of change. Underlying these criticisms are the implicit assumptions that social systems are more or less closed to their environments and unitary in nature. As long as one's system model remains open to external stresses from the environment and allows for internal strains among partially autonomous subunits, it can take account of numerous sources of change and change processes.

A final basis for convergence between these two metatheoretical perspectives on social change lies in the fact that both assume extensive exertion of social power. This assumption is explicit in the power perspective, with its emphasis on the actions of powerful subunits seeking to attain their own goals through interaction with other subunits. The assumption of power exertion is more implicit in the adjustment perspective, but is nevertheless quite evident. The compensatory actions that an organization takes as it attempts to counter disruptive tensions almost inevitably involve the exercise of power to enforce social control or to promote overall coordination. The major distinction between these two perspectives on social change therefore turns on the question of who is exerting power in a particular situation. Is the principal power wielder a total organization or one of its subunits?

An initial step toward synthesizing the adjustment and power perspectives on social change might be stated in the following manner:

PRINCIPLE 86: Social change results from the exercise of power by an organization or its subunits in an effort to cope with social tensions

[7]Pierre van den Berghe, "Dialectic and Functionalism," *American Sociological Review* 27 (October 1963): 695–705.

generated by stresses and strains that arise in conjunction with the protection of key elements or the attainment of collective goals.

Growth-Oriented Theories of Change

THE idea of organizational growth or social evolution will be discussed in more detail in the following chapter, but its central thesis can be stated quite briefly. Sociologists attempting to explain broad processes of historical change in human societies have generally viewed these trends as relatively linear and cumulative in nature. Societies and other forms of social organization have therefore been seen as tending to increase in size and complexity through time. Consequently, all of the specific theories of social change prevailing in contemporary sociology—in contrast to the two metatheoretical perspectives discussed above—are explicitly oriented toward organizational growth. In this section we shall briefly examine four major growth-oriented theories of social change: cultural accumulation, ecological development, structural differentiation, and epigenesis.

CULTURAL ACCUMULATION

The theory of cultural accumulation gained wide support among American sociologists during the 1930s and 1940s, primarily through the writings of William Ogburn.[8] This thesis begins with the assumption that in literate societies cultural knowledge—especially material and social technology—is rarely permanently forgotten or ignored. Once people begin to record their hard-won knowledge concerning the world and themselves, each new generation can in effect start out where the last generation left off. Since the technological knowledge of the past is already available, the new generation can learn it without having to rediscover it or repeat costly errors. Hence cultural knowledge tends to accumulate at an ever-increasing, or exponential, rate. Sooner or later this growing body of cultural knowledge influences and shapes social life, with a resulting evolutionary development of social organization. In short:

PRINCIPLE 87: Social change occurs as material and social technology is accumulated through time and applied to organized social life.

A challenging topic for study—about which we know very little—is why innovation (invention and discovery) occurs when it does. Ogburn points out that innovation cannot take place until the necessary back-

---

[8] Ogburn's classic statement of this theory was his *Social Change* (New York: Viking Press, 1922). For a more recent presentation, see W. F. Ogburn and M. F. Nimkoff, *Sociology*, 4th ed. (Boston: Houghton Mifflin, 1964), chaps. 23 and 24.

ground knowledge, or cultural base, has been accumulated. Any innovation is essentially an outgrowth or new synthesis of previously existing information. Once the necessary cultural base for a particular innovation has been developed, however, it appears to be only a matter of time until that innovation occurs. Ogburn attempted to substantiate his thesis by studying simultaneous inventions. Numerous inventions have been made at approximately the same time by two or more persons who worked independently of each other but who presumably shared the same cultural base of information. To cite a few examples: the printing press was invented by Coster in 1423 and by Gutenberg in 1443; photography was developed by both Daguerre and Talbot in 1839; and the telegraph was invented by Henry in 1831 and by Morse, Cooke-Wheatstone, and Steinheil, all in 1837.

This idea of cultural accumulation persists in current sociological writings, though it is now commonly incorporated within one of the other change theories. It is also being employed by several writers who stress humanity's increasing ability to harness and utilize sources of energy.[9] As a descriptive generalization of an empirical phenomenon, the thesis of cultural accumulation has considerable validity. Mankind's stockpile of technological knowledge has in fact tended to grow at an increasing rate. But as a general explanation of the process of social change, the theory contains several weaknesses. The most serious is that it does not specify how cultural accumulation becomes transformed into broader processes of social change—that is, how technological knowledge affects social organization. Nor does it deal with the question of how developing social organization influences the invention or discovery of new knowledge. For these reasons, the cultural accumulation thesis is perhaps most useful as an ancillary part of other, more inclusive theories of social change.

ECOLOGICAL DEVELOPMENT

The initial roots of this explanation of social change lie in Émile Durkheim's writings on the division of labor in society,[10] although he borrowed heavily from Herbert Spencer and other earlier theorists. Durkheim's principal argument was that expanding role specialization leads to growth in the division of labor throughout society, which in turn produces increasingly complex social organization. Whereas previous writers had generally assumed that population growth led automatically to role specialization, Durkheim pointed to increasing "dynamic density," or frequency

[9] The best known of these writers is Leslie A. White. See his *The Science of Culture* (New York: Farrar Straus & Giroux, 1949). See also Fred Cottrell, *Energy and Society* (New York: McGraw-Hill, 1955).

[10] Émile Durkheim, *The Division of Labor in Society*, trans. by George Simpson (Glencoe, Ill.: Free Press, 1933).

and intensity of social interaction, and its resulting social and economic competition, as the crucial factors in this process. He also differed from earlier writers in his insistence that growing division of labor produces not only a more complex society, but also a more cohesive society.

Contemporary ecological theory incorporates this idea of division of labor, but also stresses population growth, environmental conditions, and technological innovation as determinants of social change.[11] The major tenets of ecological theory were given in chapter 5 and need only be briefly reviewed here. Ecological theory focuses on the functional means through which a society, community, or other organization satisfies sustenance and other fundamental survival requirements. Growth in population size and density, increased abundance of resources from the natural and social environments, and accumulation of technological knowledge all act singly and in combination to stimulate the development of social organization, while the level of organizational development in turn influences each of these other interrelated factors.

Population, environmental, and technological forces affect a society primarily through its economy, and especially through its main sources of wealth and power. The more effectively the economy satisfies basic sustenance requirements, the greater the extent to which collective efforts can be diverted away from survival problems toward other activities and goals, and hence the more complex the resulting societal organization. Particularly crucial in this process are the actions of key functionaries, who control the flow of resources from the environment into the organization and perform other vital functions for the organization. Their activities largely determine the nature and direction of social change. In short:

> PRINCIPLE 88: Social change occurs as a society, acting through its key functionaries, effectively utilizes technology to cope with the task of surviving in its environment and thereby acquires surplus resources for population growth, division of labor, and organizational development.

As an explanation of social change, ecological theory contains several weak points. Most important is its treatment of changes in population size, the environment, and technology as essentially random occurrences, except to the extent that these factors influence each other. Furthermore, this theory has thus far shown only limited ability to specify the processes or forms of social organization that will develop once survival requirements have been

---

[11] The first systematic statement of ecological change theory was by Amos H. Hawley, *Human Ecology* (New York: Ronald Press, 1950), especially chaps. 10–12. An introductory explanation of the theory as it applies to social change is given by Paul E. Mott, *The Organization of Society* (Englewood Cliffs, N.J.: Prentice-Hall, 1956), chap. 3.

satisfied. Consequently, it cannot adequately explain many social changes observed in highly developed societies. Nevertheless, it does emphasize a concern with the "hard facts" of physical reality that is lacking in the other theories, and it may prove to be increasingly relevant to changing social conditions resulting from future energy shortages.

STRUCTURAL DIFFERENTIATION

By far the most popular theory of social change in contemporary sociology is structural differentiation.[12] This thesis can also be viewed as an outgrowth of Durkheim's emphasis on the division of labor, but it diverges sharply from ecological theory. The theory begins with the observation that in simply organized societies, most social activities take place within a few basic types of organization (such as the extended family or a small community). All functions necessary to satisfy individual and social requirements are performed by these "multipurpose" organizations. Such functionally unspecialized organizations tend to be rather inefficient in carrying out their diverse activities, since they cannot commit all of their resources and efforts to any one type of problem. With growing population size, cultural knowledge, and common desires for more effective operational procedures, it becomes impossible to confine all social life to a few organizations. Through a process of trial and error, an ever-increasing number and variety of new organizations is created, each of which specializes in a rather narrowly defined sphere of activity.

The principal cause of structural differentiation, especially in modern societies, is people's desires for greater functional effectiveness in the attainment of collective goals. Expressed in this manner, the process may appear to be highly rationalistic, but in practice it usually involves numerous tensions, conflicts, and social movements. The more extensive the resulting web of diversified organizations within the society, the more complex it becomes. As pointed out by S. N. Eisenstadt, however, structural differentiation often decreases the functional and normative cohesion of a society, which calls for new forms of "reintegration" if the society is to remain viable.[13] In short:

PRINCIPLE 89: Social change occurs as multipurpose organizations become structurally differentiated into numerous functionally special-

[12] For a representative sampling of this literature, see the following: S. N. Eisenstadt, "Social Change, Differentiation, and Evolution," *American Sociological Review* 29 (June 1964): 375–386; Talcott Parsons, "Evolutionary Universals in Society," *American Sociological Review* 29 (June 1964): 339–357; and Neal J. Smelser, *Social Change in the Industrial Revolution* (Chicago: University of Chicago Press, 1959).
[13] S. N. Eisenstadt, "Social Change, Differentiation, and Evolution."

ized units, each of which can more effectively perform its particular
activities as long as the total society retains adequate cohesion.

Considerable evidence has been compiled to support the thesis that
social change does frequently take place through structural differentiation,
but this statement is only an empirical generalization, not a causal explanation. What social forces, other than public dissatisfaction with existing
procedures, operate to initiate this process of differentiation? In what ways
are functionally ineffective organizational innovations discarded and satisfactory ones retained? And what factors determine the lines along which
"fused" activities become functionally specialized, or the particular forms
that structurally differentiated organizations will assume? Finally, how does
a society remain cohesive while undergoing structural differentiation? In
brief, this theory describes a general process through which social change
frequently occurs, but it does not explain this process. It tells us what
happens, but not how or why it happens.

EPIGENESIS

A fourth theory of social change is provided by Amitai Etzioni's
idea of epigenesis.[14] This thesis begins with the assumption that individuals
frequently propose, and societies or other organizations adopt, collective
goals for social life. As a means of achieving these goals, existing organizations are expanded or new ones are established. Workers form a labor union
through which to bargain with their employer, an association is begun to
promote the game of golf, or a community is founded to take advantage of
nearby natural resources. New organizations can be started from "scratch,"
but more commonly they develop as several existing organizations merge to
form a larger and more inclusive social entity. Etzioni has used this
theoretical perspective to study the growth of international confederations,
but it obviously has many other applications.

A major difference between the ideas of differentiation and epigenesis is
that the former thesis stresses only the development of new ways of carrying
out old activities, whereas the latter thesis emphasizes the creation of totally
new social activities. According to the differentiation theory, all basic social
functions are performed in even the most primitive society (though perhaps
not very efficiently), so that social change involves merely the splitting up of
these functions among more specialized organizations. The epigenesis
theory, in contrast, argues that through the collective seeking of new goals,
people establish both new organizations and new activities. Social change
is not just a matter of learning how to perform social functions more

---

[14]Amitai Etzioni, "The Epigenesis of Political Communities at the International Level,"
American Journal of Sociology 68 (1963): 407–421.

effectively and efficiently; it also adds totally new activities and dimensions to organized social life. Although the process of epigenesis may appear to be overly rationalistic, the theory largely escapes this pitfall by emphasizing the actions of organizational elites, who use their power to influence, shape, and direct the process of social organization toward the attainment of whatever goals they seek for themselves or for their organizations. In short:

> **PRINCIPLE 90:** Social change occurs as social actors, especially powerful elites, more or less purposefully expand existing organizations and activities or create new ones to achieve goals through collective action.

This theory does not attempt to explain all aspects of social change, and hence leaves many crucial questions unanswered. For instance, from what sources can leaders derive the power with which to carry out the process of organizational expansion or creation, or how do such organizations become functionally effective, or what happens when the masses of the people involved disagree with the elites? Nevertheless, epigenesis does offer a relatively straightforward explanation of at least some of the forces involved in the change of social organization.

COMPLEMENTARITY OF THE THEORIES

None of these four growth-oriented theories of social change is necessarily incompatible with any of the others, although they do emphasize different causal factors and dynamic processes. To explain any particular occurrence of social change, therefore, the sociologist can utilize and combine whichever of the theories appear to be most applicable to that situation. Moreover, all four theories are fully compatible with a social system model, since all of them point to dynamic interrelationships among system parts.

In addition, each of the four theories relies—either implicitly or explicitly—on the exercise of social power. Cultural accumulation depends on the actions of knowledgeable actors to synthesize existing information into new ideas and to transform these ideas into organizational processes and forms. The actors who perform these roles derive power resources from their possession of new knowledge, and in turn exert power as they apply this knowledge. Ecological theory assigns great importance to the activities of key functionaries who perform socially vital roles. These actors are clearly in a position to exert considerable power throughout an organization, and the success of any change effort will be directly affected by the effectiveness with which they employ their power to influence others. Structural differentiation, in contrast, is not necessarily initiated by powerful elites. But the actions of elites are crucial in maintaining societal cohesion as differentiation occurs, so that the perpetuation of this process is dependent on the exertion of power by elites. Epigenesis, finally, is usually initiated, directed, and controlled by organizational elites through the exercise of social power. In the final analysis, therefore, social change can be viewed as an outcome of power exertion in organized social life.

RECOMMENDED READING

Applebaum, Richard P. *Theories of Social Change.* Chicago: Markham, 1970.
> All of the major contemporary sociological theories of social change are described in this short text.

Cancian, Francesca. "Functional Analysis of Change." *American Sociological Review* 25 (December 1960): 818–827.
> A sophisticated examination of the adjustment perspective on social change.

Eisenstadt, S. N. "Social Change, Differentiation, and Evolution." *American Sociological Review* 29 (June 1964): 375–386.
> Analyzes the process of evolutionary social change as occurring through structural differentiation, together with the effects on society of differentiation.

Etzioni, Amitai. "The Epigenesis of Political Communities at the International Level." *American Journal of Sociology* 68 (1963): 407–421.
> Describes the epigenesis theory of social change, distinguishes it from structural differentiation, and applies it to the creation of international organization.

Moore, Wilbert E. *Social Change.* Englewood Cliffs, N.J.: Prentice-Hall, 1963, chaps. 1, 2, 5.
> An introductory presentation of the major concepts, causes, processes, and trends of social change.

Mott, Paul. *The Organization of Society.* Englewood Cliffs, N.J.: Prentice-Hall, 1965, chap. 3.
> An introduction to ecological theory as applied to the evolutionary change of social organization.

Ogburn, William F., and Meyer F. Nimkoff. *Sociology,* 4th ed. Boston: Houghton Mifflin, 1964, chaps. 23, 24.
> The most recent statement of the theory of cultural accumulation.

Smelser, Neil. "Toward a General Theory of Social Change." In his *Essays in Sociological Explanation.* Englewood Cliffs, N.J.: Prentice-Hall, 1968, chap. 8.
> Outlines a broad conceptual framework for a theoretically integrated perspective on social change.

van den Berghe, Pierre, "Dialectic and Functionalism." *American Sociological Review* 28 (October 1963): 695–705.

> Contrasts and compares the "adjustment" and "power" theoretical perspectives on social change and suggests several lines of convergence between them.

Zeitlin, Irving M. *Marxism: A Re-examination.* Princeton, N.J.: D. Van Nostrand, 1967, chap. 4.

> Evaluates Marx's thesis of dialectical social change in light of contemporary sociological thinking.

14

Social Development

OUR discussion of social change in the previous chapter was essentially ahistorical in that it did not deal with any specific historical trends. In reality, of course, social change always occurs in historical settings, and any sociological analysis of change must take account of sequences of events through which change becomes manifest. Moreover, most instances of broad-scale social change are directional in nature, so that societies are seen as developing along identifiable lines and evidencing new forms. When viewed from a historical perspective, this process is commonly described as social evolution. When viewed from the more theoretical perspective of social systems analysis, the process is often called system growth or morphogenesis. In this chapter we shall explore the nature of social evolution, analyze in more detail the two modernization trends of industrialization and urbanization, and then briefly sketch four alternative models of possible "postmodern" societies.

Social Evolution

EARLY sociological thinking was thoroughly infused with crude notions of social evolution, which were often coupled with ideas of either

353

social progress or social degeneration. The French social philosopher Auguste Comte, who is sometimes called the father of sociology, believed that all societies evolve through three cultural stages, which he called theological, metaphysical, and positive (or scientific). Herbert Spencer, the first major English sociologist, wrote that sociology is "the study of evolution in its most complex form."[1] The German theorist Ferdinand Tönnies saw social evolution as movement from *gemeinschaft* societies based on personal, communal relationships to modern *gesellschaft* societies, in which social relationships are impersonal and contractual. Émile Durkheim's thesis of the growing dominance of organic (functional) over mechanical (normative) solidarity in contemporary societies also expressed an evolutionary orientation. William Graham Sumner, an early American sociologist, tried to apply Darwin's theory of biological evolution through natural selection and survival of the fittest to the totality of social life. And most important of all, Karl Marx's contention that social dialectical processes might ultimately sweep all humanity from feudalism through capitalism to socialism is thoroughly evolutionary in nature.

THE NATURE OF SOCIAL EVOLUTION

Although sociologists still study the grand evolutionary theories of these "founding fathers," few serious attempts have been made to incorporate their emphasis on social evolution into current sociological thought. In their attempts, beginning about 1920, to make sociology "scientific," an entire generation of sociologists (with a few notable exceptions) conveniently dismissed the whole question of social evolution as too grandiose and empirically unverifiable for social science.

Since World War II, however, it has become painfully obvious that societies around the world—both "primitive" and "modern"—are attempting to "modernize" with full deliberate speed. As a belated consequence, contemporary sociologists have reawakened to the vast implications of social evolution for contemporary social life.[2] In its current guise, the thesis of social evolution is often called "modernization"—despite invidious overtones of ethnocentrism inherent in this word—but the fundamental conception remains the same. *From an evolutionary viewpoint, social change is both linear and cumulative in the long run.*[3] Social change is linear if nonrepetitive trends run throughout many diverse events and

[1] Herbert Spencer, *The Study of Sociology* (New York: D. Appleton, 1873), p. 350.
[2] A parallel trend has also occurred in anthropology, as witnessed by such books as Julian Steward, *Theory of Cultural Change: The Methodology of Multilinear Evolution* (Urbana, Ill.: University of Illinois Press, 1955), and Marshall D. Sahlins and Elmar R. Service, eds., *Evolution and Culture* (Ann Arbor, Mich.: University of Michigan Press, 1960).
[3] This discussion does not attempt to deal with the radically different thesis of cyclical evolution, which sees a certain set of processes or series of stages as being endlessly repeated throughout

alterations. Although short-term fluctuations may be observed, the broad patterns of change are neither random nor cyclical. The steady decline in the death rate that has been occurring around the world for the past century is an example of a fairly linear change, as is the steady growth of "white-collar" occupations, while periodic variations in dress style are not linear. Social change is cumulative if it builds upon itself, so that prior changes are not only retained but also influence future changes. Although cumulative change can occur in a "downward" direction toward increasing disintegration of social organization, most such change during the past several hundred years has been "upward" growth or development of social organization toward increased size, scope, and complexity. The process of industrialization, for instance, tends to be relatively cumulative as well as linear, in that the more extensively a society is industrialized, the more rapidly its economy can expand to encompass further industrial development.

More explicitly, contemporary students of social evolution or modernization point to a number of broad, long-range, nonrepetitive, cumulative changes in social organization that are becoming strikingly evident throughout the world. These trends include such phenomena as (1) increasing size of organizational units, in terms of both population and geographic area; (2) growing functional interdependence among social organizations, with attendant diminishing of functional self-sufficiency; (3) shifting of many social activities and responsibilities from small organizations such as families and neighborhoods to large social networks, national governments, and even international confederations; (4) rising functional specialization, or division of labor, among both individuals and organizations; (5) emergence of extremely complex and formal organizations, composed of many levels of interrelated subparts; (6) increasing centralized coordination and control in many types of organizations; (7) spreading cultural secularism and universalism, so that social values and norms are seen as man-made, relative, open to change, and applicable to all people and organizations; and (8) growing application of scientific knowledge and rational thought to social life.

In their attempts to free evolutionary theory from many of its older biases and limitations, contemporary social scientists studiously avoid imputing to social evolution a number of corollary ideas that were once either implicitly or explicitly assumed. The process of social evolution, they argue, does not include or imply (1) progress, or any necessary betterment in human happiness or morality; (2) teleology, or ultimate plans, purposes, or goals; (3) fixed stages through which all societies or other organizations must

---

human history. Two leading proponents of this view are Arnold Toynbee (*A Study of History*, one-vol. ed. [New York: Oxford University Press, 1953]), and Pitirim A. Sorokin (*Social and Cultural Dynamics* [Boston: Porter Sargent, 1957]).

successively pass; (4) unilinear change along any one particular path; (5) social determinism, or the idea that development is somehow inherent in social life and hence beyond human control; or (6) universality of evolution in all social organization. By rejecting notions such as these, sociologists hope to find in the idea of social evolution a theoretical key with which to unlock part of the riddle of "How has social organization changed throughout history and where is it going in the future?"

In short, social evolution is seen as one particular kind of social change—or more accurately, as a historical and theoretical perspective on social change. Not all change is evolutionary in nature, but in the broad sweep of human history we can discern crucial social trends that are both linear and cumulative and that are slowly but radically transforming organized social life.

ORGANIZATIONAL GROWTH

To place the process of social evolution within a theoretical framework, sociologists frequently employ the social system model as an analytical tool. *Evolutionary development is then described as transformation of social organization toward increased systemization*, or approximation to the social system model. Many current writers speak of this trend as growth of organizational complexity, although some prefer the more technical concept of morphogenesis.[4]

As long as one's theoretical concern remains focused on problems of system homeostasis or equilibrium, any changes that occur in the system will usually be seen as essentially random responses by the system to various stresses and strains acting upon it. Yet the phenomenon of organizational growth (including negative growth) in size and complexity is not only a persistent theme throughout human history, but is also dramatically evident in today's world. As expressed by A. D. Hall and R. E. Fagen, social systems "possess the ability to react to their environment in a way that is favorable . . . to the continued operation of the system. It is as though systems of this type have some prearranged 'end' and the behavior of the system is such that it is led to this end despite unfavorable environmental conditions."[5]

If we are to avoid imputing teleology, or intentional purposes, to social systems, we must construct a theoretical explanation of system growth as a

[4]Three significant articles on organizational growth, from which the following discussion is largely drawn, are Kenneth E. Boulding, "Toward a General Theory of Growth," in J. J. Spengler and O. D. Duncan, eds., *Population Theory and Policy* (Glencoe, Ill.: Free Press, 1956), vol. 1, pp. 109-124; Mervin L. Cadwallader, "The Cybernetic Analysis of Change in Complex Social Organizations," *American Journal of Sociology* 65 (September 1959): 154-157; and Mason Haire, "Biological Models and Empirical Histories of the Growth of Organizations," in Mason Haire, ed., *Modern Organizational Theory* (New York: John Wiley & Sons, 1959), chap. 10.
[5]A. D. Hall and R. E. Fagen, "Definition of System," *General Systems* 1 (1956): 18-28.

natural process. One suggestive approach to this problem is provided by the idea of functional effectiveness, as emphasized by ecological theory. In essence, it argues that *as actors within social systems strive to adapt to and cope with their natural and social environments, they often tend to develop increasingly effective functional procedures, which in turn generate surplus resources that can be applied to system growth.* Key functions and functionaries play crucial roles in this process, for they constitute the "cutting edges" of organizational growth. And since these sectors and actors are generally the main foci of power in society, *system growth can also be seen as a result of expansion in the total amount of power being exercised within a society.*

This thesis of growing functional effectiveness does not require any assumption of purposeful goal striving by social systems. In fact, *much system growth is probably an unintended consequence of efforts by organizations to cope with social tensions produced by external stresses or internal strains, so as to maintain overall stability and cohesion.* To manage or resolve such tensions, an organization will often create (frequently through much trial and error) new patterns of social ordering and cultural ideas. For example, the members of an association might respond to demands from other organizations in the social environment by admitting more members, enlarging the operating budget of the organization, establishing new subunits, or improving intraorganizational communication channels—all without any conscious awareness that these activities were increasing the functional effectiveness of their association and thus enabling it to grow. Moreover, to the extent that these innovations aid the organization in dealing with the current situation, they will probably be incorporated into the organization on a permanent basis. And because these innovations will likely prevent or nullify the further occurrence of the original disruptive condition, the organization will be ensured of greater functional effectiveness in the future, thus allowing it to continue growing.

If system growth is to be maintained through time, however, the system must also develop adequate information processing or cybernetic techniques. These include the ability to procure new information and generate new ideas, to store and retrieve useful information, to analyze and solve problems, to reach collective decisions, and to provide for and learn from informational feedback. Without such cybernetic techniques, an organization will blindly repeat old activities over and over again no matter how dysfunctional they are for system survival or goal attainment.

One final qualification must be added to this theoretical perspective. The process of system growth is rarely uniformly linear. In the course of coping with one disruptive force, a system might easily eliminate some previously acquired capabilities that were useful in dealing with other kinds of problems. Growth in one area of the system would be sacrificed for growth in another more pressing sector, and the system might even experience a temporary decline in overall organizational complexity and strength. Sooner or later, though, "the world bites back," and the system would be forced to correct its deficiency by creating additional functional patterns that could deal with problems in both these areas. In other words, systems frequently experience many temporary fluctuations, so that overall growth is only evident in the long run.

The essence of this functional effectiveness theory of organizational growth can be stated in the following manner:

PRINCIPLE 91: **Organizational growth toward greater systemization frequently results from efforts by the organization to cope with pressing stresses and strains by creating and retaining new procedures and forms that enable it to function more effectively, thereby expanding its ability to exercise social power and increasing its overall size and complexity.**

Modernization Trends

IN the contemporary world, organizational growth is most evident in the process of societal modernization, which has resulted primarily from the two pervasive evolutionary trends of industrialization and urbanization. Although they are distinct social phenomena, historically these two trends have become highly interwoven, so that growth in either area is quite likely to produce concomitant growth in the other also. Together, industrialization and urbanization have largely shaped the modern "Western world," and are now slowly transforming many other societies around the globe. The discussions of these trends in the following paragraphs are necessarily rather cursory, but they serve to illustrate the process of social development as it is occurring today.

INDUSTRIALIZATION

The process of societal modernization is normally initiated and propelled by widespread industrialization within that society. The "entering wedge" of industrialization is technological innovation or diffusion, so that this trend is often viewed as a purely technological development, in which the use of power-driven machinery for all kinds of economic production becomes widespread throughout a society. The replacement of handicraft production by machinery and mass-production techniques has ramifications throughout all aspects of social life, however. *With growing industrialization the economy of a society becomes increasingly effective in meeting basic organizational and individual survival requirements, so that considerable resources and effort can be directed toward many other kinds of collective activities.* The social and cultural development of a society is therefore no longer limited by relentless survival demands.

Preindustrial societies frequently remain quite stable for long periods, providing they do not encounter severe disruptive stresses such as changes in the natural environment or military conquest. In analytical terms, there can be extensive change within the society without producing radical change of the society, so that the basic feudal pattern often survives for centuries—as seen in medieval Europe. Feudal elites often maintain such pervasive control over their society that they can fairly effectively prevent any extensive social changes of the total society. Other segments of the society, such as peasants or artisans or merchants, are too weak to challenge or overthrow the rule of the landed nobility, and there are few societywide organizations such as political parties or interest associations through which members of the society might promote social change. As a broad generalization, therefore, it appears that feudal types of societies cannot usually be transformed into more modernized societies without an external impetus from material technology or the social environment. The segment of a feudal society most capable of introducing sweeping social change is the landed nobility, but their vested interests usually lead them to perpetuate the status quo as long as possible. Only with the appearance of entirely new sources of social power and power elites not dependent on ownership of agricultural land, plus attendant patterns of social ordering and culture, can feudalism be transcended and the processes of modernization begun.

Industrialization provides these new sources of power and social organization. With industrialization, wealth and other power resources accrue to those who own and operate machines rather than land, so that a new power elite emerges to challenge the control of the feudal nobility. As industrialists gain economic power in a society, they almost invariably seek to extend their influence to other realms such as politics, and hence sooner or later clash with the landed nobles. A prolonged period of extensive, violent, and even bloody conflict may ensue, but as industry grows in productivity so does the power of business leaders, until the landed nobility can no longer suppress or control them. Sooner or later the old elites will be either driven out or reduced to powerless symbolic figureheads, and radical transformations will ensue throughout the entire society.

Rather ironically, in many feudal societies the landed nobility have unwittingly hastened their own downfall. In order to expand and consolidate their power, feudal elites have sought to create large standing armies and navies. They have also felt compelled to maintain lavish courts and engage in elaborate conspicuous consumption as symbols of their status in society. But all this has required more revenues than could be squeezed out of the peasants. The nobles consequently began to tax and borrow from merchants and nascent industrialists, and thus over time became increasingly dependent upon these additional sources of income. As the old elites sought on the one side to gain power and prestige, on the other side they gradually but continually surrendered power (if not immediately prestige) to the business community.

The development of extensive industrialization within a society requires at least six preconditions: material technology, capital accumulation, agricultural productivity, social technology, political unification, and entrepreneurial values.[6]

Widespread utilization of power-driven machinery depends on the acquisition and application of a vast amount of scientific and engineering knowledge. Until such technology becomes available, either through innovation or diffusion, industrialization cannot occur. Because England was the first society to become highly industrialized, much emphasis is often placed on the inventions in the textile industry (such as the spinning jenny and the power loom) that initiated the entire process. But the industrialization of a society does not have to begin with textile manufacturing, and in fact has not done so in any other major society. Economists are generally agreed that if any one sphere of production is particularly crucial for industrialization, it is undoubtedly the manufacturing of steel. All other industries depend on steel for their own machinery, and for many it is also a basic raw material. More important than any specific form of production, though, is knowledge about and development of sources of inanimate energy. In this light, it can be argued that the steam engine was the single most important invention for early industrialization. Today many other sources of energy are also available, including oil, electricity, and nuclear fission, although their application often raises many problems for industrializing nations.

Given the necessary material technology, the principal facilitating factor in promoting societal industrialization is the rate and amount of capital accumulation. *Industrialization can proceed only as rapidly and extensively as capital becomes available for investment in productive facilities.* This holds true regardless of whether the necessary capital is being provided by private entrepreneurs or by the state. Possible sources of new capital for industrialization include untapped natural resources, economic exploitation of foreign colonies or domestic workers, surplus agricultural production, enforced savings by individuals, a favorable balance of international trade, and foreign aid. Whoever controls this new capital will be able to wield enormous economic power in a society, and will be able to direct the course of industrialization. The old land-owning elites of the preindustrial

---

[6] A concise but highly insightful analysis of requirements for industrialization is given by W. W. Rostow, *The Stages of Economic Growth* (New York: Cambridge University Press, 1964).

era could conceivably assume these emerging power roles, thus giving the society a relatively smooth transition into industrialization without excessive conflict—but also leaving the traditional stratification structure largely intact. To some degree this did occur in England, which is probably one reason why it avoided a violent political revolution in conjunction with industrialization. But this does not appear to be a common occurrence in most other nations. In the vast majority of cases the landed nobility have concentrated their efforts on resisting change as long as possible. As a consequence, they left the way open for the rise of new economic elites—either private entrepreneurs or governmental bureaucrats.

If people are to work in factories, agricultural productivity in a society must be high enough to free large segments of the population from subsistence farming. More food must be produced by fewer farmers. Mechanization of agricultural work will greatly raise productivity, but most societies in the early stages of industrialization lack the wealth to buy and operate such equipment even if it is available. They must rely instead upon the development of such practices as fertilization, crop rotation, and irrigation. Once again, though, feudal elites have frequently hurried their own downfall. In England and Europe, it was they, not the peasants, who first introduced improvements such as these into agriculture. Their clear intention was to increase their own wealth and social power as a means of combating the rising merchants and industrialists. In eighteenth-century England the nobility also passed the famous Enclosure Acts, which entitled them to fence off and cultivate land that previously had been used as communal livestock grazing pastures. Agricultural productivity was raised as a result of these various innovations, and for a time the landed nobility benefited. But in the long run they merely succeeded in freeing more peasants for work in factories.

Handicraft production in feudal societies takes place primarily within an artisan's home or small shop, with one or a few persons performing the entire operation from beginning to end. The introduction of machinery into the productive process changes all this, however. The high cost of machinery, the space it requires, and the necessity for connecting many machines to a common power plant all necessitate the building of factories. A factory is much more than a building that houses machinery; it is also a complex social organization consisting of countless novel social relationships and patterns of social ordering. Practices must be initiated and problems solved in such areas as recruiting workers into the factory and hiring them on a cash basis to work during certain specified periods of the day, supervising and disciplining workers who may never before have worked in accordance with time schedules and fixed routines, providing for the safety and welfare of employees, coordinating the many diverse activities taking place within the different parts of the factory, anticipating demands and problems so as to plan for and guide factory production, disposing of the finished products on the outside market, and in general managing a huge and highly complex organization. In short, *industrialization depends as much on developments in social technology as on those in material technology.*

Beyond these basic features of factory organization, many other forms of social technology are also involved in industrialization. Two examples are specialized mass production and the corporate form of organization. Short of complete automation, industrial production becomes most efficient when each machine (and hence each worker) performs only one or a few specialized operations, over and over again. With the addition of a moving assembly line, vast quantities of goods can be cheaply produced in this manner. But extreme division of labor introduces numerous problems of coordination and regulation, not to mention the loss of creativity and satisfaction suffered by the individual worker, who becomes a distinctly minor cog in the vast wheel of mass production. On a broader level, the corporate form of business organization has many advantages over individual ownership or partnerships. It enables the company to raise large amounts of capital through the sale of stock, it protects investors from unlimited financial liability for the business, and it gives the company legal stability despite changes in ownership or management. Moreover, this process of social innovation must extend far beyond the economy to include the legal system, government, communication and transportation facilities, the educational system, and even the family.

The small and relatively autonomous political units characteristic of feudalism are not well suited to extensive manufacturing and trade. Hence *close ties of political cooperation, if not complete political unification, are another necessary requirement for the industrialization of a society.* As long as each feudal fief is more or less politically independent of its neighbors, merchants face such problems as inadequate or nonexistent means of transportation between localities, toll charges every few miles as goods move from one principality to another, lack of a common currency with which to conduct sales, wide variations in laws and customs pertaining to manufacturing and business transactions, a limited pool of labor from which to hire workers, and severely restricted markets for sales. Political cooperation and unification on an increasingly broader scope alleviates all of these problems for manufacturers and traders, even though the ruling nobility may seek political consolidation largely for its own aggrandizement and without any necessary intention of furthering industrialization.

Finally, in addition to economic, social, and political requirements, *industrialization is dependent on a set of cultural values and norms which must be internalized by individuals so as to motivate their activities.* As conceptualized by Max Weber, these "Protestant ethic" values and norms stress the importance of hard work, self-denial, self-discipline, thrift, frugality, self-reliance, and individual initiative.[7] Industrialization requires the investment of large sums of money, or capital, in machinery, buildings, raw materials, and trained workers. Entrepreneurs must therefore be willing to forgo immediate rewards and invest their savings and profits as capital that may not begin to produce wealth for many years. Furthermore, the creation of industry always involves financial risks and requires ceaseless efforts by its founders. Weber argued that without the values and norms of the Protestant ethic, individuals lack the motivation and drive necessary to carry out the process of industrialization.

This ethic, Weber believed, was first stressed by Protestant reformers, especially John Calvin and his followers. It was for them a purely religious doctrine, and they had no intention of applying it to economic affairs. But by a historical accident, these religious beliefs were ideally suited to the emergence of industry and commerce, and hence provided the necessary cultural support for industrialization in Europe. Weber amassed vast quantities of data to support his thesis. He showed, for instance, that Protestant England, Germany, and Scandinavia industrialized earlier and more extensively than did Catholic France, Italy, or Spain. He also tried to prove that the lack of a "Protestant ethic" was the primary factor that prevented China and India from becoming industrialized long before Europe. Numerous critics have since attacked Weber's thesis, and have rather conclusively demonstrated many logical and factual errors in his linkage between Protestantism and this set of cultural values and norms.[8] Rejection of Weber's causal argument does not diminish the importance of cultural ideas such as these for industrialization, however. Under the newer names of "entrepreneurial values" or the "work ethic," they are stressed by many contemporary social scientists as a vital requirement for industrialization.

In sum, if the process of total social change associated with industrialization is to occur in a society, considerable amounts of social power must be exercised at several strategic points, including capital accumulation (which is often accompanied by restrictions on consumption), limiting the rate of population growth (to prevent the new capital from being totally absorbed in supporting the additional population), overcoming the resistance of

---

[7] Max Weber, *The Protestant Ethic and the Spirit of Capitalism*, trans. by Talcott Parsons (New York: Charles Scribner's Sons, 1958). Weber spoke only of privately owned businesses, but it can be argued that his basic thesis applies to all instances of industrialization regardless of formal ownership.

[8] The most recent and thorough criticism is by Kurt Samuelsson, *Religion and Economic Action: A Critique of Max Weber*, trans. by E. Geoffrey French (New York: Harper & Row, 1961).

existing land-based elites, promoting political unification on a broad scale, and introducing new forms of social organization throughout the society. This requirement for power exertion suggests that few of these crucial changes are likely to happen spontaneously through a more or less automatic process of social adjustment. The more probable situation is that each step of this change process will be bitterly resisted by some segments of the society—partly as a consequence of apathy or traditional orientations among the masses of people, but more directly as a result of overt opposition by established elites and all others (such as handicraft artisans) who occupy relatively advantaged positions in the old social structure. In addition, power exertion is also necessary to sustain all of these changes and ensure their continual development, at least until the society reaches a stage of relatively complete industrialization.

More briefly, the essence of this analysis of industrialization as a major developmental trend can be expressed thus:

> PRINCIPLE 92:   The growth in economic productivity resulting from the introduction of industrial technology, both material and social, throughout a society creates new power resources, new sets of dominant elites, and new forms of social organization that eradicate feudalism and produce a totally different and exceedingly more complex society.

URBANIZATION

Although cities of at least moderate size have existed since antiquity, widespread urbanization is less than one hundred years old. The explanation of this seeming paradox is that the existence of a few cities within a society does not render it urbanized. For example, Rome under the Caesars is estimated to have achieved a population of over one-half million, while in the fifteenth century Florence and Venice both reached at least 100,000 population, but Italy never has been and is not now an extremely urbanized society.[9]

As a major evolutionary trend, *urbanization is the process in which communities within a society grow in size and power until they contain a large portion of the total population and exercise functional and cultural dominance over the entire society.* Even though we often use the number and size of cities in a society as an indicator of urbanization, this developmental process is actually societywide in scope. As urbanization pro-

[9]A concise review of the historical development of urbanization is given by Kingsley Davis, "The Origin and Growth of Urbanization in the World," *American Journal of Sociology* 60 (March 1955): 429–437. For data on world urbanization, see Jack P. Gibbs and Kingsley Davis, "Conventional vs. Metropolitan Data in the International Study of Urbanization," *American Sociological Review* 23 (October 1958): 504–514.

gresses, the social life of an entire society is increasingly shaped by its urban communities.

Two aspects of this definition of urbanization require additional exploration. First, what proportion of a society's population must reside in urban communities before the society can be meaningfully described as urbanized? There is no standard criterion for urbanization in terms of population location, but rather a scale along which societies are ranked, ranging from under 10 percent in parts of Africa to over 80 percent in Great Britain. (The United States is presently set at about 70 percent urban.) These figures depend on one's definition of the minimum size of an urban community, and their significance varies from one society to another. At present a society might be considered relatively urbanized if at least 40 percent of its population lived in urban communities (this would now include only twenty to twenty-five societies), but this criterion will undoubtedly rise as urbanization progresses around the world.

Second, what is meant by "functional and cultural dominance" of urban communities over a society? Sociologists have given considerably less attention to this phase of urbanization than to the more obvious population question, even though urban dominance is the distinctive organizational feature of an urbanized society. No matter how large cities become, if they remain relatively isolated from the rest of the society—as in the case of ancient Rome—the society as a whole is not urbanized. Any city is always dependent upon the surrounding countryside for food and other raw materials, and will in turn exert some influence over its hinterland. But a nation does not become urbanized until these metropolitan influences are strong enough to affect most aspects of social life throughout the entire society. The situation is no longer one of reciprocal interdependence, but rather one-sided dominance.[10] Urban dominance can occur in numerous different activities, including politics, manufacturing and trade, education, recreation, transportation, communication, values, and "styles of life," although all such activities are usually interwoven to some extent. At the same time, the dominant urban communities become increasingly dependent upon each other and less dependent on their immediate surrounding regions. The society can no longer be pictured as a series of relatively autonomous areas, each of which centers around its own urban center. Instead, we must now see the society as an ordered and interrelated network of urbanized communities and metropolises, all of which together draw on and dominate the nonurbanized portions of the society.

[10] A comprehensive analysis and investigation of urban dominance is given by Donald J. Bogue, *The Structure of the Metropolitan Community: A Study of Dominance and Subdominance* (Ann Arbor, Mich.: Horace H. Rockham School of Graduate Studies, University of Michigan, 1950).

Given these difficulties in conceptualizing urbanization, it is not surprising that we have no reliable data on the extent of worldwide urbanization. It has been estimated, for instance, that between 20 and 25 percent of the world's people now live in cities of at least 20,000 population, with about half of these persons residing in metropolises of 100,000 or more population. But this tells us nothing about the extent of metropolitan dominance in various societies. Nevertheless, it is readily apparent that world urbanization is presently nowhere near its potential peak. The degree of urbanization around the world has been steadily rising since about 1800, but three-fourths of humanity still lives outside urban communities. If present rates continue, though, it is possible that close to half of the world's people may be urbanized by the year 2000.[11]

Several conditions must exist in a society before extensive urbanization can occur. The most important of these are high agricultural productivity, industrialization, development of transportation and communication facilities, and adoption of public sanitation practices.[12]

The necessity for rising agricultural productivity is obvious. As with industrialization, *people must be freed from agricultural work if they are to live in cities and engage in urban occupations.* This can occur only as farm operations are mechanized and techniques of scientific agriculture are discovered and applied. It has been estimated that in a typical feudal society at least twenty-five agricultural workers are required to support one town dweller, whereas in the United States one farmer can presently raise enough food for twenty-five or more urban residents. When agricultural productivity does increase to this extent, farm workers are not simply freed for urban occupations—they are forced by economic necessity to seek urban employment, since they are superfluous on the farm. The reverse side of this coin is the necessity in urbanized societies for the steady expansion of urban jobs in industrial, commercial, clerical, service, technical, and professional fields.

The growth of urbanization within a society is highly related to the development of industrialization. The reason is again readily apparent. The establishment of industrial and related business concerns provides work for those persons displaced from farms. In addition, the higher standards of living and new ways of life commonly found in industrialized communities attract increasing numbers of rural dwellers to the city, even when they are not forced to move by economic necessity. England was the first society to become fully industrialized, and since 1800 it has continually led the world in rate of urbanization. Numerous studies have found correlations above .80 between the extents of industrialization and urbanization in

---

[11]Davis, "The Origin and Growth of Urbanization in the World."
[12]Amos H. Hawley, "World Urbanization," in Ronald Freedman, ed. *Population: The Vital Revolution* (New York: Doubleday, 1964), pp. 70–83.

societies around the world.[13] And of the seventeen most highly urbanized societies at the present time, all but two are also extensively industrialized.[14] Although in most societies the process of industrialization tends to precede urbanization by a slight margin, which suggests a causal link, this is not always the case. In several South American nations, for instance, the rate of urbanization is currently running ahead of industrial development, indicating that the attractions of city life may temporarily become greater than the opportunities for urban employment.[15]

Because of the extreme degree of economic and other functional specialization inherent in urban living, *extensive networks of communication and transportation facilities are also vital requirements for large-scale urbanization.* Individuals and organizations become highly interdependent in all areas of life, and must be able to interact with relative speed and convenience. Means of transportation between the city and its hinterland are of highest necessity, since the urban community must daily import food and other raw resources and export goods and services of all kinds. Transportation and communication between cities also become important as they develop interdependent links. Extensive internal communication and transportation facilities are not needed as long as towns remain fairly small and serve primarily as trading centers for the surrounding countryside. But large urban metropolises containing hundreds of thousands of people and countless specialized activities are absolutely dependent on such devices as motor vehicles, newspapers, and telephones. Even a temporary loss of electric power, for example, can totally paralyze a modern city.

Plumbing may seem far removed from urban social organization, but *lack of adequate public sanitation has been a major hindrance to urbanization throughout history.* Medieval European towns, for example, were periodically swept by plagues, which often killed large portions of their entire populations. It would be virtually impossible for a million people to live together in close proximity without some procedures for ensuring a safe water supply, food preservation, and disposal of garbage and sewage. In addition, as cities become even larger and denser in population, public health measures to control communicable diseases become crucial.

From a demographic perspective, the process of urbanization is charac-

[13] Leo F. Schnore, "The Statistical Measurement of Urbanization and Economic Development," *Land Economics* 37 (1961): 229–245. Thomas O. Wilkinson, "Urban Structure and Industrialization," *American Sociological Review* 25 (June 1960): 356–363.
[14] The fifteen societies supporting the generalization are Great Britain, Israel, Germany, Australia, Denmark, United States, Belgium, Argentina, Canada, New Zealand, France, the Netherlands, Japan, Austria, and Sweden. The two exceptions are Cuba and Venezuela. See Wilkinson, "Urban Structure and Industrialization."
[15] James R. Wood and Omer R. Galle, "Urbanization, Industrialization, and Modernization: The South American Experience," paper read at the 1965 annual meeting of the American Sociological Association.

terized by two distinct trends in population location: concentration and dispersion. Initially, *urbanization must consist of an inward flow of large numbers of people from scattered rural areas to urban communities.* Population concentration in urban areas can be viewed as a response by many people to the requirements and benefits of industrialization. For industrialists and related businesspeople, population concentration is almost an economic imperative. They depend on access to large numbers of people to provide both an industrial labor force and a mass market, and hence have traditionally gone to great lengths to induce rural dwellers to move to cities. Moreover, it is economically advantageous for manufacturing and related business firms to be located near one another, so as to minimize transportation costs. Concentration of the population in urban centers is also desirable for governmental leaders. Industrial development creates many new demands on government for stimulation and regulation of the economy, and for the provision of many new services ranging from protection of labor unions to unemployment programs. Most such activities can be performed more effectively and efficiently in cities than in rural areas, so that political elites frequently support the efforts of industrialists to promote urban migration.

For countless individual workers, meanwhile, industrial development creates many strong inducements for movement to the cities. No matter how low factory wages may be, they are usually better than what most peasants and farmers are currently earning, and in addition are seen as providing a more secure income than is possible through agricultural work. Beyond this economic inducement, the city frequently offers many other attractions, especially to the young. It promises them a new way of life that is much more appealing than anything they have experienced in the countryside, including educational opportunities, a large pool of potential marriage partners, a wide variety of possible jobs, and countless recreational possibilities. In addition to these "pulls" from cities, "pushes" in rural areas—such as crop failures, surplus population, and loss of land—also act upon these people. The combination of all these pulls and pushes sometimes becomes so strong that the rate of urban migration exceeds the supply of jobs in the cities, creating greater urbanization than a society can adequately handle, but even this situation rarely stems the flow of migrants from farms and small towns to cities.

As individuals and organizations become increasingly concentrated within the small geographic area comprising a city, its center—or "downtown"—rapidly becomes the scene of intense social activity. Because of this concentration, land values tend to be highest near the city center and to decline in a fairly steady ratio as one moves outward toward the periphery of the community. Land values in turn influence, but do not fully determine, the social uses to which various sections of the community will be devoted. The result is that patterns of social ordering within urban communities often assume identifiable spatial forms, as determined by such factors as distance from the city center, accessibility to transportation lines emanating from the downtown area, and proximity to industrial plants and other specialized activities. Urban sociologists have proposed several theories to explain the spatial patterning of urban communities, none of which is adequate by itself, but all of which when taken together provide considerable insight into this phenomenon.[16]

Once highly concentrated urban communities have developed, the second demographic shift begins. *Individuals and organizations disperse outward from the "inner city" to the periphery of the urban community.* Dispersion does not negate concentration, since this type of movement remains within the metropolitan area and does not return people to rural locations. It does, however, profoundly affect both urban spatial patterns and urban ways of life. The predominant form of dispersion in the United States is suburbanization, in which families live in suburban communities on the outskirts of large metropolises but commute into the central city for work, shopping, and many other activities. Suburbanization is clearly dependent upon means of transportation in and out of the city, so that although a few "railroad suburbs" began to appear as early as the 1880s, the trend did not become widespread until the advent of the automobile in the 1920s. Since then, however, the peripheries of most metropolitan areas have experienced two or three times as much population growth as have the central cities.[17] The mushrooming of suburbs in this society is primarily the result of our cultural emphasis on single-family dwellings and home ownership, people's desires to escape the congestion of city life and to find adequate schools for their children, and the economic fact that the only land available at a reasonable cost for large-scale housing developments is on the outskirts of cities.

Urban dispersion can take other forms besides suburbanization, two of which are "industrial scattering" and "urban sprawl." Instead of families moving outward, industrial plants and other businesses may locate in outlying areas, with individuals continuing to reside in or near the central city. This pattern is quite common in many European cities, which developed around feudal castles and trading centers long before industrialization began, so that when factories were built they had to be located on the

---

[16] The three major explanations of urban spatial patterning—the concentric-zone, the sector, and the multiple-nuclei theories—are summarized and compared in Chauncy D. Harris and Edward L. Ullman, "The Nature of Cities," in Paul K. Hatt and Albert J. Reiss, Jr., eds., *Cities and Society* (New York: Free Press, 1957), pp. 237–247.

[17] Davis, "The Origin and Growth of Urbanization in the World."

periphery of the city. In recent years it has also become more common in the United States, as businesses have discovered the economic benefits of inexpensive land and low taxes outside the legal city. Urban sprawl, meanwhile, refers to the continual outward expansion of entire urban communities as they grow in size. Vertical expansion via skyscrapers has nowhere reached its possible limits, but it quickly becomes extremely expensive, and it cannot go on indefinitely. As urbanization proceeds, therefore, a metropolis must constantly expand outward, encompassing more and more territory. Not only families and businesses, but also retail stores, schools, churches, recreational facilities, and all other types of organizations relentlessly disperse over the countryside.

As a direct result of these various forms of dispersion, many urbanized areas in the United States presently face severe problems of political fragmentation. Although any metropolitan area is functionally and culturally a single community, in legal terms it may be divided into dozens of autonomous political units, including the legal central city, surrounding suburbs, satellite cities, specialized "authorities" for harbors, parks, water supplies, and transportation, one or more counties, and sometimes even two different states. The community faces countless problems in such areas as mass transportation, public utilities, public recreation facilities, school systems, crime, and housing, all of which can be solved only through unified communitywide programs. Yet concerted action of any kind is virtually impossible when numerous separate political units, each jealous of its own autonomy, must somehow reach mutual agreement before anything can be accomplished. The result in many cities is virtual stagnation; little or nothing is done to deal with pressing urban problems, and few attempts are made to plan for future community development.[18]

Looking toward the future, we can envision the emergence of giant "megalopolises," or "supermetropolises," resulting from the expansion and merging of what were originally several separate cities. The strips of land between these cities slowly become filled with urban or semi-urban settlements, until each community merges imperceptibly with its neighbors. Ultimately there would be no particular areas of extremely dense population concentration, but neither would there be any open rural land. This trend is already evident on the American East Coast, extending for over four hundred miles from Boston to Washington, D.C. "One can travel from one end to the other of this super city without leaving territory that is predominantly urban in its land use, its occupations, and the way of life of its people. Within the area about 20 percent of the nation's people are concentrated on less than 2

---

[18]For a detailed discussion and analysis of this situation, see Scott Greer, *Governing the Metropolis* (New York: John Wiley & Sons, 1962).

percent of its land."[19] Similar trends can be seen in southern England, northwestern Europe, around the Great Lakes, and in southern California. These are perhaps the prototypic urban communities of tomorrow.

In sum, the essence of this analysis of urbanization as a major developmental trend is as follows:

PRINCIPLE 93: As cities grow in size and complexity, they increasingly exercise functional and cultural dominance throughout the entire society, so that what begins as population migration ends in the creation of totally new forms of social organization in all realms of life.

Postmodern Development

IF industrialization and urbanization have been the major historical trends producing contemporary modernized societies, what may future "postmodern" societies be like? In what directions may social organization develop in the future? When we attempt to preview the future, we essentially project from current trends, filling in details with imaginative speculation. Nevertheless, in recent years social scientists have been giving increasing attention to future possibilities for social life. We cannot possibly review here all of the visions of the future proposed by these writers, but we can briefly sketch four contrasting types of overall societal organization that might become evident in the future as societies experiment with alternative forms of postmodern development.

The basic theoretical perspective underlying all of these projected societal models is epigenesis, or relatively purposeful development toward increasingly complex forms of social organization. They all assume that ecological concerns of survival in the natural environment will steadily diminish in importance—provided that solutions are found to the problems of population growth, scarcity of energy and other natural resources, and environmental pollution. As economic production approaches the level at which material needs are adequately satisfied, the economy will slowly lose its dominant power over the rest of society. Paradoxically, universal abundance destroys economic dominance based on scarcity. As economic productivity grows in both volume and efficiency, individuals and organizations are freed from basic sustenance and related economic imperatives, and are then able to direct more attention and effort toward securing whatever other goals they choose to pursue.

As an outgrowth of this trend, the primary basis of social power in

[19]Leonard Broom and Philip Selznick, *Sociology*, 3rd ed. (New York: Harper & Row, 1963), pp. 615–661.

society will slowly shift from control over economic processes to the exercise of political authority, so that political values and processes increasingly shape the structure of society.[20] Going further, some writers have argued that another increasingly vital power base in postmodern societies will be possession of expert technological and professional knowledge.[21] Social power, these writers suggest, will steadily pass to the scientists, engineers, professionals, educators, technicians, and other specialists who control the vast accumulations of knowledge in all realms of life upon which a highly organized postmodern society will rest. The crucial point here, however, is that both political authority and technical knowledge are potentially unlimited power resources, so that the amount of power being exerted in society could continue to grow indefinitely.

To the extent that future societies display increasingly complex patterns of social ordering and constantly expanding possibilities for pervasive power exertion, might we not witness an inexorable drift toward concentration of power in national governments? As all of the myriad subparts comprising a postmodern society become highly specialized and interdependent, there will be ever increasing requirements for overall coordination and regulation of social life if the society is to remain cohesive and successful in attaining its collective goals. Already, governments of contemporary societies are steadily performing more and more of these control functions on a national scale. Simultaneously, with the spread of popular demands for the socioeconomic benefits of the welfare state, people also look to government to provide services ranging from preschool education to retirement programs. The result of these and related trends is that in all modern societies the national government already exercises far more power than any other sector of society, and this functional dominance of government steadily multiplies. Therefore:

PRINCIPLE 94: A fundamental value issue pervading all efforts to construct models of future societies is whether we will accept extensive centralization of power in government or whether we will attempt to create new societal forms in which power is purposefully decentralized as far as functionally feasible.

The first two models of postmodern society sketched below—mass and totalitarian societies—emphasize power centralization, although to varying degrees. The latter two models—socialist and pluralist societies—emphasize power decentralization, but again to varying degrees. It is important to

[20]This thesis is elaborated by W. W. Rostow in *The Stages of Economic Growth.*
[21]The main proponent of this argument is Daniel Bell, in *The Coming of Post-Industrial Society* (New York: Basic Books, 1973).

remember, however, that the writers who have formulated these models (especially the former two) are not necessarily espousing them as desirable ideals, but are merely describing societal forms that might possibly arise in the future. No real society is ever likely to resemble any of these models in all respects, so that features of all of the models may become evident in most countries, although one or more of the models may be more closely approximated than others.

MASS SOCIETY

Sociological notions of mass society—which are derived largely from extrapolations of certain trends evident in the United States today— unfortunately differ in many crucial respects. William Kornhauser's conceptualization of this model is perhaps the most complete, however.[22]

For individuals, the chief characteristic of mass society is isolation or atomization. People are socially isolated from one another, and interact only as segmented and highly impersonal role actors. A dissolution of extended kinship and stable community ties destroys meaningful and binding social relationships among individuals, leaving them without secure "social roots" of any kind. "The chief characteristic of the mass . . . is isolation and amorphous social relationship. . . . Mass society is objectively the *atomized* society and subjectively the *alienated* population."[23] Each individual is adrift alone in a vast sea of anonymous humanity. The nuclear family may remain as a social unit in mass society, but it becomes isolated from all other social groups and cannot serve as a mediating bond between the individual and larger social organizations. The only viable social ties in a mass society are those that link each separate individual with the societal government. "Mass society is a situation in which the aggregate of individuals are related to one another only by way of their relations to a common authority, especially the state."[24]

From a broader structural perspective, the major feature of mass society is a relative absence of intermediate organizations between individuals and the larger society. Some groups—such as nuclear families, friendship cliques, or neighborhoods—are too small, weak, and transitory to have any important effects on the society. Other organizations—such as the govern-

---

[22] William Kornhauser, *The Politics of Mass Society* (New York: Free Press, 1959). Other descriptions are given by C. Wright Mills, *The Power Elite* (New York: Oxford University Press, 1956); chap. 13; Joseph Gusfield, "Mass Society and Extremist Politics," *American Sociological Review* 27 (February 1962): 19–30; Philip Selznick, "Institutional Vulnerability in Mass Society," *American Journal of Sociology* 56 (1951): pp. 320–333; and Edward Shils, "The Theory of Mass Society," in Philip Olson, ed., *America as a Mass Society* (New York: Free Press, 1963), pp. 30–47.

[23] Kornhauser, *The Politics of Mass Society*, pp. 31–33.

[24] Ibid.

ment, huge business firms, or giant metropolises—are too large, remote, and complex for individuals to exercise any influence over their activities. The intermediate associations that do exist—such as political parties, labor unions, or professional organizations—either perform no important functions in society, or else lack the several levels of successively inclusive subunits necessary for effective individual participation. In sum, the social structure of a mass society contains essentially only two types of social ordering: (1) small, shifting groups, which provide few stable or meaningful ties among individuals, and which wield no power in society, and (2) huge, centralized organizations, which impersonally control virtually all societal activities, and over which individuals can exercise no influence.

Those few persons who occupy positions at the apexes of the dominant organizations in mass society, especially governmental leaders, form a small and relatively closed elite that authoritatively rules the society. Such elites are not particularly strong, however, for several reasons. First, they have no intermediate associations through which to reach the population. They cannot effectively control individual actions or mobilize and organize the population for collective activities. Their only means of access to the people is via mass communications, which may produce widespread conformity but will not lead to viable social relationships. Second, elites find it difficult to secure and maintain legitimacy, since they lack any organized support outside the government that would sustain them during periods of severe conflict or disruptive crises. Third, they have no established means by which potential new leaders in the population can be identified and gradually given positions of increasing responsibility as they gain administrative skills. By and large, all social positions are either "elite" or "nonelite," with few intermediate gradations. Fourth, elites cannot effectively deal with public dissatisfaction or disruptions of social order. There are no institutionalized "feedback" mechanisms to keep elites immediately informed of events and problems throughout society. Instead of dealing with stresses and strains continually as they occur, elites are periodically faced with intense social conflicts growing out of unresolved tensions. Fifth, elites are open to arbitrary and extreme popular pressures, in the form of mass movements and revolutions. Because they lack the social distance and insulation from the people that intermediate organizations would provide, elites have little freedom of operation. Before undertaking any activity, they must in effect ask themselves, "How likely is this to produce a demonstration or riot?" As a consequence, many necessary but unpopular actions are never attempted.

While elites in a mass society are overly accessible to popular pressures, the masses of people are also readily available for manipulation by elites and for conformity to the anonymous dictates of mass social movements. Lack of strong attachment to immediately relevant organizations leaves the masses open to whatever influences from the larger society happen to blow upon them. These inundating pressures may consist of either appeals by elites through the mass media, or popular demands for support of and participation in mass extremist movements. In neither case can the individual exercise control over his or her own social destiny. The relentless social forces confronting one are far superior to one's lone powers of resistance—and the sources of these social pressures may be entirely anonymous. One's social world is meaningless, and one is powerless to affect or alter it. In Kornhauser's words: "Where intermediate groups do not exist or do not perform important social functions, elites and nonelites are directly dependent on one another; there is nonmediated access to elites and direct manipulation of nonelites. . . . Centralized national groups do not mitigate mass availability; neither do isolated primary groups. For the one relationship is too remote and the other is too weak to provide the individual with firm bases of attachment to society. This is the situation of mass society." [25]

Since no one has advocated "massification" as a desirable goal for society, the dissenter in this case is the writer who finds worthwhile features in the mass-society model. For instance, it has been suggested that some aspects of a mass society would tend to encourage continual (and presumably beneficial) social change, to inhibit extremist politics growing out of widely diffused social power, or to promote individual freedom of choice by providing a person with many different possible courses of action.[26] It is important to realize, though, that the conceptions of mass society held by these theorists all differ markedly from the model proposed by Kornhauser. As sketched here, mass society remains largely a "negative utopia."

The major problem of a mass society, if one should ever arise, would probably be instability. The weakness of the elites, added to the volatility of the masses, gives mass society an inherent propensity to drastic social conflict and change. A likely direction that such change might take, as elites attempted to strengthen their power or to "rescue" society from "impending social anarchy," would be toward totalitarian society.

TOTALITARIAN SOCIETY

Totalitarian society has come closer to actual realization in the twentieth century than any of the other societal models. This fact has both desirable and undesirable consequences for sociological analysis. We can describe and study many aspects of totalitarian society in considerable detail, but at the same time we may find it exceptionally difficult to maintain value

[25] Ibid., p. 100.
[26] These writings are, successively, Daniel Bell, "America as a Mass Society: A Critique," in his *The End of Ideology* (New York: Free Press, 1960), chap. 1; Gusfield, "Mass Society and Extremist Politics"; and Edward Shils, "The Theory of Mass Society."

neutrality. The two major prototype examples of totalitarianism—Germany under Hitler and Russia under Stalin—remind us, however, that this form of society can incorporate either a capitalistic or a socialistic economy. The distinctive feature of totalitarianism lies in its power structure, not in its economic order.

A totalitarian society differs markedly from a traditional dictatorship. In both types of regimes, power is highly centralized in a small governmental elite, which acts authoritatively—and often autocratically—without consulting the rest of the population. Traditional despots have sought only to rule their society, however, not to control it totally. Their power has for the most part been limited to the formal government, plus its attendant legal and military networks, supplemented by a limited amount of influence over the economy. But the rest of society has usually been left alone. Most of these dictators have ultimately been concerned with promoting their own welfare, not that of the total society, and they have sought to exercise only enough power to expropriate the available benefits and resist all attempts at social change.

Not so in totalitarian society. Given the technological facilities and complex social organization of industrialized-urbanized-bureaucratized societies, *totalitarian elites attempt to extend their control over all parts of the society and all aspects of social life. They create a "total state," in which the government, acting through the political network, absolutely dominates the entire society.*[27] The state—or more precisely, the elites who operate the government, which is the focus of the polity—controls all subordinate governmental units, all social networks throughout the society (including the economy, education, communication, religion, socialization, medicine, and so on), all associations existing in the society (businesses, labor unions, political parties, occupational and professional organizations, special-interest associations, churches, youth clubs), and, as far as possible, all families and small groups. When carried to its extreme, complete control by totalitarian elites would not even stop here, but would also influence or determine all individual behavior, and would ultimately employ socialization and propaganda techniques to mold the personalities of all members of the society. In short, totalitarian society is highly organized, integrated, and institutionalized, but it is also thoroughly dominated by the state, which is in turn completely controlled by a few elites.

These elites often attempt to justify their total control of society on the grounds that they are in the process of constructing a totally new—and

[27]The major writings on totalitarian society, from which this discussion is largely drawn, are Hannah Arendt, *The Origins of Totalitarianism*, 2nd ed. (Cleveland, Ohio: World, 1958), chaps. 10–13; and Carl J. Friedrich and Zbigniew K. Brzezinski, *Totalitarian Dictatorship and Autocracy*, 2nd ed. (Cambridge, Mass.: Harvard University Press, 1965). See also Robert Nisbet, *Community and Power* (New York: Oxford University Press, 1962), chap. 8.

highly utopian—type of society that will eventually benefit everyone. Instead of just exploiting their society, totalitarian elites are presumably seeking to promote the common welfare. Instead of defending existing social conditions, they initiate radical social changes. Totalitarian elites may genuinely believe in the utopian ideals they propound, or they may simply be using these goals as a means of gaining legitimacy, but this factor is not crucially significant. Regardless of whether they are seeking personal gain or social betterment, the society is still totalitarian.

As a prelude to the massive social changes required for the creation of a totalitarian society, most existing social ordering and culture must be severely weakened or destroyed. Established relationships and organizations are subverted or eliminated, leaving the ground bare and fertile for the growth of totalitarianism. At this point coercion and violence may be used, although events such as wars and depressions might produce the same effects. "The political enslavement of man requires the emancipation of man from all the authorities and memberships . . . that serve, in one degree or another, to insulate an individual from external political power. . . . The monolithic case of the totalitarian State arises from the sterilization or destruction of all groups and statuses that, in any way, rival or detract from the allegiance of the masses to [the] State." [28] Thus it is that mass society, with its atomization of individuals and absence of intermediate associations, is often described as particularly ripe for the emergence of totalitarianism.

Destruction of the old order and creation of an organizational void is only the first step on the road to totalitarianism, however. The controlling elites must now endeavor to create an entirely new structure of groups, associations, classes, networks, and other types of social organization throughout society. This elaborate set of organizations is established and thoroughly controlled by the state. The ruling elites determine what functions each organization is to perform, what its values, goals, and norms are to be, how it is to operate, whom its membership shall include, what power it is to wield, and which individuals shall act as its leaders. In short, *every organization within the society is merely an extension of the state, acting as its agent.* All organizations comprising the society function solely for the benefit of the state, never for their individual members.

The unique characteristics of a totalitarian society can be briefly summarized under three headings: a monolithic political party, a pervasive ideology, and unlimited social control. [29] There is only one political party in totalitarian society, and it brooks no opposition. Although limited in size to a small percentage of the population, it is the single most powerful

---

[28] Nisbet, *Community and Power,* pp. 202 and 205.
[29] For more extensive discussion of these various features, see Friedrich and Brzezinski, *Totalitarian Dictatorship and Autocracy.*

organization in the society. Party membership is the first requisite for all important social positions, and all members are expected to exhibit both loyal dedication and active participation. In its operation, the party is highly authoritarian, with all power exercised downward from a tiny inner circle through several successively broader but less influential levels of party membership and organization. The inner circle of elites that directs the party, and hence the entire society, may act as a collective unit or may select one or more of its members to be the head of state, but in either case the elite group as a whole remains the final seat of power. Totalitarian "supreme leaders" are always highly dependent upon their "coelites."

In practice, if not also in ideology, the party is superior to the formal government in totalitarian society. For all practical purposes, the party is the ruling political unit, which then acts through the formal government and other agencies of the state, which in turn pervades all organized social activities. The formal government is thus reduced to being largely an administrative organ, while all major policy formation and decision making originates within the higher levels of the party. To maintain total control over the government as well as the rest of the society, the party assigns one or more of its members to every governmental bureau and office, and to every factory, business firm, military unit, youth organization, professional association, court, newspaper, broadcasting station, and other such organizations it considers important. This party agent does not directly rule the organization or unit to which he is assigned, but rather acts as an observer and liaison to pass on party directives, to ensure that party rules are enforced, and to report back to the party any problems or "deviations" that occur. Because of this intricate web of party observers, and also because of the fact that key governmental offices are often duplicated by parallel party units, totalitarian society is sometimes said to have a "dual social structure."

All societies have ideologies, or sets of interrelated values that explain, justify, and guide social activities. But totalitarian ideologies are distinctive in several ways: (1) they are proclaimed by the elites as the official values of the whole society; (2) they are utopian in nature, calling for complete reconstruction of the society along entirely new lines, and supposedly leading ultimately to an ideal way of life; (3) they are totally inclusive, pertaining to virtually all areas and aspects of human life; and (4) they are frequently universal in scope, appealing to all humanity. These ideologies serve primarily to legitimize the power of the elites and the totalitarian movement. By establishing goals for social action that are believed to be morally perfect, they justify all means required to achieve them. Their constant rejection of the present society for the sake of grandiose schemes of social reconstruction and societal betterment provides the moral basis for the unlimited extension of totalitarian power to all parts of the society. Totalitarian elites may not privately accept their ideologies at face value, but in public these ideas are incessantly preached to the people as ultimate truths to be accepted unquestioningly.

To propagate their ideologies and enforce their power, totalitarian elites use every available means of social control. They operate the educational and communications networks as vehicles for propaganda, allowing the public to receive only selected items of information. Teachers and writers must be approved by the party, their actions are continually monitored, and everything they present is censored. In addition, schools and youth organizations are used as socialization agents to mold each new generation into loyal supporters of the regime. There is an elaborate code of laws pertaining to every conceivable event, these laws are rigidly enforced, and violators are judged by courts wholly controlled by the party. Besides the usual civil and criminal statutes, an extensive list of party rules and regulations is rigorously enforced, so that a majority of all "deviants" are classified as "political criminals." Public "show trials" and self-confessions are used as aids in sustaining the legitimacy of the state. And unlike traditional dictatorships, in which the military provides much of the backing for the political rulers and hence retains considerable autonomous power, totalitarian regimes bring the military firmly under their control and employ military force as a coercive sanction.

Beyond all these pervasive techniques of social control, totalitarian elites also rely, in varying degrees, upon the exercise of terror by secret police. These police are responsible only to the party leaders, and their victims have no means of resistance or defense. Their terror tactics may include planting informants in private groups, electronic spying, arbitrary arrest and imprisonment, inquisitions to wring information or confessions from suspects, capricious harassment of individuals, deportation to concentration or "work" camps, individual "liquidation," and mass "extermination." The main purpose of all such terror is to frighten the population into willingly obeying the dictates of the party and its leaders.

From a purely functional point of view, it is rather difficult to find fault with the totalitarian model. This type of society uses to the full all known techniques of sophisticated social organization on a vast, highly complex, and completely centralized basis. Overall, the resulting society may operate with relative efficiency in the attainment of whatever goals it seeks, may remain fairly cohesive, and may evidence considerable stability. Given enough time, a totalitarian regime might become overly rigid and incapable of adjusting to changing social conditions, but even this weakness is perhaps not inevitable. In any case, the elites' complete monopoly over all means of social control, including military coercion if necessary, makes popularly based resistance extremely difficult if not impossible. Only an organized counterelite within the party can realistically hope to succeed in overthrowing the ruling leaders, but such "palace revolutions" rarely produce major alterations in society.

Criticism of the totalitarian model must therefore be essentially valuative in nature. If we reject totalitarianism it is primarily because we dislike it, not because it will not work. And if we do reject this model on the grounds that it violates many values we hold to be crucial for social life, it becomes imperative to develop alternative blueprints for future societies. Otherwise, totalitarianism is only too likely to emerge, as it has done repeatedly in the twentieth century. Any nontotalitarian model of society must incorporate some organized means of resolving the dilemma between the functional necessity for centralized coordination and regulation and the desire for the benefits of power decentralization.

SOCIALIST SOCIETY

Socialism means many things to many people, so that there are almost as many different conceptions of a socialist society as there are writers on the subject. Nonetheless, *the ultimate goal of most forms of socialism is full enjoyment by all individuals of whatever economic and social benefits their society can provide.* Exploitation, deprivation, and human misery are to be eradicated as far as is humanly possible. A socialist society, it is argued, will exist to serve all persons, not just a few privileged elites, so that everyone will be given the opportunity to maximize life to the fullest possible extent. Individual and collective social responsibility will replace self-interest as the basis of social life.[30]

If exploitation and special privileges are to be eliminated, socialism must eventually come to grips with such issues as centralization of collective decision making, selection of public leaders, and methods of formulating common goals. At the present time, however, little consensus exists among proponents of socialism as to how these problems should be met. Presumably, a socialist society would adopt whatever political arrangements most effectively promoted its overall goal of full individual and social development. But who can decisively determine what these specific arrangements might be in any given situation? As a consequence, we find socialist thinkers arrayed across the entire spectrum of political philosophy, from "mass democracy" in which all issues are resolved by popular vote, to "paternalistic oligarchy" in which a small elite determines what is in the best interests of the entire society. On the whole, nevertheless, a socialist society would

---

[30] For more extensive discussions of socialist society, see Robert Heilbroner, *The Future as History* (New York: Grove Press, 1959), pt. 2; Paul E. Mott, *The Organization of Society* (Englewood Cliffs, N.J.: Prentice-Hall, 1956), chap. 20; and Joseph Schumpeter, *Capitalism, Socialism, and Democracy* (New York: Harper & Row, 1950).

presumably evidence considerably less power centralization than mass or totalitarian societies.

Underlying all of the diverse conceptualizations of socialist society is the fundamental proposition that the goals of socialism cannot be realized as long as economic injustice prevails. Since wealth is a primary resource for social power, its production, distribution, and use will inevitably influence most other aspects of social life. Socialists therefore argue that it is pointless to speak of political democracy if the economy benefits primarily a small elite sector of the population. Alternatively, given an economy that serves the welfare of the entire population, any form of government must of necessity operate for the most part in the public interest. Hence the immediate goal of all forms of socialism is economic reform and reorganization. *In a socialist society, the economy is oriented toward public rather than private concerns, so that it benefits the entire society.* The antithesis of socialism is not necessarily capitalism, but rather private exploitation of the economy by a few economic dominants for their own selfish interests.

A wide diversity of specific procedures and social arrangements have been proposed as means of achieving the goal of a publicly oriented economy. Following Marx and other nineteenth-century writers, governmental ownership of all means of economic production has often been advocated as a mandatory requirement for reaching this goal. Governmental ownership is only one of many possible procedures, however, and a growing number of socialists today argue that it is not even necessary. Other proposals for achieving a socialist society include the following:

1. Governmental control of only certain key industries, such as steel mills, which dominate most other parts of the economy.
2. Governmental regulation, but not control, of important economic activities, from banking to transportation.
3. Societywide economic and social planning.
4. Income, inheritance, and other graduated taxes.
5. Promotion of full employment.
6. Social welfare programs of all types, to protect individuals against poverty, unemployment, old age, serious medical crises, and similar problems.
7. Establishment of producer and consumer cooperatives.
8. Full opportunity for education and technical training to the limit of one's abilities.
9. Abolition of all class, racial, religious, and other barriers to equal participation in the economy.
10. A guaranteed minimum income for all individuals.
11. Direct involvement of workers in the management of their employing organizations.

12. Creation of occupational associations to protect the rights of all individuals engaged in each type of work.

All of these proposals, it must be reiterated, are merely suggested means for attaining a socialist society, and should not be viewed as ideological imperatives.

Although many people equate socialism with communism, for objective analysis we must distinguish between these two related but distinct philosophies. *Three critical differences between socialism and communism pertain to the distribution of wealth, governmental ownership of industry, and the nature of social change.* First, under socialism the benefits of the economy are to be used for the common welfare, but wealth need not be distributed equally among all individuals. A key phrase to describe the goal of socialism might be "economic justice for all." Each individual is to have full opportunity to enjoy the benefits of the economy, but each person will not necessarily receive the same income. Communism, in contrast, states that wealth must be shared among individuals strictly according to personal need. All significant economic differences among individuals are to be eliminated. Second, governmental control of all industry is for socialism only one possible means to a broader goal. For communism, though, it is an absolute requirement that must be realized before any other steps will become meaningful, since only in this way can social classes and class conflict be eradicated. Third, socialism tends to be evolutionary in nature, seeking its goals through gradual social change within existing political frameworks. Communism, in contrast, claims that economic, political, and social change are all inseparable, so that the entire society must be altered at once, often through revolution. Socialism thus provides the more general model of a possible future society, with communism being an extreme but not inherent version of this model.

The major theoretical criticism of the socialist model is that many of the specific measures it envisions—though not necessarily its overall goal of economic, social, and political justice—require action by the national government. If carried far enough, would not socialism place overwhelming power in the hands of the government, so that political elites would be in a position to direct the economy, if not the entire society, in any direction they wished? At the very least, would not socialism increase markedly the power of government in relation to other parts of the society, thus furthering the process of power centralization? This fear that socialism could lead eventually to totalitarianism is undoubtedly one of the main reasons for the widespread opposition to socialist ideology in the United States. This is a quite realistic concern, especially if socialism were to take the extreme form of state-controlled communism. But that outcome is not inherent in the idea of socialism, nor is it the goal of democratically oriented socialists. On the contrary, they argue that full-scale "economic democracy" would provide a strong foundation for meaningful political democracy and power decentralization.

Contemporary experiments with workers' councils within industries, employee ownership of the firms in which they work, self-directed work groups, guaranteed annual incomes, and similar procedures are all seeking more effective ways of decentralizing economic and organizational power as extensively as possible. In turn, as individual workers and consumers acquired greater ability to exercise control over their economic fate, they would presumably become increasingly active in the political arena and demand a more meaningful role in shaping the political policies of their communities and society. A certain amount of centralized governmental planning and regulation would still be a vital necessity, but socialism might provide a viable check on the unlimited expansion of governmental power.[31]

PLURALIST SOCIETY

A central concern of political philosophers since antiquity has been how to limit the powers of rulers so as to prevent tyranny. The idea of differentiating various governmental functions can be traced back at least as far as Aristotle, while the importance of embodying legislative, executive, and judicial powers in separate units was stressed by Montesquieu in the eighteenth century. Division of political power is also embedded in the federal type of government, in which the national state shares sovereignty with one or more levels of local government.

These forms of pluralism are all limited to politics, however. Although a broader conception of pluralism can be seen in James Madison's *The Federalist*, No. 10, it was Alexis de Tocqueville who first gave clear expression to the idea of social pluralism as a model for an entire society.[32] He argued that social pluralism—including, but not limited to, political pluralism—is absolutely necessary for the realization of democracy. To counter the growing power of centralized government in modern societies, individuals of all ages and social conditions must constantly form, maintain, and act through private, voluntary special-interest associations. These associations provide a check against the power of government, and hence limit any tendencies toward despotism. "Amongst the laws which rule human societies there is one which seems to be more precise and clear than all others. If men are to remain civilized, or to become so, the art of

---

[31] For a more extensive elaboration of this thesis, see Carole Pateman, *Participation and Democratic Theory* (Cambridge, England: Cambridge University Press, 1970).
[32] Alexis de Tocqueville, *Democracy in America* (New York: Schocken Books, 1961).

associating together must grow and improve, in the same ratio to which the equality of conditions is increased."[33]

The importance of social pluralism for the preservation of highly complex societies was further stressed by Émile Durkheim: "Where the State is the only environment in which men can live communal lives, they inevitably lose contact, become detached, and thus society disintegrates. A nation can be maintained only if, between the State and the individual, there is intercalated a whole series of secondary groups near enough to the individuals to attract them strongly in their sphere of action and drag them, in this way, into the general torrent of social life."[34]

As suggested by Tocqueville and Durkheim, *a pluralist society would contain a vast network of voluntary interest associations, each of which possessed its own power base and hence could function relatively independently of government.*[35] Sometimes called "intermediate organizations" because of their structural location between the citizens and the government, these associations must rest on voluntary membership derived from shared interests and concerns. They must be entirely private, or outside the formal government, to ensure their functional autonomy. Each association must be limited in its sphere of activities, so that it does not become too inclusive of its members' lives. Either separately or through interlocking linkages, these organizations must extend from the grass-roots level of individual participation up to the national level where they interact with the government. And most important, if they are to affect political decision making, these intermediate organizations must possess sufficient resources to be able to exert influence on governmental bodies and leaders.

Some of these intermediate organizations, such as political parties, political action groups, and lobbies, may participate regularly in the political system. But most of them will normally be nonpolitical in nature, entering the political arena as "parapolitical" actors only when their particular organizational interests are involved. Such parapolitical associations might include labor unions, business and professional associations, or even churches. Regardless of how frequently or extensively these organizations become politically active, however, the crucial feature of the pluralist model is that all of them remain voluntary and autonomous, to provide citizens with independent power bases from which to interact with government.

[33] Ibid., vol. 2, p. 133.
[34] Émile Durkheim, *The Division of Labor in Society*, trans. by George Simpson (New York: Free Press, 1933), Preface to the Second Edition, p. 28.
[35] Contemporary theorists who have contributed to this formulation of pluralist society include Robert A. Dahl, *A Preface to Democratic Theory* (Chicago: University of Chicago Press, 1956); Kornhauser, *The Politics of Mass Society*; Nisbet, *Community and Power*; and David B. Truman, *The Governmental Process* (New York: Alfred A. Knopf, 1951).

To prevent a highly pluralist society from being torn apart by intense conflicts arising among its component organizations as each one seeks to attain its own particular goals, the model also incorporates several necessary cohesive conditions. These include cross-cutting rather than cumulative interests on various issues, to prevent cleavages among organizations from becoming too deep or irreconcilable; overlapping memberships, with individuals (and especially leaders) belonging to several different organizations; interdependent activities, to keep organizations functionally interrelated; and general consensus on a shared set of procedural rules for resolving conflicts and reaching collective decisions.

The intermediate organizations comprising a pluralist society prevent excessive power centralization in society by enacting a mediating role between individual citizens and the societal government. Each special-interest association brings together a number of people with similar concerns and goals, provides means through which these members can acquire information about relevant public issues, enables them to pool their resources to generate greater collective influence than could be exercised by any single individual, and provides an established channel through which they can exert this influence "upward" on political decisions and policies. They also protect individuals from direct manipulation by elites through the mass media or state-controlled programs. At the same time, intermediate organizations serve governmental leaders by providing necessary information about public interests and needs, as well as an established means through which these leaders can reach "downward" to large numbers of constituents in order to deal effectively with their problems and concerns. Governmental leaders are simultaneously insulated from immediate dependence on mass public opinion and fear of overthrow by mass movements or revolution, which enables them to take socially necessary but unpopular actions. In short, *the exercise of power by both elites and citizens is thoroughly embedded within an established web of organizations,* so that no single small group or organization can dominate the total society.

The essence of this mediation process is that it bridges the influence gap between citizens and the government that is ignored by traditional democratic theory, making it possible for individuals to exercise far more extensive and meaningful influence on political decisions and policies than would ever be possible through occasional mass voting or sporadic mass movements. As expressed by Robert Presthus: "According to pluralist theory, voluntary groups play a critical role in a democratic system. Linchpins between government and the individual in a complex society, they become the most important means of direct access to those with political power. In the sense that they help shape public policy, they are parapolitical. By hammering out a consensus among their members, which then becomes part of the raw materials from which political parties manufacture their policies, they become part of the political system. . . . In sum, voluntary organizations are essential instruments of pluralism because they make possible citizen influence on government." [36]

Several theoretical criticisms are frequently made of the pluralist model of society. First, it assumes a "natural harmony of interests" among all parts of the society, or consensus on basic values, lack of deep social cleavages, and absence of strong ideologies and extremist politics.[37] Only under such conditions will diverse actions by competing, self-oriented, special-interest organizations result in social unity and promotion of the general welfare. Lacking these conditions, pluralism can either paralyze or destroy a society, since attachment to intermediate associations does not by itself ensure commitment to the total society. As society changes, some organizations are bound to feel adversely affected and deprived, while others will develop new aspirations and goals. In both cases, these organizations may decide that the existing social and political orders are not adequate, and reject them in favor of extremist ideologies, bitter intergroup conflict, and radical social change.

Second, to the extent that pluralism relies upon and promotes extensive functional specialization and structural differentiation, it increases the necessity for overall, centralized coordination and administration if the society is to remain cohesive. A potential outcome of pluralism might thus be greater centralization—which is contradictory to the basic values of pluralism. Following the argument of Robert Michels, this tendency might even lead to oligarchy.[38] Is it possible to have unified coordination, regulation, and planning without also imposing centralized authoritarian control?

The third criticism of pluralism pertains to its practicality. In contemporary nations, in which the state predominates over all other parts of society, how effectively can private, limited-interest associations influence the government? Are not all intermediate organizations relatively powerless on the societal level, acting only as peripheral spectators in the arena of national affairs? In short, it is sometimes argued that pluralism is unworkable in modern complex societies.[39]

Although pluralism is perhaps the unofficial sociopolitical philosophy of the United States, does this society today even approximate the pluralistic model? Two observers have recently claimed that the United States no longer resembles this model—if indeed it ever did—although they disagree in their descriptions of current conditions. C. Wright Mills has suggested that

---

[36] Quoted in David Berry, *The Sociology of Grass Roots Politics* (London: Macmillan & Co., 1970), p. 241.

[37] Joseph Gusfield, "Mass Society and Extremist Politics."

[38] Robert Michels, *Political Parties*, trans. by Eden and Cedar Paul (New York: Free Press, 1966).

[39] Nisbet, *Community and Power*, chap. 11.

pluralism does continue to operate below the "power elite," in the "middle levels" of power: in Congress, state and local governments, political parties, labor unions, and other voluntary and occupational associations.[40] In reality, though, this middle level of power is largely controlled by the "power elite," he argues. Although these organizations do wield some power within their spheres of special concern, they rarely exercise much power over the total society. Instead, the "power elite" operates through them, using them as administrative vehicles for carrying out predetermined policies and as mechanisms for controlling the rest of the society. David Riesman disagrees sharply with Mills, in that he does not believe that any unified, national "power elite" actually exists in the United States.[41] He claims, instead, that power in this society is diffused throughout a vast number of separate "veto groups," each of which acts only when a public issue impinges upon its particular area of interest. Most significantly, though, this complex of veto groups—which corresponds rather closely to Mills's "middle level" of power—is not seen as wielding its power in a positive sense, seeking to impress its myriad concerns on the total society, as called for by the pluralist model. Rather, as Riesman's term implies, the power of veto groups is strictly negative in nature; the most these organizations can do is to block programs or activities that they oppose. There are many other observers who maintain that the United States does in many ways approximate a pluralistic society, but Mills and Riesman have alerted us to the fallacy of blindly assuming that complete pluralism presently exists in American society.

These various criticisms of the pluralist model indicate that it is not an ideal blueprint for containing power centralization and promoting political democracy in postmodern societies. Indeed, if political elites were capable of infiltrating and gaining control of the major interest organizations in a society, they could conceivably convert a pluralist society into a totalitarian state under their complete direction. Nevertheless, the pluralist model does suggest that a viable network of autonomous intermediate organizations throughout a society might provide a means of diffusing the exercise of social power among many different parts of society, thereby giving individual citizens numerous opportunities to participate in the governmental process. If this model were effectively implemented in postmodern societies, it could provide an organizational foundation for both political democracy and meaningful involvement by all citizens in the operation and continual transformation of their society.

[40] C. Wright Mills, *The Power Elite*, chap. 11.
[41] David Riesman et al., *The Lonely Crowd* (New York: Doubleday, 1954), chap. 10. The observations of Mills and Riesman are compared and contrasted by William Kornhauser, "'Power Elite' or 'Veto Groups'?" in Seymour Lipset and Leo Lowenthal, eds., *Culture and Social Character* (New York: Free Press, 1961), pp. 252–267.

The central theme running throughout all four of these models of possible future societies is as follows:

> **PRINCIPLE 95:** **Postmodern societies will be shaped largely through the exercise of authority based on political legitimacy and expert knowledge, but the distribution and consequent usage of this power may take any of several alternative forms depending on the values and goals of a society.**

RECOMMENDED READING

Bell, Daniel. *The Coming of Post-Industrial Society*. New York: Basic Books, 1973.
> An extensive analysis of current social trends that are shaping emerging postmodern societies.

Berry, David. *The Sociology of Grass Roots Politics*. London: Macmillan & Co., 1970.
> Elaborates and examines the pluralist model in terms of current social and political conditions.

Birnbaum, N. "Conflicting Interpretations of the Rise of Capitalism: Marx and Weber." *British Journal of Sociology* 4 (June 1953): 125–141. (Also Bobbs-Merrill reprint S-26.)
> Compares and contrasts the theories of Marx and Weber concerning social and cultural factors influencing the development of capitalistic industrialization.

Boulding, Kenneth E. "Toward a General Theory of Growth." In J. J. Spengler and O. D. Duncan, eds., *Population Theory and Policy*, vol. 1. Glencoe, Ill.: Free Press, 1956, pp. 109–124.
> A highly sophisticated attempt to construct a general theory of growth applicable to all open systems.

Davis, Kingsley. "The Origin and Growth of Urbanization in the World." *American Journal of Sociology* 60 (March 1955): 429–437. (Also Bobbs-Merrill reprint S-66.)
> Reviews the historical development of urbanization, its current extent and major trends, and its future possibilities.

DeGré, Gerard. "Freedom and Social Structure." *American Sociological Review* 11 (October 1946): 529–536. (Also Bobbs-Merrill reprint S-70.)
> Compares several different models of society, with emphasis on pluralism.

Friedrich, Carl J., and Zbigniew K. Brzezinski. *Totalitarian Dictatorship and Autocracy*, 2nd ed. Cambridge, Mass.: Harvard University Press, 1956, chap. 2.
> An overview of the major characteristics of totalitarian society, pointing out ways in which it differs from a traditional dictatorship.

Hawley, Amos H. "World Urbanization." In Ronald Freedman, ed., *Population: The Vital Revolution*. New York: Doubleday, 1964, pp. 70–83.
> A discussion of the historical development of world urbanization, with emphasis on social requirements for urbanization.

Heilbroner, Robert L. *The Future as History*. New York: Grove Press, 1959, pts. 2 and 3.
> Contemporary economic and social trends, in both emerging and modernized societies, are used as a basis from which to project future possible societal development under socialism and capitalism.

Kornhauser, William. *The Politics of Mass Society*. New York: Free Press, 1959, chaps. 1, 2, 3.
> A rigorous analytical discussion of the mass-society model.

Mills, C. Wright. *The Power Elite*. New York: Oxford University Press, 1956, chaps. 1, 6, 9, 10, 12.
> An analysis of the growing centralization of power in the United States in the areas of government, business, and the military, leading to the emergence of a national "power elite."

Nisbet, Robert A. *Community and Power*. New York: Oxford University Press, 1962, chaps. 3, 8, 11.
> A penetrating analysis of the consequences for social life resulting from mass, totalitarian, and pluralist social organizations.

Rostow, W. W. *The Stages of Economic Growth*. New York: Cambridge University Press, 1964, chap. 3.
> Summarizes the major economic, social, and political conditions necessary for the beginning of sustained industrial development.

Wilensky, Harold L., and Charles N. Lebeaux. *Industrial Society and Social Welfare*. New York: Russell Sage Foundation, 1958, chaps. 3, 4.
> Examines early and later effects of industrialization on society from a sociological point of view, then evaluates traditional thinking about urbanism.

15

Social Guidance

INSOFAR as social organization is a dynamic process that is continually being created and recreated through time, it is always open to purposeful social guidance. Consequently, social change can be not only developmental in nature, but also intentionally directed toward desired social goals. Purposeful guidance is not necessary for the development or perpetuation of social organization, and much organized social life has undoubtedly resulted from the actions of persons who "muddled through" from one day to the next, without much awareness of, or concern for, long-range goals. But it is also possible to establish desired goals for collective action, to rationally plan organized activities that will effectively attain these goals, and then intentionally create social organization that will embody our goals. Purposeful guidance of the process of social organization and social change, especially on a societal scale, is still a rather rare occurrence in today's world. Nevertheless, part of the evolutionary trend of modernization has been a slow movement toward social planning and guidance. We are gradually coming to the realization that it may be possible for humanity to willfully plan and guide the future course of social organization.

Social Choice

THE first step in the process of social guidance is choosing desired goals for social life. *Goal setting rests on the assumption that meaningful choice is possible within social organization.* Although we are all born into a social world we did not create and that is largely shaped by pervasive and impersonal historical trends, these forces are not totally immutable. As expressed by Edward Lehman: "Inherent in all distinctively sociological perspectives is the assumption that however much human actors are the creatures of society, they can also be its creators. Indeed, once we acknowledge that the ultimate 'stuff' of social life is human interaction . . . then we can see that although we did not make today's world, the consequence of our behaviors, and the behaviors of groups we belong to, function either to sustain, to modify, to weaken, or to overthrow the existing order. Paradoxically, although we did not make the world we live in, we are the world we live in and hence the creators of tomorrow's world."[1]

To effectively make and then carry out choices concerning our social lives and our societies, we must be able to exercise social power. Choices made in a power vacuum are merely daydreams. These dreams become viable goals for purposeful social action only to the extent that we can influence others and control the process of social organization. Indeed, if we accept Malcolm Walker's definition of social power as "the potential ability to choose, to change, and to achieve the goals of a system,"[2] then the exercise of power is seen as an inherent feature of all meaningful social choices. The ability to exert power is thus a bridge to desired future social conditions, and to be powerless is to be defuturized.

GOAL SETTING

Two models of social organization that have pervaded much sociological thinking have conceptualized goal setting in sharply differing terms. The rational, or bureaucratic, model treats organizations as closed systems in which some internal part—usually formally designated authorities or other powerful elites—sets goals for the entire organization. According to this model, the organization is then structured and operated to achieve those goals as effectively and efficiently as possible. In contrast, the open system model sees organizations as continually interacting with their environments in a problem-solving manner. Organizational goals, therefore, are largely imposed by the demands of the external environment, to which the organization must respond in some manner.

[1] Edward W. Lehman, *A Macrosociology of Politics* (New York: Columbia University Press, 1977), chap. 6.
[2] J. Malcolm Walker, "Organizational Change, Citizen Participation, and Voluntary Action," *Journal of Voluntary Action Research* 4 (Winter–Spring 1975): 4–22.

At first glance, these two organizational models may appear irreconcilable, but James Thompson has fused them with the concept of "bounded rationality." He conceives of organizations as "open systems, hence indeterminate and faced with uncertainty, but at the same time as subject to criteria of rationality and hence needing determinateness and certainty."[3] In other words, because real organizations are always open to their environments, they are constantly faced with changing external conditions that impose a degree of uncertainty on all their activities. Nevertheless, most organizations do attempt to set goals for themselves and to act as rationally as possible (within existing conditions) to achieve those goals by creating norms and rules that will give them at least temporary and limited certainty in their activities. As a consequence, organizations commonly pursue "satisfying" rather than "maximizing" operational procedures that permit adequate if not ideal goal attainment.

With Thompson's approach, *goal setting is accomplished largely by organizational leaders, but these goals are always fluctuating outcomes of interaction between the organization and its environment.* The setting of organizational goals is therefore a continual process that is always highly sensitive to impinging social forces. Organizational leaders must constantly be alert to, and take account of, changing environmental conditions as they are constantly formulating and reformulating goals for their organizations.

In some circumstances, an organization may be able to act with relative autonomy in setting its action goals, while in other circumstances this process may be largely dictated by external demands. Thompson and William McEwen suggest four alternative strategies that organizations can employ in their dealings with other organizations, arranged in order of increasing environmental control over organizational goal-setting processes: (1) *competition,* or rivalry between two or more organizations as mediated by neutral third parties—which prevents unilateral or arbitrary goal choices by the competing organizations; (2) *bargaining,* or negotiation between two or more organizations for the establishment of exchange relationships—which limits an organization's goal-setting activities by committing some of its resources to situations over which it does not have complete control; (3) *co-optation,* or the absorption of threatening outside elements into the leadership ranks of an organization in order to blunt their attacks—which further diminishes organizational autonomy in goal setting as "outsiders" are given a direct voice in the process, and as organizations become tied together through overlapping memberships; and (4) *coalition,* or the formation of temporary working partnerships between two or more organizations—

---

[3] James D. Thompson, *Organizations in Action* (New York: McGraw-Hill, 1967), p. 10.

which eliminates autonomous organizational control over goal setting, since all decisions must now be made jointly with the coalition partners.[4]

This conceptualization of the goal-setting process can be summarized as follows:

> **PRINCIPLE 96:** **Organizational goals are largely set by leaders or other members capable of wielding power in the organization, but must be constantly modified to take account of changing environmental conditions and the demands of other interrelated organizations.**

MACROSOCIETAL GOALS

Most writings on organizational goals, including those of Thompson mentioned above, deal only with relatively formal associations that are designed to attain specific goals. Larger and more inclusive organizations such as communities and total societies often do not formulate collective goals in such a precise manner. It is quite possible for such organizations—usually acting through their governmental units—to establish broad goals for themselves, however. The process of national goal setting is becoming increasingly evident in modern societies. Three such macrosocietal goals that are frequently discussed in the contemporary American setting are social equality, quality of life, and personal freedom.

Herbert Gans has described the current struggles for racial, economic, and sexual equality as the beginning of a long-term "equality revolution." "In a large and complex society, inequality and the lack of control over one's life are pervasive, and are often thought to be inevitable by-products of modernity and affluence. The protest that began in the sixties suggests, however, that they are not inevitable, and that there can be more democracy, autonomy—and equality—but only if enough people want them and are willing to act politically to achieve their demands."[5] This emerging social movement may likely take many different forms, including income redistribution, realignment of social privileges and prestige, or shifts in social power structures, but the underlying emphasis throughout is on collective action to reduce existing patterns of inequality in social life. Although total equality of all persons may never be possible or desirable, there is clearly much room in all modern societies for considerable movement toward greater social equality.

The goal of improving the quality of life is a much more nebulous

[4] James D. Thompson and William J. McEwen, "Organizational Goals and Environment: Goal Setting as an Interaction Process," *American Sociological Review* 23 (February 1958): 23–31.
[5] Herbert J. Gans, *More Equality* (New York: Pantheon, 1968), p. 8.

ideal, but that has not prevented the concept from becoming a pervasive social theme in the past decade. Initially, quality of life was often equated with a rising gross national product and personal incomes. More recently, however, this goal has been expanded to include the quality of public services, community organization, recreational opportunities, personal development, protection of the natural environment, and subjective satisfaction with one's personal life and the functioning of society.[6] There is still little consensus on the full meaning of this concept, but the current emphasis on assessing the potential social impacts of all proposed public projects and programs is forcing both social scientists and public officials to come to grips with the question of what constitutes quality of life in modern societies.

The desire to maximize personal freedom within organized social life, in contrast, is an ancient ideal that has intrigued social philosophers since antiquity. The long history of intellectual debate on this issue can very briefly be summarized in the form of five conditions that must be satisfied before meaningful personal freedom can be attained. (1) As emphasized by German philosophers beginning with the Reformation, the individual must be aware of, and committed to, some transcendent values with which he or she can judge passing historical events. (2) Thinkers of the Enlightment added the necessity of possessing adequate rational and scientific knowledge to enable the individual to translate his or her values into social action, and thus bring the world more in line with his or her ideals. (3) Liberal political theorists such as Locke argued that the individual must also be freed from constraining external restraints on his or her activities, so that it is realistically possible to take action to achieve one's goals. (4) More recent philosophers such as Marx have insisted that these actions can only be successful to the extent that the social world is organized in such a way that instrumental activities will result in desired ends. (5) Finally, contemporary psychologists influenced by Freud have added the observation that the individual will still be incapable of acting in an autonomous manner until he or she has achieved sufficient personality development to be capable of assuming the burdens of independent action without relying on external supports. Taken together, these ideas suggest that personal freedom requires transcendent social values, adequate practical knowledge, absence of external constraints, an ordered social environment, and a high level of personal maturity, all of which demand an elaborate degree of societal development for their fullest expression.[7]

[6] Angus Campbell, Philip E. Converse, and Willard L. Rogers, *The Quality of American Life* (New York: Russell Sage Foundation, 1976), chap. 1.
[7] This thesis is elaborated in greater detail in Marvin E. Olsen, "The Mature Society," *Michigan Quarterly Review* 3 (July 1964): 148–159. See also Erich Fromm, *Escape from Freedom* (New York: Rinehart, 1941).

Social Planning

THE second step in the process of social guidance is to devise plans for collective action that will result in desired social goals. In recent years, numerous writers have begun to ask how social scientists might bring their knowledge and skills to bear on these planning efforts.[8]

DIFFICULTIES OF SOCIAL PLANNING

Social planning cannot be contemplated, let alone attempted, as long as cultural values and norms are viewed as sacred commandments. Only as culture becomes secularized and as conformity to ancient traditions ceases to be a moral virtue does rational social planning become credible. A strong impetus was given to social planning by the "rationalists" of the Enlightenment movement in Europe during the seventeenth and eighteenth centuries, although their ideas were in many ways oversimplistic. Reacting against the medieval view of social order as preordained and immutable, many writers of this period argued that social organization is created by human beings and hence can and should be altered as we see fit. The naiveté of this view lay not in its justification for rational social planning, but in the belief that, given a minimum of rationality and consensus, any desired change could easily be accomplished.

The Romantic movement of the nineteenth century arose as a direct challenge to these conceptions. A host of philosophers and social theorists insisted that the development of social organization is largely beyond human control. Our societies may not be the direct expression of divine providence, but they are the outcomes of imponderable natural or historical forces that are incomprehensible and unalterable. We can have no more effect over the course of social evolution than over biological evolution. Hence social planning is futile.

Despite the calamities of the twentieth century, *contemporary social science holds that purposeful social planning is feasible, although we now have a more sophisticated realization of the limitations and enormous complexities of this process.* People are not free to order social activities in whatever ways they might fancy. Historical trends and the ever-present weight of established social ordering and cultural ideas severely limit the extent to which any generation can alter the course of organizational development. We cannot today, for example, undo the effects of a century or

---

[8] Much of the following discussion of social planning is adapted from Ronald Freedman et al., *Principles of Sociology*, rev. ed. (New York: Holt, Rinehart, and Winston, 1956), pp. 566–569. See also Bertram M. Gross, *Social Intelligence for America's Future* (Boston: Allyn & Bacon, 1969); and Alfred J. Kahn, *Theory and Practice of Social Planning* (New York: Russell Sage Foundation, 1969).

more of expanding industrialization and urbanization. Nor can we, by simple fiat, change basic societal values and norms, as Prohibition dramatically illustrated. Within these broad limits, however, men and women can do much to affect, at least slowly and moderately, the social organizations within which they live—provided that we have acquired the necessary scientific knowledge and social technology.

Present-day criticism of social planning tends to stress not its futility, but rather the argument that it restricts individual freedom of action. Collective planning, it is said, denies the individual control over his or her own life, and forces one to conform to the dictates of others. There is an undeniable kernel of truth in this proposition. Consider a few typical instances of social planning: city authorities set aside a plot of land for a park, and deny business people the right to construct a shopping center there; the national government institutes an old-age pension program, and requires all workers to contribute to it; because of the importance of education in contemporary society, a community establishes schools and expects all children to attend them until a certain age; a law is passed requiring stores to serve all customers, regardless of race or religion. In all of these cases, individuals are denied certain "freedoms" their ancestors once enjoyed. But to focus exclusively on the negative side is to miss the point of social planning. *While restricting some individual rights, social planning can have the simultaneous benefit of greatly expanding the scope of activities open to all persons.* By surrendering certain small individual privileges, we can all gain vast new opportunities, as the examples above illustrate. In other words, we can gain much more than we lose through purposeful social planning.

Notice, though, the use of the provisional word "can" in the previous statements. Whether or not planning does result in expanded social freedoms depends on how that planning is carried out. Social planning is just as feasible in totalitarian as in democratic societies, but it will not have the same consequences for individuals. Democratic social planning, as opposed to autocratic dictates, is intended to promote the welfare of all people according to their own common wishes. But how are these wishes to be ascertained? The process of social planning is only a means of rationally and effectively directing social organization toward the attainment of whatever goals people desire. By itself, it says nothing about the nature or desirability of these goals. We could just as feasibly develop plans for the elimination of humanity from the face of the earth as for any type of human betterment. To achieve democratic social planning, therefore, we must establish universal decision-making procedures through which common wishes can be determined and collective goals can be set. Only in this way can we ensure that planned social activities will benefit rather than restrict all persons.

GUIDELINES FOR PLANNING

Democratic, as opposed to autocratic, social planning is often fraught with conflict among interest organizations, public officials, and professional planners. Traditional approaches to planning have commonly sought to minimize conflict as much as possible and to achieve consensus at virtually any cost. Contemporary social planners are increasingly recognizing, however, that *conflict is an integral aspect of social planning and can be effectively utilized to enhance that process.* From this perspective, Walter Jewell has outlined a set of guidelines to increase our ability to use conflict constructively.[9] They are as follows:

1. Avoid monolithic goal definitions. Remembering that society is complex, don't try to force onto it artificial structures for behavior that ignore the empirical realities of the society.
2. Cohabit with goals; don't marry them. As development unfolds, be prepared to alter goals to meet emerging needs.
3. Don't plan on development that is presumed to solve problems or establish an effective structure for the next generation, the next decade, even the next five years.
4. Monitor conflict not as a means of eradicating it but as a means of telling where you've gone wrong.
5. Work toward a broader, more diffuse and less structured definition of change goals. . . . Work not toward the structuring of society but toward increasing its ability to utilize the dynamic tensions, the conflict, within it to maintain a flexible, adaptive pattern of human interrelationships.
6. Create adaptable development plans. In no society does a single development scheme operate uniquely on the social structure.
7. Utilize conflict in the innovation process, whether with the development organization or the target context, to require a continual reevaluation and rethinking of the original development analysis.
8. Welcome defeat. Defeat is often a good way to get things done. . . . Remember that defeat changes the victor, generally to the victor's surprise. Losing the battle may be the best way to win in the long run.
9. Be a good micro-politician. Know the source and location of conflict in society at a microscopic level of analysis. Let that conflict work for you.
10. Remember that massive, violent change may be required to open society up to new initiatives. . . . Revolution perceived as rapid change within which there are limits on violence, but nonetheless

[9] Walter O. Jewell III, "Social Conflict as a Contributor to the Success of Planned Development," paper presented at the Eighth World Congress of Sociology, 1974.

much creative conflict, . . . can be extremely effective in producing functional change.

Jewell's summary statement is also worthy of note: "The concept of creating and maintaining a truly revolutionary society in which flexible adaptation is the fundamental structure of the system of human relations based on a continuous working out of interactive agreements between the actors and units of the social system, in which conflict is normal, remains a challenge to planners and developers who have for too long looked at the form of human relations and ignored its content."   ˙

SOCIAL SCIENCE AND SOCIAL PLANNING

What place is there in the process of social planning for the professional social scientist? How can his or her expert knowledge be used without infringing upon democratic goal determination and decision making?

The distinction between the roles of expert and citizen is crucial for this question. Social scientists, acting as professional experts, have two responsibilities for social planning in a democratic society. First, we must seek to gain as much knowledge as possible concerning social processes and problems, so as to increase our understanding of these phenomena. Second, we must use our expert knowledge to suggest various plans for achieving whatever social goals are being sought, and also to evaluate the advantages and disadvantages of each of these proposed courses of action. In sum, the social scientist must act as both a researcher and a planner, But one's role as an expert ends there. The social scientist's special competence in technical matters does not qualify or authorize him or her to determine social values or formulate overall goals for society, although one may certainly participate in these activities in one's role as a concerned citizen. Final decisions concerning the ends toward which social planning will be directed—which ultimately rest on shared social values—must in a democratic society be made by all citizens. In short:

> **PRINCIPLE 97:** The role of the social scientist is to provide necessary scientific and technical information for social planning, on the basis of which citizens select a final plan, which public officials and organizational leaders then translate into concrete programs of action.

Social Activation

THE third—and perhaps most vital—step in social guidance is activation of citizens and leaders for collective decision making and program implementation. This role is frequently carried out solely by public officials, but the outcome is then autocracy rather than social guidance. Three critical aspects of social activation are citizen participation, functional organization, and dynamic leadership.

CITIZEN PARTICIPATION

Traditional democratic theory allows citizens to participate in collective decision making only sporadically through elections, choosing public officials but not directly deciding public issues. With the advent of public polling in the 1930s, citizens acquired a means of expressing their opinions on current issues, but these preferences are never binding on governmental officials. The introduction of the public referendum did give citizens a direct role in public policy formation, but only on a very limited basis. In recent years, however, this notion of active citizen participation in all realms of public planning and decision making has gained increasing acceptance in the United States and other modern societies. In analytical terms, this reformulation of the meaning of political democracy is commonly called the *theory of participatory democracy.*[10]

Terrence Cook and Patrick Morgan define participatory democracy as "decentralization of power for direct involvement of amateurs in authoritative decision making."[11] Key features of this process include: (1) political leadership that is open and responsive to citizen activities; (2) a public goal-setting procedure that takes into consideration all segments of a community or nation; (3) citizen participation in public-policy determination and decision making, on either a "co-determination" basis with officials and experts, or a "self-determination" basis in which citizens exercise final authority; and (4) involvement of citizens and private interest organizations in all phases of public program development and implementation. In short, *the essence of citizen participation is greater dispersion of political power throughout society.*

In practice, citizen participation programs have taken many forms, such as (1) public meetings at which officials describe proposed plans or programs and ask for questions and comments from the audience; (2) formal hearings sponsored by governmental agencies at which "intervenors" can respond to

---

[10] The major theoretical work on participatory democracy is Carole Pateman, *Participation and Democratic Theory* (Cambridge, England: Cambridge University Press, 1970). See also Terrence E. Cook and Patrick M. Morgan, *Participatory Democracy* (San Francisco, Calif.: Canfield Press, 1971). Discussions of current citizen-participation efforts include the following: Alden Lind, "The Future of Citizen Involvement," *The Futurist* 9 (December 1975): 316–328; Carl W. Stenberg, "Citizens and the Administrative State: From Participation to Power," *Public Administration Review* (May/June 1972), pp. 190–197; and Jon Van Till and Sally Bould Van Till, "Citizen Participation in Social Policy: The End of the Cycle?" *Social Problems* 17 (1970): 313–323.

[11] Cook and Morgan, *Participatory Democracy*, p. 4.

proposed policies or projects in a quasi-legal manner; (3) workshops at which citizens, planners, and public officials jointly discuss and develop action programs; (4) citizen advisory councils that meet regularly with officials to formulate public policies for specified issues; and (5) citizen control boards that exercise final decision-making powers in various areas. With the exception of citizen control boards, however, all of these procedures allow citizens to exercise only reactive, suggestive, or advisory roles, not actual decision making, which has led some critics to describe most citizen participation programs as "pseudo participation."[12] If participatory democracy is to be fully realized, there is clearly a pressing need to devise and implement additional procedures for including citizens in public decision making. In other words:

> **PRINCIPLE 98:   Citizen participation will result in meaningful partici-patory democracy to the extent that all concerned citizens are given full opportunity to become actively invoved in all phases of the public decision-making process.**

FUNCTIONAL ORGANIZATION

The idea of functional social organization has early roots in G. D. H. Cole's[13] writings on guild socialism, and more recently has been espoused by such writers as Peter Drucker[14] and Carole Pateman.[15] This thesis argues that *the major subunits of society should be networks of interrelated organizations that perform specific social functions*—such as economic networks, legal networks, medical networks, educational networks, communication networks, and numerous others. The organizations comprising these networks would be partially private, in the sense that they would operate with considerable autonomy and would be expected to be financially self-supporting (though not profit-generating), but they would also be partially public, in the sense that their prime responsibility would be to serve public needs and interests. These networks of functionally specialized organizations would replace much of the present system of federal, state, and local governments. Government could then give its full attention to the direct process of governing—including social planning, public policy formation, and societal decision making—and would not become involved in functional activities such as operating railroads or providing medical services or constructing housing.

---

[12] J. Malcom Walker, "Organizational Change, Citizen Participation, and Voluntary Action."
[13] G. D. H. Cole, *Social Theory* (London: Methuen, 1920).
[14] Peter Drucker, "New Political Alignments in the Great Society," in Bertram M. Gross, ed., *A Great Society?* (New York: Basic Books, 1968), pp. 198–215.
[15] Carole Pateman, *Participation and Democratic Theory.*

Extensive functional organization throughout a society would promote societal guidance by actively involving all kinds of groups, associations, and other organizations in a common effort to attain collective social goals. Unlike the relatively weak special-interest associations emphasized by traditional pluralistic theory, the networks of functional organizations comprising such a society would all control considerable resources for exercising power vis-à-vis each other and the government. This power would be derived from the fact that each network and every organization within it performed a functionally necessary service for society. Since all the component parts of the society would be highly specialized and interdependent upon one another, each part would control a leverage point for exerting power in the form of functional dominance. Indiscriminate or irresponsible use of this power by any one part would be held in check by the fact that many of the other parts could in turn exert countervailing power on it, if needed.[16]

With widespread functional organization throughout a society, the specialized organizations and networks that comprised the total societal system would ultimately provide routes by which the interests of all individuals would be represented in decision-making processes—and backed up with sufficient influence to ensure that they were taken seriously. To the extent that a person took an active part in any functional organization and exercised influence over its activities through normal role performances, he or she would also be actively involved in the societal political system. In short:

> PRINCIPLE 99: **Functional organization maximizes the opportunities for individuals to exercise social power by actively including all organizations in societal decision-making and goal-attainment efforts.**

DYNAMIC LEADERSHIP

Both active citizen participation and extensive functional organization facilitate the attainment of collective societal goals, but one additional ingredient is needed if effective social guidance is to be realized. As expressed by Amitai Etzioni, "To the degree that a society is able to act in unison at all, it has some mechanisms for converting the aggregate demands of its members into collective directives."[17] *The effectiveness of these collective action mechanisms depends on the quality of leadership exercised by organizational leaders.*

The key feature in Etzioni's conception of societal guidance is the

---

[16] John Kenneth Galbraith, *American Capitalism* (Boston: Houghton Mifflin, 1952).
[17] Amitai Etzioni, *The Active Society* (New York: Free Press, 1968), p. 430.

ability of elites in all realms of social life to exert dynamic and responsible leadership through a two-pronged process. On the one hand, they are able to exercise the social control necessary to direct collective activities toward common goals through judicious employment of cybernetic information flows, efficient mobilization of resources for effective power exertion, and establishment of responsive decision-making procedures. On the other hand, they are continuously sensitive to the need to maintain adequate consensus on basic values and goals among all the component segments of society, so as to avoid alienating the population and losing public support. In short, *societal guidance is "a combination of downward control and upward consensus-formation processes."* [18]

This is no small order, but it is nevertheless a prime requisite for the creation of what Etzioni calls an "active society" characterized by viable societal guidance. In contrast to this ideal of an active society, Etzioni describes three other types: "(1) those low in both control and consensus-building, passive societies, a type approximated by many underdeveloped nations; (2) those whose control capacities are less deficient than their consensus-building mechanisms, overmanaged societies, a type approximated by totalitarian states; (3) those whose consensus-building is less deficient than their control capacities, drifting societies, a type approximated by capitalistic democratic societies." [19] He does not believe that any existing society presently approximates the active ideal, but he does hold out the hope that "the active society, one that is master of itself, is an option the post-modern periods opens." [20]

The kind of dynamic public leadership required for effective societal guidance in an active society is undoubtedly more easily attained in a political democracy than under an autocratic regime. But the vital key to the realization of such leadership in future societies will lie primarily in the ability of those entrusted with leadership roles to use their power vigorously and responsibly in ways that will promote the attainment of such collective goals as greater equality, an enriched quality of life, and maximum personal freedom for all people. As great leaders have probably always known:

> **PRINCIPLE 100:** The essence of dynamic and effective leadership is the ability to move ahead of the public and guide it toward the goals it seeks through a skillful blending of control-exertion and consensus-building.

Let us close this exploration of the process of social organization with the realization that collective social life can be shaped and directed by

[18] Ibid., p. 670.
[19] Ibid., pp. 466–467.
[20] Ibid., p. vii.

concerned men and women—by choosing the goals they wish to seek, rationally planning courses of action to attain those goals, and purposefully creating requisite patterns of social ordering and cultural ideals. But this requires both scientific knowledge about social life and unending concerted effort by all citizens. The future of human social organization is within our hands—if we can rise to the challenges confronting us!

RECOMMENDED READING

Etzioni, Amitai. "Toward a Theory of Societal Guidance." *American Journal of Sociology* 73 (September 1967): 173–187.
> Describes the idea of societal guidance as the central feature of an active society.

Himes, Joseph S. *Social Planning in America.* New York: Doubleday, 1954.
> Describes and explains the relationship of social planning to social change, the nature of social planning, the method of social planning, and the enactment of social planning in the United States.

Kahn, Alfred J. *Theory and Practice of Social Planning.* New York: Russell Sage Foundation, 1969.
> A comprehensive text on social planning from both a theoretical and practical perspective.

Lind, Alden. "The Future of Citizen Involvement." *The Futurist* 9 (December 1975): 316–328.
> Reviews the current state of citizen participation practices, mentioning eighteen ways in which citizens can become involved in public decision making.

Olsen, Marvin E. "The Mature Society: Personal Autonomy and Social Responsibility." *Michigan Quarterly Review* 3 (July 1964): 148–159.
> An attempt to portray the main features of a societal model in which both personal autonomy and social responsibility would simultaneously be maximized.

Pateman, Carole. *Participation and Democratic Theory.* Cambridge, England: Cambridge University Press, 1970.
> The major theoretical statement of the theory of participatory democracy, emphasizing functional organization.

Stenberg, Carl W. "Citizens and the Administrative State: From Participation to Power." *Public Administration Review* (May/June 1972): 190–197.
> Sketches the development of citizen-participation practices in the United States.

Thompson, James D. *Organizations in Action*. New York: McGraw-Hill, 1967.
        Develops a comprehensive theory of organizational goal attainment,
        stressing goal setting and power exertion.

Walker, J. Malcom. "Organizational Change, Citizen Participation, and Voluntary
Action." *Journal of Voluntary Action Research* 4 (Winter–Spring 1975): 4–22.
        Contrasts and compares the relevance of citizen participation and
        voluntary action organizations in promoting fundamental social
        change.

Index